The Metropolitan Tower

To Jean-Louis Cohen,
Nikos Ktenas,
Gwenaël Clément,
Édith Girard.

First published in French in 2012 by Éditions Recherches, Paris:

Set in Whitney. Design: Pauline Nuñez

The Metropolitan Tower

A Pedagogical Research Initiated by Michel Kagan

Edited by Nathalie Régnier-Kagan

Translated by Christian Hubert

PARK BOOKS

D'un continent à un autre, d'un individu à un autre individu, les idées voyagent, sont modifiées par les médias, réinterprétées par de nouveaux protagonistes; elles sont en constant devenir. C'est en cela que l'on est moderne, dans la mise en doute des vérités, dans cette nouvelle critique de l'expérience vécue et de celles à venir.

From one continent to another, from one individual to the other, ideas do travel, they are modified by the media, reinterpreted by new protagonists; they are in constant becoming. This is where we are modern, in the questioning of truths, in this critical movement of lived experience and the one to come.

— M.W.K.

Contents

3/ Sharing the Project

4/ Practicing the Project

Foreword

Pierre-Alain Croset

This polyphonic book demonstrates the extent to which Michel Kagan's architectural work, thought and teaching continue to play a major guiding and reference role. It is based on a pedagogical experiment that he initiated in the 1980s across the Atlantic at the very start of his teaching career, and which he developed and refined during his years as a professor at the Belleville School of Architecture. The book's title—*The Metropolitan Tower* — should be interpreted not just as the title of a project exercise, but as a much broader notion that could be used to describe Michel Kagan's obsession with a profoundly urban and modern form of spatiality, at the service of the European city. His constant experimentation with new forms of 'vertical composition' of architecture goes well beyond purely typological research into the architecture of "towers". No longer seen as an isolated, self-referential object, the 'metropolitan tower' creates a critical tension with the urban context, introducing a parcel of density that enriches the spatial experience of the city interpreted as an opportunity for three-dimensional composition. In this respect, it would be fair to speak of a veritable strategy of urban acupuncture that reaches into the deepest stratifications of the city, all the way up to the sky, to link human beings together.

Originally published in French by Éditions Recherches in 2012, this book is now available in an English edition that has been extensively revised and expanded with new essays that demonstrate the extent to which Michel Kagan's architectural and urban thinking remains relevant today. Many architect-teachers continue to draw inspiration from his pedagogical research, in particular the group of teachers who continued this exercise at the École de Paris Val-de-Seine, from 2013 to 2023: Nathalie Régnier-Kagan, Jean Mas, Pierre-André Comte, Laurent Beaudouin and Jean-Michel Veillerot. A complete reading of all the texts shows how the rich network of relationships between architects, teachers and schools on both sides of the Atlantic, in Europe and around the world, in the cities visited by Michel Kagan and Nathalie Régnier-Kagan (New York, Montreal, Geneva, Turin, Milan, Seoul, and of course Paris), could develop a positive and creative energy around the question of Towers, to improve their knowledge, and the ability of future architects to master their monumental and human scale.

To conclude this brief foreword, I would like to pay tribute to Jean-Louis Cohen, a mutual friend who, better than anyone else, found the right words to accurately describe the exceptional coherence between Michel Kagan's design practice and his pedagogical ethic:

"The coherence between the strategies developed as designer and teacher, an attainment that remains an inaccessible objective for most architects, is something that he has built up over twenty-five years through the intertwining of a constructive imagination and a didactic discourse. Rare are the successful examples of such a combined approach that incorporates design methods, the underlying and justifying theories and the operations used to transmit the ideas, without reducing them to a simplifying catechism."[1]

It's in this spirit of "theoretical practice" that we need to approach this teaching, which allows free experimentation but is always rooted in reality.

1. Jean-Louis Cohen, "W for Wunderkind", in *Kagan Architectures 1986–2016*, ed. Nathalie Régnier-Kagan (Bruxelles-Paris: AAM-Ante Prima Editions, 2016), 14.

Architecture to Come

Édith Girard

This book is a tribute to the immense contribution of Michel Kagan, architect and professor, to the emergence of a future architecture, in which elegance and virtuosity are essential to make the earth more beautiful.

Through its formal qualities as a plastic object in resonance with its context, "The Metropolitan Tower" has the capacity to transform the surrounding space as a shining example of the vertical continuity of the public space. It makes a place through its porous habitability and the way it captures light.

Do the exemplary didactic qualities of this project exercise initiated by Michel Kagan constitute a pedagogical utopia? Asking the student to achieve the impossible, to confront the contradictions inherent in the subject, leads him to surpass his or herself, to resolve simultaneously conditions of use, the formal dimension, the relationship to the urban landscape, and structural logic.

From the menhir to the "Endless Tower", vertical architecture is monolithic. In its singularity, the tower marks an anchoring spot, and as a finished totem, it becomes the center of the horizon, avid of the ground, marking the space of our lives. To reach the sky, which is not humanity's natural habitat, housing and offices vie for maximum compactness in the face of mutant climates, that are even hostile to moving too far from the ground. In its solitude, the Skyscraper is intoxicated by its useful surface, makes the most of the extent of its base and sets out to conquer the sky, to be seen from afar and to reveal from above the territory that is offered to it. The texts gathered here should enlighten students, architects and critics on the question of vertical architecture and overcome the current debate, too simplistic, opposing the object to space, image to use.

In Search for Metropolitan Towers

Henri Bresler

Throughout this journey, the metropolitan tower is the object of an ongoing quest, with an understanding that constantly shifts, transforms, and transposes. Michel Kagan and the authors of this book describe a moving target. They do not seek ready-made answers that would allow the tower to be permanently set into a preconceived mold. On the contrary, they constantly and iteratively question its essence, its form, and its materiality. As part of their contextualist priorities, the tower is necessarily subordinated to the site, the city, the territory.

The results are towers that are not just towers but towers that exalt their verticality; "towers" that are "plots", standards for buildings or high-rise buildings, singular, dual or plural architectures; some that accentuate their function as urban signs; others that function in counterpoint; and still others that modestly try to blend into the interstices of the city. The list of towers given to the students at the outset of the exercise was indicative of this state of affairs. Indeed, the non-exhaustive and partial list presented buildings, completed or not, ranging from the 20th century to the present day, and including the most diverse typologies and functions. It is therefore not surprising to see that the American Folk Museum, designed by Tod Williams and Billie Tsien in New York in 2001, figured prominently[1]. This building, extremely refined, both in its interior spaces and in its envelope, is inscribed in a longitudinal parcel while its façade on the street asserts a verticality.

In 1981, Michel Kagan found himself in New York. During his wanderings through this city in perpetual mutation, he sensed the very essence of a "metropolitan tower". By calling this tower *metropolitan*, he assigned it a quasi-mythological role, as if born of the mater polis where the primordial rock gives it its reason for being, its energy, its vitality. Like the architect Erich Mendelsohn who, during his initiatory trip to the United States in 1924, frantically captured shots of New York skyscrapers[2]. Michel Kagan

1. On his last trips, Michel Kagan, was able to appreciate all the qualities of this exemplary achievement.

2. Erich Mendelsohn, *Amerika, Bilderbuch eines architekten*, Berlin, Rudolf Mosse Buchverlag, 1926 (first edition), Expanded edition, 1928. The latter was the basis for the French publication: Erich Mendelsohn, *Amerika* (Paris: Les Éditions du Demi-cercle, 1992).

was fascinated by the upwelling of these vertical constructions and their potential autonomy. This gave rise to his vision of a "cubist city" with kaleidoscopic volumes emerging from a rather low horizon merging with the ocean.

However, these constructions are based on a very old urban grid, dating from 1804. At the beginning of the 1980s, this relationship between the buildings and the urban structure was crucial to the debate on architecture and the city. The result was a new "quarrel between the ancients and the moderns" in which Michel Kagan, a student of Henri Ciriani, deliberately chose the camp of the "moderns". The "ancients" refer to an architecture based on the relationship between "architectural typologies"—in this case the skyscraper—and "urban morphology"—the New York grid. The "moderns" relied much more on the "contextuality" of the site as a trigger for the project. From then on, our architect, an ardent defender of Russian constructivist architecture, looked for exceptions, intrusions, and incongruities in the orthonormal grid of Manhattan that would alter the established type of "skyscraper" and give it a singular volumetric form, a scale in relation to its site, and an envelope that was in touch with the earth and the sky.

At the beginning of the 20th century, two buildings, located respectively at the intersection of Broadway with 5th and 7th Avenues, were already emblematic of their particular situation; the famous "Flatiron Building" in Madison Square, built in 1902, and the "Times Building" in Times Square, built in 1904, transformed in 1965, and subsequently demolished. These buildings fully occupied the triangular shape of their parcel of land while enhancing, from the urban space, the perspective of their volumetry. Moreover, the "Times building" was topped by a large belfry, allowed it to resonate with the city. In light of these historical examples, the metropolitan tower, still in its infancy, would have the vocation of assuming the specificity of the site and its relationship with the surrounding context.

The concept of the metropolitan tower has a date of birth: during an architectural competition in 1984, for the triangular plot of land freed by the destruction of the Times building, the architect Raimund Abraham proposed, a project for a tower that would stack seven identical theaters in the same volume—42nd Street obliged! This proposal was presented in 1985 at the IFA in Paris during the exhibition "*Nouvelles directions de l'architecture moderne*" (New Directions of Modern Architecture) and published in a prominent place in the accompanying publication. It rightly fascinated the two curators, Kenneth Frampton and Michel Kagan[3]. The latter proposed it as a paradigm of the metropolitan tower. Indeed, this exemplary tower, which rises like a monolith, clearly refers to the Flatiron, but the voids of the vestibules are dug out from the underside of each auditorium, sculpting the overall volume and giving it an almost totemic form, like Brancusi's "Endless Tower". Thus, the tower rises in one fell swoop between earth and sky, and erases the conventional ternary divisions of the skyscraper.

This new tower, which is informed by the Flatiron and positioned in Times Square, functions as a removable entity that can move around the Manhattan grid at will, like a chess piece on its board. These simple effects of metamorphosis and displacement give the project its status as an eminently cerebral "exercise" that gives it all its theoretical validity.

During his first pedagogical experiences as Kenneth Frampton's assistant at Columbia University, Michel Kagan was confronted with the intense debates that animated the University at the time. Just as in France, the "Modern Movement" found its ardent detractors. Richard Plunz, a professor at Columbia, who published an excellent book on the

3. Kenneth Frampton and Michel Kagan, *Nouvelles directions de l'architecture moderne* (Paris, Milan: Electa Moniteur, 1985). (See also New York: Rizzoli Intl Publishers, 1985).

institutionalized forms of New York housing, 1850-1950[4], painted a bleak picture of the urban achievements initiated by Robert Moses, the promoter of post-war modern urbanism in New York.

Plunz came to somewhat hasty conclusions in which the towers and slabs of social housing were singled out in the same way as Le Corbusier's *Cité Radieuse.*

In relation to the block morphologies analyzed by Richard Plunz and those proposed as subjects of study to the students at Columbia, Kenneth Frampton and Michel Kagan preferred the closed perimeter block—which proved to be the most relevant for consolidating the existing grid[5]. But Michel Kagan, in his design teaching with Michael Mostoller, proposed to open up this type of block in order to be able to implant some high-rise building functioning as a "pivot" —with the capacity to requalify the entire surrounding building. *May the cubist city perpetuate itself!*

It was only in 1998, when he entered the Paris-Belleville School of Architecture, that the metropolitan tower became the subject of his master's degree and final diploma. However, at the end of the 1990s, the tower was still a taboo subject, still banished from the Parisian landscape... all this since 1973, with the first oil crisis that sounded the death knell of the *trente glorieuses*, and the following year, with the election to the presidency of Valéry Giscard d'Estaing, follower of a new urban policy called "human scale".

For Michel Kagan, the theme of the metropolitan tower could not be translated into a few heroic gestures, a few futuristic digressions, a few technical feats. This new tower, actually rather small in scale, needed to be capable of drawing inspiration from the city itself. It was therefore necessary to choose a site that could convey its full relevance.

Kagan was interested in a particular site, at the conjunction of the Bastille Viaduct, the *Quinze-Vingts* Hospital, the Opera House, and above all, at the convergence of different urban fabrics. This site remains today in a state of incompletion as if divergent interests had frozen it forever.

The presence of a simple tower on this site manages to unite heterogeneous fabrics, to introduce a verticality in relation to the adjoining monumentality, and above all to address the different referent grounds: that of the city, that of the viaduct. Given such a situation, the tower project can only become more complex. However, the reduction of the program to the simple superimposition of movie theaters, in reference to Raimund Abraham's project, is not neutral, because it makes it easy to test the plastic effects of the stacking, to introduce subtle interior/exterior relations, and to grasp the relationship that the tower has with the ground and the sky. The result is a unique tower that stands out as a signal, even a sign.

As this book shows, Michel Kagan's teaching was nourished by all the paradoxes mentioned above. The result is an open pedagogy. Thus, during the "critique" sessions, the various modalities of resolution for the project were identified. From then on, the student was asked to validate his or her own choices and to deliberately assume control of the project. This active pedagogy is based more on questioning than on certainties, in order to give the student both theoretical and practical autonomy in the implementation process at the end of his or her studies. The metropolitan tower project would subsequently be taken up many times in other schools, in numerous workshops, in France and abroad, as all so many contributions to the development of a subject that is not set in stone, but remains in permanent evolution. For more than ten years, the metropolitan tower project, also planned for other Parisian sites, benefitted from close and fruitful

4. Richard Plunz, *A History of Housing in New York City* (New York: Columbia University Press, 1992).

5. The proposed typologies included the Carpet type, the Superblock Type, the Mews Block, and the Perimeter Block.

collaborations between teachers: Pierre-Alain Croset, Hervé Dubois, Cyril Faivre, Miguel Macian, Jean Mas, Nathalie Régnier-Kagan...

Michel Kagan never sought to dissociate his practice as an architect from his teaching. Thus, the metropolitan tower was already in the making in the *Tête Défense* competition designed in New York in 1984 with Studio 7, as well as in his first project, completed in 1991, for the the Cité Technique et Administrative de la Ville de Paris [Technical and Administrative Centre] located beyond the ring road, in the 13th arrondissement. In the competition for the *Tête Défense*, the high-rise standard building is reminiscent of El Lissitsky's "floating constructions". In the *Cité Technique*, one of the volumes reserved for offices and which assumes a relative verticality, will be qualified as a "tower"; its purpose is to reinforce the visual effect of the ensemble which, perceived from the quays, resembles an urban gateway.

But the metropolitan tower will really be present in the various proposals of the recent Osan project in Korea. Can we consider this unrealized project as an experimentation of the "contemporary city" towers initiated by Le Corbusier?

At a time when the densification of the city is the order of the day and high-rise buildings are becoming less and less taboo, the metropolitan tower must take root in European cities. However, it still oscillates between myth and reality. So how can we apprehend and tame these architectures, which must fit precisely into the interstices of the city? According to Michel Kagan: "These are innovative architectures, but also dialectical architectures, attentive to the program. Made of contextual insertions, of very measured heights, of diversified volumes keeping the same architectonics as integrated urban enclaves, they give meaning to a revisited critical regionalism"[6].

6. Michel Kagan, "La torre metropolitana", *Giornale dell'Architettura*, March 2008. See "European Towers versus High-Rise Buildings", p. 65.

The Shadow of the Vertical

Nathalie Régnier-Kagan

It is not a question of adhering to this or that doctrine, but to maintain a constant dialogue with oneself. The activity of thinking is to be two in one.[1]

Hannah Arendt

The "Metropolitan Tower" was the theme of a design exercise assigned by Michel Kagan over the course of his ten years of teaching at the Paris-Belleville School of Architecture. This publication had been in the works for more than a year before he passed away in 2009. Michel Kagan had wanted to make his pedagogical research more widely known and to mark a stage in his theoretical thinking on architecture and the city. The format and content were entirely conceived on the occasion of this publication, based on the statements or list of references distributed to the students, the pictures of projects we had kept, as well as the article written by Michel Kagan, on Pierre-Alain Croset's commission for *Il Giornale dell'Architettura*[2].

The authors of this book shared important moments with Michel Kagan in his pedagogical reflection and his practice as an architect. They shared a common passion with him and moments of friendship. Architects, practitioners and teachers, former students, or former collaborators of the agency, all agreed to my request that they bring their own contributions and interests to this theme, in order to compose the most complete picture possible. This entailed going beyond hagiographic accounts or so-called "scientific" research and paying homage to Michel Kagan's personality—to his commitment as a human being, an architect, and a teacher—by assembling a didactic work useful to future generations.

This pedagogical exercise, anchored in reality, but carrying with it a "measured" utopia, has undoubtedly been his most personal and accomplished contribution to the teaching of the project and deserves to be transmitted and presented in depth. I picked up threads from our discussions and our readings in this publication, Michel Kagan was not a loner. He thrived on relationships and dialogue as part of the creative process. For twenty years he and I shared our life's work: a creation and a passion for architecture. We built a career together, searching for truths we could share, through continuous dialogue, never in a facile manner, but with a common desire to communicate and transmit. In this, we complemented each other's strengths perfectly: his ability to speak, and mine to write.

1. Quoted in Nicolas Weill, "À propos d'Hannah Arendt", *Le Monde*, October 20, 2005.

2. Michel Kagan, "La torre metropolitana", *Giornale dell'Architettura*, March 2008.

fig. 1. Studio atmosphere, with Gwenaël Clément, EAPB 1999

We worked together at the agency and shared teaching moments: with him in Belleville, and me in Versailles, sharing the European architectural and urban studio, the workshop in Bergamo, the study trips to Barcelona, New York and Chicago, the exercise of the Metropolitan Tower...

After teaching the Metropolitan Tower for two years in 2005 and 2006 at the Versailles School of Architecture with Jean Mas and Jean-Pierre Laute, and organizing joint juries with the Paris-Belleville School of Architecture, and after the death of Michel Kagan, I decided to offer this teaching in the Master's program at the Paris-Val de Seine School of Architecture, where I was teaching at the time, and we have been doing it for ten years from 2013 until now. It's this fruitful experience that I wanted to share, taking the opportunity to re-publish this book, in a completed and updated version, this time in English to encourage university exchanges.

This exercise was never simply a structural, dimensional, or formal feat for Michel Kagan. He was interested in this urban form for its capacity to respond to specific situations—for example at the end of the Avenue Daumesnil promenade—to condense architectural intentions through the vertical superposition of a program, to free up public space and to create landmarks in the city (fig. 1). Like the constructivists, he considered the metropolitan tower a "social condenser." We reinforced this teaching with the contribution of engineers, to anchor it in reality. This is the meaning of his "theoretical practice". Speculative opportunism for high-rise buildings in Paris was never his intent, and he kept his distance from proposals for neighborhoods of towers over 200 m high. He preferred to speak of the need for the "*invention of the European tower*"[3], adapted to the historic city, with its ancient layouts, and more human dimensions. This teaching should be considered an architectural reflection on the possibility of densifying the city through its "vertical extension".

The exercise also entailed learning a method of composition: repeating modules, hierarchy, scale, relationships to nearby and distant landscapes, accommodation of use at the scale of the city, but also at the human scale. "*The characterization, the creation of a type, is indeed the most important moment of the creative work in art and architecture*"[4] said Peter Behrens in 1912. It is also the opportunity to create tension between

3. Ingrid Taillandier, Olivier Namias, and Jean-François Pousse, eds., *L'invention de la tour européenne* (Paris: Éditions du Pavillon de l'Arsenal / Picard, 2009).

fig. 2. The Green Grid. Student projects, EAPB 2002-2003.

fig. 3. Michel Kagan teaching his students, EAPB 2007-2008.

architectural spaces: vertically by superposition, and horizontally in relation to the ground and its topography. It should also be kept in mind that this exercise was to be systematically accompanied, in counterpoint, by a project entitled *"the green grid"*, that addressed the needs of social housing for facilities (nursery, gymnasium, neighborhood house, workshops, shops, etc.). Through a framework of green spaces developed as *"green corridors"* on an urban grid, this device developed a theme introduced by Le Corbusier and the constructivists through the concept of the *"linear city"*[5] or *"green city"* —a reflection on the *"horizontal extension"* of cities in harmony with nature (fig. 2). *"For agglomerations of a certain size, the reform will be in the construction of* vertical garden cities *taking here the relay of* horizontal garden cities"[6]. The exercise of the *"green grid"* links a predefined urban figure of the *"redent"* type, as described by Le Corbusier in *"Les Trois établissements humains*[7]*"* and as developed by the architects of the GATEPAC[8], that opens on to public spaces on alternating sides of an axis, so as to define an urban structure

4. Quoted by J.-L. Cohen, "Américanisme et modernité" in *Scènes de la vie future*, Paris, Flammarion/CCA, 1995.

5. Le Corbusier, *Les Trois établissements humains*, (Paris: Éditions de Minuit, 1968).

6. Le Corbusier, *Manière de penser l'urbanisme*. (Paris: Gonthier, 1972).

7. Le Corbusier, *Les Trois établissements humains*, op. cit.

8. A group of Spanish architects who founded the Spanish branch of the CIAM during the 1930s. See article p. 175.

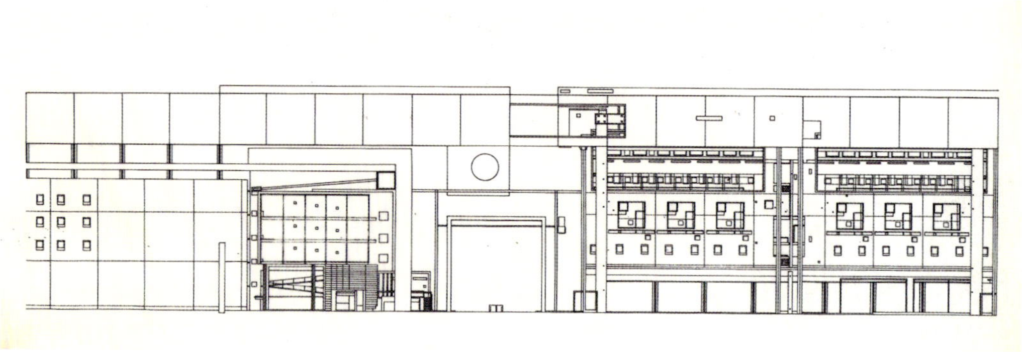

able to give a measure to the diffuse city, to contain density, as well to consolidate and maintain sufficient breathing space. The *redent* is an urban type, just like the "perimeter block", the "manzana", or the "urban room". Its minimum size is R+4, its perimeter 185 m × 55 m. It questions sites such as Plaine Saint Denis, the Batignolles site, Île Seguin... It is a question of understanding the territorial dimension of contemporary urban space, and knowing how to combine it with the quality of housing (spatiality, interiority, habitability)... the micro-scale and macro-scale of contexts in the midst of reconversion, or mutation...

In other words, these two exercises define the framework of a reflection on the development of cities, their growth, the balance between density and natural spaces: the urban question is central to it...

This teaching, practiced with 4th and 5th year students (fig. 3), was developed over time by Michel Kagan during his years of teaching in New York, Geneva, Lille and Paris-Belleville: it is the culmination of his pedagogical thinking. The methodology used in this exercise is the fruit of all his previous experiments and his practice as an architect and marked by all these issues. The exercise of the tower, with its subtitle *"Megaform as urban structure"*[9], entails a focused reflection on the territory of the city, and on shaping spaces for the "little man" —that is to say, a construction where one can no longer clearly distinguish where the building ends and the landscape begins, where the topography extends inside the spaces, and in which the inhabitants can move freely, in a privileged relation with the horizon of the city.

We can take a moment here to refer to some important milestones in Michel Kagan's trajectory. The seven lectures I gave in seven French architecture schools between May 2010 and July 2011, that accompanied the exhibition *Être et transmettre*[10] allowed me to summarize them over time.

The years of training with Henri Ciriani gave birth to Michel Kagan as an architect. He has always recognized that this contact with his teacher gradually transformed his vision and sensitivity as a painter into the qualities of an architect. He learned rigor, precision, the structuring of space in three dimensions, the workings of light; and he discovered the work of Le Corbusier. I have often heard Henri Ciriani say that in order to know how to teach, one must have had a master, and have received a real education oneself. Le Corbusier himself considered that each architect is a link in a chain, which has nothing to do with academism: *"tradition is the unbroken chain of all innovations and, therefore, the surest witness to the projection into the future."*[11]

9. Kenneth Frampton, *Megaform as urban landscape. Raoul Wallenberg Lecture.* (New York: University of Michigan A. Alfred Taubman College of Architecture + Urban Planning, 1999).

10. Exhibition "Être & transmettre, hommage à Michel Kagan", Ensa Paris-Belleville, EnsaP Lille, Ensa Bretagne, Ensa Marseille, Ensa Toulouse, Ensa Paris-Val de Seine, Ensa Nancy, May 2010-July 2011.

11. Le Corbusier, *Entretien avec les* étudiants *des écoles d'architecture* (Paris: Éditions de Minuit, 1993).

fig. 5. Artists' studios, Paris 15th, 1992. Facade on the Parc Citroën Cévennes.

fig. 6. Artists' studios, interior of the courtyard.

left

fig. 4. Drawing by Mr. Kagan, diploma project, Michel Kagan and Laurent Salomon, 1979.

In the late 1970s, after the oil crisis, student projects were by contrast utopian, and their scale often disproportionate: Michel Kagan and Laurent Salomon's 1979 diploma project developed a kilometer-long building (fig. 4)... It was a more modest project, a house designed with Bernard Desmoulins in 1977, that was awarded during the Alberti competition, with the presence of Bernard Huet and Kenneth Frampton on the jury, and then the grant from the Villa Medici *"hors les murs"* in 1981, which opened the doors to America...

Michel Kagan's first teaching experiences took place between 1981 and 1984 as an assistant to Kenneth Frampton at Columbia University in New York. For Michel Kagan, his American years were a time of deepening modern architectural culture, through the *"comparative critical analysis"* of remarkable buildings of the 20th century. He always evoked the

12. Studio 7: Michel Kagan, Brigitte de Kosmi, Colin Cathcart, Ted Kruger, John Loomis, Peter Pfau, Faye Sueltz *in* "Portrait: Michel W. Kagan", *Archi Cree* 211 (April-May 1986).

treasures he discovered in the Avery Library during this period, and how the critical eye and analytical methods of Kenneth Frampton, architect and historian, helped him understand the importance of developing a student's instrumental capacity through a formal culture of buildings and their representation—in plans, sections and axonometric drawings. It was also through his contact with Frampton that he developed a taste for the philosophy of Paul Ricœur and Hannah Arendt. During this period, some remarkable competition projects were proposed with the architects of "Studio 7"[12]: the international competition for the Peak, the project for the Tête Défense, the Cité de la musique, and some concrete achievements. He also discovered an America far from the usual clichés, in which teaching and urban concerns, at Columbia University in particular, were largely devoted to social housing, and to the question of the perimeter block as a city unit. Michel Kagan was always fascinated by the "cubist" vision offered by the urban grid of the American metropolis. He was also interested in the "five architects"[13] of New York, their reinterpretation of modernity, and the teaching of John Hejduk at the Cooper Union. He spent a short time at Peter Eisenman's office, as part of a research project for the IAUS[14]. We both shared a great admiration for the American architect Richard Meier; I worked for him in 1990 and Michel Kagan always showed the Bronx Development Center in his classes as a prototype of the "urban room".

In 1986, he was invited to UQAM[15] in Montreal by Georges Adamczyk and François Giraldeau. This was the first time Michel Kagan would conduct a studio on the theme of the metropolitan tower. This experience was to be foundational; but Michel Kagan would have to wait until his arrival at the École d'architecture de Belleville in 1998, to teach this project again it and make it his favorite exercise.

His return to France in 1987 was marked by a strong desire to build. The competitions held at that time were for housing projects and public

13. Kenneth Frampton, "Frontality versus rotation", in *Five architects: Eisenman, Graves, Gwathmey, Hejduk, Meier* (New York: Oxford University Press, 1975).

14. Institute for Architecture and Urban Studies.

15. Université du Québec à Montréal.

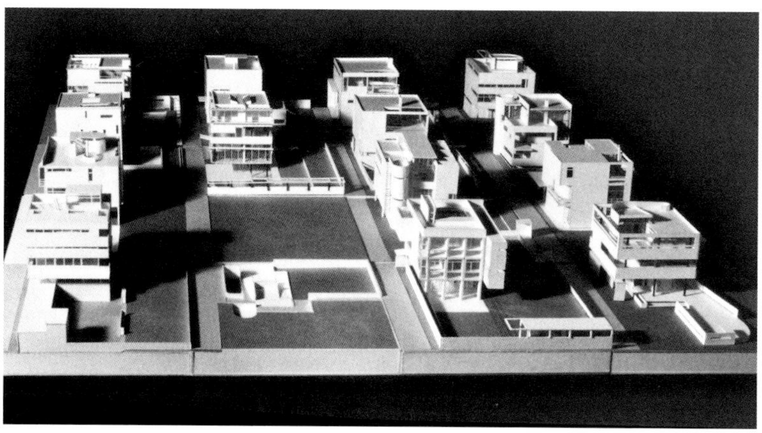

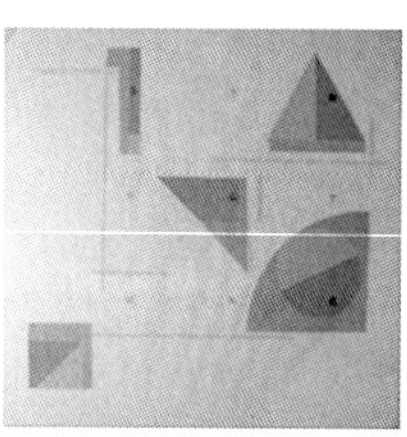

fig. 7. "Gainsborough": modern village of architectural culture, Geneva School of Architecture.

fig. 8. The spatialized image, Sandra Parvu, EAG, 1992.

fig. page de droite

fig. 9. The French Pavilion at the Venice Biennale, Lille School of Architecture.

fig. 10. A house for 3 generations in Pessac, EA Lille.

fig. 11. A house at the Weissenhofsiedlung, EA Lille.

fig. 12. The relief plan in Euralille, EA Lille.

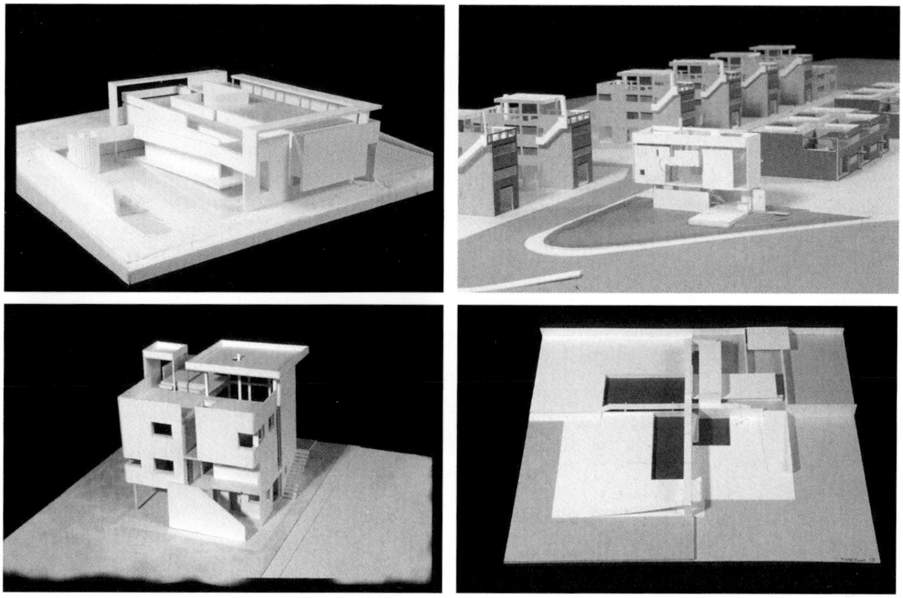

facilities in France, led to the first commissions: the Cité Technique et Administrative de la Ville de Paris [Technical and Administrative Centre] in the 13th arrondissement, and the Cité d'Artistes [City of Artists] in the 15th arrondissement (fig. 5 and 6), with the RIVP[16] as the contracting authority.

From 1989, during 20 years of teaching in Switzerland and France, Michel Kagan had the opportunity to develop a complete pedagogical program of project teaching, from the first year, to the diploma:

> In Geneva from 1989 to 1994[17] (fig. 7), the first year program, the learning of the *"Elementary Forms"*, started with the exercise of the *"nine squares"*, followed by the exercise of the *"spatialized image"* (fig. 8); then the exercise of the *"magic box"*, development in 3 dimensions of an architectural promenade, starting from the preceding exercises, and finally, the "minimum-maximum house" introducing the notions of use, dimensions, and spaces in relation to a natural landscape, on the model of Le Corbusier's *cabanon*, an exercise further nourished by Thoreau's famous book *Walden*[18]. Influenced by the experiments of John Hejduk at the Cooper Union and those developed by Henri Ciriani with the Uno group at UP8, these exercises draw on the pedagogy of the Bauhaus and the writings of Paul Klee and Kandinsky...

> The second year program, *"Se nourrir de l'histoire"* (Feeding on history) which was held in Lille from 1994 to 1998[19], could be divided into three main themes: *"critical addition"*, *"historical substitution"*, and *"theoretical affirmation"*, to occur in real existing contexts. The confrontation with a building or a district of the "learned" architecture of the 20th century was to lead the student to analyze and "understand" it, according to the famous phrase of André Lhote: *"To imitate is to understand"*[20]. These included the design of a *"house for three generations"* in Le Corbusier's Cité Frugès in Pessac, or Mies van der Rohe's Weissenhof in Stuttgart;

16. Régie Immobilière de la Ville de Paris.

17. With: Jean Mas, Hervé Dubois, Miguel Macian, Jean-Paul Brusson, Donato Severo.

18. Henry David Thoreau, *Walden or Life in the Woods* (1854).

19. With Bernard Bassez, Antoine Béal, Hervé Dubois, Miguel Macian, Pascal Quintard-Hofstein, Jean-Pierre Massenot, Donato Severo.

20. André Lhote, *Traité de la figure* (Paris: éditions Floury, 1950).

fig. 13. Extension of the *Immeuble Clarté* of Le Corbusier, EA Lille.

the creation of the French exhibition pavilion in the gardens of the Venice Biennale (fig. 9 to 11); the extension of Le Corbusier's *Clarté* building in Geneva (fig. 13), or of Roland Simounet's Museum of Modern Art in Villeneuve d'Ascq; Learning history is always linked up with the pleasure of creation. This applies as well to the development of the "relief plan" concept in the park of Euralille (fig. 12), or how to "build the site" from a specific work of the ground, according to a grid of 16 squares, etc.

From 1998 to 2009, The fourth and fifth-year programs in Belleville[21] were the years of *"theoretical practice"*, through the exercises of the *"metropolitan tower"*, the *"green grid"*, and the *"European architectural and urban studio"*, mentioned above. In retrospect, it is clear and obvious that these three exercises were the fruit of years of previous experience. They also reveal a more particular contribution of Michel Kagan to the teaching of the project, stemming from his own personal path.

People tend to believe today that art is born of individual fantasy, rather than from learning. In this book, I must insist on the importance that giving a structured framework to his exercises had for Michel Kagan—as a means setting the best conditions for allowing the student to save time and exercise his creativity, without getting lost. *"The more constraints one imposes, the more one frees one's self of the chains that shackle the spirit."*[22] Freedom is always the reward for effort (fig. 14). Michel Kagan always said learning how to do a project required constant practice. He preferred action in the student to a flood of useless words. His was a didactic and ethical teaching, where the search for formal pleasure was compatible with the search for meaning. This led him to create a theory course, entitled *"The State of Things"* in reference to Wim Wenders' film: it was more of a conversation with the students than a lecture, in which he shared his questions about the city and contemporary architecture, favoring a humanistic approach.

Michel Kagan and I shared an aversion to the "kitsch" architecture disseminated by the media. It was important to us to promote a trans-European, rationalist architecture, in a search for modernity, based on consideration of space, structure, light, use, and place. In addition to friendship, we maintained a relational network of architects, in the utopian dream that Michel Kagan carried in him to create "new CIAM[23]", an international of the spirit, a space of exchange and discussion between architects and urban planners of the whole world, escaping the official network and the French architecture milieu. Seeking universality, he liked to quote the Portuguese writer Pessoa, when he said: *"The universal is the local without the walls"*. But universality did not have to mean a culture without particularity: *"Universality supposes the fruitfulness of a widespread and communicated culture, whereas cosmopolitanism foresees neither action*

21. Depending on the year, with Miguel Macian, Cyril Faivre, and the engineers: Marc Saluden, Pierre Bismuth, Jean-Marc Weill, and subsequently Jean-Pierre Laute.

22. Igor Stravinsky, *Poetics of music in the form of six lessons.* (Cambridge: Harvard University Press, 1970).

23. Congrès International d'Architecture Moderne.

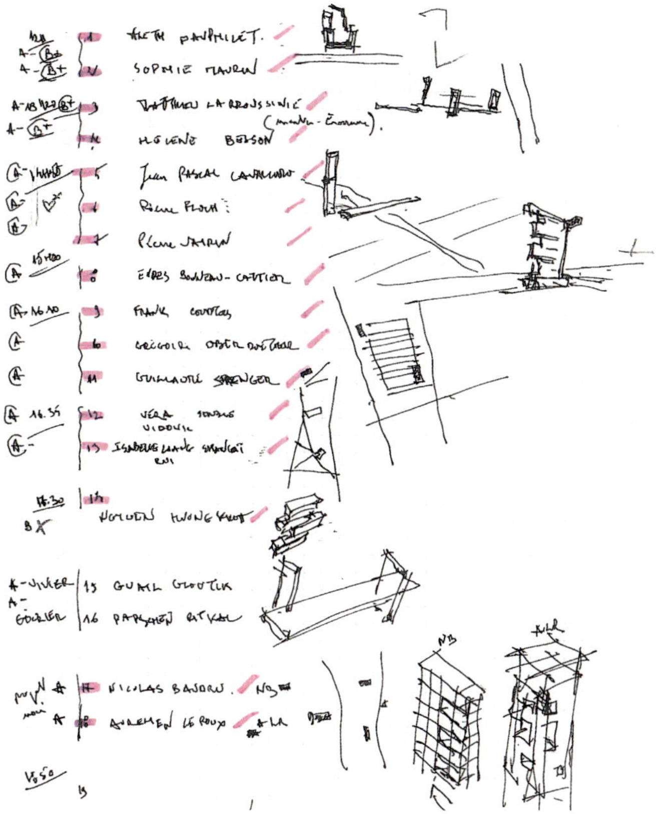

fig. 14. Student evaluation, sketchbook, M. Kagan 2009.

nor doctrine, and leads to the indifferent passivity of a sterile eclecticism"[24].

Michel Kagan's pedagogical work is characterized by knowing how to encourage the student to discover the desire to learn, to respect the powerful requirement to articulate the universal and contingent culture. Socrates thought that wisdom consisted in perceiving what one does not know. He presented himself in the face of intellectual conformism, with a freedom of tone and thought, emphasizing the creation of one's self, making one's life a work of art. For Michel Kagan, too, teaching is only true by example: he built his life as a work, and himself as a "work of life". The teacher is a messenger, who learns from his students as much as they learn from him. Persuasion is the motor. *"The written word stops, immobilizes the discourse, does not take into account questions or objections. Oral teaching allows for face-to-face interaction, like a free exchange without rhetoric."*[25] Michel Kagan sought to build a shared culture, a culture of relationship, against the stigmatization of the old, and the blind optimism of the new, beyond individualism and opportunism. As in classical art, he thought that the culture of modernity should be collective and shared: the essence of his transmission was to define *"how man makes himself eternal"*[26], in the architecture of our time. He never understood modernity as a historical period, but more as a space, *"a constellation of points in movement"*[27].

Our experiences at the École d'Architecture de Paris-Val de Seine have been part of a progressive approach from the first year of the bachelor's

24. Igor Stravinsky, op. cit.

25. George Steiner, *Lessons of the masters. Charles Eliot Norton lectures 2001-2002.* (Cambridge: Harvard University Press, 2003).

26. George Steiner, op. cit.

27. Jean-Hubert Gailliot and Sylvie Martigny, "Être éditeur, au-delà des modes", *Libération*, September 30, 1999.

degree through to the master's degree, through a series of exercises designed and taught by a group of teachers[28]. I personally took part in the first-year project initiation program, whose first semester devoted to the discovery of "Spatial Sequences", with three linked exercises: the first, "Between nature and culture", a public outdoor installation, organizing an urban itinerary, that enabled us to discover the importance of the ground, the foundation of all architecture; The second exercise, "Rooting" (fig. 15), an underground exhibition gallery, inspired by the famous book by Pierre von Meiss[29], again insisting on the theme of the itinerary, natural light, and interior space in relation to the work to be exhibited, and finally, the third exercise: "Urban Emergence", which consisted in installing a "guinguette", an open-air café according to a free plan, at the exit of the exhibition hall, integrating the three exercises in a spatial continuity, in a specific site along the Seine, opposite the Grande Bibliothèque, close to the School to facilitate on-site visits.

The second semester takes up the theme of "The minimum-maximum habitat" (fig. 16), again with three linked exercises. the first consists of the "Analysis of a prototype house" from 20th or 21st century architecture, the second: "the minimum-maximum cabin", a minimum living space installing the functions of dwelling in a relationship with a natural landscape, quite similar to the exercise Michel Kagan gave in Geneva, and finally, the third, "A house for three generations" or a "house / workshop" on a real site, which could serve as a common exercise for the whole school.

Several other exercises punctuated the Val de Seine Bachelor's degree, representing fundamental stages in the students' training, particularly in the second year: "From the intimate to the shared", a pedagogical exercise developed with Jean-Michel Veillerot and Thomas Heuze. This involves designing a student residence associated with a community house (fig. 17), in a project process that starts with the student's room, its assembly, repetition and vertical and horizontal distribution, arranging the common spaces along an ascending path in a given parallelepiped (15 × 30 × 30 m), ending on the roof of the building and determining its relationship to the territory; the relationship to

28. A-Ito Group: Laurence Allegret, Laurent Beaudouin, Hervé Dubois, Thibaut David, Thomas Heuzé, Cyrille Faivre, Jean Mas, Nathalie Régnier-Kagan, Simon Rodriguez, Emmanuelle Sarrazin, Jean-Michel Veillerot an also Paolo Amaldi, Sébastien Blondiau, Pierre-André Comte, Martine Weissmann.

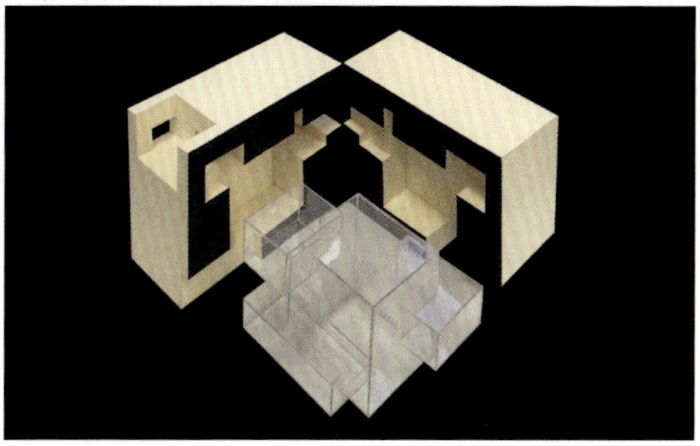

opposite

fig. 15. Spatial Sequences, Kévin Pinto, Ensa PVS.

fig. 16a. & 16b. The minimum-maximum habitat, "Cabanon", Théo Metalli, Raphaël Boussange, Ensa PVS.

above

fig. 17. Students dwellings and community center, Andy Cinna, Ensa PVS.

fig. 18. "The Case and The Crystal", Ensa PVS.

fig. 19. Collective space, Simon Mullot, Ensa PVS.

the ground is defined by the community center program, in which the student definitively establishes the building's location on the plot, by means of a "spatial figure", which anchors the geometry of the program's organization, in relation to the site.

Another generic exercise consists in developing the typology of three dwellings: T3, T4 and T5 in a cube with imposed dimensions (12 × 12 × 12 m), each dwelling having to offer four (or even five) orientations, an exterior extension, double height, and natural lighting in all rooms, including bathrooms. Finally, a highly visual exercise, developed in the third year by Laurent Beaudouin and Cyrille Faivre, involved the design of a public building, its natural light, interior space and itinerary, based on a cube, and work on fullness and emptiness, embodied by "the case and the crystal" (fig. 18 and 19), in order to explore the notion of "*foyer spatial*"[30].

The aim of these exercises is to introduce students to architectural design, so that they arrive at the Master's level with the know-how they have acquired in working with space and its representation, capable of tackling more complex real-life situations, and integrating other issues more closely related to current affairs. The Paris Val de Seine School of Architecture, having established a principle of plurality and diversity in its training, and seeking to break away from the old vertical workshops inherited from the Beaux-Arts, has favored a free and self-chosen student pathway. This progressive pedagogy has benefited a large number of students (nearly a third), and has influenced the whole school in a diffuse way, to the benefit of the general level.

29. Pierre von Meiss, *De la cave au toit* (Lausanne: EPFL, 1991).

30. The notion of "foyer spatial" (spatial foyer) was developed by Henri Ciriani within the Uno group.

1/ Nourishing the Project

fig. 1 Mies van der Rohe, Glass Skyscraper, 1920.

High-Rise Form in the Continuity of the City[1]

Kenneth Frampton

fig. 2 Louis Sullivan, Guaranty Building, Buffalo, New York, 1896.

High-Rise Form in the Continuity of the City 1896–1997

It is arguable that the aesthetics of modern high rise construction begins with Louis Sullivan's seminal essay of 1896, "The Tall Office Building Artistically Considered"[2] wherein he differentiates between the base and the shaft of his 13 storey Guaranty Building, completed in Buffalo in the same year; a work which, by today's standards, would hardly qualify as a high rise at all. Nevertheless the format of the Guaranty represents a significant conceptual advance over what was then the received idea of handling a high building, namely, to divide it into bottom, middle, and top; a formula naively predicated on the sub-division of a classical column into base, shaft, and capital.

In the Guaranty Building Sullivan emphasized the verticality of the shaft by suppressing the floors through recessed spandrel panels and by doubling up the mullions at twice the interval of a standard span in steel frame construction; that is to say, behind every other mullion there was no actual frame. This aesthetic subterfuge was implicitly revealed through the direct expression of the steel frame through fat, cylindrical, fireproofed columns on the lower two floors while simultaneously rendering the blocky podium as a four-square monumental form (fig. 2). All of Sullivan's medium to high rise commercial structures after 1896 adopt and express the

1. Essay published in *SOM Journal* 7 (November 2011).
2. Louis Sullivan, The Public Papers, Chicago University Press, 1988.

fig. 3 Louis Sullivan, Schlesinger & Mayer Store, Chicago, 1903.

standard bay spacing of a steel frame thereby coming to represent the breadth as well as the height of the structure. Nevertheless, in the Bayard Building New York of 1899, a sense of height will still be conveyed by alternating the thickness and depth of the vertical piers, clad in terracotta. The tectonic probity of the frame was eventually most directly expressed by Sullivan in the horizontal mass-form of his Schlesinger and Mayer Store completed in Chicago in 1903, with the large, plate glass display windows of its two storey base being echoed above by the typical tripartite Chicago window which became the primary motif determining the overall proportion of the building (fig. 3).

The expression of the steel frame *in se* was totally abandoned a decade later in the 55 storey, Neo-Gothic Woolworth Building designed by Cass Gilbert and realized in downtown Manhattan in 1913. With considerable prescience, Gilbert opted for reiterating the piers of a Neo-Gothic terracotta skin whereby the vertical proportions of a Gothic stone shaft could be extended ad infinitum to emphasize the height of the building while suppressing the floors.

A further refinement of this historicizing Neo-Gothic syntax was arrived at in the winning entry of the Chicago Tribune Competition of 1922 which may now be seen as the cultural breakpoint in which the scholarly Neo-Gothic of Hood and Howells' design for the 34 storey newspaper building was countered by Eliel Saarinen's second prize design which stressed the profile of the shaft through stone faced monumental corners and gathered up clustered, Neo-Gothic piers so as to form a series of setbacks culminating in a shallow-pitched pyramidal roof.

In retrospect, one may claim that this inspired design plus the set-back requirements of the1917 zoning code crystallized into the format of the Art Deco skyscraper as this format came to be variously elaborated in the rival 75 and 85 storey Chrysler and Empire State Buildings, respectively designed by William Van Allen and by Shreve, Lamb, and Harmon, both being realized in Manhattan towards the end of 1920. The Saarinen high rise formulation of 1922 was taken to its ultimate resolution in the 70 storey RCA Building erected as the centerpiece of Rockefeller Center which was at the heart of a much larger complex, amounting to some 14 buildings of varying height, erected on the eight block site in the center of Manhattan between 1930 and 1940 (fig. 4). The picturesque potential for a city made of comparable developments became evident in the Neo-Aztec, Piranesian imagery of Hugh Ferris' phantasmagoric perspectives that illustrated his book The Metropolis of Tomorrow of 1929 (fig. 5). While this highly romantic vision was hardly a realistic proposition, the idea of planned cluster development, involving more than one high rise at a time would resurface, here and there, throughout the rest of the century.

The two structures, which recast the aesthetic ground rules for high-rise steel frame construction after the Second World War were Mies Van der Rohe's twin 10 storey apartment towers built at 860 and 880 Lake Shore Drive, Chicago and SOM's 23 storey Lever House in

fig. 4 Associated architects, Rockefeller Center, New York, 1931–1939.

fig. 5 Hugh Ferriss, *The Metropolis of Tomorrow*, New York, Washburn, 1929.

New York designed by Gordon Bunshaft, both works being completed in 1951 (fig. 6 and 7). In retrospect it is hard to imagine two works that were more categorically opposed in aesthetic terms despite the fact that they were both predicated on standard steel frame construction. Where Lever House consisted of an hermetic glass wall projected in front of the frame, and sub-divided by thin metal mullions to culminate in a prismatic flat-topped form, Mies' twin towers on Lake Shore Drive were of a more nuanced expression in which standard, steel frame construction was brought into a syncopated relationship with the H-sectioned steel mullions of the floor to ceiling, by virtue of being welded to the steel face plates covering the fire proofed structural columns and the edge beams throughout. Conversely, by totally suppressing the structural frame, Lever House presented its 20 story abstract form as a skin tight, reflective prism suspended above a two storey, plate glass podium upon which it would ostensibly depend for its support. The overall figure of Lever House was very ambiguous since its form remained uneasily suspended between the repetitive horizontality of the green spandrel panels at every floor and the overall verticality of the slab, covered in a seamless glass skin. In contrast, the mullion versus structural frame counterpoint in Mies's facades on Lake Shore Drive was a tectonic solution of exceptional sophistication. By hoisting pre-welded sections of the steel curtain wall into position on top of the fireproofed steel frame, Mies was able to express both the repetitive rhythm of the vertical mullions and the regular bay spacing of a standard steel frame, creating a kind of dematerialized Neo-Suprematist relief, comparable in its overall plastic density to the stone *modenature* of a typical Art Deco skyscraper.

While Mies would ring the changes on this format in one high-rise after another, he would never again approach the purity of his initial twin towers on Lake Shore Drive, not even with the magisterial, 60 storey Seagram Building realized in New York in 1959 (fig. 8). In this last work, Mies would employ the bronze, anodized, rolled steel mullions in a particularly consistent manner in as much as the curtain wall was projected in front of the steel frame. Unlike Lever House, however, the mullions, in this instance, established the unequivocal verticality of the form by emphasizing the re-entrant

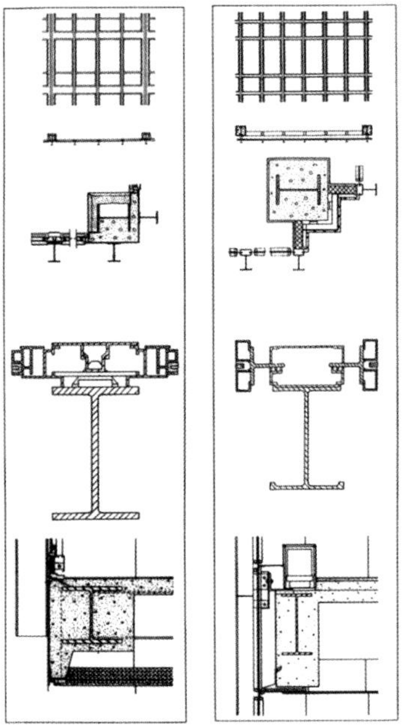

fig. 6 Gordon Bunshaft (SOM), Lever House, New York, 1951.

fig. 7 Mies van der Rohe, Modular metal frame, detail of windows and corner design at 860 Lake Shore Drive and Seagram Building.

fig. 8 Mies van der Rohe, Seagram Building, New York, 1959.

steel corners of the vertical shaft as it was set back before a plaza opening onto Park Avenue. It is significant that Mies built a large, all metal model of the Seagram so as to simulate the way in which the bronze anodized steel components would fuse with the brown tinted glass of the curtain wall thereby to yield a megalith that was as homogenous in its overall character, as the stone-faced, bronze-plated façade of Hood's RCA Building of 1936.

Of the eight major high-rise structures that were designed and realized by SOM in the space of three intense years between 1958 and 1961, the most tectonically innovative was the 19 story Inland Steel Building, Chicago, that was finally completed in 1965 (fig. 9 and 10). The most

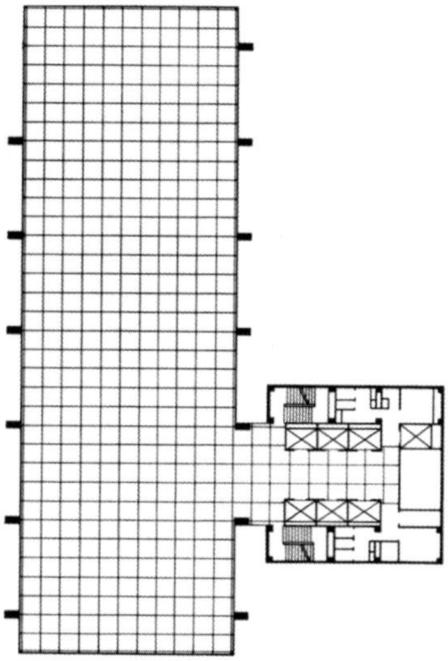

fig. 9. & fig. 10. SOM, Inland Steel Building, Chicago, 1965.

radical aspect of this design was the 60 foot clear span, steel girders, welded to seven pairs of composite steel columns on either side of the slab, thereby yielding 10,200 square feet of column free office space on each floor, with a separate, free-standing 25 story service tower set to the rear of the slab. Seemingly inspired by the pioneering exo-skeletal structure of the PSFS office slab, built in Philadelphia to the designs of Howe and Lescaze in 1931. Inland Steel, unlike either Mies's 860–880 Lake Shore Drive or Bunshaft's Lever House, differentiated absolutely between the framing interval of the vertical, basic structure and the recessed spandrels of the curtain wall. This perennial, expressive tension between the structural frame and the curtain wall will be obviated entirely in SOM's 11 story Pepsi Cola Building, erected on Park Avenue in the same year as the Seagram (fig. 11). In this instance, five pairs of fire proofed steel columns carry a concrete floor plate, with a 39 foot mid-span and 13 foot cantilevers to either side. The street elevation of this proto-'minimalist' work consisted of five spandrels, framed by aluminum mullions carrying single panes of clear glass, measuring 9 feet by 13 feet, a proportion which approximated to the classic golden section.

SOM will return to the format of Inland Steel in their last major high rise of the late 50's, above all in their 60 storey Chase Manhattan Bank built in downtown Manhattan in 1961 (fig. 12). Its much larger footprint necessitated four lines of columns at 18 foot centers with the out riding columns assuming the form of an exoskeleton. As in Inland Steel this expression was emphasized by short, cantilevered overruns at the ends of the slab. For its part, the virtually mullion-less, abstract format of the Pepsi-Cola building will be taken a step further, in the 20 storey Hartford Insurance Company Building, realized in Chicago in 1961. This was an atypical, exposed reinforced concrete structure, in which the structure itself predominated while the floor to ceiling glazing was set back behind the structure on all floors. Here, an unusual balance between horizontal and vertical elements of the concrete structure recalled the equitable proportions of Sullivan's Schlesinger and Mayer Store of sixty years before.

The European Interregnum, 1914–1965

The idea and image of the skyscraper would virtually haunt Europe from the time of Antonio San't Elia's set-back skyscrapers featured in his Futurist Citta Nuova of 1914 to the outbreak of the Second World War of 1939. The image of an all glass high-rise first appears in Mies's sheer glass curtain wall high rises of somewhat unspecified height and structure, dating from 1920 (fig. 1).

Auguste Perret's proposition for a city of towers dating from around 1915, was depicted in a remarkable aerial perspective, drawn by Jacques Imbert and published in the magazine *Wendingen* in 1923 (fig. 13). This envisaged an avenue of 70-storey towers, spaced out at intervals on either side of a high-speed traffic boulevard which was wider and longer than the Champs-Élysées. The high rises that made up this futuristic vision, published barely a year after Le Corbusier's Ville Contemporaine, were to have been executed in a Beaux Arts neoclassical manner closer to the stone faced work of McKim, Mead, and White than to the classical rationalism of Perret in his prime. They manifest a transatlantic Romanticism which will be entirely absent from Mies's speculations about glass skyscrapers of virtually the same date. With its pierced windows and its skeleton framed *modenature*, there was nothing particularly American or Miesian about Perret's only realized foray into a high-rise form, as we find this in his 25-storey tower realized in Amiens in 1954, the year of his death (fig. 14).

Other than the 15 story Unité d'Habitation at Marseille of 1952 and four other variations

fig. 11 SOM, Pepsi-Cola Building, New York, 1959.

fig. 12 SOM, Chase Manhattan Building, New York, 1961.

fig. 13 Jacques Imbert & Auguste Perret, City of Towers, 1923.

fig. 14 Auguste Perret, 25-story Tower, Amiens, 1954.

of the same type that he realized between 1952 and his death in 1965, Le Corbusier never realized a high-rise building. However, his 60 storey, so called, Cartesian skyscraper, first projected in the drawings for his Ville Contemporaine of 1922 and later elaborated in his Plan Voisin of 1925, was predicated on a Hennebique concrete framing system in which a reinforced concrete structure was cantilevered out on all four sides; a proposition that in terms of providing a continuous, uninterrupted, curtain-wall membrane was close to Mies' hermetically glazed skyscrapers of 1920 and his Friedrichstrasse office block project of 1922.

Perret's tower in Amiens will be fenestrated with pierced square windows, as will Ernesto Roger's Torre Velasca built in the center of Milan in 1958 (fig. 15). This steel-framed, 28-storey Tower may be seen in retrospect in that the form mimics the profile of a fortified tower. At the same tower, the structure is more overtly tectonic, in the manner of Perret rather than Le Corbusier.

Perhaps the most radical aspect of Le Corbusier's so called Cartesian skyscraper of the early 20's was the clustering of its form as into 24 glistening glass towers conceived as the administrative core of the Ville Contemporaine. In this instance, each tower with the same cruciform serrated plan, rose to the same height so as to establish a new horizontal datum some 60 stories in the air. He will continue to assert this strategy throughout his ambitious urban proposals of the next two decades, as these will be eventually assembled into his book *La Ville Radieuse* of 1934. The type-form of the Cartesian skyscraper will be modified at around this time from a cruciform plan with a serrated perimeter to a smooth-surfaced, Y-shaped plan, providing exceptionally well-lit office space of relatively shallow depth, illuminated from both sides. While this variation would have entailed a highly uneconomic form of development in terms of square footage, it will be given a decidedly iconic importance in the four towers that make up the center of Le Corbusier's plan for Paris of 1937. One should

also note that the aesthetics of Le Corbusier's Cartesian type, irrespective of whether its plan was cruciform or Y-shaped, was equally concerned with the horizontal spread of the form as with its height and with the clustering of such forms, having the same height so as to create a new urban profile. It is to be regretted that this civilized concept should only have been realized on one or two occasions during the entire span of the 20th century; most notably in the serried ministerial slabs lining both sides of the monumental axis in Brasilia and in the four slabs rising to the same height that make up the Segelgatan development in Stockholm realized between 1955 and 1965.

Le Corbusier will first confront the aesthetic challenge of the featurelessness, skin-tight undifferentiated curtain wall of limitless height in the one-off skyscraper that he projected for the Quartier de la Marine, Algiers in 1938. Here in a project for a free-standing, 50-storey office slab with a lozenge-shaped plan he divided up the overall height into three equal sections above an initial 6 storey podium base (fig. 16). Each of these sections were to have been separated one from another by interstitial floors

fig. 15. Ernesto Rogers (BPPR), Torre Velasca, Milan, 1958.

fig. 16. Le Corbusier, 50-story Tower, Naval Zone, Algiers, 1938.

that were to have been treated as single-storey, opaque bands with pierced windows, ostensibly to be assigned to the accommodation of archives, although they could just as easily have been handled as intermediate service floors. It is striking that, as in his free-standing, Cartesian skyscraper model of virtually the same date, he found it necessary to give his prototypical, singular slab a central focus, which took the form of a recessed opening in the center of the main facade. In a later high rise projected for Algiers, this focus was extended over the entire middle section of its tripartite façade to form a syncopated relief through the manipulation of *brise soleil* in front of the glass. In fact, through the rhythmic application of such sunbreakers, two plastic manipulations were envisaged as operating together; the first was a vertical, counter-changing *brise soleil* running up for the full height of the building, the second was a horizontal elaboration of the central third of the form which suggested a modification of this somewhat unprecedented formalism in the work of Le Corbusier can surely only be accounted for in terms of a kind of *horror vacuii* which is inherently latent in the form of high-rise structures, made up of nothing but the repetition of anonymous floors.

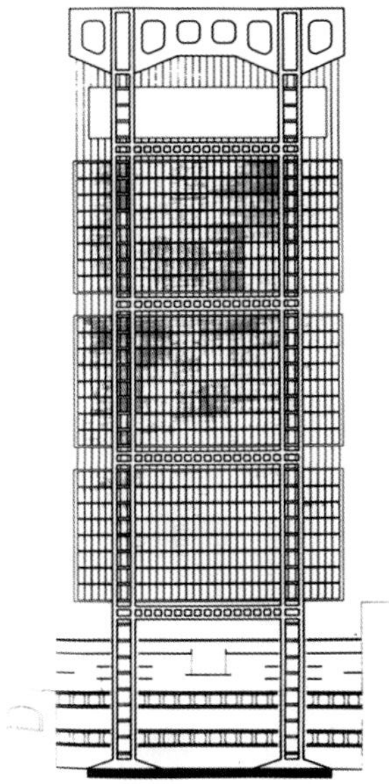

fig. 17. Amancio Williams, Project for a 28-story skyscraper, 1948.

fig. 18. Louis Kahn, Project for a 35-story skyscraper, Kansas City, 1966–1973.

Structure and Space-Form in the Late Modern Skyscraper 1948–1997

The idea that a work of great height could be modified by a giant structural frame lying outside the body of the building is first fully articulated by Amancio Williams in his 1948 proposal for a 28-storey high-rise structure for an unspecified site in Argentina (fig. 17). The text that he publishes in Zodiac 16 of 1964 says everything one might need to know about the raison d'être behind this particular form: "The project is based on two very different elements: the supporting structure of reinforced concrete composed of four huge pillars and two big beams and the building itself, a clear steel and glass construction hanging from the beams. The concrete structures were to be built in place. The steel tension bars and the glass curtain were to be fabricated in factories and workshops."

While the exoskeleton was a little more complicated than Williams' initial description would suggest, the proposition remained that most of the floors would be carried by tensile suspension rods rather than by compressive columns which would enable certain savings with regard to the structure.

Over a long gestation period, lasting from 1966 to 1973, Louis Kahn and his engineer Auguste Komendant will work on the development of a 35 storey high rise for Kansas City where in respect of a square plane, the principle was to suspend the floors on wire cables from four inverted, reinforced concrete, bow-string

trusses each one spanning across one side of the square plan with the compressive loads being carried down to the ground by eight coupled columns, two at each corner of the square (fig. 18). The aesthetic aim here was to terminate the top of the building with bridge-like, catenary spans and hang the curtain-walled floors beneath, contained by the monumental, compressive column clusters at the corner.

Norman Foster's 41 storey Hong Kong and Shanghai Bank, under development for a prominent site in the center of Hong Kong from 1979 to its completion in 1985, would be inspired by William's unrealized exo-skeleton high-rise proposal of 1948 (fig. 19a). What Foster was able to realize in Hong Kong integrated two ideas which had long been at issue in the evolution of high-rise office buildings. These were, first, how to modulate the height of a building through its structure, and second, how to introduce semi-public uses and volumes with which to mediate the only too privatized accommodation of repetitive bureaucratic floors.

fig. 19a Foster Associates, Hong Kong & Shanghai Bank, Hong Kong, 1979–1985, overall view.

fig. 19b Foster Associates, Hong Kong & Shanghai Bank, Hong Kong, 1979–1985, view of the escalator connecting the atrium and the public space.

The second of these aims had been achieved, in principle, in Frank Lloyd Wright's six-storey Larkin Building, Buffalo of 1904, which, while hardly a high rise, was nonetheless a multi-level office building in which the processal anonymity of the repetitive office floors was mediated by the full height, semi-public space occupying the heart of the building. It is just this paradigm that Foster will apply to the core of the HSBC headquarters in Hong Kong.

Like Amancio William's exo-skeleton high-rise project of 1948, the multi-layered Hong Kong and Shanghai Bank, with its three slab segments rising to 28, 35 and 41 stories, respectively, comes to be modulated in terms of

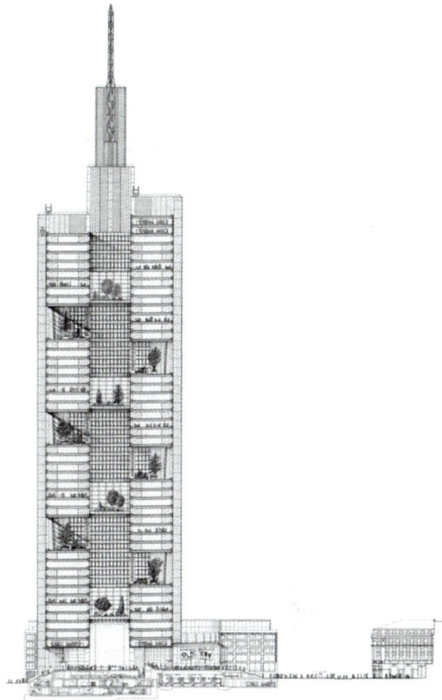

its height by tubular steel, triangulated trusses, each spanning 38 meters, from which the repetitive office floors are suspended on wire cables. It is significant that the building spans over a time-honored public space in downtown Hong Kong and that a semi-public void, running up inside the structure will be connected by escalators to the civic space situated immediately beneath the building (fig. 19b).

Foster will return to the same high-rise, composite theme, namely the mutual modulation of both the height of the structure and the space within, in his 45 storey Commerzbank built in downtown Frankfurt in 1997. This last is a multi-storey office building predicated on a triangular plan, in which the office floors make up three sides of an equilateral triangle, enclosing a void throughout the full height of the building. The service cores, that is the elevators stairs and lavatories, are relegated to the points of the triangle while the void consists of a 45 storey, public atrium covered by a glass roof. While the actual structure supporting the floors

fig. 20a Foster Associates, Commerzbank, Frankfurt, 1997, overall view.

fig. 20b Foster Associates, Commerzbank, Frankfurt, 1997, section.

is of conventional construction, the height of the building is broken up by seven, two storey, staggered "sky gardens" alternating from one side of the building to the other; thereby affording green semi-public, garden terraces for the benefit of the bank employees (fig. 20a and 20b). It is just these "hanging" gardens which will break up the height of the Commerzbank in such a way as to relate the remaining six storey segments of bureaucratic space between the terraces, back to the average height of the surrounding residential fabric. In this one piece, for a single instance, the high-rise finds itself tentatively reconciled to the continuity of the city. High-rise finds itself tentatively reconciled to the continuity of the city.

fig. 1. Le Corbusier, The Horizontal and Vertical of Buenos Aires by Night, sketch, 1929.

The Skyscraper According to Le Corbusier[1]

Catherine Carpentier

Le Corbusier worked at every scale of architectural and urban practice, from the simple armchair to the apartment building, from the individual villa to a city for three million inhabitants. Skyscrapers marked a series of milestones in his professional career, with an approach that was always global: from solving a façade detail, to integrating one or more of these urban objects into some of the most important cities in the world at the time.

A tool for urban planning

As early as 1921, in the fourth issue of the magazine *L'Esprit Nouveau*, Le Corbusier published a drawing of a "city of towers"[2]. The drawing was the outcome of a project that Le Corbusier presented at the *Salon d'Automne* in 1922 under the title "*Ville Contemporaine de trois millions d'habitants*". The project was intended as an entire city, in a totally theoretical context, whose guiding principles were the decongestion of the city center, the increase in density, the means of circulation, and planted areas—comprising twenty-four skyscrapers, each sixty stories high, located in the center of the city, designed to accommodate 10,000 to 50,000 employees each. They were cruciform in shape (for high stability), stepped (for large window development), had their first floors on stilts for circulation, and were 150 to 200 m high. They were to contain 64 elevators and 12 large fire escapes. The first floor was to include 3,640,000 square meters of gardens, squares, and parks, with terraces, restaurants, cafés and luxury shops. "*Already softened by the blue sky in the distance, the skyscrapers raise up their large geometrical sections all in glass. In the glass that covers their facades from top to bottom, the blue glows and the sky sparkles. Dazzling. Immense, but radiant prisms.*"[3] Unlike Perret, Le Corbusier believed that skyscrapers were not suitable for family life. They were therefore intended for offices, and thus, of the three million inhabitants, two million would actually be installed on the outskirts in the garden cities.

1. This article is a condensed version of Catherine Carpentier's diploma thesis, "*Les projets de Gratte-ciel de Le Corbusier*" [Le Corbusier's skyscraper projects] discussed in March 1997, at the École d'architecture de Paris-Belleville, supervised by Marie-Jeanne Dumont.

2. The title is identical to that given by his former mentor Auguste Perret to his 1920 project for the Paris-Saint-Germain axis. See K. Frampton,'High-Rise Form in the Continuity of the City', p.39.

fig. 2. The business District of Paris, le Plan Voisin, model photograph, 1925.

In 1925, in the Plan Voisin, Le Corbusier confronted the theory of the City of Three Million Inhabitants with the Parisian context, by installing a 240-hectare business city in the heart of the city center on the one hand, and a residential city on the other, at the center of which was an underground train station. "*This plan attacks the worst neighborhoods, the narrowest streets. [...] This city, which has been creeping up until now, suddenly rises up in the most natural order, and momentarily surpasses our imagination, which is limited by age-old habits*"[4] (fig. 2). In both cases, the skyscrapers are containers, modern technological tools whose purpose is to free up the historical city, asphyxiated by its overpopulation. The impression they convey of their highly technical construction and the importance of their transformative role defines their aesthetic.

But during his trip to South America in 1929, Le Corbusier did not so much confront problems of congestion or overpopulation, but rather nature itself. A series of ten conferences took him from Buenos Aires (Argentina) to Montevideo (Uruguay) and São Paulo (Brazil). These cities struck him with the immensity and strength of their natural settings, yet each of them seemed to ignore its environment. Of Buenos Aires, he wrote: "*Buenos Aires has neither picturesqueness nor variety. It is a simple meeting of the Pampas and the Ocean, in one line, lit up at night from one end to the other*"[5]. Montevideo, on the other hand, is perched on a promontory, detached from its port below. As for São Paulo, it is located on a high plateau, at an altitude of 800 meters, surrounded by numerous hills and valleys.

Faced with such strong contexts, Le Corbusier set out to confront natural magnificence with human ingenuity. The built work was to compensate for the difficulties of the

3. Le Corbusier, *Urbanisme* (Paris: Flammarion, 1994), 166.
4. Le Corbusier, op. cit., 267-268.
5. Le Corbusier, *Précisions sur un état présent de l'architecture et de l'urbanisme* (Paris: Altamira Éditions, 1994), 200.

natural environment (topography, distance) while enhancing each of the sites. He envisioned a very great density for Buenos Aires, and designed high skyscrapers, near the port, and even on a pier extending into the sea, whose verticality was meant to contrast with the horizontality of the water: *"an immense block raised by man in the water of the Rio and standing in the sky of Argentina"*[6] (fig. 1).

In Montevideo, he proposed to horizontally extend the main street that comes down from the countryside and for it to cross the city above the port. Thus, from cars driving 80 m above the sea, *"we will go down to the offices. For the offices will be the immense spines of building that carry the street above"*[7]. These "seascrapers" were intended to make up the business city and allow it to be located near the port.

Finally, in São Paulo, to relieve the roads that come to the city after crossing a multitude of hills and valleys, he envisaged the creation of elevated highways laid from summit to summit. These gigantic viaducts would be supported by "landscrapers", reinforced concrete structures that containing offices in the center of the city, and housing on the outskirts.

Skyscrapers, seascrapers, and landscrapers would all have the same objective: to offer these cities-in-the-making an urban typology of their own that would allow them to live up to the destiny that Le Corbusier foresaw for them. These monuments would create the necessary conditions for the advent of their national and even international influence.

Evolution of a type: the Cartesian skyscraper

Le Corbusier's first thoughts on the "Radiant City" began to appear in 1930. Presented at the third CIAM in 1930, they appeared in several articles in the magazine *Plan* in 1931 and were published in 1935 and 1964. This city, whose main difference from the city of three million inhabitants is that it is linear and not concentric, is made up of zones laid out along the main axis: the business city, the residential city, manufacturers, and finally, heavy industry. The train station, the airport, the hotels and the embassies are located between the business city and the residential city (fig. 3).

Within the comprehensive framework of this urban reflection, and by a logical, rational, and mathematical reasoning, Le Corbusier described very precisely for the first time what he called *"the Cartesian skyscraper"*. This goal of this type was to *"decongest the center of cities by increasing density to reduce distances"*[8], and to constitute the business center of the region or the country. It would allow the entire ground surface to be returned to circulation and to bring air, light, quiet, and vast horizons to the workplace. The skyscrapers were to be placed every 400 m (equivalent to the average distance between two Parisian subway stations), in a staggered or checkerboard pattern. Their footprint represents only 5% of the area allocated to them. They are cross-shaped to avoid courtyards, to develop a maximum facade surface (thus of light) and to present an optimal resistance to the wind. Built in glass and steel, they rise to a height of 220 m and their enclosed spaces start at 5 or 7 m from the ground and leave free passage underneath. The layout of the skyscrapers creates a special traffic system, where cars and pedestrians do not cross paths and each skyscraper has 3,000 parking spaces. Thus, concludes Le Corbusier: *"the skyscraper is a function of content (the premises) and of the surface area of the free ground at its foot. A skyscraper that does not achieve this function in harmony is a disease. It is the very disease of New York"*[9]. He would return to the subject at length following his trip to New York in 1935[10].

All the precepts of the Cartesian skyscraper described here were already present in the examples studied earlier. Thereafter,

6. Le Corbusier, *op. cit.*, 204.

7. Le Corbusier, *op. cit.*, 239.

8. Le Corbusier, *Plans,* nº7, July 1931, 6.

9. Le Corbusier, op. cit., 10.

10. See: Le Corbusier, *Quand les cathédrales étaient blanches* (Paris: Denoël/Gonthier, 1983).

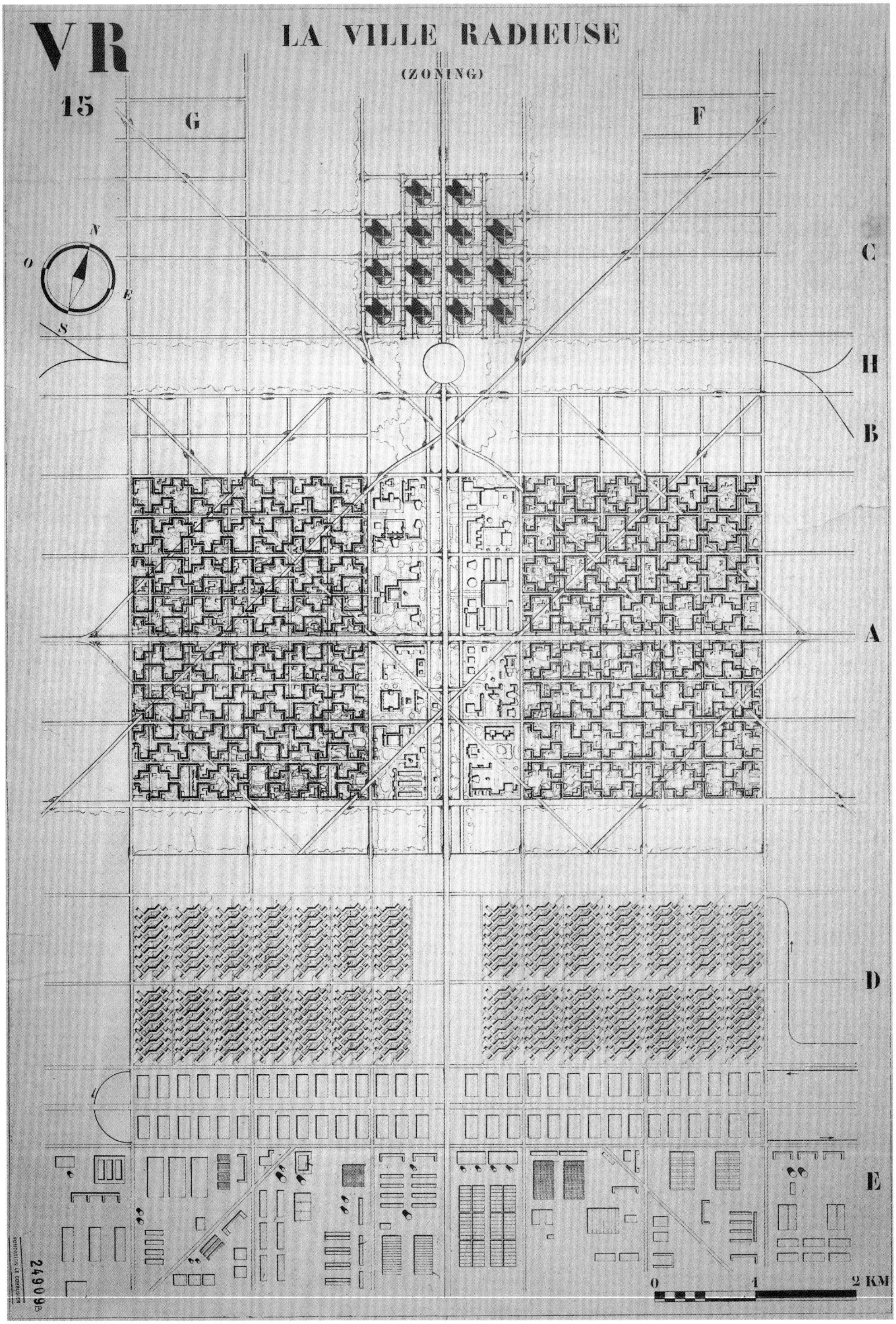

fig. 3. The Radiant City, plan, 1930.

fig. 4. The Cartesian skyscraper, 1932.

he continued to call the different skyscrapers imagined in specific contexts as "*Cartesian*". Their own typology evolved, but they all had in common the same notion of a containing object, the "*mature fruit of a machinist evolution*"[11], and a "*tool for putting precise urban phenomena in order*"[12].

For example, in 1932, for the new urban plan of Barcelona, Le Corbusier proposed a new type of skyscraper for the business city facing the sea. A large parallelepiped with its ends inclined at 45°, to which another smaller volume is attached in its center, forms the "hen's foot" building, which responds much better to the path of the sun than the cruciform skyscraper. This new typology would be used several times by Le Corbusier in the following years (fig. 4).

The advent of a symbol: Algiers

Le Corbusier's longest and most productive urban study was in Algiers (1932–1942). This city saw its population grow from 77,500 to 257,000 in the space of 50 years, and in 1931, Algiers with its suburbs was the fourth largest city in France, after Paris, Marseille, and Lyon. Le Corbusier developed five successive urban projects, during which the typology and symbolism of the skyscraper itself evolved considerably.

The first stage (project A) echoes a Regional Plan drawn up earlier, which suggested replacing the Quartier de la Marine, which was close to the sea and overpopulated by the local population, with affordable housing. Le Corbusier was opposed to this arrangement, which perpetuated the "bottleneck" created by this district, cutting the city in two. Here, as in South America, nature could not be left out: "*The joy of Algiers is in the sea and the sky. The principle: each window must be full of*

11. Le Corbusier, *Plans*, op. cit., 6.

12. Le Corbusier, *Œuvres complètes*, Vol. 3, (Zürich: Éd. d'Architecture Artémis), 75.

sky and sea, the worker's window a priori"[13]. But land for building was scarce, so the architect proposed very long buildings for housing, all of a piece, and forming a promontory to free up circulation and parks below. The business district was then established in the liberated Quartier de la Marine: the building rises from hill 12 to hill 158, from which a footbridge extends towards the hill of Fort l'Empereur, at the foothills of the Quartier de la Marine. This footbridge is supported by substructures that potentially constitute future building lots. The building of the business city assumes the founding role of a device that simultaneously solves the problems of housing and circulation. In this version, it is parallel to the coast, with trapezoidal slopes on the land side and a smooth face on the sea side. It measures approximately 500 m long, 58 m wide (including 25 m of projection of the redents—steps) and 150 m high.

Projects B and C reduce the importance of the business city. Le Corbusier was inspired by the construction system of the Italian architect-engineer Guido Fiorini's "cantilever"[14] bridges. He created an H-shaped building, combining two elements of Fiorini's skyscraper (103 × 84 × 158 m high). At the height of 100 m, at the junction with the first viaduct, the skyscraper is pierced by a loggia three levels high, a huge window on the sea (fig. 5)

These three projects did not come to fruition, and at the end of 1937, Le Corbusier was appointed by the government as a member of the new Permanent Planning Commission for the Algiers region. New urban measures were taken, completely freeing up the area of the Quartier de la Marine. The business city, the main concern of the D project, could then be freely installed there. Le Corbusier discarded the H-shaped typology and introduced the "tripod" typology, a version of the "hen's foot" skyscraper, in order to improve the sunlight of the building. The axes of this skyscraper are arranged according to the medians of an equilateral triangle inscribed in the part of the Quartier de la Marine that projects out to sea. It is 150 m high: "*Equipped in this way, the Quartier de la Marine clearly becomes a place of high significance; it expresses Algiers—Capital of Africa*"[15].

Project E, whose centerpiece is the skyscraper, would confirm this symbolic distinction. Taller than Project D, the 45-storey building takes the form of a spindle, 87 m long and 37 m wide at its two ends and 43 m in the center. The central part is used by the vertical circulation core; offices are distributed to either side. The layout of the facades is symmetrical.

Over the course of the studies, while the internal structure of the skyscraper evolved little, its facades became asymmetrical: "*Intervention of plastic. Everything seemed implacably ordered by the succession of rational events. A decision of a poetic nature intervenes: the plan was rigorously symmetrical. But through a golden section, the attitude of the façade became asymmetrical. The form seems to swell on the left, to taper on the right. Response to a double call of the site: the cliff and the sea*"[16]. It is in this form that the project was installed, as part of the master

13. Le Corbusier and Pierre Jeanneret, *Plan d'Aménagement de la ville d'Alger* 1931-1932 offered to the municipality, 26.

14. This static layout in iron and steel uses tie rods to transfer the weight of each floor onto a central core, that alone supports the effects of compression. Except for this core, which must be progressively cemented during the progress of the construction, all the rest of the building can be prefabricated in series, which not only brings a substantial economy but also frees up the ground level, the whole of the upper floors being suspended.

15. Le Corbusier, *Œuvres complètes*, Vol. 3, op. cit., 103.

16. Quoted in Jean-Pierre Giordani, *Le Corbusier et les projets pour la ville d'Alger 1931-1942* (IIIrd cycle thesis, 1987), 364.

fig. 5. Project B for the Marine district of Algiers, "Showing the road works necessary and sufficient to supply a population of 200,000 on the grounds of Fort l'Empereur," perspective, 1932-1942.

fig. 6. Study for the Marine district in Algiers, perspective, 1938-1939.

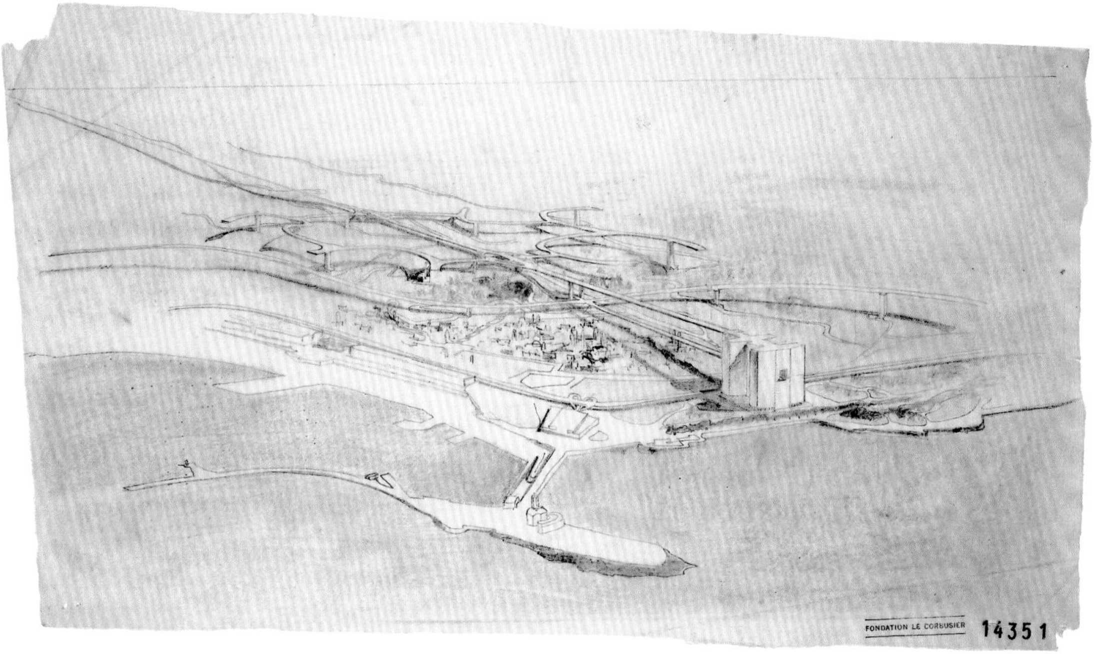
FONDATION LE CORBUSIER
14351

AL
3517
14594
FONDATION LE CORBUSIER

plan of 1942, on the new site of the business district at the foot of Laferriere Boulevard, still facing the sea.

Thus, the thick façade becomes the interface between the intrinsic structure of the skyscraper, its "Cartesianism", and the response to a precise geographical situation: a site (the cliff and the sea); an exposure (the dimensions of the *brise soleils* are calculated according to the orientation of the sun and the depth of the premises); and a culture (reinterpretation of the loggia, a traditional architectural element). This skyscraper combines modern western technical means (reinforced concrete) with a plasticity referring to the local architecture. It echoes the sky, the land and the sea; its location and its construction link the two continents of Europe and Africa. Le Corbusier said of it that it is "*a true biology*"[17] because it respects the material requirements of the Cartesian skyscraper, while responding perfectly to its particular context (fig. 6).

From Theory to Practice: American Projects

The Ministry of National Education in Rio de Janeiro

In parallel with his studies in Algiers, Le Corbusier was brought to work in Rio de Janeiro, through Lucio Costa and in collaboration with Oscar Niemeyer, on the construction of the Ministry of National Education and Public Health, built in 1943. This project, which is not a skyscraper per se, is the most convincing testimony of the application of his theories to the high-rise building. A simple 14-story parallelepiped is set on 10-meter-high pilings and articulated perpendicular to a low volume forming a plinth containing the conference and exhibition rooms. The open space around the building, a large public square with a sculpture by Celso Antonio, gives it a monumentality that suits its program. Here again, *brises soleils* are used to respond to the Brazilian climate, and Le Corbusier encouraged the integration of local materials (azulejos, pink granite from Carioca for example), as well as local skills for the exterior spaces (garden designed by Roberto Burle Marx) (fig. 9). The building marked the culmination of fruitful exchanges between Le Corbusier, Oscar Niemeyer and Lucio Costa[18], and gave birth to a new Brazilian school. By combining contemporaneity and tradition, the building was quickly perceived as a manifesto of South American modernity.

The UN project in New York

But an even more prestigious institution than the Brazilian ministry offered Le Corbusier the opportunity to crystallize his twenty years of reflection on the theme of skyscrapers. Although the final design of the construction escaped him, it seems appropriate to return here to the genesis of this exceptional project, developed in record time. The United Nations, whose purpose is to "*save succeeding generations from the scourge of war, which twice in the space of a human lifetime has inflicted untold suffering on mankind*"[19], was to be headquartered in the United States, in Manhattan, on land acquired with the help of the wealthy John D. Rockefeller. Le Corbusier, sent by France in 1946, participated in the first commission that chose the site. He was enthusiastic about it: "*Don't make it the cradle of the United Nations, make it the immediate 'battle station' that you will build tomorrow. And when you get tired of New York, you will sell it at a profit because it will consist of the best offices and auditoriums*"[20].

17. Le Corbusier, *Œuvres complètes*, Vol. 3, op. cit., 50.

18. See on this subject the letters from Lucio Costa and Oscar Niemeyer, in Le Corbusier, *Œuvres complètes*, Vol. 4, (Zürich: Éd. d'Architecture Artémis), 90.

19. Preamble of the United Nations Charter, quoted in Serge Berstein and Pierre Milza, Histoire du vingtième siècle. 1. La guerre et la reconstruction 1939-1953 (Paris: Hatier) 277.

20. *Architecture d'Aujourd'hui*, n° spécial Le Corbusier, 1948, 109.

fig. 7. United Nations, Project n° 23, proposed by Le Corbusier, model, 1947.

A group of ten international architects, including Oscar Niemeyer and Le Corbusier, was hired to develop the project[21]. They formed the Building Plans Department, under the direction of Wallace K. Harrison, the architect of the Rockefeller Center. They were appointed in February 1947, but Le Corbusier, who had been there before, drew up the first sketches that would guide the group's work. For four months, 45 meetings punctuated this collective work in which each architect contributed to the common work.

Le Corbusier quickly set up the Secretariat in a skyscraper whose dimensions he studied: 60 × 25 × 130 to 140 m high to accommodate 5,000 people in 10 m^2 offices. Around the building, the various functions of the Organization were housed in separate entities, with a particular relationship to the horizontality of the nearby East River. With a built front on the First Avenue side to protect against it, and an opening towards the river, he wished to create the "Valley of Nations", a name later abandoned. Various sketches show a square containing the Council Chambers and the General Assembly, the Secretariat skyscraper, two small skyscrapers for the Specialized Agencies, a curved hotel and a hill of terraces for the restaurants. These elements, like pawns, are interchangeable. The skyscraper is almost always designed in the shape of a diamond ("lens" skyscraper) with a grid system on the facade reminiscent of the *brises-soleil* of Algiers.

On April 3, 1947, Le Corbusier presented his project (called No. 23) at the 26th meeting of the Plans Department, with the following objectives: to create an obvious relationship between the different buildings, to leave plenty of room for circulation, to separate the pedestrian and car entrances, to create a single large hall with separate entrances for the press, the public, and the delegates, and to create an open-air amphitheater on the roof of the General Assembly. The volumes, although economical and compressed, preserved an excellent relationship between the three constituent units of the Organization. (fig. 7)

On April 25, Niemeyer made his own proposal (project no. 32) and questioned the location of Le Corbusier's buildings. He placed them near the edges of the plot to free up an esplanade. "*The idea was to have a good overview of the site, and to place the buildings in such*

21. Gyle Soilleux (Australia), Gustave Brunfaut (Belgium), Oscar Niemeyer (Brazil), Ernest Cormier (Canada), Ssu Ch'eng Liang (China), Le Corbusier (France), Sven Markelius (Sweden), Howard Robertson (United Kingdom), Julio Vilamajo (Uruguay), Nikolaï D. Bassov (USSR). As Germany and Finland are not part of the UN, architects such as Aalto, Gropius or Mies van der Rohe could not be selected.

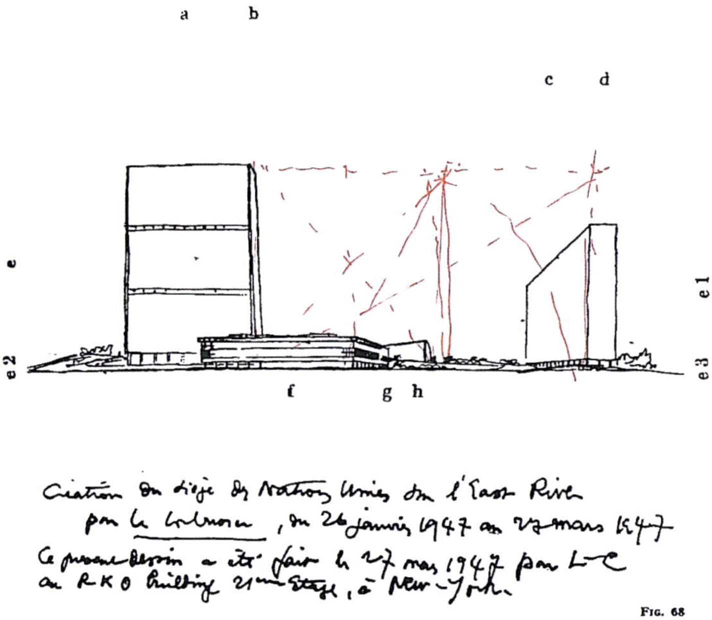

fig. 8. Creation of the United Nations headquarters on the East River, Le Corbusier, 1947. In red, annotations by M. Kagan.

a way that when people arrived they could see them all and understand their functions"[22].

From that time on, Le Corbusier's presence on the architectural team became difficult. Having been on site for several months, he felt he had the overriding opinion. In 1950, in *Le Modulor*, he wrote on the subject: "*I have inscribed here a series of dimensions: a, b, c, d, e (e1, e2, e3), f, g, h, which should and could make the mathematical radiation burst through space. This space is 450 m in length, 150 m in depth, 200 m in height. The appeal to the numbers, alas! will not be made, because those who remained the masters of the enterprise, after the manipulations which sometimes triumph in such occasions, are indifferent and foreign to this quality of spirit which it would be necessary to require, to this sharpness, to this astuteness, to this curiosity, which engage 'to cross the door of the miracles'*"[23] (fig. 8).

Finally, on May 7, 1947, the two architects reached a compromise, project 42 (or 23-32), the basis of the final project, with the following objectives: the Secretariat, the place of daily work, cannot have a pre-eminent place and is placed at the periphery of the organs that symbolize the United Nations; the General Assembly is in the center of the site because it is the main element of the UN.

Work continued on this principle until June 9, the date of the last meeting, and the beginning of the finalization of the programmatic, technical and architectural details, without the help of the consulting firm. Le Corbusier quickly returned to Paris, thinking that he would remain in contact with Wallace K. Harrison, at least for the development of the skyscraper and its indispensable brise-soleil. But despite an abundance of correspondence from Le Corbusier to Harrison, Rockefeller and even Trygve Lie, the first Secretary General of the UN, he did not participate in the design of the building, nor in the construction. In 1948, drastic budgetary restrictions caused the Secretariat to lose two floors (from 41 to 39), four conference rooms (from 22 to 18) and 500 parking spaces (from 2000 to 1500). Work began in September 1948 and was completed in 1952, without the Secretariat's sunshades. During a stay in New York in 1950, Le Corbusier wrote: "*The diamonds of New York*

22. Le Corbusier, op. cit., 234.

23. Le Corbusier *Notebooks 2*, 1950–1954, fig. 255.

fig. 9. Ministry of National Education, Rio de Janeiro, 1943. L. Costa, O. Niemeyer with Le Corbusier.

are lost here because Harrison put blue glasses. Everywhere else the skyscrapers radiate 'luminous' (and yet the luminescence reigns everywhere: proof that Harrison has sown the 'blues" with such strong blue glasses)"[24].

After the UN experience, and as part of the post-war reconstruction, Le Corbusier would again try to promote the interest of the skyscraper as a "model building of the administration"[25]. In Marseille Vieux-Port in particular, in 1947, he designed a skyscraper similar to the one in Algiers, which could have been its counterpart: two lighthouses facing each other on each side of the Mediterranean. Le Corbusier had even imagined a line of force between cities by raising skyscrapers in strategic points: Le Havre, Paris, Lyon, Marseille and Algiers. Because if the typology of the skyscraper is a research in itself, it is especially the symbolic role that this one can bring to the city which is most important.

"One speaks, to untie the embrace of the cities and to bring the joy of living, to build, under certain conditions, apartment buildings of fifty meters high..."[26] *"How to avoid that our cities spread and dilute, lose their form and their soul?"... "In opposition to this great dispersion of the city, we have to build a new city. In opposition to this great scattering of panic, a natural law must be evoked: men like to group together to help each other, to defend themselves and to save their efforts"... " To raise in the sky, in the middle of space some buildings that we will qualify a priori as beautiful and worthy, proofs of optimism, of technical and sensitive capacity..."*[27] For Le Corbusier, as early as 1946, these high-rise buildings without unnecessary excess are the appropriate response to the current issue of the proliferation of housing estates that leads to the "*unhealthy swelling of cities*" and the waste of transport and networks that he mentioned in *Manière de penser l'urbanisme*.

24. Le Corbusier, *Œuvres complètes*, Vol. 4, (Zürich: Éd. d'Architecture Artémis), 133.

25. Le Corbusier, Le *Modulor* (Paris: Éditions Architecture d'Aujourd'hui, 1983), 167.

26. Le Corbusier, *Manière de penser l'urbanisme*, (Paris: Gonthier, 1972).

27. Le Corbusier, op. cit.

fig. 1. Raimund Abraham, Times Square project: perspective view in context, 1984.

Vertical Horizon

Pascal Hofstein

Context

European architecture schools in the 1980s were scarcely involved in the adventures of vertical modernity. In some American universities, a few exercises about vertical projects were given as studio projects at Columbia University and Cornell, but their ambition relied on the tower as a singular object, thereby exploring various ways of solving the eternal tripartite division of the vertical building: feet, body and head. This teaching of the vertical building was often limited to redesigning the tower while trying to exhaust its articulations of form, detailing, and composition.

One can understand the fascination that a European architect eager for modernity might feel when discovering the island of Manhattan. As a "standing city", it invents its skyline with the skyscraper as one of the most salient elements of the transformation of the grid. The place of the tower in the urban space—the tower as an object, the tower as an ideal ideogram—*functions* as a recognizable model of the New York landscape and as a subject for conquest.

Another modernity is revealed there, one transforming the constructive advances and architectural preoccupations of the old continent, one that engages in what the grid on the ground allows, a freedom of its transformation in the conquest of the sky. Manhattan is thus posed as a laboratory of multiple potentials.

Swing

Broadway Boogie Woogie, by Piet Mondrian, unveiled in 1943 a ballet of lines, voids and colored masses where multiple centralities occupy the space of the canvas. The pictorial space plays with multiple centers, displaced foci in movement. In a vocabulary of lines, rotations and instabilities, the exploded center of modern pictoriality afforded a possible spatiality, an invention to seize upon.

"The failure of postmodernism is that it does not recognize that the heart of things is hollow. At the center of meaning remains mystery. Profound insight understands there is no need to fill up everything, especially the new, the unknown, and the unsolved with pieces from and references to

a comforting past" wrote Jonathan Friedman in 1984 in his text "Wright explodes the box"[1].

In a direct reference to Frank Lloyd Wright's sublime text, "the exploded box", Jonathan Friedman reminds us that the human heart, "The center of the organism," is an empty muscle. In the same way, Wright's hearth, the spatial center, possesses comparable qualities—an empty space, built hollow and offering itself as available, irrigable...

Friedman points out that "the heart(h) is hollow"[2] and reinforces the idea that architectural space is defined by this contained explosion, or rather this implosion, which characterizes the void as a material for the construction of space, a void that must be qualified, occupied, and not saturated. Frank Lloyd Wright, born in the year when dynamite was invented, is the architect of controlled explosion, of interior space in movement, which offers domestic spatiality an unexpected quality of instability and great dimension.

Resulting from the layout of the grid, the question of the center of Manhattan rarely arises. On the other hand, the question of a center in Manhattan recurs. Which one, where, who celebrates what, etc.

On the Manhattan grid, there are several identifiable centers, all scattered: Lincoln Center, Rockefeller Center, Central Park, Grand Central Station, to name a few. Each of these centers is remarkable and above all essential. Essential because they offer a breath of fresh air to the Manhattan grid. Each center aims to enlarge the grid, to give it an extension, another limit, and another light. For it is by embracing the idea of being central that one offers oneself to the world as radiant... Lincoln Center offers a front to the Opera, Rockefeller Center the space of a skating rink and a belvedere, Central Park a great nature, Grand Central Station, a hollow void surmounted by a midnight blue ceiling where the constellations shine...

Each remarkable center in Manhattan proposes a radiance and is accompanied by an empty, generous space, producing an explosion of the grid in the urban space, a breath of air within what Rem Koolhaas celebrated in *Delirious New York*[3]—its congestion.

Times Square

In 1984, a question was raised regarding the center of Times Square. The Architectural League of New York launched a competition for an empty lot, at the corner of Broadway, Seventh Avenue and 42nd Street.

Times Square, the theater and cinema district, is above all the tourist center of Manhattan. Every year, the famous half-ton ball slowly descends from the top of the "One Times Square" tower during the last minutes of the countdown to December 31, to produce the fireworks explosion that celebrates the New Year.

Raimund Abraham was the winner of this competition that took place in a specific American cultural moment—during the profusion of so-called postmodern buildings. These examples were totally refractory to the innumerable possibilities of the Modern Movement, its plastic discoveries, and its social proposals. In other words, modern aesthetics and ethics were petrified in Beaux-Arts images totally disconnected from constructive reality.

Raimund Abraham proposed a project for a building that the members of the jury would qualify as obvious. Obvious, first of all, because it seemed to fit the place (fig. 1).

A vertical sequence of seven theaters in the middle of Times Square is relevant from the outset. It is contextual. The program of the street is repositioned, converted[4] to the vertical, transformed into architecture.

1. Jonathan Friedman, "Wright Explodes the Box", in *Abacus*, (New York Institute of Technology, 1984).
2. "The heart, but also the hearth, is empty." Ibid.
3. Rem Koolhaas, *Delirious New York a retroactive manifesto for Manhattan* (New York: Monacelli Press, 1994).
4. Philippe Potie, "Le nègre et le Schizophrène", *Le Visiteur* 16, 2010.

Obvious as well because it denatures the tower as a simple object placed on the grid. Another tower in Times Square, even the most beautiful one, would have been banal. Abraham freed himself from the tower as a solid building and proposed the construction of a vertical series of cinemas, an ascending architectural promenade punctuated by voids. It suggested that going to the cinema, enjoying leisure time, could become a new experience, a transformation of what used to take place at street level below. Another experience of "entertainment" is also the conquering of height, moving vertically, discovering, and conquering a Manhattanian space, establishing a contact with the sky. Even though Jean-Paul Belmondo could not take any more running[5], one could still imagine him here, never ceasing to climb, descend, stay... walking in the air.

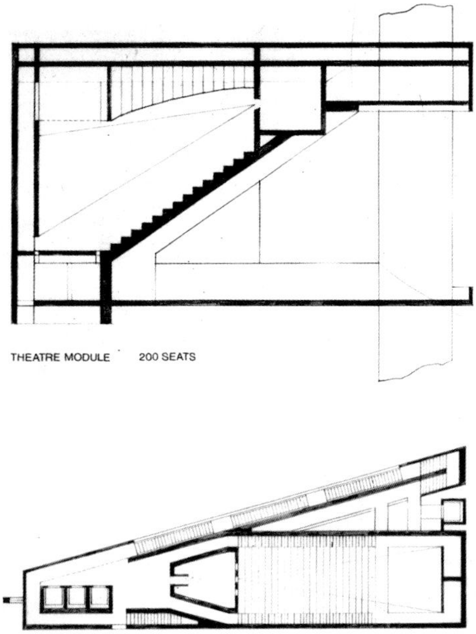

fig. 2 & 3. Raimund Abraham, Times Square model, 1984. Section and plan of one of the cinema amphitheater modules.

Sky

As a tourist in Manhattan, one can recall countless visits to the twin towers of the World Trade Center. The visit to the "World Trade Center One" tower promised a "sky-lobby" on the 87th floor. This fabulous name aroused a sense of wonder, which was immediately reduced to disappointment when it became clear that this sky lobby was only the reception area of a renowned law firm. There, the carpet was thicker, softer, richer... But we will remember this evocative wording of an inventive spatial possibility—the promise of a celestial entrance, at the foot of the clouds, and a possible vertigo.

For it is indeed the sky that is at stake. The Skyscraper, the one that scratches the sky, but also El Lissitzky's Skyhook, the one that wanted to cling to the sky. If the sky becomes the field of reference, then the vertical space can achieve its conquest.

The sky is no longer obliged to be only above. The vertical space summons the sky inside, transforms a limit that one wants to reach into spatial matter, and invents a function in the air. The sky can then be inside and not simply above, and the conquest of vertical space can risk "making the sky the most beautiful place on earth[6].

In the center of Times Square, in the center of the entertainment district, Raimund Abraham proposed a building constructed with voids, intermediate skies, small "sky-lobbies". The undersides of the cinemas are the upper limits of a void in height that opens like a balcony onto the urban space, creating a trapezoidal hollow. The geometry of the ground plot is also trapezoidal. The form of the plot changes into an empty volume, a hollow spatial fig., a double exploit within an overcrowded urban space at street level.

The vertical form, the tower erected by entablatures of horizontal levels on top of

5. Philippe de Broca, *L'Homme de Rio (That Man from Rio)*, film, 1964.

6. Air France advertisement, 1997.

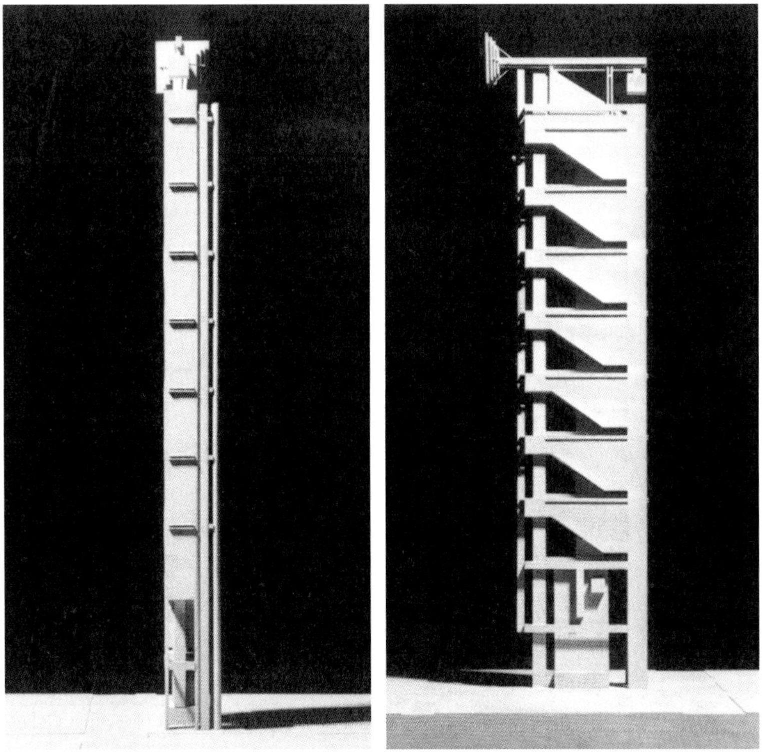

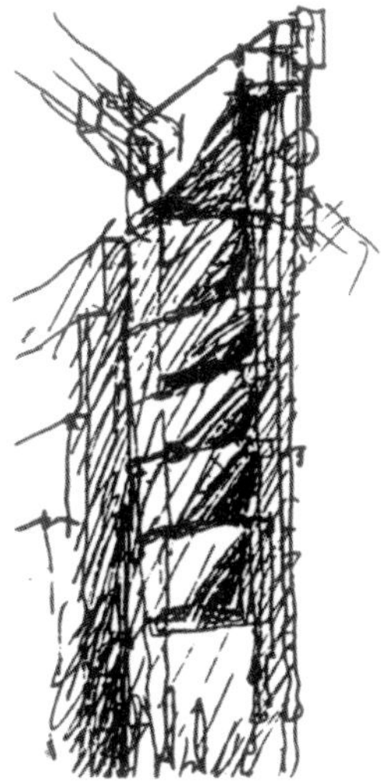

each other and achieving verticality only by the multiplication of horizontal layers, yields to the serialization of spaces built by voids (fig. 2 to 6). Verticality as an emblem capitulates before verticality as a space, as a limit towards the sky, inventing throughout its course a different perception of the horizon according to the different levels of the ascent.

Raimund Abraham ordered his proposal according to three criteria: "Ascension, support, and suspension". Playing with the narrowness of the plot, he succeeded in flanking a staircase along the cinemas, an essential element in the building's journey. Each cinema rises above its neighbor, has its own exterior lobby, and erects a series of voids, of vertical breaths. Cinema and empty space form a dependent couple, the fundamental element of the construction of the building. Suspended in space, each small lobby carries its own cinema, allowing it to defy gravity and thus becoming indispensable. (fig. 7)

fig. 4a & 4b. Raimund Abraham, Times Square, model, 1984. Elevation on 7th Avenue and 42nd Street elevation.

fig. 5. Raimund Abraham, Times Square study sketch, 1984.

All

Jean Baudrillard[7] had noticed that the American nutritional habitus does not tolerate half measures: according to him, whether they are obese or anorexic, Americans gobble up food or deprive themselves of it completely. In either case, these are phenomena of excess. It is in such excess that the means justify the end: wanting to eat everything or eat nothing comes to the same result: annihilation.

American towers perpetuate this model of disproportion. The first towers made the sky

7. Jean Baudrillard, *America*, translated by Chris Turner (London, New York: Verso Books, 1989). First published as *Amérique*, (Paris: Grasset, 1986).

fig. 6. The successive horizons of New York.

too profitable. They wanted to build everything, or at least the maximum possible, by piling up horizontal layers without the slightest void. Louis Sullivan was the first architect of this Taylorization. In symmetrical opposition to this model, John Portman built hotels in Atlanta and Manhattan with colossal voids, from floor to roof, sometimes without any obstacle that could have deflected their ascents, voids with nothing in them. The first proposal is to build everything, the second to empty everything. No void, or all void, we remain there in the field of the exploit, outside of the field of the architecture, of that learned, correct and magnificent play...

The project of Raimund Abraham proposes a learned dosage. A balance is achieved, a vertical sequence of the inseparable couples "cinema-sky lobby", an organization made of full and empty spaces, of ground and sky. Moreover, it also consists of a cycle based on the number seven and its setting in series. Seven is a prime number, indivisible. The seven programmatic entities propose a singular and finite development, a game of Happy Families whose extension leads to the discovery of the multiple horizons of Manhattan.

Utopia

This drawing (fig. 8), reproduced by Rem Koolhaas in *Delirious New York*, conveys an image of the American dream with house and yard, generated together in a vertical series, one on top of the other. Illustrating the maximum profitability of a new territory imagined in conquest of the sky, the drawing shows neither beginning nor end. Rural life remains in suspension, totally floating in the space of cumulus. The introduction of the metal framework allows this utopia. Each floor is a separate domain, a property raised in the air, autonomous, free of neighbors. This image cannot be understood as only a vision, or a celestial dream. It is a real utopia, not a hallucination.

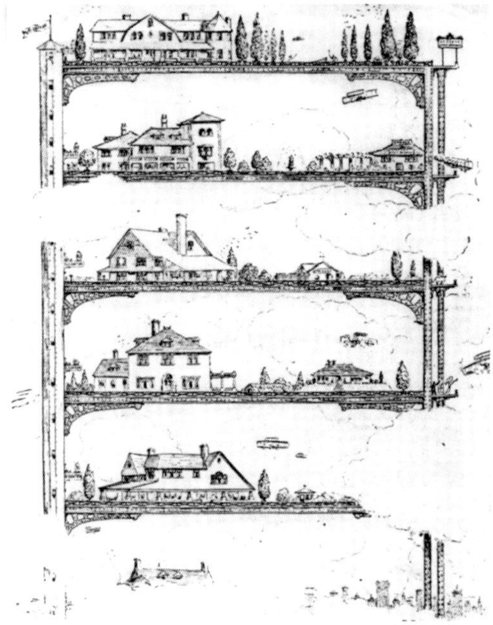

fig. 7. The 1909 theorem: the skyscraper as a utopian invention allowing the production of an unlimited number of virgin sites on a given location, anonymous.

It is a vision, along with a thought about the possibility of its realization in a *topos*, a place. That place is here the sky, the ideal place for what Raimund Abraham defined as Architecture: a "man-made landscape"[8]. The vertical landscape has become the subject of exploration.

Project

The 1990s were a fertile time for vertical explorations. José Oubrerie assigned students at Columbia University in 1988 a project entitled "the vertical monastery". It was recast as a "Center for Architectural Studies," so as not to trigger immediate criticism of the monastic universe, of autonomy in relation to the world, etc. Oubrerie needed to *reattach* the project to a more Manhattan-friendly reality. By calling the project a study center, he asserted the feasibility of utopia (fig. 9).

Nonetheless, the subject entailed thinking about the vertical series, about the construction and transformation of a building that until then had been erected on the ground (fig. 10 and 11). The monastic cells became student rooms, common spaces found a place within the vertical composition, chapels and crypts were transformed into amphitheaters or meeting rooms. The purpose of the exercise changed from the realization of a monastery to the construction of a building where vertical space, rare in Manhattan, became the type.

Canvas

New York is a metropolis where several modes of pictoriality confront each other: Cubist for Delaunay, romantic and beautiful at night for Hugh Ferris, underground for Diego Rivera, Art Deco for the WPA (Works Progress Administration). If New York is a space for painters, it also became the terrain of architects for whom painting supplied the medium for a spatial quest. Indeed, one will remember the first works of John Hejduk and his transformations based on the lessons of purism and Corbusian pictoriality. In the same vein, the publication of the work of the Five Architects[9] in 1967, as well as the text of Colin Rowe and Robert Slutzky on transparency[10] invoked the importance of what spatial manipulation owes to Cubism. It is no longer a question of analyzing the painting, but of problematizing its impact, its effect on the construction of space. The vertical space of the island of Manhattan and the perception of the skyscrapers by the painters proposes a cubist vision of their ascension. The towers are cubist objects. More specifically, the vision of their upwards deployment, of the simultaneous movement of object and space towards the sky is linked to

8. Raimund Abraham, Interview by Carlos Brillembourg, *Bomb*, 77, 2001.

9. Peter Eisenman, Michael Graves, Charles Gwathmey, John Hejduk, and Richard Meier, *Five Architects* (New York: Oxford University Press, 1975).

10. Colin Rowe, and Robert Slutzky, "Transparency: Literal and Phenomenal", written in 1955, and published in *Perspecta* 8, *The Yale Architectural Journal*, 1964.

fig. 8. Student work directed by José Oubrerie, model, 1988.

fig. 9a. & 9b. Student work directed by José Oubrerie, cross-section and longitudinal section, 1988.

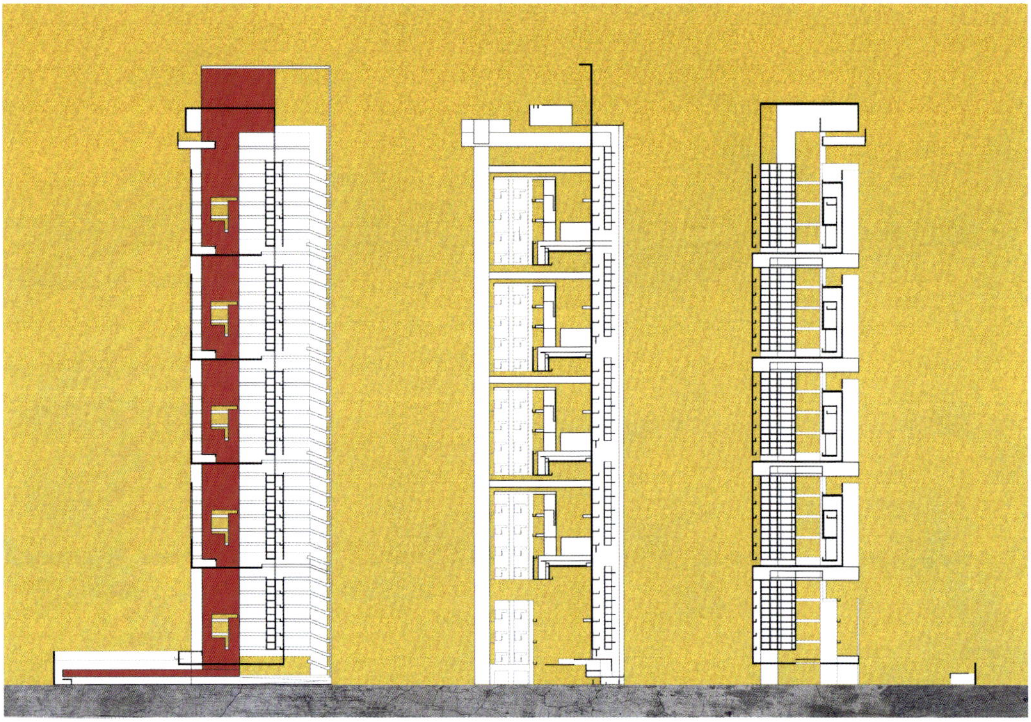

fig. 10a., 10b. & 11. Dwelling towers, third year design studio, Marin Segal, Nora El-Assaad, ENSA Paris-La Villette.

Cubist pictoriality. This perception of the space of the city serves as a springboard for the idea of an extension of vertical space through successive horizons (fig. 12).

Metropolitan Tower

"A question of desire: to enter a section cut is to find the space of the question" said Roland Simounet.

While we recognize the freedom afforded by Manhattan for having anchored the Tower as an *icon*, we must pose the realization of the vertical space as a *question*. In other words, the architectural work consists indeed of conquering a freedom, of conjugating the audacity of the construction of a building in height with its vertical dimension. The project of the metropolitan tower engages a conception of vertical space and a construction of great height. It is based first of all on Raimund Abraham's building in Times Square as the first register of its invention. The vertical series of seven amphitheaters or seven cinemas, or theaters, perpetuates the Manhattan model and opens itself to the realization of a public program.

Nevertheless, there is an invention in the statement of this exercise that transforms Raimund Abraham's proposal. Certainly, the Metropolitan Tower deals with the vertical assembly, the elevated architectural walk through the building, the construction of the necessary voids and the realization of the series. But the ambition of this project lies in the resolution of a metropolitan space, a space belonging to the city that would be relocated within the boundaries of the building. The building offers a center to the city, a weightless center, a center within, an abstract, vertical, and measured space. In the metropolitan tower, the urban is no longer on the ground. It is in motion and inside. The space

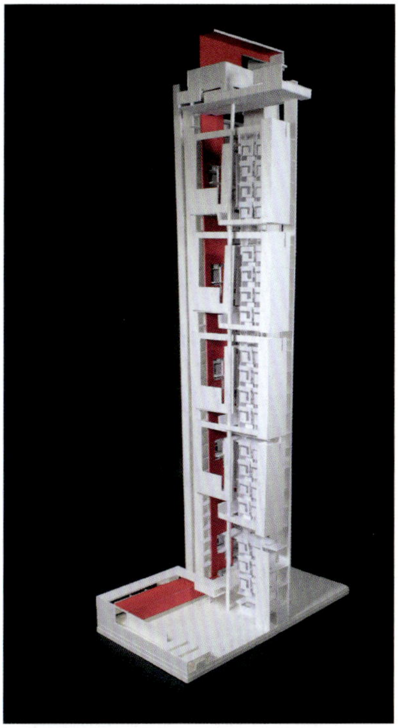

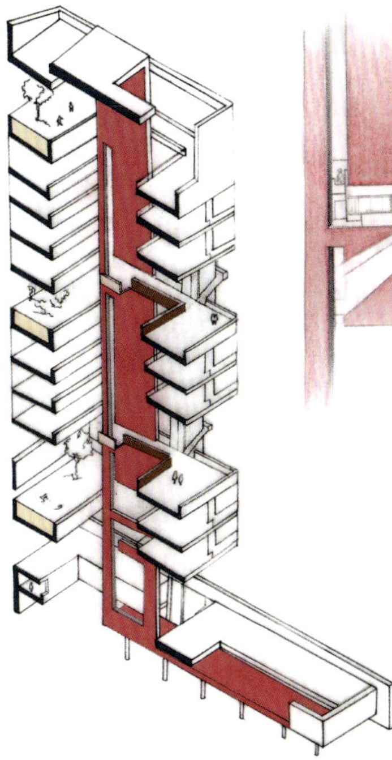

of the city is not simply staged. It contributes to the definition of a landscape, "man-made"[11] to use Raimund Abraham's words; a skyline, the intersection of several programmatic dimensions. The architectural promenade is an ascent by levels, by sequences, by vertical successions.

The section cut becomes the primary means of investigation, the necessary tool for the discovery and construction of this "space of the question", without which the building loses its meaning.

Let us keep in mind that the project of the Metropolitan Tower given by Michel Kagan has always been situated: Paris has been its terrain, which seems to be the most suitable for the exercise. But we must absolutely understand that in New York, Paris or elsewhere, the richness of the project lies in the idea of an interior vertical metropolitan space. It could be understood as a prototype project, an indispensable exercise for any investigation on the space of verticality. With its capacity to possess several sites, the tower will be able to launch itself to conquer the clouds of so many metropolises.

Paris La Villette

Inspired by Michel Kagan's project, we have developed in some 3rd year design studios a similar endeavor.

Since 2018, along with Gwénaël Clément and Nabil Hamdouni, we have launched the project of a tower, focusing on the construction of the vertical assemblage of housing units, all build as family dwellings with a mandatory double-height.

As mandatory programmatic outlines we emphasized the need for an urban space built within the body of the tower. To imagine the city moving upwards conquering the sky, thereby achieving the indissociable trio: each space should be "programmatic, pragmatic and poetic".

11. Raimund Abraham, Interview with Carlos Brillembourg, *Bomb*, 77, *op. cit.*

from left to right, top to bottom

fig. 1. Reuben Street Housing, Dublin by FKL architects, 2006.

fig. 2. Urban development in the vicinity of Piet Heinkade, Claus en Kaan Architecten, 2000–2006.

fig. 3. Hinna Brygge Housing, Brandsberg-Dahls Arkitekter, 2006–2007.

fig. 4. Housing ZAC Masséna-Bruneseau, Paris, Beckmann N'Thépé, 2007.

European Towers versus High-Rise Buildings[1]

Michel W. Kagan

Does the tower inescapably return as the image of urban renewal at the beginning of the 21st century, to be inscribed in the context of the contemporary European city? Or is there, on the part of architects like those who build in China or Dubai, a search for validation, in wanting to build fragments of a vertical city at the thresholds of the horizontal European city?

The paradoxical stimulus to build high in a world of horizontal extension interests both private developers and public building contractors, who seek attractive images, a differentiated way of life, and the possibility of a city with greater urban and speculative density. The dream of building a new, idealized architectural type is extraordinary. It reminds us of San Giminiano, because now we see many projects of towers built in the largest capitals of Europe, such as Barcelona, London, Vienna, Frankfurt, Malmö... Even in Paris, where the "rabbit cage" tower was banned in the seventies, many competitions to design the "humanized" tower have recently been announced. This new skyline of the European city would be the leitmotiv of a "different" city, which would increase in height in order to be sustainable and compact and would occupy the thresholds of the city (described by Sergio Crotti[2]). Why the thresholds? They are the future places of a nodal modernity and the phenomenological meeting points of the past and the future. It is necessary to densify to accommodate the thousands of inhabitants to come, to make communications and transportation faster, more immediate and less expensive; to develop mixed cities, no longer separating dormitory towns from office areas, leisure centers and the historic city... It is necessary to find available surfaces on the outskirts of the city. "Living well in the city" would be the recurring theme of the European 21st century tower if it could also be an ecological tower. After Le Corbusier and his Voisin plan for Paris, Mies Van der Rohe and his 1922 Berlin tower, El Lissitzky's "Proun" for Moscow, Frank Lloyd Wright's Baskerville tower and its mixed-use program combining housing and offices, or William Lescaze and Georges Howe's PSFS in

1. This article was commissioned by Pierre-Alain Croset, and was published in Italian in *Il Giornale dell'Architettura* in March 2008.

2. Sergio Crotti, *Figure architettoniche: Soglia / Architectural figures: the Threshold,* (Milano: edizioni Unicopli, 2000).

Philadelphia, which is linked to a subway station, we rediscover that towers can limit urban sprawl and give a future to the contemporary city, if they are totally rethought. The low-rise city could well become a contradiction in terms, as it would consume an enormous amount of land and privatize the surface of cities.

The cubist city

The tower has only one context—the contemporary city, which is also the historical city. Research on the tower contributes to a new urbanism that is emerging with the ecological corridors of Bernardo Secchi's "diffuse city,"[3] one that calls into question the scale of the city and its landscape to determine a reasonable and ultimately controllable measure of its development. With the tower, we must conceive our cities in section as well as in plan. Thickness can be revealed again with another aesthetic of the dense city because it can become a vertical city; the three-dimensional city would take precedence over the city of the 18th century, the Haussmannian city, or the city of *Mitteleuropa* all conceived in two dimensions. The city can become a polycentric archipelago, dominated by thresholds that the landscape and the history of the city have set for it in today's context. Reflection on great height is therefore an "off-topic" subject, but of great interest for architects: either the question of height is secondary to a design that decisively determines it, or the height depends on an urban project that precedes the design and imposes a common rule offsetting the personal and stylistic expression of architects. In this new generation of towers, the single tower can no longer be isolated in the environmental contexts of contemporary European cityscapes, except if it is a public building. The mix of scales as well as the mix of urban activities come together in a conception of the tower whose role in the urban fabric and public space is an integral part of its design. If the tower emerges above its own base, it is always to orient or reorient itself, to announce its presence in a dimension that contrasts and adapts; the tower becomes cubist, unless it is the city in the process of becoming that takes shape as a "cubist city".

However, this new commitment to the tower raises many questions about its long-term consequences. Should there be forests of towers as Jacques Ferrier, author of the Hypergreen tower, suggests? It is true that the question of the tower in the European city comes down to determining what relationship the height of the tower can have with a context or an existing landscape that was not originally designed, as in New York, for implanting dominating structures that create shadows in their immediate environment? The site constraints are particularly strong when one does not have the benefit of the "American grid", but dedicated urban layouts instead, with the most recent ones dating from the 19th and 20th centuries. With the possible exceptions of Barcelona and Rotterdam, or in recently urbanized territories, the tower can develop in the chaos of the city without limits, as derived from the last fifty years. The tower project is necessarily metropolitan; that is why we will distinguish the metropolitan tower from other towers that cannot be considered without a relationship to the ground and a relationship to the sky. The goal is precisely to establish a limited but significant contact with an existing urban fabric, and always to build, complete and consolidate a fabric. If every urban fabric is in the process of becoming, the tower grafts a new relationship on the existing conditions and becomes a new founding theme for the European city.

Thus, Sullivan's precepts, which advocated a base, a main body, and a top, could be reviewed and corrected to meet a new

3. Bernardo Secchi, *Première leçon d'urbanisme* (Marseille: Parenthèses, 2006). First published as *Prima lezione di Urbanistica* (Roma, Bari: Laterza, 2000).

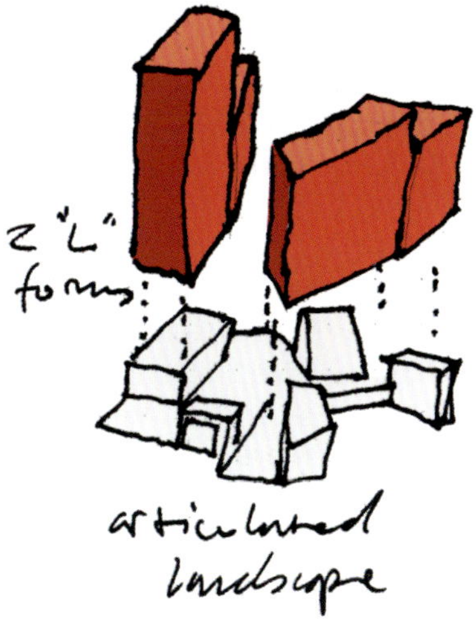

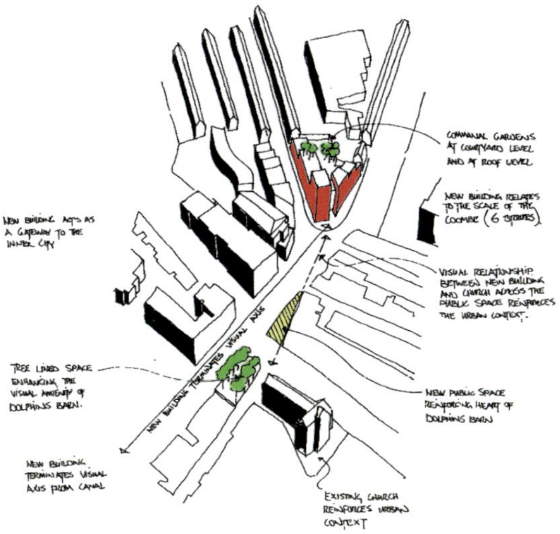

Reuben Street Housing Project, Dublin by FKL architects, 2006

fig. 5a. Relation to the industrial and urban context of the neighborhood.

fig. 5b. The urban room, concept sketch.

fig. 5c. Situation in the city, concept sketch.

demand: to create a new urban landscape with close views of the historical context and distant views of the formerly hidden dimension of today's city. The worldwide proliferation of ever taller, more aesthetically pleasing, and—why not—ecological towers flood the magazines as a new and unquestionable Eldorado of architectural production. It was Tadao Ando who, after Sir Norman Foster had built the famous "Hong Kong Shanghai Bank", refused to build another tower for the same client, that was meant to be much higher than the previous one. After having refused to build it, Tadao Ando's ethics led him to say to Kenneth Frampton on that occasion: "Above a certain height, a tower is no longer architecture!" However, the exhilarating novelty of vertical architecture is exciting because we are led to rediscover an abandoned source of modernity that only crossed the Atlantic. The criticism of the vertical style is always present because towers have a bad reputation! They remind us of an "international style" unsuited to the urban condition, such as the urban imbroglio of the La Défense district in Paris, the urbanism of energy-guzzling towers and bars, where the elevators never work!

Strong form

Should we build towers on the fringes of the city and spare the center, apart from London perhaps, and favor the development of areas penalized by the presence of heavy infrastructures? Some European architects from very diverse architectural movements have recently built towers that do not simply fill these waiting voids. They share an idea of the "metropolitan tower" situated in the new contexts of the "cubist city," where they locate their projects. It is an architecture that may recall the cubist collages of the nineteen twenties, but only to a limited extent. They are innovative architectures but also dialectical architectures, attentive to the program. Made of contextual insertions, of deliberately calculated height, of diversified volumes, with the same architectonics, and elements of integrated urban enclaves, they give meaning to a revisited critical regionalism. The distinctive conceptual characteristic of these towers is the will to seek a "strong form" and, more subtly, to multiply scales, volumes, materials, fragments, and continuities. The result is a pure cubist and urban architecture composed of strict dimensional relationships. A real urban presence emerges at the corners of the streets and produces an ascending volumetric vision clearly linking the horizontal lower city to the vertical upper city. The four projects presented here are part of this formal register, whether in Dublin, Paris, Amsterdam or Stavanger.

Four tower projects

The project by Irish architects Michelle Fagan and Paul Kelly at the corner of Reuben Street and Dolphin Barn Street in Dublin is a small "urban piece," as Henri Ciriani called this type of urban project, which is intended to constitute large or small, open or closed blocks to consolidate an urban fabric beyond city walls. (fig. 5a). The building is conceived as two unequal "L" shaped blocks that open towards each other and align with the two adjacent streets, whose height rises from 8 to 10 floors at the main corner. A bridge between these two forms connects them and supports a work of art (fig. 5b and 5c). The program consists of two commercial units and 64 residential units consisting of studios and two-room apartments. The facades are all made of traditional bricks, renewing the use of this thousand-year-old material. They have random openings of two kinds set with aluminum joinery: either square with a small loggia or vertical to light a room. The composition of the volumes, according to the architects, is designed to reflect the industrial aesthetics of the neighborhood, and to establish a positive comparison with the industrial brick buildings of the Guinness breweries located nearby. These two "L"

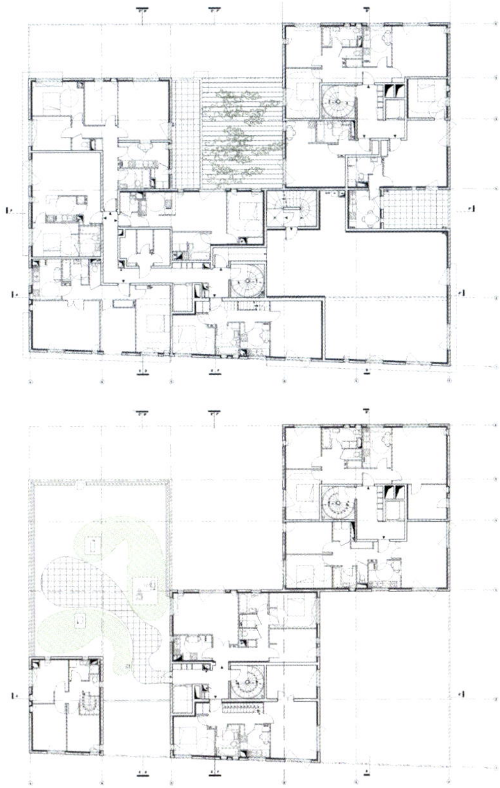

Housing ZAC Masséna-Bruneseau, Paris, Beckmann N'Thépé, 2007.

fig. 6a & 6b. Self-compacting concrete and work on textures, first floor and 4th floor plans.

shapes construct a specific architectural landscape in this outlying location and are inspired by Diener & Diener's early work in a strong, restrained, and modest instrumental vocabulary.

In contrast, the project by French architects Beckmann N'Thépé is not an isolated act of architecture but is integral to the urban ambitions of the new Masséna district in the 13th arrondissement of Paris. As the authors of the project point out: *"According to the principles imagined by Christian de Portzamparc, the project is cut, refined, and sculpted to reinforce its simplicity in an elegance that is its own. Each new construction is a further milestone in this part of the city of* 'Age 3'". The layout on the street is laid out in strict alignment; however, the overhangs, the recesses, the play of terraces and a fault form the expression of plots to make the neighborhood benefit from the idea of *"an open heart of the block"*. Self-compacting colored concrete provides a finish, purity, and unity to a very varied composition (fig. 6a). Large first floor glazed facades lift up the buildings and play with a certain immateriality. The random play of windows responds to a concern for close or distant views, and making the floors disappear. This cubist and critical architecture eschews the archetypes of style and representation: 48 dwellings, business premises, and shops give this inhabited complex the urbanity of a contemporary street (fig. 6b).

The so-called "Hinna Brygge" dwellings by Norwegian architects Ingar Svinterud, Hans Jorgen Moe, and Brandsberg-Dahls in Stavanger are located in a new development area (fig. 7a). They mark the entrance to the harbor, near a former construction dock for oil platforms in the North Sea. The two towers run along the water on three sides and are accessible by a walkway 1.5 m above sea level. They invert and turn toward each

Hinna Brygge housing development, Brandsberg-Dahls Arkitekter, 2006–2007

fig. 7a. Placement in the site.

fig. 7b. View from one of the units.

fig. 7c. Facade and openings.

other to provide views from each apartment (fig. 7b) and the best sunlight conditions for both buildings. One block has copper facades while the other facades are lead, introducing a variety of materials when they are otherwise identical. The horizontal arrangement of the façade materials and the verticality of the buildings' bodies create a contrast that nevertheless reflects the local tradition. The windows are, as in the previously described projects, randomly positioned to provide rhythm and light vibrations on the facade skin (fig. 7c). The entrances are at the lowest pier level with access to boat parking on both sides. Each tower contains 32 units, with a four-room and a two-room on each level and a very large apartment on the top floor. These two towers act as a gateway to the city from the sea and recall by their back and forth movement the origin of the city of Stavanger and its intimate relationship with the sea.

The hotel project by Dutch architect Kees Kaan and architects Mauro Felix Claus and Jaap Gräber, with Katrin Weber and Roland Rens, is a complex located at Piet Heinkade near the "waterfront" and the central station of Amsterdam. It consists of 4 independent buildings that rest on a common and single base (fig. 8a). This base accommodates several public functions, including the cruise ship passenger terminal, a music center, convention spaces, and a multi-level parking garage. From the base upwards (fig. 8b and 8c), we move to a semi-public domain and the hotel function. Set on a glass volume perpendicular to its horizontal orange base, the 400-room tower-hotel has a composite cladding of green granite, white marble, and white cement that opposes and confronts the two superimposed volumes on which it stands. This play lightens the prismatic volume of the tower and detaches it from its relationship to the urban ground to seek distant views from each of its rooms. Here is evoked a major theme of the metropolitan tower that was so elegantly addressed with SOM's Lever House in New York, the theme of the geometric and spatial intersection between high and low volumes through a major public space that is integrated with it: the patio.

Urban development around Piet Heinkade, Amsterdam, Claus en Kaan Architecten, 2000–2006

fig. 8a. Confrontations of orientation and materials between the base and the hotel.

fig. 8b. Semi-public promenade above the plinth.

These four projects determine a new "society of rooms", as Louis Kahn could call them, which are all new "city fronts" located within the domain of the contemporary city. They allow for urban renewal within the thickness of the historic city without having to overwhelm it. They demonstrate that projects with "strong forms", according to Martin Steinman's terminology, and with carefully reasoned scales can fit into the landscape of our European cities by abandoning the question of the "mega-structure" dear to Archigram for the more innovative and contextualized "mini-structure". To complete Kenneth Frampton's argument, if the "megaforms are necessarily horizontal forms that take on the dimension of urban landscape infrastructures", the "mini-forms", represented by this morphology of metropolitan towers, are plural forms and "elegant solutions" (cf. Le Corbusier), vertical and horizontal, that condition the modification of the landscape of the historic city bequeathed by the 20th century.

fig. 1. Skyline of New York, the UN seen from Roosevelt Island.

Discovering Architecture

Nathalie Régnier-Kagan

The journey shifts references and recomposes the gaze; it induces cultural or institutional comparisons and thus proves to be a producer of critiques and alternatives to the horizon of departure. But the journey in space is also coupled with an exploration of time: if America is often considered in the nineteenth and twentieth centuries as scenes of future life, to use Georges Duhamel's image, Italy remains rather the scene of the reconstruction of history; to Italy, then, the nostalgia of the past, and to America this nostalgia of the future judiciously evoked by Colin Rowe.

Jean-Louis Cohen[1]

This quotation from Jean-Louis Cohen concludes his introductory article for the catalog of "New Directions in Modern Architecture: France / USA"[2], an exhibition that marked the conclusion of Michel Kagan's four years of teaching at Columbia University in New York, before disseminating it for nearly two years in Europe, South America and in several American and Canadian universities. The quote sums up the two major cultural axes that nourished his training and our subsequent travels during 20 years of teaching: travels in Italy—to discover the work of Terragni and Scarpa—to Switzerland and Ticino; explorations of the European city: Barcelona, Madrid, London, Helsinki, Athens, as well as the American metropolises of New York and Chicago, all inexhaustible sources of knowledge and discovery.

"*Architecture as something indivisible, something you cannot separate into a number of elements. Architecture is not produced simply by adding plans and sections to elevations. It is something else and something more... On the whole, art should not be explained; it must be experienced.*"[3] These words of Steen Eiler Rasmussen speak to us of the importance of actually being in spaces, of experiencing them in order to understand them. Visiting remarkable buildings and urban spaces is part of every architect's apprenticeship (fig. 1 and 6). In the age of the virtual, these remain indispensable for the student of architecture. Our trips focused on understanding the architecture of the 20th century, without of course neglecting the previous centuries. Architectural modernity is still too often lacking from general French culture; this ignorance is the cause of frequent misunderstanding by the general public, when faced with an abstract, contemporary production. Taste must be educated and slowly refined, through practice and contact with recognized environments. Travelling allows one to overcome the fear of the new, of the unknown, of what one does not understand. Modernity has not yet reached its "classic" age, when it can be recognized and appreciated by all, according to shared criteria and valiues. The "modern" architect

1. Quoted by Kenneth Frampton and Michel Kagan in *Nouvelles directions de l'architecture moderne*, France/USA, (Milan, Paris: Electa Moniteur, 1985), 23.

2. K. Frampton and M. Kagan, op. cit.

3. Steen Eiler Rasmussen, *Experiencing architecture* (Cambridge: MIT Press, 1959).

fig. 2. R. Meier, M. Kagan, N Régnier-Kagan with students.

fig. 3. Richard Meier & Partners Agency, 2004.

fig. 4. & 5. Tod Williams & Billie Tsien Agency, 2007.

is still a pioneer. Our trips consisted of visiting cities, remarkable buildings, and important architectural agencies. We introduced our students to the offices of Livio Vacchini in Locarno, Richard Meier and Tod Williams in New York, Carlos Ferrater in Barcelona, Alberto Campo Baeza in Madrid, Norman Foster in London, and Christian Gulligsen in Helsinki (fig. 2 to 5)...

The discovery of the great American metropolises is a fundamental part of the education of an architect: in their time, Adolf Loos, Erich Mendelsohn and Richard Neutra embarked on the initiatory travels to America. In the light of the prestigious architectural past of Europe, it is legitimate to doubt the capacity of modern architecture to produce harmony and beauty. To be convinced of this, one must go and discover the American city: New York, Chicago, San Francisco... The layout of the urban grid is characteristic of American urbanism; *"as in all the periods of generalized colonization in the history of the world, the old colonial cities, then the frontier cities, were laid out according to a geometric mode in rectangular blocks, straight streets, and intersections at right angles"*[4] — for reasons of economy, simplicity, and ease. These grid plans, heirs to the Roman city and the cardo-decumanus, also produced large green spaces, vast public places, and alternating squares. The beauty of these metropolitan cities, which developed mainly in

4. John W. Reps, *The Making of Urban America: A History of City Planning in the United States*, (Princeton: Princeton University Press, 1965).

fig. 6. Michel Kagan, Sacha and Sonia, Crown Hall, Chicago, 2009.

the nineteenth and twentieth centuries under the pressure of immigration, is based on the strong resonance of this geometric pattern with a particular geography: Lake Michigan for Chicago, or the island of Manhattan, whose limits are clearly defined. There is a specifically American city: the grid is its system, the skyscraper its architectural model. Both egalitarian and democratic, but also a framework for individual freedom, in opposition to the radio-concentric plan, typical of European cities, centralized and authoritarian. The grid is what separates and connects the blocks between them: it is the city's ongoing durability. It can also generate anarchy in three-dimensional space, becoming a "fairy-tale catastrophe"[5] according to Le Corbusier, or a "delirium"[6] according to Rem Koolhaas.

The vertical city was born in America. New York and Chicago are not alike. Their rivalry to determine which of the two metropolises is to be considered the birthplace of the skyscraper has been described by many writers; some consider the origin of the skyscraper in the structural honesty, the metal frame, functionalism, and the appearance of the elevator in Chicago. Others highlight the historicist eclecticism, the great size, and the visual pleasures of New York. Their differences, linked to geographyical and historical conditions, produced two distinct kinds of cities.

5. Le Corbusier, *Quand les cathédrales étaient blanches* (Paris: Denoël/Gonthier, 1983).

6. Rem Koolhaas, *Delirious New York* (New York: Oxford University Press, 1978).

fig. 7. Flatiron, New York, 1986. .

fig. 8. Aerial view of New York.

Revisiting New York

In the context of teaching the metropolitan tower, New York is a must[7]. A *"standing city"*[8] according to Le Corbusier, or a *"horizontal city"* according to Paul Morand, the beauty of Manhattan comes from its landscape, its "skyline" and its contours: *"It is the city that makes the skyscraper, not the skyscraper that makes the city,"*[9] remarks Hubert Damisch. *"The city makes the skyscraper, but it is the architecture (because that is what it is all about, as Le Corbusier understood) that makes the site, whether it reveals it or produces it."*[10] Michel Kagan, fascinated by a cubist vision of the city, is both attached to its geometric framework, an orthonormal reference point in three dimensions, and attracted by the formal freedom it allows: the intersection of the horizontal and the vertical, the "spatial cross" dear to Frank Lloyd Wright.

"New York is not a finished city,"[11] said Le Corbusier. An aerial view of the city gives the impression of looking at a carpet that is worn in places (fig. 8). In Manhattan, whatever the nature of the architectural event, it will have to intervene within the limits of the 2,028 blocks that make up the grid. The meeting of two different grids, New Amsterdam to the south, and the 1811 plan that subdivides the entire island, causes the separation between "downtown" and "uptown", creating a typical urban form. Broadway Avenue, the only oblique in the orthogonal grid, is a generator of urban events. It causes accidents in the urban

7. Trip to New York, EAPB April 2004-June 2007.

8. Le Corbusier, *Quand les cathédrales...*, op. cit.

9. Hubert Damisch, Preface *in* Jean-Louis Cohen, *Scènes de la vie future* (Paris: Flammarion, CCA, 1995).

10. Hubert Damisch, op. cit.

11. Le Corbusier, *Quand les cathédrales...*, op. cit.

fig. 9. Aerial view of Chicago.

fabric, giving rise to squares, gardens or corner buildings (fig. 7). Broadway is an element of Manhattan's urban form. Similarly, Central Park is an event in the urban grid, from 59th to 110th Street, between 5th and 8th Avenues. Fifth Avenue is neither east nor west: it is Avenue Zero. Times Square is the intersection of 7th Avenue, Broadway and 42nd Street: a crossroads of theaters and cinemas, it is the "heart" of Manhattan. *"The beauty other cities only acquired over centuries has been achieved by New York in fifty years"*[12] says Baudrillard.

Chicago-Athens, from progress to origins

It is difficult to detach the pedagogical experience from the events lived: last summer, last trips[13], return to the sources of modernity and antiquity. In Americanism and Modernity, Yannis Tsiomis compares Athens and Washington and notes that *"the ideology of progress would not exist without the other constant, that of the origin"*[14]. He speaks of *"two perfections, one ancient, (classical), the Greek, the other new, (modern), the American"*[15]. Both are found in the energy deployed, through a regulatory route, at different times, to conquer wild lands, to move the boundaries of civilization. The parallel with Chicago is striking: even more than Washington, could Chicago not represent the city of the

12. Jean Baudrillard, *America* (London, New York: Verso, 1988).

13. Trip to Chicago, July 2009, as part of the Metropolitan Tower course at ENSAPB, and "Athens beyond history" workshop, July 2009, organized by Nikos Ktenas.

14. Yannis Tsiomis, "Athènes et Washington, ou comment confondre l'origine et le progrès", in *Américanisme et modernité* (Paris: EHESS, Flammarion, 1993).

15. Yannis Tsiomis, op. cit.

fig. 10. & 11. The "Loop", Chicago in 2009.

Modern Movement par excellence, the *"city of the Athens Charter"*[16]?

In Chicago, the grid spreads out infinitely, like a grid of lights that squares the night as seen from the air. *"The broad lines of the urban grid seem to merge into the Jeffersonian grid of the Great Western Plains, visible to the horizon."*[17] Horizontal expansion has found another limit to overcome: height. *"The skyscraper gives the scale of the new times."*[18] A vertical thrust in the center of the city impels a deformation of the skyline facing the lake, contrasting with the flatness of the Prairie (fig. 9). On top of the perpendicular grid of the city center, the loop of the "Loop" is superimposed, an aerial subway that encircles a narrow city center (fig. 10 and 11). Chicago, built on wetlands, is an example of an urban slab, in which the transition between the different strata of the city's soil is seamless. It is common to think of the Chicago School as a school of architectural rigor in cast iron and steel. But rather than Sullivan's adage: *"form follows function,"* should we not also say *"form follows finance"*[19]? Both New York and Chicago produced the *"vernacular urban forms of capitalism"*[20].

In Chicago, Miesian thought found a favorable terrain for its development. Michel Kagan saw in Mies not only a great architect, but also an outstanding urban planner: according to him,

16. Ibid.

17. Hubert Damisch, op. cit.

18. Jean-Louis Cohen, *Scènes de la vie future*, op. cit.

19. Carol Willis, *Form follows finance* (New York: Princeton Architectural Press, 1995).

20. Ibid.

fig. 12. Federal Center, Mies van der Rohe, Chicago.

fig. 13. The Parthenon, Athens, in 2009.

Mies van der Rohe's urban spaces are the prototypes of the places of modernity. The plaza between the towers of the Federal Center in Chicago (fig. 12), or the forecourt of the Seagram Building in New York, illustrate the effectiveness of these modern public spaces that function in resonance with the buildings that surround them, as an extension of interior spaces that are both noble and generous. In every Miesian building, the urban void it produces is paramount.

Invited by Nikos Ktenas in July 2009 in Athens, as part of the workshop "Athens beyond history", we return to the foundations of architecture. In Athens, the urban grid is a still living device, which regulates the development of the city and ends against the hills that surround it. The Parthenon, *"pure creation of the mind"*[21], said Le Corbusier, its geometry in harmony with the landscape, still resists the hordes of tourists, and the eternal consolidation works (fig. 13). Michel Kagan particularly appreciated the perspective of the buildings in the site, *"sculpture in full geography and topography"*[22], the intervention of Pikionis in this unique setting, the paved path on the hill (see p. 89), the restaurant below.

His sketchbooks make very little reference to these trips, always devoted to his future projects, buildings in gestation, and theoretical reflections. From these visits, he will *"fill his bag with emotions"*, as Le Corbusier used to say, aware that the only way to renew a gesture is to find a new way of doing it.

21. Le Corbusier, *Vers une architecture* (1923; repr. Paris: Flammarion, Champs, 1995).

22. Jean-Jacques Deluz, "Quelques réflexions sur Le Corbusier et l'Algérie" in *La Méditerranée de Le Corbusier* (Aix-Marseille: Université de Provence, 1991).

fig. 14. Frankfurt skyline, 2014.

"Is academic", said Le Corbusier in 1929, *"he who does not judge by himself, who admits the effect without controlling the cause, who believes in absolute truths, who does not involve his 'self' in every question..."*. Michel Kagan has always been convinced that *"there is creation only when there is transgression of the model"*[23].

The project given to the students on the Lycabettus Hill was meant to be a counterpoint to the Acropolis: a taut line on the ridge, towards the Mediterranean, a backbone organizing buried infrastructures, with a public esplanade open to the landscape, the project reunited by a virtual layout the new districts of Athens according to the 4 cardinal points. The verticality is expressed here in negative, in the depths of the earth...

Last trip, like a hat pulled, a reverence to the architecture, last glances on the horizon, facing the sunset...

European Towers

Our student travel programs for students from Paris Val de Seine School of Architecture focused on European cities: Amsterdam, Basel, Barcelona, Berlin, Copenhagen, Frankfurt, Göteborg, Marseille, Milan, Lisbon, London, Porto, Rotterdam, Zürich... Three days of intensive visits in each city enabled all our second-year undergraduates (250 to 300 students) to discover noteworthy architectural accomplishments, in record time, and in groups of twenty—each of them led by two teachers. Routes were calculated on maps, and transportation carefully studied before departure. Our groups of students criss-crossed Europe's capital cities at breakneck speed, on foot, by metro or by bus, in order to *"learn to see architecture"*[24]. Sometimes, a quasi-military organization was required, to "respect" the program. Each year, a presentation in the school's main hall enabled all the groups to share their experiences, supported by photos, films, drawings and models.

Over the course of our excursions, we saw contemporary towers gradually emerging in the skyline of European cities and competing with the spires of Gothic cathedrals. In the 1920s, under the influence of the avant-garde,

23. Ibid.

24. Bruno Zévi, *Apprendre à voir l'architecture* (Paris: éditions de Minuit, 1959).

American skyscrapers were proposed for the "old continent", to be inserted into the historic fabric and symbolize its renewal. Definitively inscribed by the Athens Charter into the landscape of reconstruction, as *"Cartesian, rational, orderly"*[25] bearers of an explicit social will, they became part of the urban form of Europe's capital cities. The "vertical urbanism" of the '60s and '70s became widespread, with the aim of increasing density while conserving land. The Barbican district[26] in the heart of London was one of the most controversial icons of this trend. Both hated and admired, it is now one of the city's most desirable neighborhoods, and it has been a protected heritage site since 2010. Not to be outdone, Berlin's Hanse district or "Hansaviertel" has also been listed as a historic monument.

The construction of high-rise buildings has been booming since the 2000s. They have proliferated in European cities and have been both contested and have become veritable tourist attractions. These include Norman Foster's Commerzbank in Frankfurt (1997), Swiss Re in London (2004), Jean Nouvel's Torre Agbar in Barcelona (2005), Rem Koolhaas' "De Rotterdam" tower in Rotterdam (2011), The Renzo Piano's "The Shard" in London (2012), Stefano Boeri's "Bosco Vertical" in Milan (2014). As an object of communication, the tower ratifies the change in scale of the European city and begins a new chapter of urban history. At the same time, in Germany, France and Switzerland, we are witnessing the regeneration of high-rise neighborhoods, and in particular, their public spaces in areas such as Olympiades and the Front de Seine in Paris. The "regeneration" of high-rise buildings: the GSW headquarters in Berlin (1999) by Sauerbruch and Hutton, the Bois le Prêtre tower in Paris (2009) by Druot, Lacaton and Vassal, are all opportunities to rebuild the city on the city.

After the "Covid years" (2020-2021), the transitional journey needs to be reinvented: into something more sober, slower, more in-depth, less far-flung, with small groups of motivated students. It remains one of the essential moments in the training of architects, to see architecture... for as Viollet le Duc put it, *"to see is to know."*

25. Ingrid Taillandier, "Acclimatation d'un modèle, 1893-1945 ", in *L'invention de la tour Européenne* (Paris: Éditions du Pavillon de l'Arsenal-Picard, 2009).

26. Architects: Chamberlain, Powell and Bon.

Captions on the following pages

p.84 1., 2. Crown Hall. **3.** Students, 2004. **4**. Students, Chicago, 2009. **5., 6., 7.** Cooper Union. **8.** Columbia University. **9.** Students, Chicago, 2009.

p.85 New York 1., 2. ONU. **3.** Bleeker St., Pei arch. **4.** New York by Gehry. **5.** Chrysler Building. **6.** Whitney Museum. **7.** 432 Park Avenue. **8.** Brooklyn Bridge. **p.86 1.** American Radiator Building. **2.** M. Kagan au MoMA. **3.** Skyline. **4.** Maison W. Lescaze. **5.** Skyline. **6.** New Museum of Contemporary Art. **7.** Downtown New York.

p.87 Chicago 1. Chicago skyline. **2.** Marina City. **3.** John Hancock Tower. **4.** Metropolitan Correctional Center. **5.** Wrigley Building. **6.** Chicago skyline. **7.** Aqua Tower, Gang arch. **p.88 1.** Michigan Avenue. **2.** Skybridge. **3.** Lake Point Tower. **4.** North Lake Shore Drive. **5.** Lake Shore Drive. **6.** Chicago River. **7.** Unity Temple. **8.** Johnson Wax Building. **9.** St. Regis Chicago.

p.89 Athens 1. Athens, panoramic. **2., 3.** Former Agora. **4.** Urban grid. **5.** Paving detail beneath the Acropolis.

p.90 Amsterdam 1. Silodam, MVRDV. **2.** IJ Tower, Neutelings & Riedile. **3.** Bank "La Bochère", HOK. **Basel 4.** St Antoine Church, Karl Moser. **5.** Novartis, Herzog & de Meuron. **6.** Meret Oppenheim Hochhaus, Herzog & de Meuron. **Barcelona 7.** Tour Agbar, J. Nouvel. **8.** Hotel Arts & Torre Mapfre, B. Graham, Ortiz & de Leon.

p.91 Berlin 1. Sony Center. **2.** Debis Tower, R. Piano. **3.** GSW Hauptverwaltung, Sauerbruch & Hutton. **Copenhagen 4.** Metropolis housing, Futur systems. **5.** SAS Royal Hotel, Arne Jacobsen (Now Radisson Hotel). **Frankfurt 6.** Skylight tower, R. Rodgers. **7.** Commerzbank, N. Foster. **8.** Students group, Ensa PVS 2014.

p.92 Göteborg 1., 2. Brf Viva housing, Malmström & Erdström. **Lisbon 3.** New University, Aires Mateus. **Porto 4.** Office & Trade bdg Burgo, Souto de Moura. **London 5.** Barbican center, Chamberlain, Powell and Bon. **6.** London skyline. **7.** One Crown plaza, KPF.

p.93 Marseille 1. CMA CGM, Zaha Hadid. **2.** La Marseillaise, J. Nouvel. **Milan 3.** Bosco verticale, S. Boeri. **Paris 4.** Front de Seine. **5.** La Défense. **6.** Paris Courthouse, R. Piano. **Rotterdam 7.** De Rotterdam, R. Koolhaas.

Travel Notebook I

New York

Chicago

thens

Travel Notebook II — European Towers

Amsterdam

Basel

Barcelona

Berlin

Copenhagen

Frankfurt

Frankfurt

Göteborg

Lisbon

Porto

London

London

Marseille

Milan

Paris

Rotterdam

Museum of American Folk Art

fig. 1a. View of the main façade in bronze panels.

Singular Towers

Nathalie Régnier-Kagan

The three projects presented here, the American Folk Museum, the Perry Street Condominium in New York, and "The Contemporary" in Chicago, are not skyscrapers per se. We particularly appreciated them with Michel Kagan during our study trips. They represent, by their proportion, a height that largely exceeds the Haussmannian template, and could come close to the concept of "metropolitan tower" that Michel Kagan claimed for Paris: "miniforms" of towers, "elegant solutions" with reasoned scales. Although they differ in their program—one is a museum, the other two are apartment buildings—and in their facades—one is very interiorized, the other two are open to the urban landscape—they nevertheless have many points in common, such as the work on the cross-sectional spaces, a very clear expression of the structure and materials, the use of the free plan, and a language that is both rational and poetic, without formal "expressionism". In this respect, it seemed appropriate to me to present them in this book, to illustrate our point with concrete and real examples of what a city conceived in three dimensions could be, of a dialectical architecture, attentive to the program, scale and use... Since 2014, a new line of very tall, very slim towers has been changing the skyline of Manhattan: "pencil towers" are sprouting up all over the metropolis' urban landscape, giving the skyline an unruly and uncontrolled look. At the same time, under pressure from real estate development, the American Folk Museum vanished from the capital's architectural heritage without a trace.

Museum of American Folk Art, New York, NY

Tod Williams and Billie Tsien, 2001
(demolished 2014)

The American Folk Museum, completed in 2001 by architects Tod Williams and Billie Tsien and since demolished, was the first new museum built in New York City in over three decades. Located on 53rd Street, on a 40-foot-wide by 100-foot-long (12 m × 30 m) plot, surrounded by the Museum of Modern Art on three sides, the building's eight levels gave it the proportions of a small metropolitan tower, a moment of rest in the vertical city (fig. 1a).

The four upper levels were entirely dedicated to permanent and temporary exhibition spaces. The upper mezzanine contained a small café overlooking 53rd Street, with

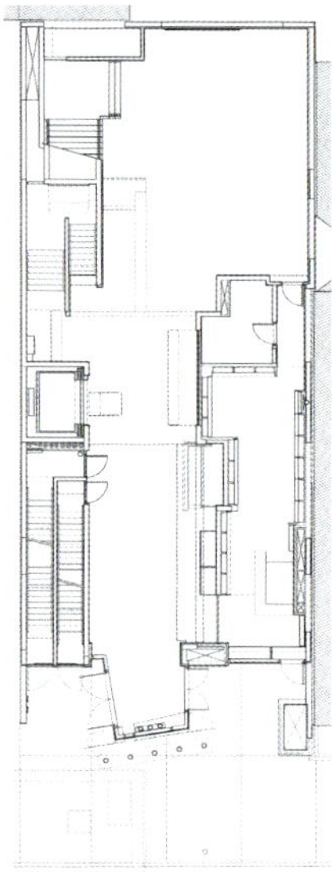

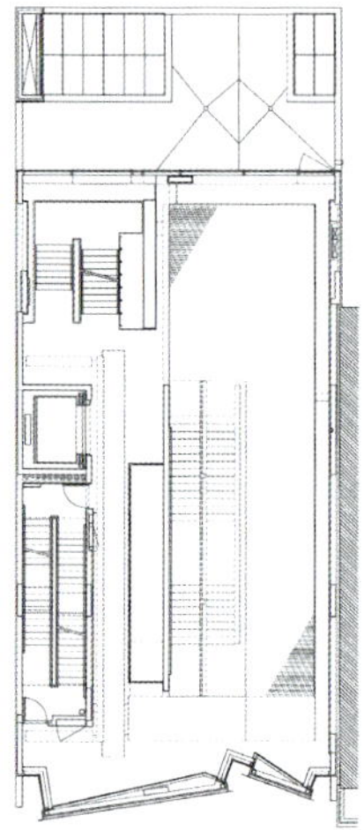

Museum of American Folk Art

fig. 1b. Circulation and exhibition spaces.

fig. 1c. Plan of the second floor.

fig. 1d. Plan of the second floor.

fig. 1e. East-West section looking north.

fig. 1f. North-South section looking west.

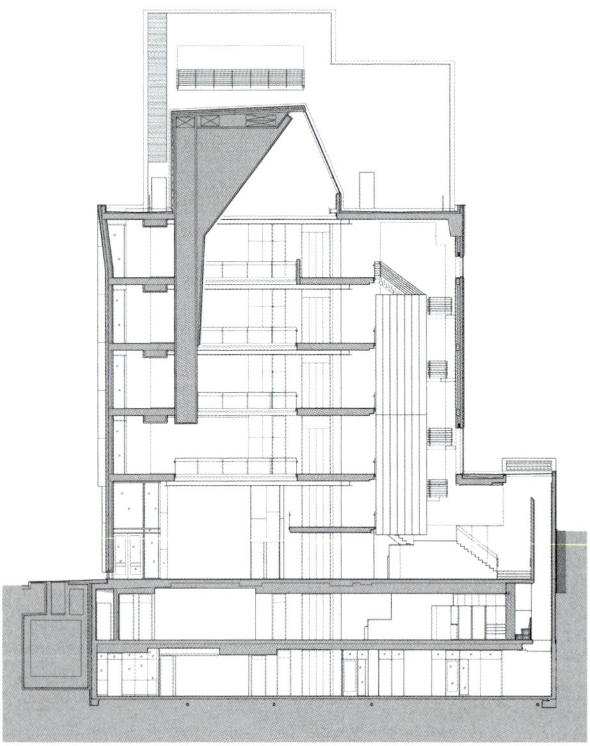

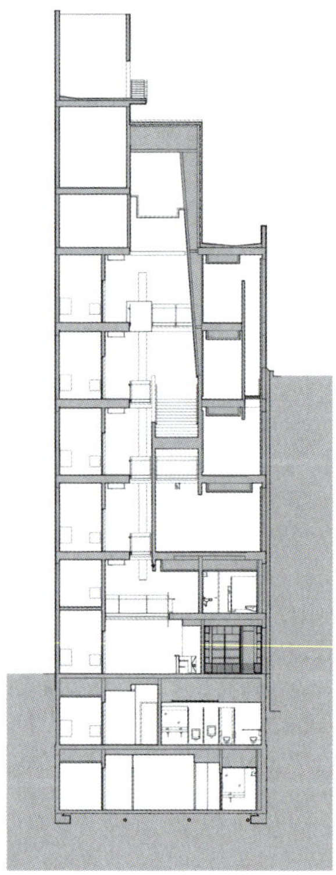

views of the double-height atrium. Two basement levels provided space for the auditorium and classrooms, while the lower level housed the museum offices, library, and archives. The store was located on the first floor and remained accessible outside of public hours through a separate entrance.

The building occupied the entire depth of the plot, and through a refined work on the cross-section, proposed an architectural promenade that wrapped around a central void according to a free path that visitors could choose; the skylight above the grand staircase expanded in the upper parts and compressed towards the bottom, allowing natural light to penetrate deeply into the interior space of the hall, and to illuminate the galleries through a skylight (fig. 1e and 1f). The placement of another skylight at the back of the plot brought light to the 2nd basement. The exhibition spaces and built-in display cases developed along these vertical faults, which split the building into a lamellar space (fig. 1b, 1c and 1d).

Perry Street Condominium

fig. 2a. View from the Hudson River, the impact of Perry Street Towers on the neighborhood skyline.

The façade of the Folk Art Museum expressed a certain sculptural autonomy within its context. It consisted of faceted metal panels of white bronze, fabricated in an ironworks, that folded inward toward the museum's interior. The variations in surface textures were achieved by using molds from different concrete textures. Depending on their orientation, the panels reflect a particular light, depending on the rising and setting sun, which varies with the seasons. According to the architects: "It is an idiosyncratic idea for a singular art". It was one of their most successful works, a little jewel chiseled in the heart of Manhattan.

Things have changed since then: due to the small institution's financial difficulties, the American Folk Museum was sold to MOMA in 2011 and to the developer Gerald Hines, in order

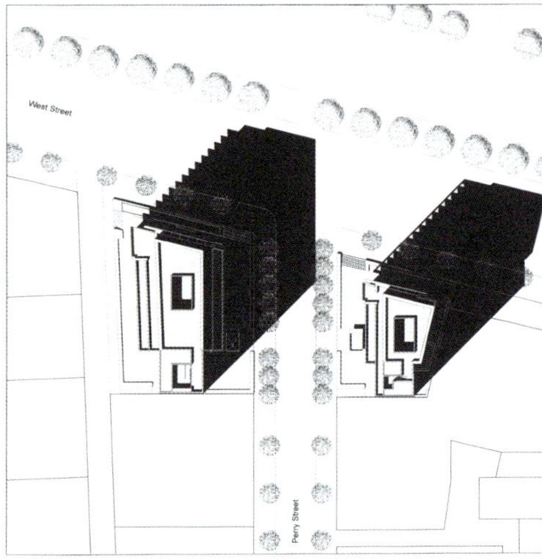

Perry Street Condominium

fig. 2b. West facades of the twin towers.

fig. 2c. Ground plan.

fig. 2d. Current floor plans of the 173 and 176 Perry Street Towers.

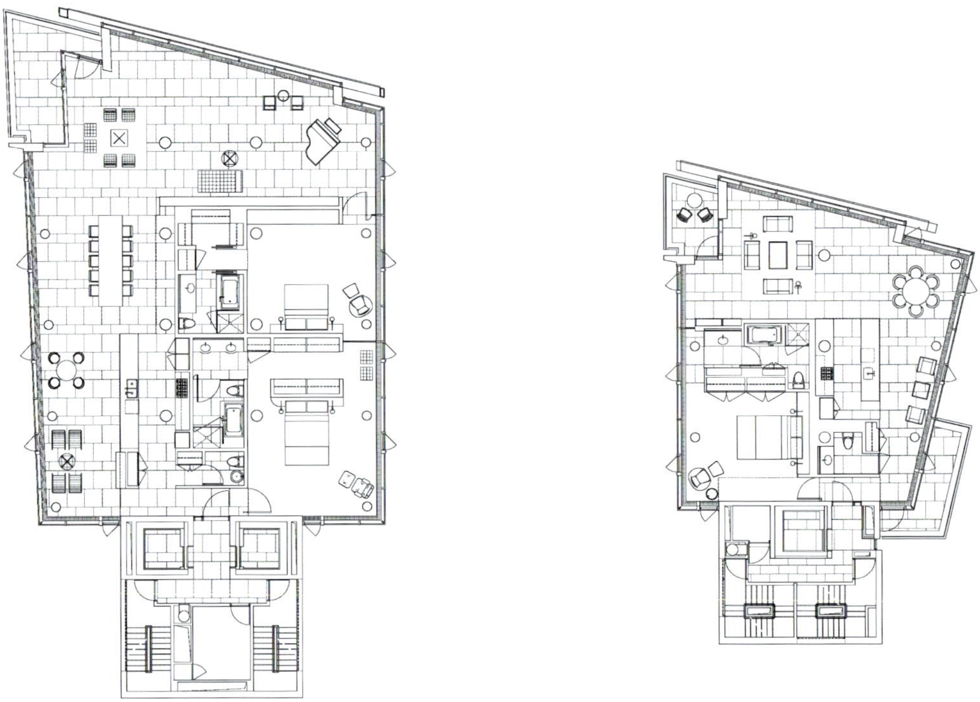

to increase MOMA's exhibition space, and to carry out a major real estate operation on the adjoining plot to the west, which was entrusted to the French architect Jean Nouvel, in which MOMA's galleries were also to be extended. Barely 13 years after its completion, despite protests from the architectural community and architecture critics, and despite attempts by the architects Diller and Scofidio to integrate the building into the new extension, the real estate pressure was too great, and the opportunity to give the building a new life failed: the small museum was demolished in May 2014. "*Demolishing this uniquely constructed, human-scale building is a great loss for New York City in terms of diversity of scale and texture in the Midtown neighborhood, which is in danger of becoming increasingly homogenous*"[1], lamented Tod Williams, invited in February 2014 to Paris to participate in an International Workshop jury at the Paris Val de Seine School of Architecture. When Tod Williams and Billie Tsien were approached about retaining the façade elements, they preferred not to compromise the integrity of the building. Today, MOMA's gigantic galleries occupy the plot, without distinction of scale, to accommodate the hordes of visitors: with some extra effort on the part of the Director of the Institution, a part of the museum dedicated to smaller works, or perhaps an architecture gallery, could have seen the light of day in this building, to the benefit of the exceptional architectural heritage represented by this small museum, and its transmission to the general public.

« The Contemporaine »

fig. 3a. Dynamics of the corner treatment.

Perry Street Condominium, New York, NY

Richard Meier & Partners, 1999–2002

This twin-tower residential complex in Greenwich Village, which borders the Hudson River, is a recent project designed by Richard Meier in Manhattan since the Westbeth project of social housing for artists in the 1960s. The 16-story towers are located at the north and south corners of Perry and West streets in the West Village. Their minimal, transparent form is an important contribution to the profile of the New York skyline on this side of the river, characterized primarily by lower 19th-century red brick structures (fig. 2a).

The buildings face not only the neighborhood's pedestrian promenades, but also the recently renovated Hudson River Park, which provides a mix of green space and paved walkways for passersby, joggers, and sportsmen of all kinds who travel from Battery Park City to 59th Street.

Each building is clad in insulating laminated glass and white aluminum millwork; the facades are curtain walls modulated by openings in a floor-to-ceiling pattern, enveloping the entire building, interrupted only by the open-worked slab nosing cassettes, metal panel balcony

1. Lecture by Tod Williams, feb. 2014, Ensa Paris Val-de-Seine.

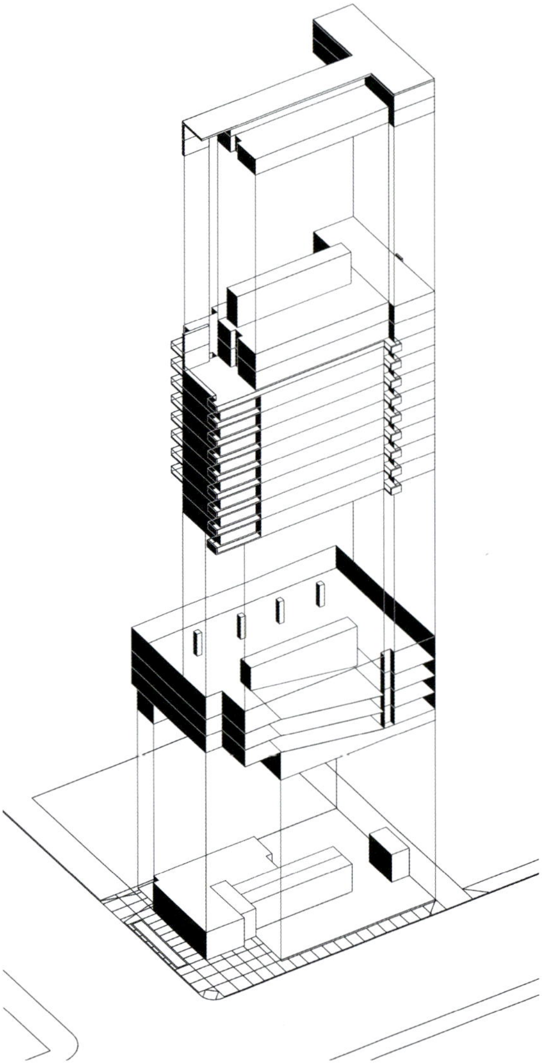

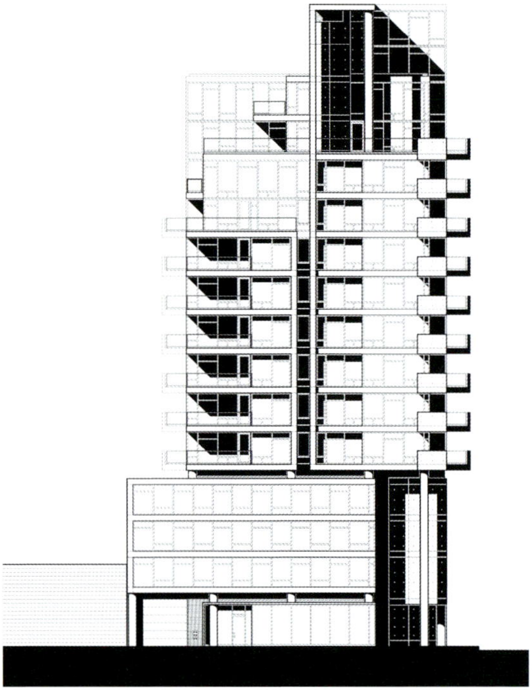

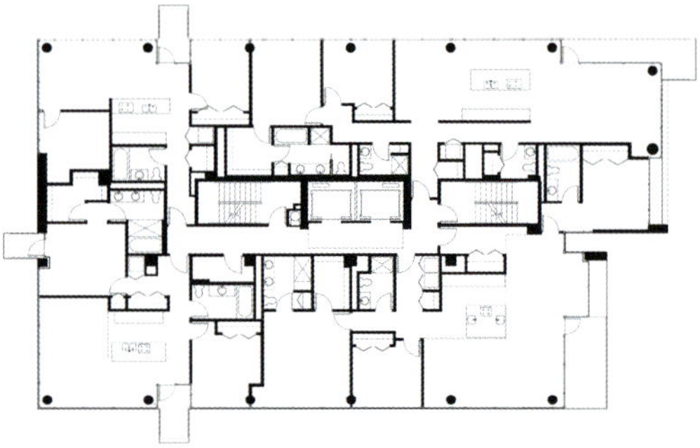

« The Contemporaine »

fig. 3b. Axonometry of the building. Urban collage strategy and different types of programs.

fig. 3c. East elevation

fig. 3d. Current floor plan

fig. 3e. View of one of the apartments

columns, and exposed raw concrete circulation to the east. With ceiling heights of more than 10 feet (3 m), the apartments offer continuous panoramic views of Manhattan, the Hudson River, and the New Jersey shoreline. The extensive use of glass was made possible by perimeter floor heating (fig. 2b).

Arriving from Perry Street, residents pass under a canopy, before entering their respective "lobbies." Each floor was designed to accommodate a single three-way apartment of 170 square meters in the north tower at 173 Perry Street, and 350 square meters in the south tower at 176 Perry Street. The service ducts and vertical distributions are located to the east, so as to free up views of the river as much as possible (fig. 2c and 2d).

A third tower came later to complete the other two, which does not have the quality of the first two; it seems that its realization escaped its author...

fig. 3f. View of the North façade

"The Contemporaine", Chicago, IL
Perkins + Wills, 1999–2002

The Contemporaine by Perkins & Wills, built in 2002, is a residential building located on the corner of a parcel in a neighborhood north of the Chicago River. The challenge of the dense and constrained site contributed to the development of an architecture with sculptural qualities (fig. 3a). In response to the varied scales and uses of the surrounding warehouses and converted stores, the design of the complex adopts the strategy of a mixed function and a highly expressive urban composition. The building is a tower of concrete, metal and glass, with eleven levels of housing, and four levels of parking and shops.

The articulation of its programmatic components allows the building to calibrate the different scales existing in the immediate surroundings.

The four floors of the parking lot and the commercial first floor respond to the pedestrian scale with facades animated by glass panels arranged over the entire height of the floors and punctuated by the noses of the slabs. The narrowness of the plot of land did not allow for a car ramp at the heart of the building, so it was moved to the periphery of the building and is visible from the street, adding a diagonal movement to an otherwise rectilinear structure (fig. 3b).

The eleven levels of residential units above the parking lot are detached by a thin rift, while the commercial floor is placed at the base. The series of superimposed balconies projected outward breaks the mass effect at the corner. The east-facing facade recedes deeply to allow views towards the city skyline. Two concrete bracing walls and the roof plane frame the ensemble and create a distinctive silhouette from Wells Street. The glass panels punctuated by window modules accentuate the interplay between solids and voids and animate the façade. The dynamic energy of the building culminates at the northeast corner with the emergence of a 45-foot (13.50 m) high exterior column that anchors the tower to the ground. The recessed corner, structural expression and balcony overhang compose a clear and powerful urban bias through the simple implementation of materials. The apartments have open plans, thanks to a "free plan" structure that underscores their adaptability. Four rooftop penthouses develop double-height living spaces to capture light and views (fig. 3c, 3d and 3e).

This building echoes the "Skybridge", another high-rise apartment building in Chicago, also built by Perkins & Wills, in an identical formal vocabulary.

"Towers that grow like hardy perennials"[2]

For several years now, a new strain of skyscraper has been springing up in New York, taking advantage of Manhattan's famous urban regulation allowing the transfer of air rights from neighboring plots. New silhouettes of towers are emerging in the New York skyline, signed by the great names of international architecture, defying the scarcity of land, and taking advantage of constant advances in technology to build extremely high. In many cases, these new buildings are no more than reflections of the ongoing investments that are shaping our cities, much more than architecture.

One of the first of its kind, Portzamparc's "one 57", whose final design was completed in 2009 after several years of research, just after the financial crisis, has been built in 2014, with a 75-storey, 306 m-high hotel and residential program, by the company Extell Development. Frank Gehry's 2011 building at 8 Spruce St, south of Nassau Street, features a residential program combined with a hospital, a school and a fitness center: it rises to a height of 267 m. Its undulating facade, like the surface of water, is often compared to the Aqua building designed in 2009 by architect Jeanne Gang in Chicago.

Architect Rafael Viñoly's **432 Park Avenue** remains the icon of this new generation of supertall buildings, towering over the others at a height of 425 m, with a slenderness ratio of one in fifteen. It stands out for its geometric purity, based on the Pythagorean theorem, and for its exposed structural concrete facade, which expresses the regularity of the Manhattan grid, laid out around a central core and creating column-free interiors to house 104 luxury apartments. The floor plan offers total flexibility for customized remodeling. The Tower's six volumes are divided by open intermediate levels, intended to deflect wind pressure and to achieve structural stability. The first levels are dedicated to services and facilities such as conference and meeting rooms, a restaurant, a spa with a fitness center, a swimming pool and underground parking. At ground level, the building creates a landscaped outdoor space opening onto Park Avenue, while a self-contained, fully glazed commercial volume marks the entrance to the site. But the problems encountered by this supertall construction (deafening

2. Dominique Machabert, "À New-York, les tours semblent pousser naturellement, comme des plantes vivaces", interview with Alvaro Siza, *AMC*, 284 (February 2020).

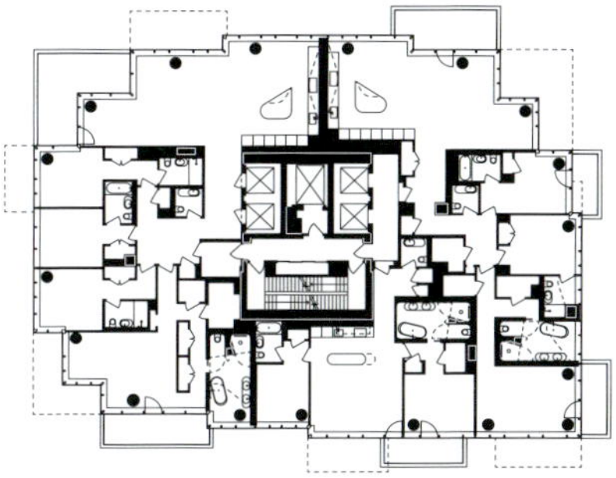

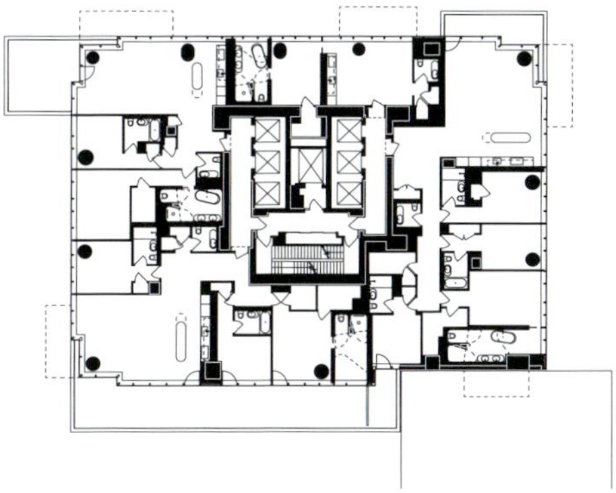

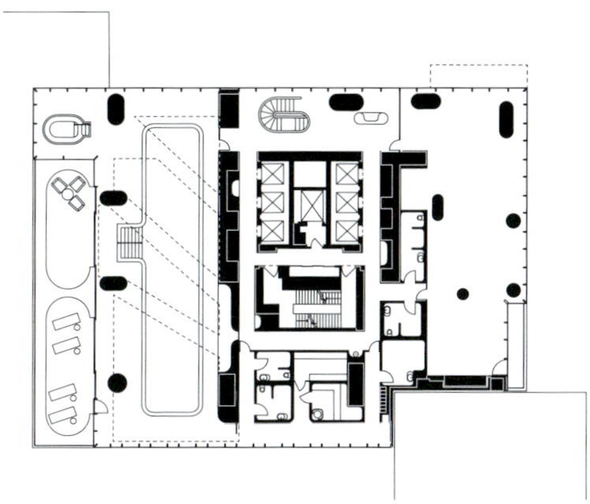

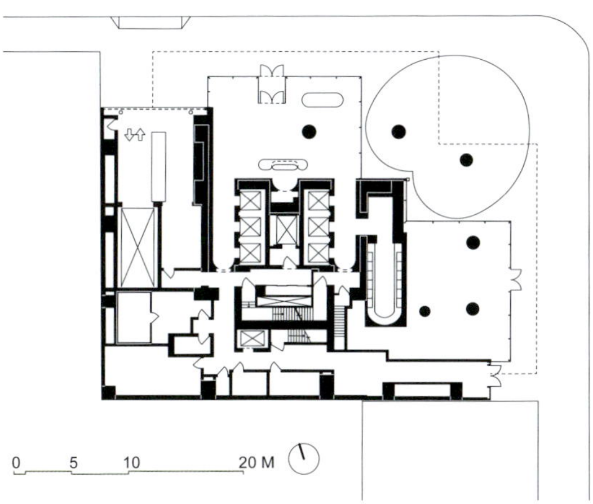

56 Leonard Street

fig. 4a. Zone 4, level 34, floor plan.

fig. 4b. Zone 1A, level 8, floor plan.

fig. 4c. Base, level 7, floor plan.

fig. 4d. Base, level 1, floor plan.

fig. 4e. View from Greenwich Street.

fig. 4e. Façade detail.

611 West 56th Street

fig. 5a. View from the west, façade.

fig. 5b. View of Hudson River.

fig. 5c. View of Midtown.

fig. 5d. South elevation.

fig. 5e. 25th to 28th floor plan.

fig. 5f. 8th floor plan.

fig. 5g. 4th floor plan.

fig. 5h. 1st floor plan.

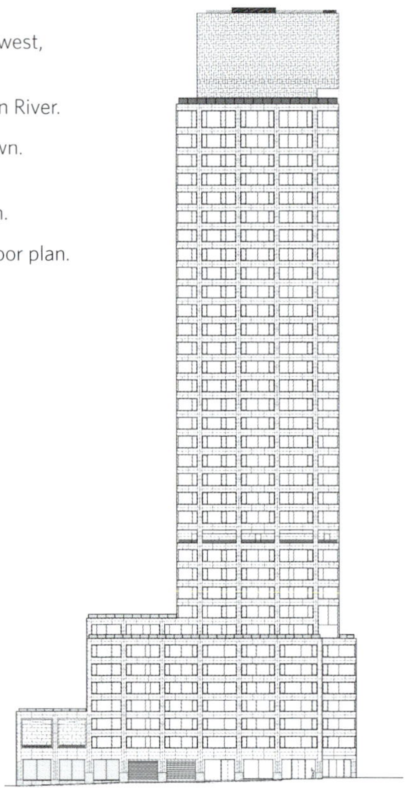

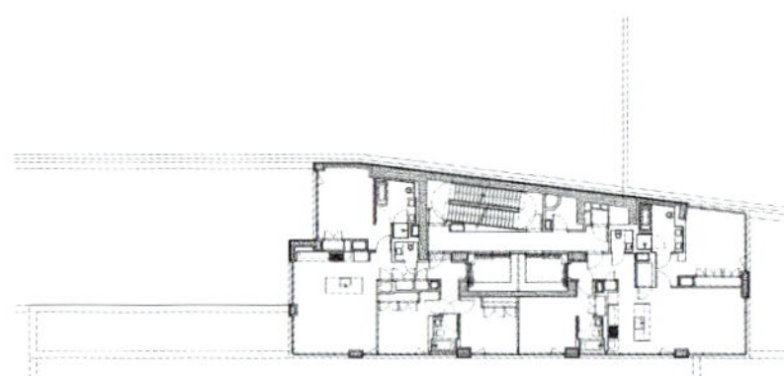

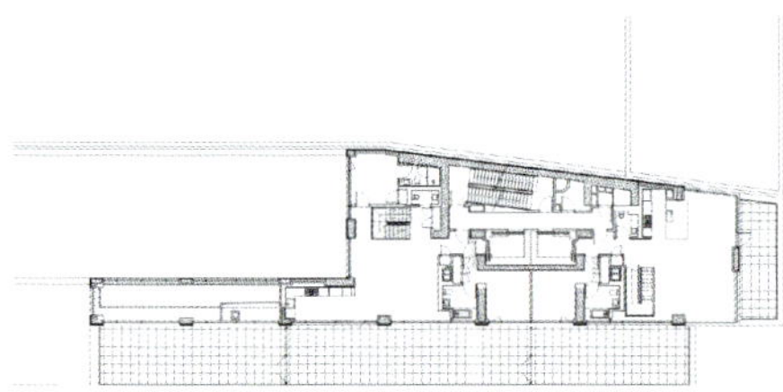

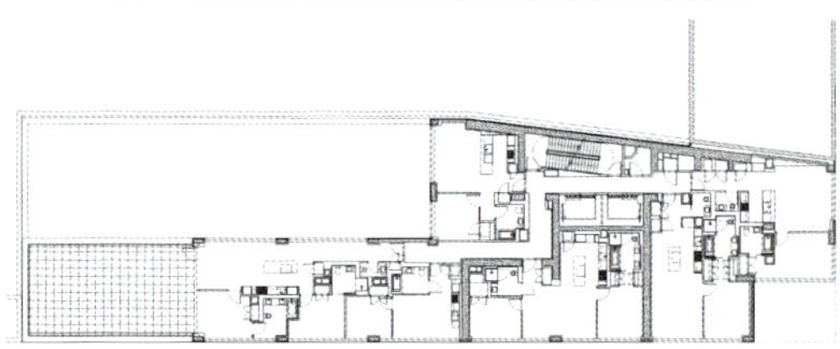

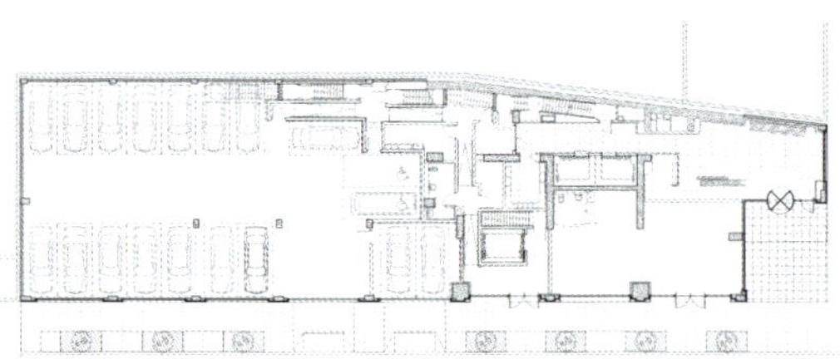

noise in the evacuation ducts, jammed elevators, vibrations) would contribute to making this tower the symbol of the extreme limits of capitalism.

In 2016, the Swiss architects Herzog and de Meuron designed and built a 60-storey, 250 m-high tower in the Tribeca district, at **56 Leonard Street**. Presented as "houses stacked in the sky" or "sky villas", it quickly took on the name of the "Jenga" tower in the image of the sets of wooden bricks that are stacked irregularly. Rising above the heart of the financial district, the building features 145 luxurious apartments with exceptional views of Manhattan and the Hudson, and an Amish Kapoor sculpture at its foot.

The project is designed as a stack of individual, identifiable rooms, creating different individual conditions for each flat, and breaking the tendency towards anonymity and repetition in residential towers. The external spaces provide direct and indirect visual links between people, while avoiding overlooking. The sculptural top, made up of ten cantilevered penthouses, is the most expressive part of the project, reviving the tradition of New York's iconic towers. The base responds to the distinctive character of Tribéca, reflecting the different scales of the neighbourhood, from small town houses to large industrial blocks. *"The overall appearance of the tower is very much a result of accepting and pushing to the limit simple and familiar local methods of construction. As a volume, the building has extreme proportions—at the very edge of what is structurally possible—and given its relatively small footprint, is exceptionally tall and slender. The building also shows its structural 'bones' and does not hide the method of its fabrication underneath layers of cladding. Instead, exposed horizontal concrete slabs register the floor-by-floor stacking of the construction process and exposed in-situ concrete columns allow the scale of the structural forces at work to be experienced from within the interior."*[3]

611 West 56th Street is a slightly different example in this race to the sky. It's an 80-unit residential tower designed by Portuguese architect Alvaro Siza, with interiors by the New York design firm Gabellini Sheppard, and built by developers Saif Sumaida, Amit Khurana, and Leny. At just 138 m tall and 38 stores, the building is much less dizzying than the others, is resolutely south-facing, and offers a new way of living, with sophisticated design and a variety of apartment typologies with unobstructed views over Midtown, Downtown, and the Hudson River.

"In New York, it's clear that economic dynamism is at the heart of the city's formation, not only in reality, but also in the myth of the New World, which seems to be just as active. This explains why skyscrapers spring up like perennial plants," explains Alvaro Siza. *"There's a kind of spontaneity to this architecture, the great heights seem almost natural* [...] *The visual spontaneity we witness* [...] *calls for very strict regulations, such as the stepped setback of facades as the towers rise to compensate for the narrowness of the streets, the maximum height of the buildings and the authorized variations, fixed in advance."*[4]

The building is a structure that stands out, not only in its immediate environment, at the intersection of the Midtown and Upper West Side districts, through a particular work on the angle, but in the whole of New York, asserting a refined and timeless architecture, more attached to detail than to grand gesture, displaying a discreet character, more in tune with the "post-covid" zeitgeist, resolutely more human and reasonable than its competitors. "*The angle allows us to work on the building's identity, just like the tops of skyscrapers*"[5], recalls the architect. The residence includes magnificent apartments ranging from one to four rooms, as well as duplexes and maisonettes, and a large penthouse at the top. With an average of only two apartments per level in most of the building, and the elevator often opening directly into the units, the sense of privacy is total. The building envelope is treated in stone with a granite base, like a white monolith with very pure contours, while the top cuts into the sky, adding a sculptural element to the ever-changing Manhattan skyline, a unique work in the architect's career.

3. Herzog et de Meuron.
4. Dominique Machabert, interview with Alvaro Siza, op. cit.
5. Ibid.

2 / Teaching the Project

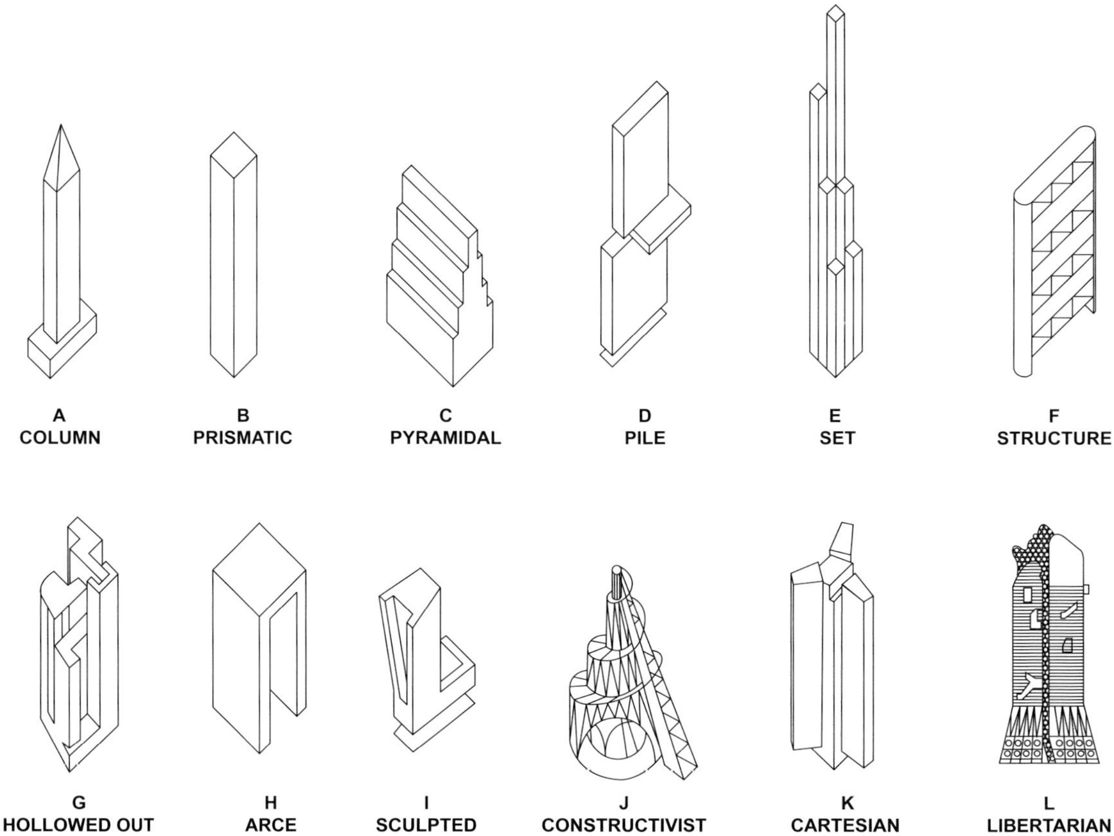

fig. 1. Typological inventory, Jean-Christophe Quinton, EAPB diploma 2000.

A Theoretical Exercise "Megaform as Urban Landscape"[1]

M. W. Kagan & N. Régnier-Kagan

It's simply a matter of learning—to be able to do. The project is the modus operandi of this "doing", a process that is cognitive as well.

C. Devillers[2]

Phase One: Critical analysis of built form, search for mental figures

The study of written texts and architecture from the 20th and 21st centuries provides an opportunity to take stock of current architectural research, based on the culture of the project: the meaning and significance of contemporary architectural space, its rationality, its poetics, its functional, constructive, and architectonic structuring, as well as its use. Analysis demonstrates that the relevance of an architecture must be developed through a critical apparatus; its development is based on multiple inter-relationships: site, geography, climate, questions of space and light, economics, construction, cultural and social context, relationship to the old city, history, references...

1. Typological inventory

Each student is to analyze an example of a tower chosen for its prototypical value. Presentation: The analysis is presented in horizontal A3 format (excluding the models), with the following information on the cover page: a 2 cm title strip with the student's name, the name of the building, the year, the location, the name of the architect, a list of the documents presented and the names of the teachers.

1. Analytical drawings:
   site plan, ground floor plan, typical floor plan, programmatic cross-section, structural plan, indicating main dimensions.
2. Study models and / or axonometric diagrams.
3. Photographs: The student is asked to initiate research, starting with a photographic work, a photomontage, then to experiment in model and folding.

1. Kenneth Frampton, *Megaform as urban landscape. 1999 Raoul Wallenberg Lecture*. New York: University of Michigan A. Alfred Taubman College of Architecture + Urban Planning, 1999.

2. Christian Devillers, « Sur l'histoire et l'analyse architecturale, Lettre à Françoise Choay », in *Les Cahiers de la recherche architecturale: L'histoire, approches et connections*, 26, (Marseille: Éditions Parenthèses, 1990), 95-103.

2. Methodological summary:

1. Isolate the relationship to the ground: "building the site."
2. Isolate the relationship to the sky: "pathway to the terrace".
3. Highlight the vertical space (interiority) of the lobby: "the outside is an inside."
   The relationship with gravity: the act of raising up a volume above the ground.
4. Highlight the relationship between frontality and rotation: "frontality versus rotation."
5. Highlight the geometric and constructional structure of the project: mental structure / constructional structure / spatial structure, the question of measurement and constructional unity.
6. Highlight vertical and horizontal divisions by visualizing the modeling of envelope and its architectonics.
7. Bring out the spatial theme and conceptual matrix
   "Proof of existence" through a specific section / the question of size: scales, proportion / the matrix or generating figure.
   Give the tower a specific category: column, prism, pyramid, stack, assembly, "hollow" structure, arch, sculpture, constructivist, Cartesian, libertarian...
8. Redefining the program or "reprogramming". Highlight the internal typological organization at functional and spatial levels.
9. Demonstrate, through a series of 5 ideograms the following 5 project elements:
   Site / Program / Structure / Membrane / Space
10. Highlight the systematic pattern of repetition:
    Structural elements, volumes, bays, floors...

These ten elements of analysis are to be revealed through:

> Study models

> Figures (diagrams, concepts)

> Photomontage

> Drawing

fig. 2. Photographic work on verticality.

Phase Two: Research verticality, the transition from the horizontal to the vertical

1. Photographic report

> 20 slides, classified as to whether they were taken on site, in the street, in a building or in an interior, deliberately framed or cropped, with successive cuts or montages.

Classify a minimum of 20 architectural elements to help us see them in space, according to a scenario expressing the different elements that make up the expression of height. The photographic work consists of identifying geometric elements in our environment that qualify vertical space: select 20 photographs (images, taken in a freely chosen environment, to evoke the idea of verticality. The chosen photos are intended to challenge the eye and prompt a re-reading: an interpretation that transforms reality. The framing is done to reveal a new vision: a spatiality in search of verticality.

Visual means to be used:

> Transparent and opaque views, through filters, of constructed urban landscapes
> Studies of light and shadow, inside or outside, depending on the walls and their openings...
> Spaces and objects seen through superimpositions and interpositions
> Location plan for shots / plans, sections, elevations, perspective sketches
> Indication of shooting angles, frontal or rotational
> Explain structural order
> Define the specific spatial theme of the vertical space in question
> Match the plastic and public quality of the spaces

2. Model experiments: 1 to 6

Once the elements have been identified, a scale model will be created, that attempts to render the desired vertical space as abstractly as possible.

Goals

Folding, unfolding, folding... Folding is a discipline that enables you to move from one planar orientation to another, without breaking the material by successive cutting. From the horizontal (natural or artificial ground) to the vertical (depth of space upwards). A tower is a metropolitan public space containing volumes; the exercise consists of developing a sensitive work on space, based on the vision of a human on the move, in an interior space that is a continuation of the space of the street.

Research into vertical space will be based on successive "matrix models":

Model 1: relationship to the ground. View from below. Dimensions: 5 cm × 5 cm × 25 cm.

Model 2: relationship to the sky. View from above. Dimensions: 5 cm × 5 cm × 25 cm.

Model 3: folded synthesis of the first 2 models. Dimensions: 5 × 5 × 25 cm.

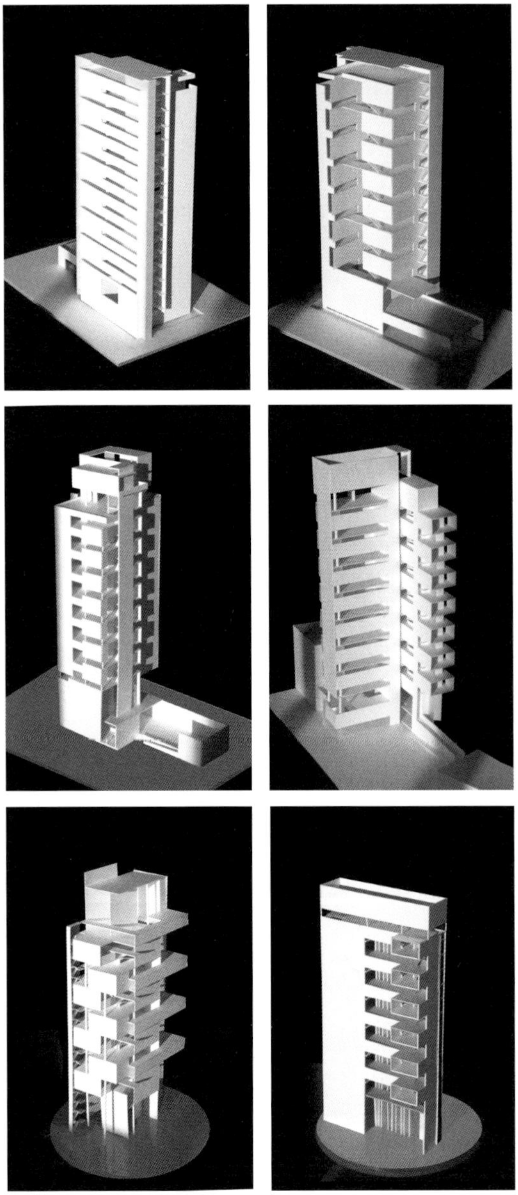

fig. 3. Taking reality into account: working with models, ENSAPB, 1998–1999.

An interpretation of the gaze will transform the vision of reality, allowing us to invert the models until we find a unifying element that gives order and meaning to a space, a structure, and a body. This new vision will reveal an exterior as well as an interior spatiality in a duality in search of verticality.

Model 4: This model explores the question of repetition as a modus operandi, bringing out 5 to 7 volumes, identical or otherwise, to create a structuring sequence for the tower.

Model 5: highlights the structure and vertical distributions.

Model 6: scaled to 1/500th and 1/200th. This model will summarize the theoretical studies, integrating structure and program distribution.

3. Placement in space to produce a project model from the transformed site.

A final stage will enable us to develop a territorial hypothesis: the confrontation with the site and an analysis of the context should lead to a transformation of the theoretical project that addresses the orientation, the immediate context, the urban fabric, the relationship to the territory, and the functional requirements in order to provide a direction for the project, which may call into question the theoretical project, distort it, or reverse it.

Presentation elements:

> Analysis of references: present the study in a slide show with a short oral presentation.

> The concept of "verticality", illustrated by a photo plate summarizing the spatial and structural intentions: name it. This can be accompanied by a short text.

> The 6 models:

— Present all the stages of the models, with their relationship to the ground and relationship to the sky, as well as the series and the structure (5 models, 5 × 5 × 25 cm).

A synthesis model of the "theoretical project", scaled to 1:500, is also to be presented, including the structure and distributions.

> Consideration of the site:

— A 1:1,000 scale model of the site with the "conceptual figure" of the project inscribed in the model.

— A 1:500 scale master plan, a cross-section, axonometries and perspectives to complete the presentation.

— A 1:500 scale model of the territorial hypothesis.

Phase Three: taking reality into account

1. Registration on the site

Site integration: This involves making choices, which may call into question certain principles of the theoretical project—re-dimensioning it, transcending it... A program must be proposed that addresses: lifestyles, mixed uses, new typologies that are suited to the context and the building: how to live, work, relax in a high-rise? How can we use the distributions, the parking lots, the lobbies on a daily basis, in relation to their context?

For this transition from theoretical discourse to concrete realization, it's essential to make the right choices in terms of typology, structure and materials. Given the multiplicity of techniques available today, rather than speaking of "truth in construction" or the expression of construction, it is important to focus on the coherence of the choice of construction -- the right use of any material, and its suitability to meet functional and emotional needs. The aim is to design a high-rise building to meet a specific urban situation. The design of this project is a back-and-forth dialogue between a program, a site, a spatial and emotional hypothesis, and a constructive approach: the ultimate aim is to combine them as a unit.

This theme is a pretext for designing constructive and spatial structures capable of illuminating both communal and private spaces, in order to integrate a technical approach in conjunction with the use of materials, their structural logic, and the implementation of their opacities and transparencies according to plastic desires, and in resonance with a particular context. The qualities of internal use, of responding to functional needs, are to be considered concurrently with the concern to modulate light, views and textures, and at the same time, to establish relationships between interior and exterior, and to create architectural promenades. The building's scale gives it a prominent role in the city, and therefore an eminently public character:

the site enables a territorial approach to be combined with the development of interior spaces and constructive principles.

2. From overall project to detailed design

This involves highlighting the major structural choices, on the one hand, and the distributions, envelope choices, opacities, transparencies, and luminosity, on the other: these choices will help determine the "architectonics" of the project, i.e. its materiality associated with its spatial design. Similarly, the question of technical ducts, their dimensions, compliance with standards, fire safety and IGH regulations, will be addressed in the general design of the building.

The detailed project: the assemblies and a few significant details of the project must be thought through as far as possible to define the materials, development and fine-tuning of lighting systems, envelopes, and structures. This work will include fine-tuning of construction details, cross-sections, and axonometric studies

Work on the project will be combined with courses to provide the knowledge needed for its development: knowledge of structural systems, knowledge of concrete, "solidity, stability", principles of fire safety in a high-rise building, and will include visits and lectures on high-rise districts in Paris.

Presentation requirements:

Inscription in the site

- Shaded site plan at 1:500 scale
- 1:500 scale site model

Overall project at 1/200 scale

- Plans, Sections, Elevations in context.
- Scale model of overall project (1:200)

Detailed project, 1/100th or 1/50th scale

- Hall plans
- Plans of a typical level
- Top floor plan
- 2 sections
- Model of main hall and intermediate halls
- 1:50 scale model of a module
- Axonometry of the structure
- 2 Perspectives (at least one exterior and one interior view of the project)
- Texture and appearance of materials: 1:20 scale cross-section
- 1 short text on the architectural and construction project
- Provide a title

Photos opposite: 1. Michel Kagan, Jean Pierre Bobenriether, Pierre Bismuth, EAPB 1999. **2.** EAPB 1999. **3.** Nathalie Régnier-Kagan, Henri Bresler, EAV 2005-2006. **4.** Michel Kagan, Jean Pierre Bobenriether, EAPB 1999. **5.** Michel Kagan, Pierre-Alain Croset, EAPB 2008.

Models p. 108: 1. Fung Tat Wai, EAPB 2006-2007. **2.** Fred Einaudi, 2008-2009. **3.** Matthieu Janmot, 2006-2007. **4.** Cédric Thomas, 2005-2006. **p. 109: 1.** EAPB 2001-2002. **2.** Jiong Jia, EAPB 2001-2002. **3, 4, 5.** Fung Tat Wai, EAPB 2006-2007. **6.** Thorsten Mischo, EAV 2004-2005. **7, 8, 9, 10, 11.** Sinda Tobni, Xabi Claverie, Bastien Bergramian, Alexis Bueno, Marie Vosguimoroukian, EAV 2004-2005. **12.** EAPB 2006-2007.

Project Notebook I

Model Experiments
Models 1 to 6

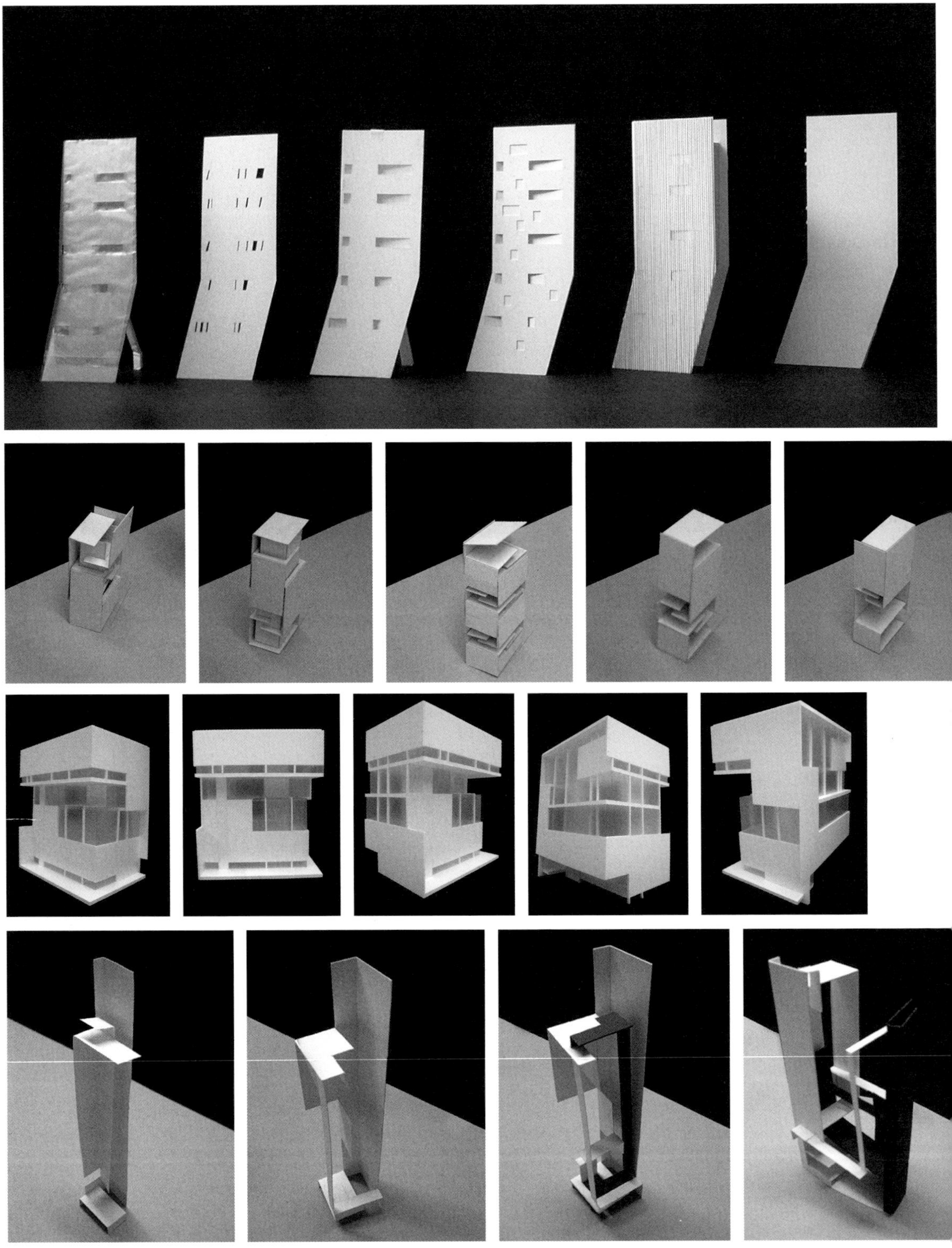

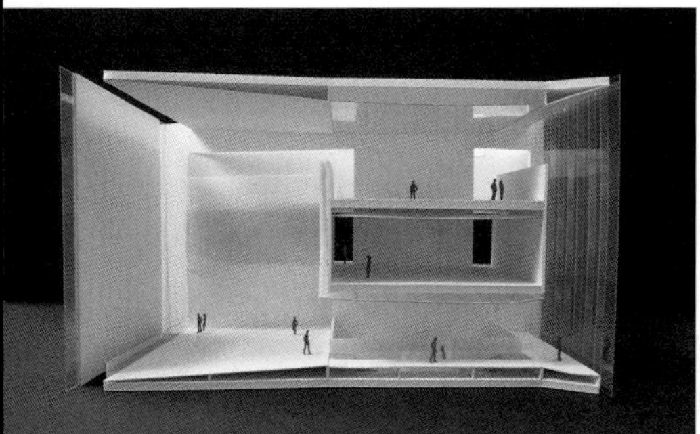
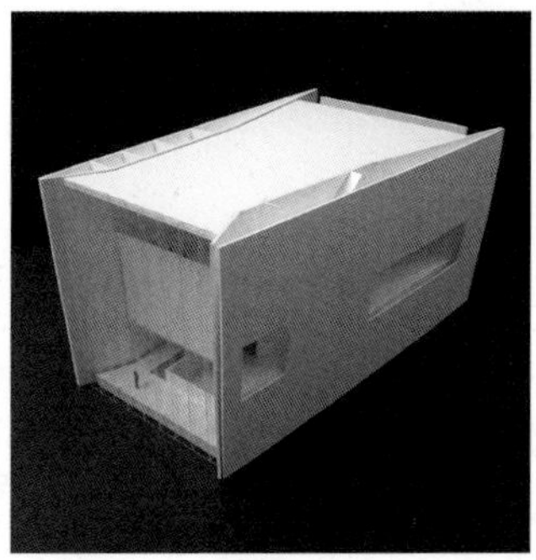
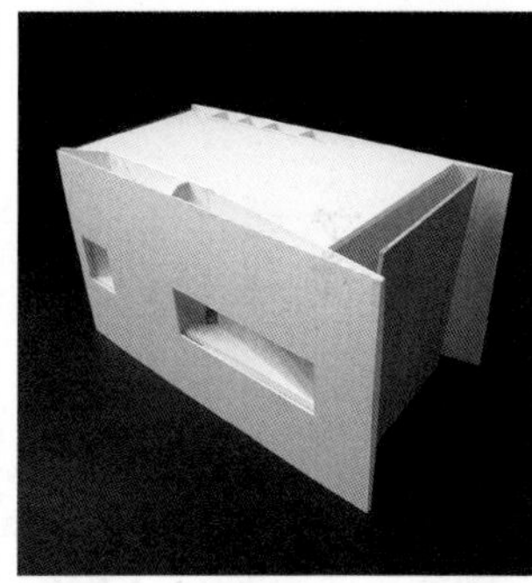

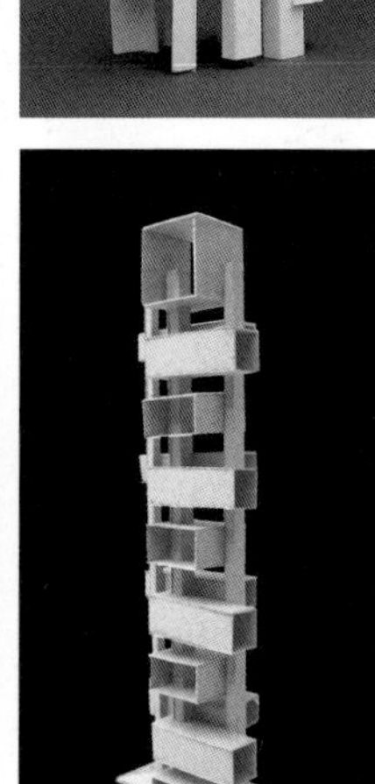

Registration on the Site

Bastille - Avenue Daumesnil

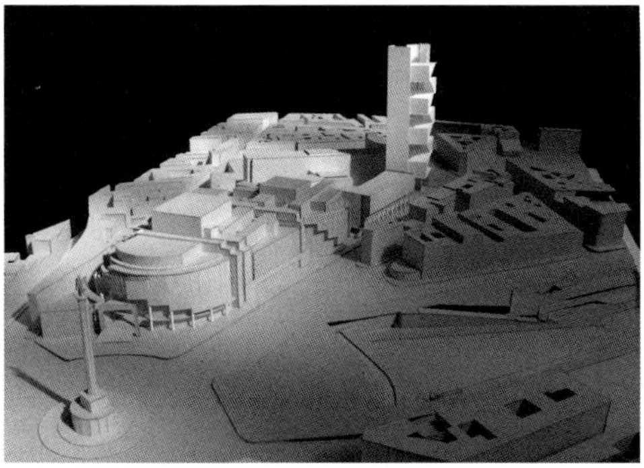

EAPB 2004-2005

Masséna - Bruneseau

1. and 2. Matthieu Janmot **3.** Steve Balme

Porte Maillot

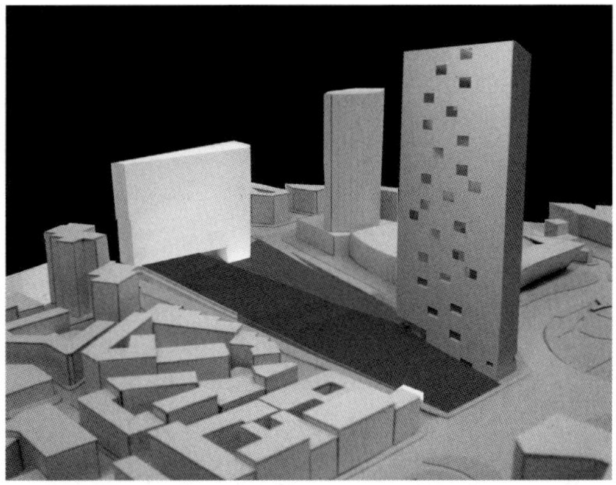

. Elena Fontanella, EAPB 2006–2007. **2, 4.** Alice Sin Ha Chau, EAPB 2007–2008. **3.** Fung Tat Wai, EAPB 2007–2008.

Front de Seine

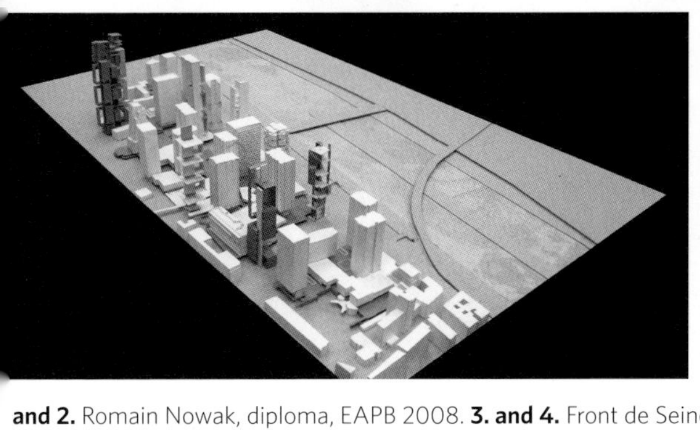

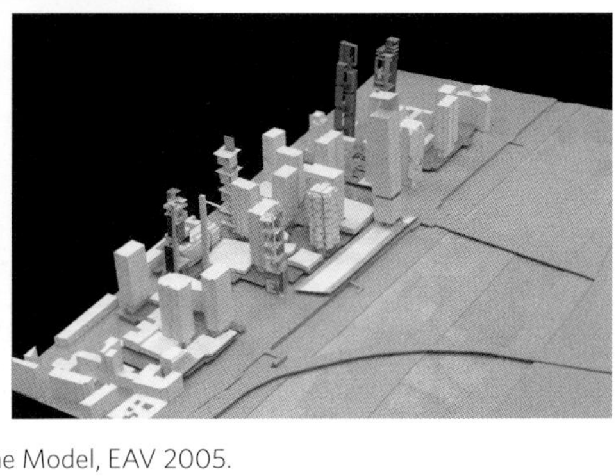

and 2. Romain Nowak, diploma, EAPB 2008. **3. and 4.** Front de Seine Model, EAV 2005.

From Global to Detailed Project

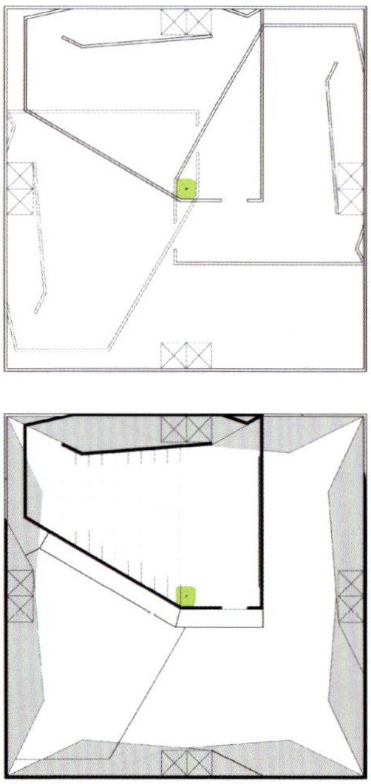

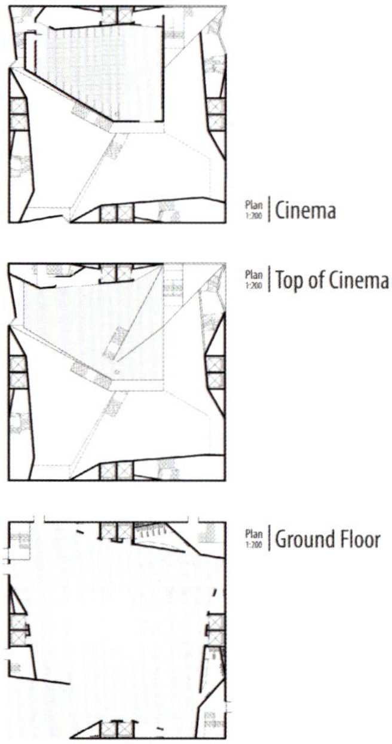

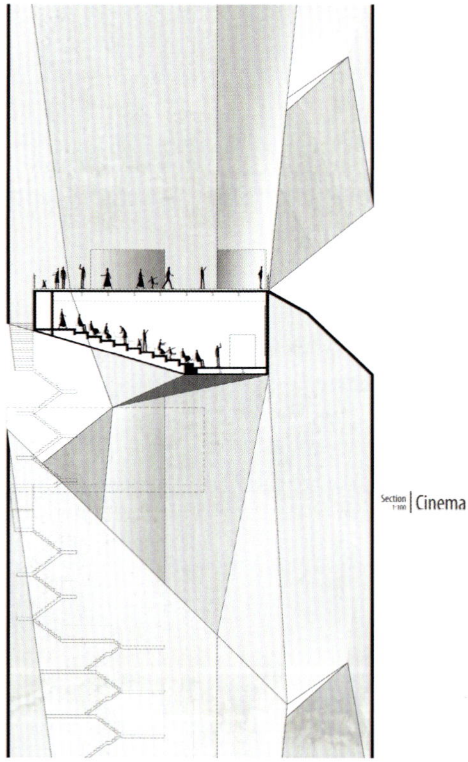

Fung Tat Wai
EAPB 2007–2008.
Plan, section, model.

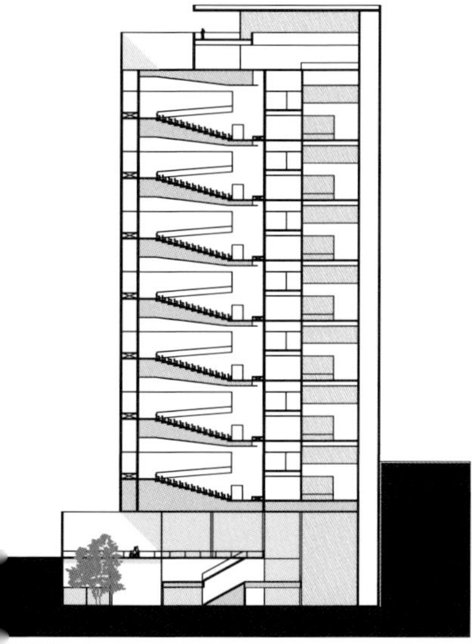

OUPE AA

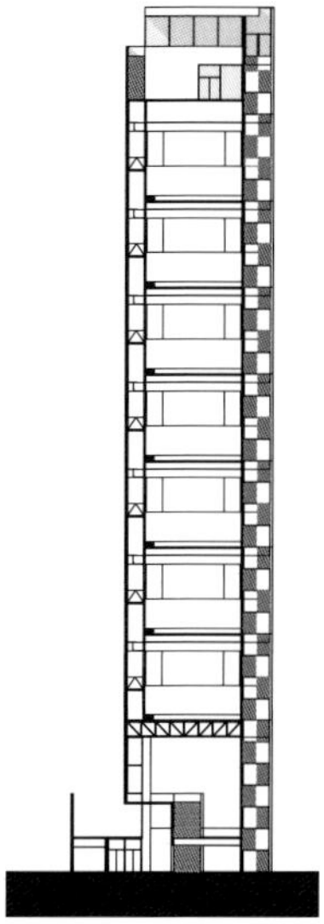

COUPE CC

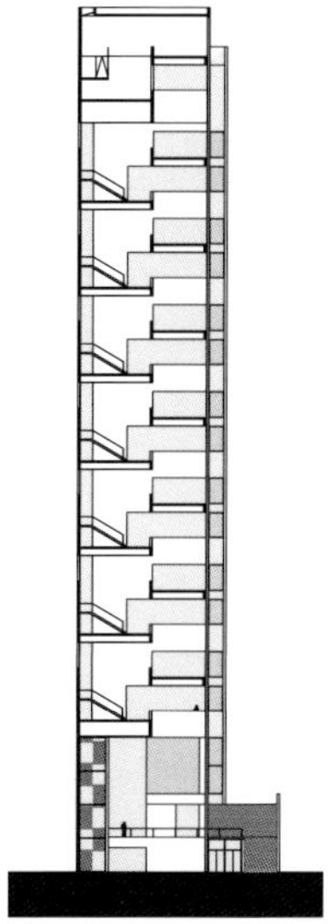

COUPE DD

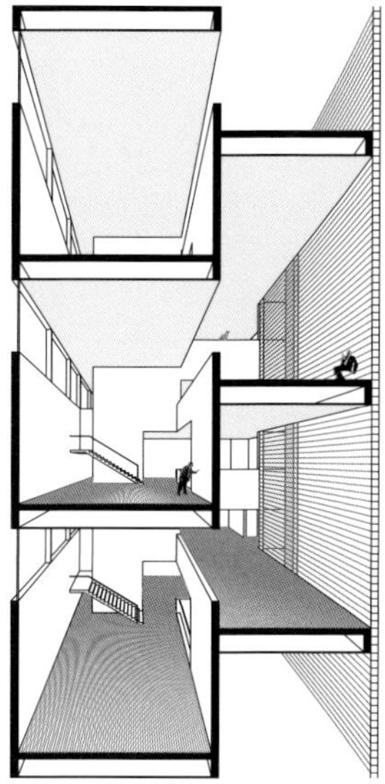

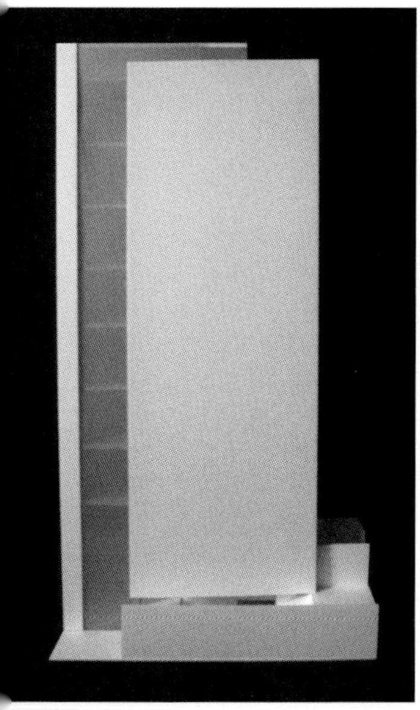

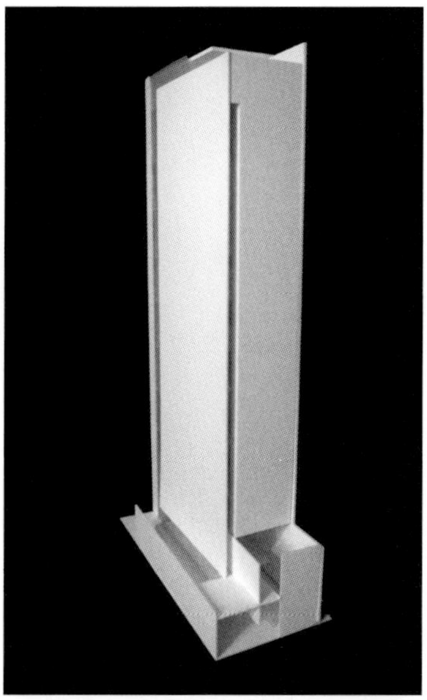

Benjamin Cros,
EAPB 2009.
Models and sections.

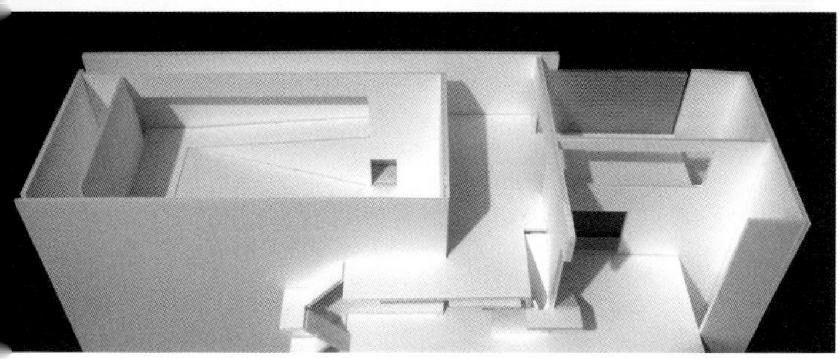

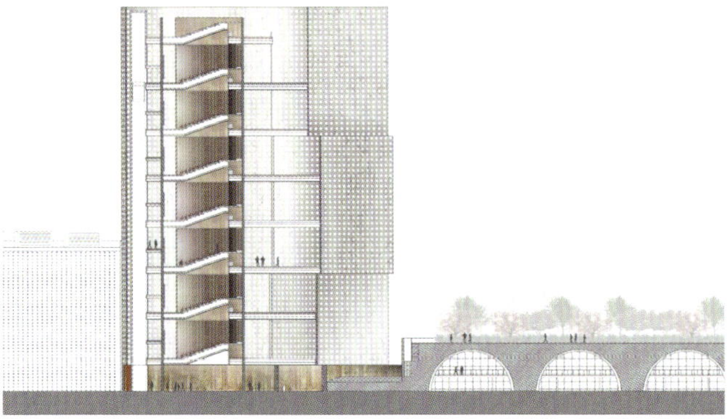

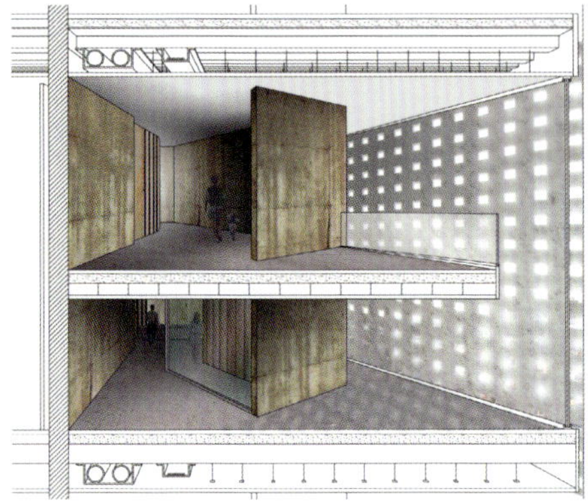

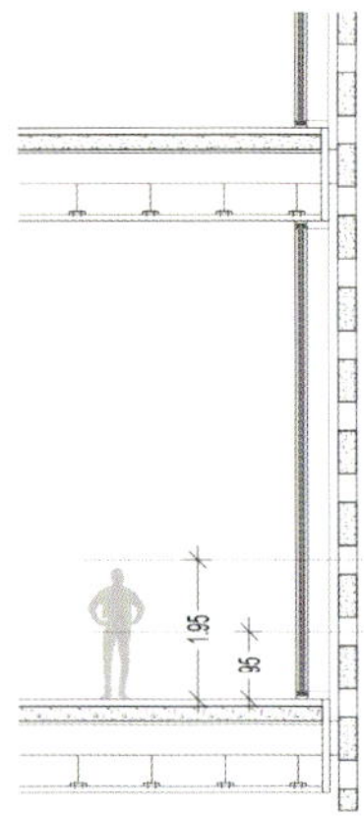

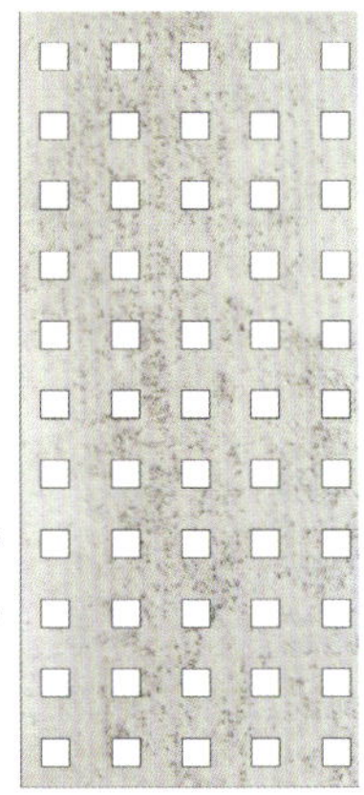

above Mathias Gervais de Lafond, EAPB 2007–2008.

below Jiong Jia, EAPB 2001–2002.

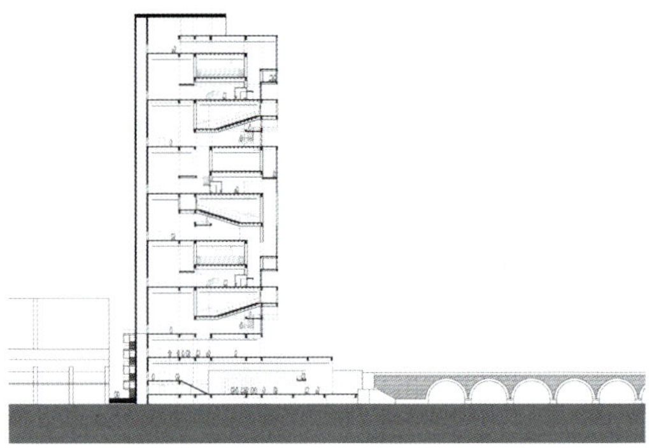

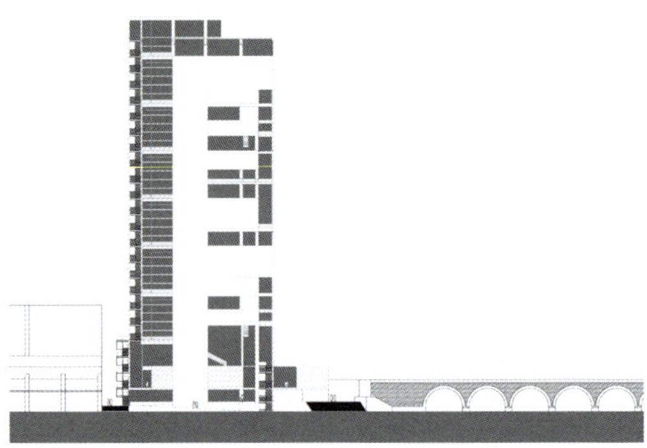

The Structural Aspect

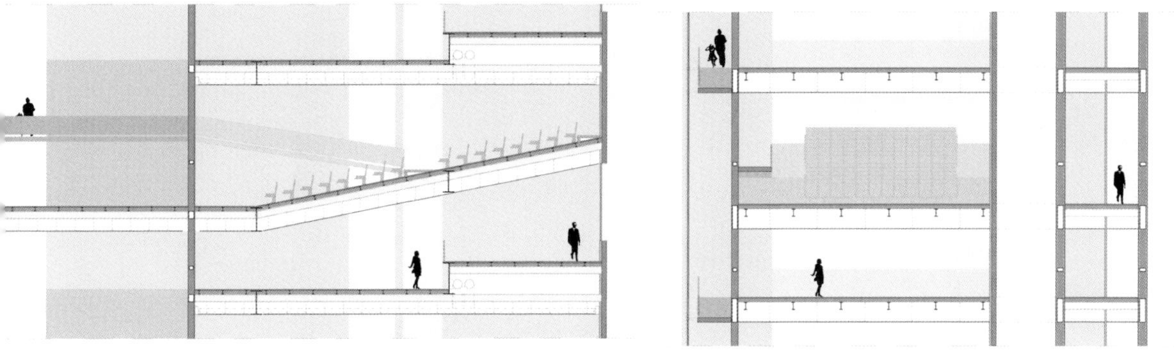

Maxime Gil, EAPB 2008.

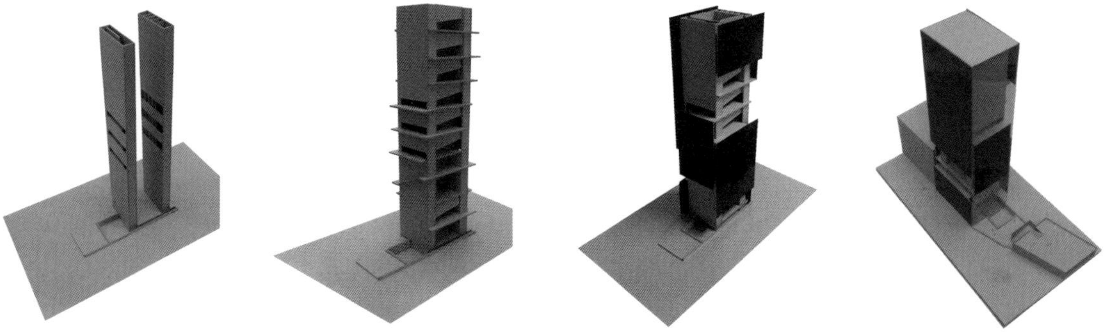

Fred Einaudi,
EAPB 2007–2008.

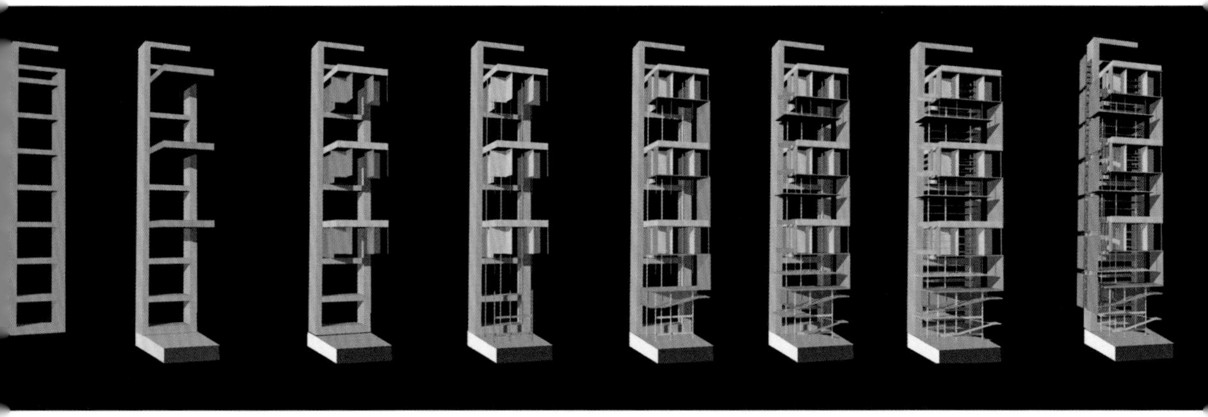

Florian Foucault and Florian Mathieu,
EAV 2004–2005.

fig. 1. Henri Ciriani. "Architecture at height, when the equivalence of horizontals and verticals make a 'city' for the man who flies". Sketch, mixed techniques, 2008. Offered for the publication.

A Few Tower References[1]

Michel W. Kagan, Nathalie Régnier-Kagan

A

Alvar Aalto
Aalto Hochhaus (housing and shops), Bremen, Germany, 1958–1962

Raimund Abraham
Times Square (cinemas), New York, USA, 1984 (project)

Austrian Cultural Center (museum), New York, USA, 1998–2002

Édouard Albert (with Robert Boileau and Jacques-Henri Labourdette)
Tour Croulebarbe (housing), Paris, France, 1956–1961

Michel Andrault and Pierre Parat
Tour Totem (housing), Front de Seine, Paris, France, 1975–1978

Université de Tolbiac, Paris, France, 1970

Roger Anger and Pierre Pucinelli
Tours résidentielles de l'Ile Verte (housing), Grenoble, France, 1963–1967

Wiel Arets architects
KNSM Island Skydome (housing), Amsterdam, Netherlands, 1990–1996

B

J. B. Bakema and J. H. van der Broek
Hansaviertel tower (housing), Berlin, 1957–1960

BBPR (Gian Luigi Banfi, Lodovico di Belgiojoso, Enrico Peressutti and Ernesto Rogers)
Torre Velasca (mixed use: shops, offices, housing), Milan, 1956–1958

fig. 2a & 2b. Charles Correa, Kauchaujunga Apartments, Bombay, India, 1970–1983.

1. Non-exhaustive list of towers, chosen for their structural, programmatic or typological interest, listed in alphabetical order by name of the architect or the architectural practice, then: name of the project (type of programme), location, date, project (if not completed). If several projects/architect, in chronological order.

Emmanuelle et Laurent Beaudouin
Tour Esch Belval (project), Luxembourg, 2004
(fig. 11)

Stefano Boeri
Vertical Forest (housing), Milan, Italy, 2007–2014

Ricardo Bofill
Walden 7 (housing), Barcelona, 1970–1975

Daniel H. Burnham
Fuller Building, known as "Flat Iron Building" (offices), New York, USA, 1902

C

Alberto Campo Baeza
Telefonica towers (offices), Madrid, Spain, 1999 (project)

Peter Chamberlain, Geoffry Powell & Christoph Bon
Residential towers of the Barbican (mixed use), London, UK, 1956–1976

David Chipperfield
Kaisstrass Studio (offices), Düsseldorf, Germany, 1994–1977

Jannowitz tower Berlin (offices), Germany, 2019

Morland Mixité Capitale (renewal), Paris, France, 2015–2022

Henri Ciriani *(fig. 1)*
Residential towers (housing), Groningen, Netherlands, 1988

38-unit residential building, The Hague, Netherlands, 1995

Charles Correa
Kauchaujunga Apartments, Bombay, India, 1970–1983
(fig. 2a & 2b)

fig. 3. William Lescaze et George Howe; PSFS, Philadelphia Saving Fund Society Building (offices), Philadelphie, USA, 1930–1932.

fig. 4. Ernö Goldfinger, Trellick Tower high-rise housing, London, United Kingdom, 1967–973.

F

Norman Foster

Head office of the Hong Kong & Shanghai Bank (offices), Hong Kong, China, 1979–1986

Millenium Tower (mixed use), Tokyo, Japan, 1989 (project)

Commerzbank head office (offices), Frankfurt, Germany, 1991–1997 *(fig. 13)*

Jiushi Corporation head office (offices), Shanghai, China, 1995–2001

Swiss Re HQ (offices), London, United Kingdom, 1997–2004

G

Studio Gang

Aqua Tower (mixed use: offices, housing), Chicago, USA, 2010

Xaveer de Geyter

Chassé Park Apartments, Breda, Netherlands, 1996–2001

Frank Gehry

8 Spruce Street (mixed use), New York, USA, 2011

Bertrand Goldberg

Marina City (parking and housing), Chicago, USA, 1959–1967

Ernö Goldfinger

Balfron Tower (housing), Rowlett Street, Poplar, London, United Kingdom, 1964–1966

Trellick Tower (housing), Edenham Street, West London, United Kingdom, 1967–1973, *(fig. 4)*

Ernest R. Graham (with Peirce Anderson)

Equitable building (offices), New York, USA, 1913–1915

Bruce Graham (SOM)

John Hancock Center (offices), Chicago, USA, 1965–1969

Sears tower (mixed retail and residential), Chicago, USA, 1974–1976

Walter Gropius

Metlife Building, former Pan Am Building (offices, shops, restaurants), New York, 1963

fig. 5. Erkki Kairamo, Itäkeskus (offices and shopping centre), Helsinki, Finland, 1984–1987.

H

Harrison & Abramovitz

United Nations Headquarters (offices), New York, 1949–1950 (based on the concept by an international team of architects)

John Hejduk

Kreuzberg Turm, (housing), Berlin, Germany, 1983–1988

Herzog & de Meuron

56 Leonard Street (housing), New York, USA, 2012–2017

fig. 6. El Lissitsky, « Skyhook » or « Wolkenbügel », Moscou, former USSR, 1924–1925, draft.

fig. 7. Kevin Roche & John Dinkeloo, Ford Foundation Headquarters (offices), New York, USA, 1967.

HPP-Hentrich, Petschnigg & partner KG
Thyssenhaus (offices), Düsseldorf, Germany, 1957–1960

Raymond Hood
Mc Graw Hill (offices), Manhattan, New York, USA, 1931–1934

Rockefeller Center, New York, USA, 1940

Raymond Hood & John Howells
American radiator building (offices), also known as American Standard Building, New York, USA, 1924

J

Arne Jacobsen
SAS Royal Hotel, Copenhagen, Denmark, 1956-1960

K

Erkki Kairamo
Itäkeskus (offices and shopping centre), Helsinki, Finland, 1984–1987 *(fig. 5)*

Kisho Kurokawa
Nakagin Capsule Tower (housing), Tokyo, Japan, 1972 (demolished 2022)

L

Morris Lapidus
Fontainebleau Hotel, Miami Beach, USA, 1952–1954

Henning Larsen,
Ferring International Center (offices, auditoriums), Copenhagen, Denmark, 2002

Denys Lasdun & Fry, Drew, Drake
Cluster Block at Claredale street (housing), Bethnal Green, London, UK, 1954–1957

Le Corbusier
The Cartesian skyscraper, 1930–1932, project

Quartier de la Marine, Alger, Algeria, 1932, 1940 (projects)

Unité d'habitation (mixed use), Marseille, France, 1946–1952

Le Corbusier, Lucio Costa and Oscar Niemeyer
Ministry of National Education and Public Health (offices), Rio de Janeiro, Brazil, 1936–43

Yvan Leonidov
Lenin Institute for Bibliographic Sciences (university centre), Moscow, Russia, 1927, diploma project

Narkomtiajprom, Commissariat for Heavy Industry (police station), Moscow, Russia, 1934, project

William Lescaze and George Howe
Moma, Museum of Modern Art, New York, USA, 1930–1931 (project)

PSFS, Philadelphia Saving Fund Society Building (offices), Philadelphia, USA, 1930–1932 *(fig. 3)*

Môrice Leroux
Skyscrapers in Villeurbanne (social housing), Villeurbanne, France, 1927–1931

El Lissitsky
Skyhook, or Wolkenbügel (mixed use), Moscow, former USSR, 1924–1925, draft *(fig. 6)*

Raymond Lopez—Frédéric Druot, Anne Lacaton & Jean-Philippe Vassal
Tour Bois Le Prêtre (housing), Paris, France, 1959, 2005–2011 (renovation)

fig. 8. Richard Rogers, Lloyds of London, Insurance Company (offices), London, 1978–1986.

M

Jean de Mailly, Jacques Depussé & Jean Prouvé
Tour Nobel, then Tour Nexity, then Tour Initiale (offices), La Défense, France, 1966

Georges Maillol
Les horizons (housing), Rennes, France, 1970

Richard Meier
Madison Square Garden (masterplan), New York, USA, 1987 (project)

Perry Street Condominiums (housing), New York, USA, 1999–2002

Ludwig Mies van der Rohe
Hochhaus Friedrichstrasse, Berlin, Germany, 1921 (project)

Lake Shore Drive Apartments, Chicago, USA, 1950–1951

Seagram Building (offices), New York, USA, 1954–1958 (with Philip Johnson)

Dominion Center (masterplan), Toronto, Canada, 1967–1969

IBM Building, currently 330 North Wabash (offices), Chicago, USA, 1969–1973

Westmount Square (offices), Montreal, Canada, 1964–1967

Chicago Federal Center (offices), Chicago, USA, 1959–1974

Promontory Appartments (housing), Chicago, USA, 1949

Luigi Moretti
Multifonctionnal complex (mixed use), Milan, Italy, 1949–1956

C.F. Murphy Associate
Civic Center (offices), Chicago, 1965 (with SOM, Loebl, Schlossmann & Bennett)

fig. 9. Paul Rudolph, The Colonnade Condominiums, Singapore, 1980.

Eduardo Souto de Moura
Burgo Tower (shops and offices), Porto, Portugal, 2006-2007

MVRDV
Mirador (housing), Madrid, Spain, 2005

N

Oscar Niemeyer
Edificio Copan (mixed use), Sao Paulo, Brazil, 1951-1966

Edificio Niemeyer (housing), Belo Horizonte, Brazil, 1954-1955

Jean Nouvel
La tour sans fins (offices), La Défense, France, 1989-1992 (project)

Torre Agbar (offices), Barcelona, Spain, 1999-2005

Tour Signal, La Défense, France, 2008 (project)

Tour La Marseillaise (mixed use), France, 2018

Tours Duo (mixed use), Paris, France, 2011-2022

Neutelings Riedijk Architects
IJ Tower (housing), Amsterdam, Netherlands, 1993-1998

O

Francisco Javier Sáenz de Oiza
Torres Blancas (housing, services), Madrid, Spain, 1968

Banco de Bilbao (Offices) Madrid, Spain, 1971-1980

OMA—Office for Metropolitan Architecture
Fondazione Prada (museum, gallery), Milan, Italy, 2008-2018

De Rotterdam (mixed use), Rotterdam, Netherlands, 1997-2013

CCTV headquarters (offices), Beijing, China, 2002-2012

P

Ieoh Ming Pei
100-110 Bleecker Street (housing), New York University, USA, 1966

Overseas-Chinese Banking Corporation Center (offices), Singapore, Republic of Singapore, 1976-1980

Bank Of China (offices), Hong Kong, China, 1985-1990

Pei Cobb Freed and Partners
Tour EDF (offices), La Défense, France, 1995-2001

César Pelli
Museum of Modern Art Tower (housing), New York, USA, 1984

William Pereira
Transamerica pyramid (offices), San Francisco, USA, 1969-1972

Perkins + Wills
Contemporaine (mixed use: parking, shops, housing), Chicago, USA, 2004

Skybridge, One North Halsted (mixed: parking, shops, housing), Chicago, USA, 2003

Auguste Perret

Tour Perret (offices, housing), Amiens, France, 1948-1954

Residential towers, Le Havre, France, 1945-1955

Renzo Piano Building Workshop

Debis Tower, The Daimler Benz Headquarters (offices) Potsdamer Platz, Berlin, Germany, 1999

Aurora Place (mixed use: offices and housing), Sydney, Australia, 1996-2000

New York Times Building (offices), New York, USA, 2000-2007

The Shard—London Bridge Tower (mixed use: housing, shops, restaurants, and hotels), London, UK, 2008-2012

Paris Courthouse, Paris, France 2017

Gio Ponti (Pierre Luigi Nervi engineer)

Pirelli skyscraper (offices), Milan, Italy, 1951-1961

Christian de Portzamparc

LVMH Tower (offices), New York, USA, 1995-1999

One57 (housing and hotel), New York, USA, 2014

Fernand Pouillon

Résidence du Point du jour (housing), Boulogne-Billancourt, 1957-1963

Résidence Le Parc (housing), Meudon La Forêt, France, 1957-1962

R

Paulo Mendes da Rocha

Edificio Guaimbê (housing), São Paulo, Brazil, 1964

Edifício residencial Jaraguá (housing), São Paulo, Brazil, 1984 *(fig. 14)*

Kevin Roche & John Dinkeloo

Ford Foundation Headquarters (offices), New York, USA, 1967, *(fig. 7)*

Knights of Columbus Headquarters (offices), Yale, New-Haven, USA, 1965-1969

Richard Rogers

Lloyds of London (offices), London, United Kingdom, 1978-1986 *(fig. 8)*

fig. 10. Frank Lloyd Wright, Price Tower (offices), Baskerville, USA, 1952-1956.

Paul Rudolph

The Colonnade Condominiums, Singapore, 1980 *(fig. 9)*

S

Kazuyo Sejima + Ryue Nishizawa / SANAA

New Art Museum, New York, 2007

Eero Saarinen

CBS building (offices), New York, 1968

Moshe Safdie

Ardmore habitat, (housing), Singapore, 1980-1985

Habitat 67 (housing), Montréal, Canada, 1964-1967

Sauerbruch Hutton architekten

GSW-Haupt-Verwaltung (offices), Berlin, Germany, 1992-1999

fig. 11. Emmanuelle et Laurent Beaudouin, Tour Esch Belval, Luxembourg, 2004

fig. 12. Woha, Newton Suites (housing), Singapore, 2008

fig. 13. Norman Foster, Commerzbank head office (offices), Frankfurt, Germany, 1991–1997.

Hans Scharoun, Wilhem Franck
Romeo and Juliet (housing), Stuttgart, Germany, 1954–1959

Schipporeit (Heinrich Associates with Graham, Anderson, Probst & White)
Lake Point Tower (housing, offices, shops, restaurants, swimming pool), Chicago, 1968

Todd Schliemann
Standard Hotel, New York, 2008–2009

Nicolas Schoeffer
Tour Lumière Cybernetique (urban sculpture), La Défense, France, 1963

Harry Seidler & Associates
Horizon Tower (housing), Sydney, Australia, 1998

Josep Lluis Sert, Jackson & Gourley
Peabody Terrace (housing), Harvard University, Cambridge, USA, 1962–1964

Alvaro Siza
611 West 56th Street (housing), New York, USA, 2015–2022

New Orleans tower (housing), Rotterdam, Netherlands, 2003–2010

Luigi Snozzi
Proposal for a residential tower (student project), 1957

Skidmore, Owings & Merrill (SOM)
Lever house (offices), Manhattan, New York, USA, 1951–1952 (Gordon Bunshaft architect)

Inland Steel Building (offices), Chicago, USA, 1956–1958

Pepsi-Cola Building (offices), New York, USA, 1959

Union Carbide Building (offices), New York, 1960

One Liberty Plaza (offices), New York, USA, 1973-74

One Chase Manhattan Plaza (offices), New York, USA, 1961

Hotel Arts (hotel), Barcelona, Spain, 1992

Broadgate tower(mixed-use), London, UK, 2008

Al Sharq Tower (mixed-use), Dubai, United Arab Emirates, 2008–2009 (project)

Rolex Tower (mixed use: offices, housing), Dubai, United Arab Emirates, 2008–2009

Starett & Van Vleck
Downtown Athletic Club, (mixed use: sports facilities, offices, hotel, housing), New York, USA, 1929-30

Hugh Stubbins Jr (in collaboration with Edward Larrabee Barnes Associates)
Citicorp Center (offices), New York, USA, 1974-1977

V

Rafael Viñoly Architects
432 Park Avenue (housing), New York, USA, 2015

W

Harry Weese and Associates
Metropolitan Correctional Centre (federal jail), Chicago, USA, 1973-1975

Amancio Williams
Proposal for a skyscraper (unknown programme), Argentina, 1948 (project)

Tod Williams and Billie Tsien
Museum of American Folk Art, New York, USA, 2001

André Wogenscky
Hauts-de-Seine Prefecture (offices), Nanterre, France, 1965–1972

Woha
Newton Suites (housing), Singapore, 2008 *(fig. 12)*

Met Tower (housing), Bangkok, Thailand, 2003-2009

Frank Lloyd Wright
Price Tower (offices), Baskerville, USA, 1952-new 1956 *(fig. 10)*

Johnson Wax Research Tower (offices), Racine, USA, 1944–1951

One Mile Tower (mixed use: offices, hotel, housing), Illinois, 1956 (project)

Y

Minoru Yamasaki
World Trade Center (offices), New York, USA, 1966–1973 (demolished 2001)

fig. 14. Paulo Mendes da Rocha, Edifício residencial Jaraguá (housing), São Paulo, Brazil, 1984

fig. 1. Location of sites throughout Paris.

The Parisian Context

Nathalie Régnier-Kagan

What will Paris be like tomorrow? How will the Parisian metropolis evolve in the early 21st century? The Haussmannian city, with its uniform template, does not accommodate the differentiation necessary to tackle the issue of urban scales within the city, or the conservation of green spaces on the outskirts of the ring road, in areas undergoing rapid change. Historian and architect Jacques Lucan describes today's Paris as "three sedimented worlds": the homogeneous Haussmannian city produced by regulations, the heterogeneous city of villages and suburbs, and the "modernist" Paris of post-war urban renewal. The "Trente glorieuses"[1] saw a flowering of high-rise buildings (Jussieu, Maine Montparnasse, Porte Maillot, Olympiades, Front de Seine, Place des Fêtes, Orgues de Flandre...). In 1977, a presidential decree put an abrupt end to all so-called "modernist" operations in Paris: neo-Haussmanism was imposed, with a return to the street, the plot, the continuity of the urban fabric, alignments, and traditional templates for three decades until the 2000s. *"It was a strange situation for French architecture in those years, when towers were banned, while extraordinary ones were being built elsewhere: by Norman Foster for the Hong Kong and Shanghai Bank (1986), and by Ieoh Ming Pei for the Bank of China (1989)"*[2].

In one of the first indications of a change in mentality, Édouard Albert's Croulebarbe Tower (1961), Paris's first 67 m-high residential "skyscraper", was listed as a historic monument in 1994. In addition to its innovative construction principle for the time, this building is exemplary in being particularly well integrated into its urban fabric. At the beginning of the 2000s, the Parisian municipal authorities reopened the question of building height in Paris, putting high-rise buildings back into current fashion (*"L'air du temps"*). It was in this context that Yves Lion proposed a district of towers around the ring road in his urban project for "Masséna Bruneseau" in eastern Paris, and that the exhibition "The Invention of the European Tower" was presented at the Pavillon de l'Arsenal.

1. "Thirty glorious years" Period of growth between 1945 and 1975.

2. François Chaslin, "Hauteurs de Paris" *in* Bruno Marchand & Christophe Joud (ed.), *Surélévations, conversations urbaines* (Paris: In Folio, 2018).

fig. 2. Tour Albert, Paris.

In 2008, the Swiss architects Herzog and de Meuron unveiled their project for a 200 meter tall triangular tower at Porte de Versailles; in 2010, Renzo Piano was commissioned to design a 160 m tower for the Tribunal de Grande d'Instance at Porte de Clichy, on the outskirts of the Batignolles district, to be completed in 2017. Finally, Jean Nouvel's Duo towers won the competition in 2011 to build two towers measuring 120 m and 180 m on rue Bruneseau, in line with avenue de France, to be inaugurated in 2022. Several factors triggered this phenomenon: in 2014, the Alur law, by abandoning the floor / area ratio, (known as the COS rule, or Coefficient d'occupation des sols), opened up new building potential, in a bid to combat urban sprawl. For the municipality, the aim was to maintain its place among Europe's capital cities, develop its status as the world's leading tourist destination, and create housing, with the objective of achieving 30% social housing by 2030...

"With the Greater Paris project, the effects of densification, which reduces green spaces and does not take into account roads, parking and facilities, are beginning to be felt,"[3] deplores Dominique Lorrain. The development of the Paris region is now seen as an asset in the context of global competition between very large metropolises. But there can be no change without a prior vision for designing a sustainable city, at the risk of seeing green spaces diminish and the living conditions of the Paris region's inhabitants deteriorate inexorably. The high-rise projects that were still on the drawing board in the Bercy-Charenton district are now being called into question by local residents. Housing will not exceed 50 m in height, and 37 m for offices, while green spaces will be increased. Beyond past mistakes, the quest for densification cannot overlook architectural quality, urban integration, and building continuity, in the quest for a balanced urban landscape that integrates nature and a diversity of scales.

We need to consider the possibility of vertical extension within Paris: this is the goal of the "metropolitan tower" exercise, a counterpoint to reflection on the horizontal extension of the city: the "green grid" exercise: an urban figure capable of conquering and urbanizing the limitless territories of the *"città diffusa"* of

3. Dominique Lorrain, *L'urbanisme 1.0, Enquête sur une commune du Grand Paris* (Paris: Raison d'Agir, 2018).

Greater Paris, in a city / nature balance essential to the harmony of human development.

The "metropolitan tower" was created on four sites in Paris and later on a site on the outskirts of the city, all of which are "case studies" representative of a particular situation and where the installation of towers is a possible response. The goal is not to generalize high-rise urban planning in Paris at all costs, but to identify sensitive areas where the installation of a vertical structure can untangle an urban situation, create a symbolic presence, and allow for measured densification. The first four sites present a specifically Parisian problematic: Avenue Daumesnil near Place de la Bastille, the Front de Seine, Porte Maillot and the Masséna-Bruneseau district. The last site is in Ivry, to the Southwest of Paris.

The Avenue Daumesnil site is typical of the urban layout of the historic city, in a central district with a Haussmann-style layout. The Front de Seine district is representative of the modern slab-and-tower urban planning of the 1960s, inspired by the Athens Charter. The Masséna-Bruneseau and Porte Maillot sites deal with the boundaries of Paris to the east and west, and the relationship between Paris and its suburbs along the peripheral boulevard.

The last site we worked on at Ensa de Paris-Val de Seine is typical of the inner suburbs of Paris: it is an urban wasteland in the heart of Ivry-sur-Seine, to either side of the railway tracks coming from the Gare d'Austerlitz. It includes the Parc des Cormailles in the center, and is bounded by avenue Georges Gosnat to the southeast, avenue Daniele Casanova to the southwest, rue Ledru-Rollin to the northwest, and rue Molière to the northeast.

On these five sites, the metropolitan tower project represents a fundamental challenge for intervening in the city on a territorial scale.

fig. 3. Duo Towers, Paris, Jean Nouvel.

fig. 4. Paris Courthouse, Renzo Piano.

fig. 5. Photograph of the site on avenue Daumesnil, Paris 12th.

fig. 6. Cadastral map, Bastille-Daumesnil, Paris 12th.

Bastille-Avenue Daumesnil

The Avenue Daumesnil site is the starting point for the exercise, and the initial focus of experimentation with the tower as an "urban densifier". The site extends the arcades of the 19th-century *"Petite ceinture"*, now transformed into the *"Viaduc des arts"*. The demolished railway station was replaced by the Opéra Bastille, leaving a residual space behind the building, between an awaiting gable, the viaduct, and the *Quinze-vingts* hospital. This urban void could be densified, stitching together the surrounding fabric, to articulate and qualify this derelict area, and create a landmark by terminating the horizontal line of the viaduct with a vertical line. Here, the metropolitan tower, with its program of seven superimposed cinemas, is designed to intensify social and urban life: it is a signpost in the city, like the towers of medieval towns at street corners. The public space on the ground is extended vertically, to foster internal and external relations. Near the Bastille, this small cinema tower is meant to open up existing neighborhoods, offering the possibility of lively urban life behind the Opera House. At the same time, the complexity of the structures to be implemented adds a further element of reflection and expression to the project, resonating with the context.

Front de Seine

Here, the metropolitan tower is set against the "*Front de Seine*" district, typical of Paris's urban renewal policy at the end of the 1950s, featuring high-rise residential and office developments with uniform 100 m heights, public amenities, and "slab" treatment of public spaces. This urban planning was inspired by the urban utopias of the '60s, which vertically separated pedestrian and automobile traffic. The aim of the exercise was not to call the existing neighborhood into question, but to add a few new towers to resolve the 6 m thick pedestrian slab situation with the street level. After analysis, several problematic locations were identified and studied: the siting of a new tower should improve conditions in the existing area, without adding to urban congestion. The program includes a mix of housing, activities, facilities, and offices. The infrastructure of the slab is taken into particular account in the development of the project, to improve the relationship with the old blocks, and to better articulate the tower complex.

fig. 7. Cadastral map, Front de Seine, Beaugrenelle, Paris 15th.

fig. 8. Photograph of the Front de Seine site, Beaugrenelle, Paris 15th.

Porte Maillot

At the Porte Maillot, a well-established neighborhood, the issues are quite different. Located on the main Parisian thoroughfare running from the Louvre to La Défense, the site had already been the subject of debate, particularly during the architectural competition to erect a monumental and symbolic entrance to western Paris, as proposed by Léon Rosenthal in the 1930s, and to "form a junction between the Paris of yesterday and the Paris of tomorrow". Robert Mallet-Stevens, Henri Sauvage, Auguste Perret, Le Corbusier as well as many other architects after them proposed high-rise buildings, but their projects never saw the light of day. The infrastructure project that eventually came to fruition marked the triumph of the road issue. It consisted of a traffic circle and plaza linking the Avenue de la Grande-Armée to La Défense above the buried ring road, as well as the creation a green entrance to the Bois de Boulogne. Setting up a tower at Porte Maillot means taking the measure of the 134 m-high Hotel Concorde Lafayette, built in 1974 by Guillaume Gillet, on a triangular plot of land bounded at its base by the recently extended Palais des Congrès. In this context, the idea is to propose one or more metropolitan towers, to give the square a distinct and urban quality, and to assert a strong architectural presence for this entrance to Paris. In the meantime, the city has abandoned its ambitions

fig. 9. Cadastral map, Porte Maillot, Paris 16th.

fig. 10. Photograph of the Porte Maillot site, Paris 16th.

fig. 11. Photograph of the Seine Rive Gauche site, Masséna-Bruneseau, Paris 13th.

fig. 12. Cadastral map, Seine Rive Gauche, Masséna-Bruneseau, Paris 13th.

to build the "thousand trees" project, a bridge-building over the ring road: the project is limited to re-establishing the major axis, and bringing the Bois de Boulogne into Paris, by replacing the roundabout with a new axis embellished with a central median strip and a forecourt to the north. The plant continuity is accompanied by the development of a multi-nodal hub underground, with new interconnections between the metro, tramway, motorway, and airport stations.

Masséna-Bruneseau

The fourth site selected, Masséna-Bruneseau, is located in the 13th arrondissement, a developing district bounded by the quays between the Boulevard des Maréchaux and the Boulevard périphérique, and including the Rue Bruneseau interchange, a favorite site for Michel Kagan, since it was here that he built his first building, the Cité Technique et Administrative de la Ville de Paris, in 1991, and the student residence in 1991 (see p. 288). The Avenue de France, a new boulevard built on an elevated slab over the existing rail network of the Gare d'Austerlitz, is a new urban thoroughfare that marks the boundary to the south. This vast fragment of inward-looking, virtually landlocked territory has the morphological character of a former industrial wasteland, the scale of which makes urban redevelopment difficult. It is a vast "open plan" where individual buildings take on a relative autonomy. The project is part of Yves Lion's *"urbanisme de tours"* (tower urbanism) project: the principles developed are mixed use and height to reinforce density, with an environmental approach, in order to create a central focus at the intersection of Boulevard du Général-Jean-Simon and Avenue de France, with the possibility of locating a major facility there. The infrastructures and buildings already on the site, such as the Hôtel Industriel built by D. Perrault, as well as future buildings, should, through the effects of densification, contrast, and tension, make up an innovative urban and landscape entity, creating a new "skyline" for the capital, with the towers considered not as solitary objects, but as elements of a landscape built at the scale of the territory, and with the capacity of challenging the urban project as defined.

The Seine Rive-Gauche "Bruneseau Nord" urban project was halted with the completion of architect Jean Nouvel's Tours Duo and the Covid crisis. High-rise buildings are limited to the 50 m-high apartment blocks built along boulevard Jean Simon. The development of the land to either side of the ring road and the Paris-Ivry alley that now links the 13th arrondissement and Ivry remains to be done.

Ivry-centre: around Parc des Cormailles

The site studied covers an area that includes, to the north: an SNCF relief zone with former industrial warehouses along rue Molière, and to the south: the 5.3-hectare Parc Départemental des Cormailles, the city's main green space, developed in 2003 and 2006 by the Ter agency on a former wasteland and a mound of earthworks, accessible from rue Georges

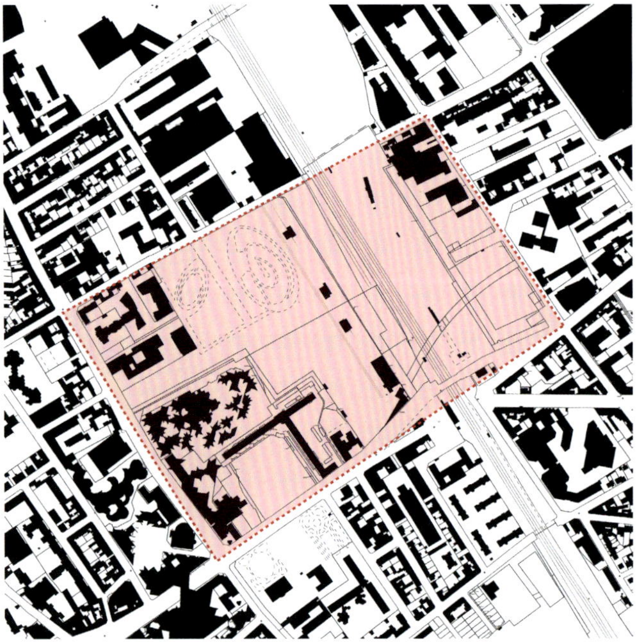

fig. 13. Cadastral map, Ivry.

fig. 14. Photograph of the Ivry site.

fig. 14. Tours EDF, Atelier Montrouge, Ivry-sur-Seine, 1967. Renovated in 2016 by Paul Chemetov.

fig. 15. The Lénine and Raspail towers, Renée Gailhoustet, 1968–1970 and "Les Étoiles" Daniele Casanova project, Jean Renaudie, 1972.

Gosnat. The park was built on a complex of underground hydrotechnical structures designed to regulate the flow of rainwater into the Seine and prevent flooding of the city center.

The park is surrounded by major real estate projects, representative of the city's post-war commitment to build innovative social housing at the time of Reconstruction, in particular the Cité Maurice Thorez, built in 1953 by architects Henri and Robert Chevalier. This was the first high-rise building in Ivry, a vertical T-shaped housing block between a bar and a tower, reaching a height of 60 m and ranging from 8 to 14 stories, and built with a reinforced concrete frame and red brick infill. The building was awarded the *"Patrimoine du XX*e *siècle"* label in 2008, and will be renovated in 2023. Atelier de Montrouge's small housing is also a remarkable reference in this context (fig. 14).

The Lénine and Raspail towers, built in 1968 and 70 by architect Renée Gailhoustet, extend the town council's commitment to urban renewal and housing experimentation, with a layout of half-duplex apartments in a highly Corbusian vocabulary, and noted by architectural critics. They are set against the backdrop of the Daniele Casanova project, nicknamed "*Les Étoiles*", built in 1972 by architect Jean Renaudie (fig. 15), which borders the Parc des Cormailles to the south, and presents itself as a hill of triangular terraces arranged in a pyramid shape, built in reinforced concrete, a veritable "manifesto" against the monotony of large housing estates. The 82 apartments are all different, with large windows and multiple orientations, and feature generous, planted outdoor spaces, like hanging gardens. The building also offers a mix of activities and shops, as well as pedestrian walkways, transitional spaces between the private and the public, generating social exchanges between residents. These unprotected buildings are currently in a serious state of disrepair, and are in need of renovation.

In this eclectic, predominantly railway-oriented environment, the heart of Ivry is the focus of the city's efforts to complete the urbanization of the industrial zones and the renovation of the city center. The architecture of Renaudie, the tall silhouette of the brick housing of the Cité Maurice Thorez and the rest of the city do not form a coherent whole around the Parc des Cormailles. Our pedagogical project is to propose urban densification around the central park, with housing programs based on horizontal and vertical development, combined with facilities and shops, to improve the relationship between the northern and southern neighborhoods on either side of the railroad line. The siting of towers in strategic locations was intended to articulate the existing development, to preserve and reconfigure the park in continuity with the existing buildings, in keeping with the original ambitions of the town of Ivry.

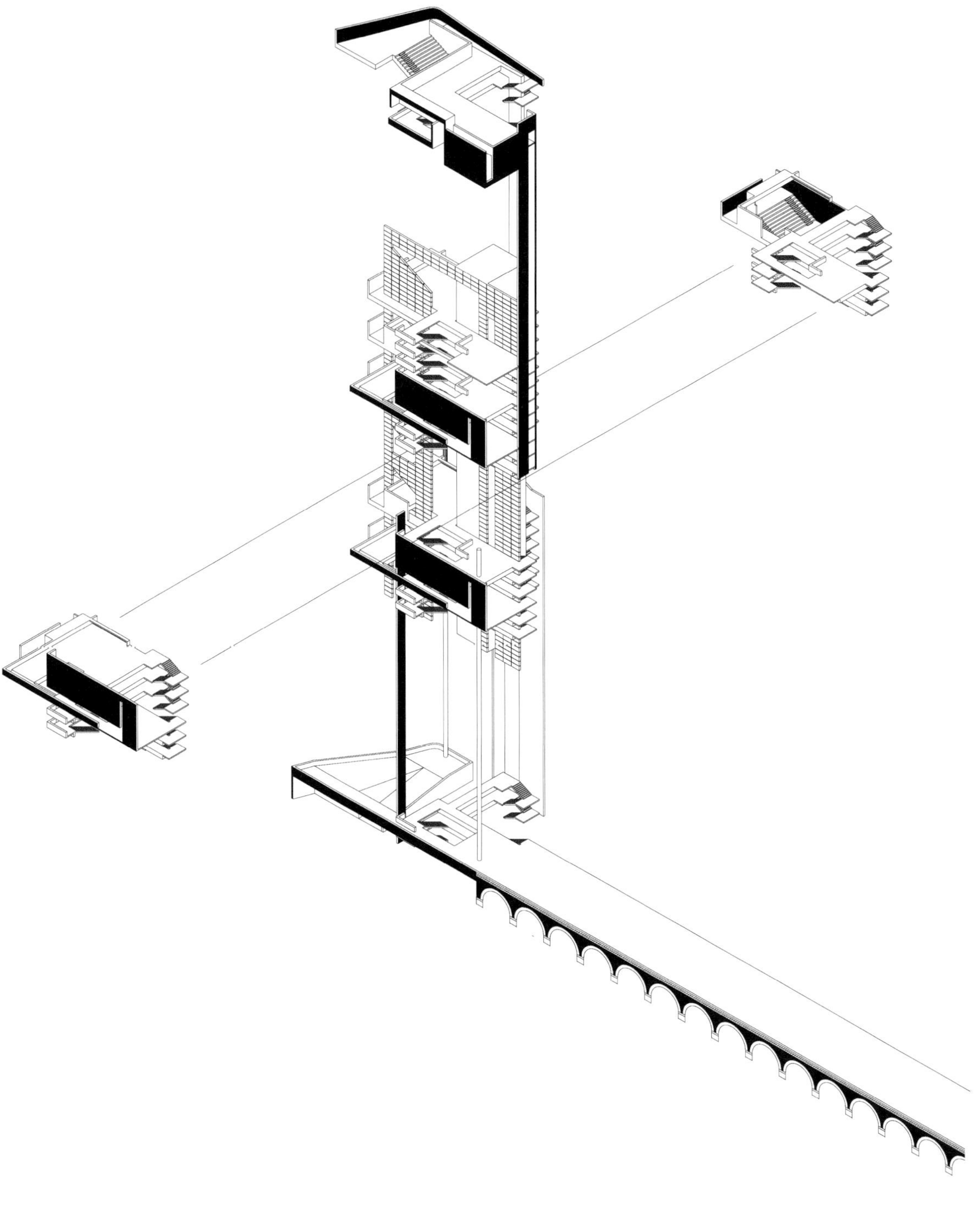

fig. 1. Exploded axonometric of tower components, G. Clément, EAPB, 1998–1999.

A Site, a Program

M. W. Kagan, Gwenaël Clément

A Site

In the Bastille district, at the crossroads of rue de Lyon and the avenue Daumesnil, this potentially exemplary space is a still-unfinished void between three facilities: the Opéra Bastille, the Hôpital des Quinze-Vingts and the Coulée verte René Dumont, an elevated walkway over the recently rehabilitated arcades of avenue Daumesnil. This ongoing vacancy is an indication of the inability of Haussmannian urban planning to respond to the specific issues of the contemporary city.

At the crossroads of contradictory interests, a tower in scale with this context would be a masterly demonstration of the ability of vertical architecture to provide an appropriate response through the basic concept of a "small skyscraper" (50 to 70 meters high).

The metropolitan tower is both a support for fiction and a powerful signalling device, transforming the city on the city. The aggregation of elements in a vertical line creates a relationship between horizontal and vertical sections. Considering the different views of near and far creates a duality of design on the territorial scale of the city, in relation to the scale of the neighborhood. Enhancing a derelict site of no major interest will enable us to renew the "urban fabric" and to redefine it by asserting an unprecedented urban potential.

A Program

The very principle that distinguishes an ordinary building from a high-rise is called into question: the stacking of repeated floors over X floors, the neutral exterior cladding: stone facade or curtain wall, the non-existent relationship to the ground… (see the office tower district built around the Gare de Lyon railway station).

The distinctive features of this project are made through the expression of a program: seven volumes of theaters or cinemas, amphitheaters or recording rooms, auditoriums or exhibition halls, superimposed and detached from the ground to compose a spatial figure made up of discrete elements, as the basis of a constructive repetition (fig. 1).

In the basement, a multi-level all-night retail outlet (like New York's Tower Records) will direct the public downwards, while a bar-restaurant on the highest level could complete the complex.

fig. 2. Perspective view of the tower in its context.

opposite

fig. 3. Superimposed of different elements.

fig. 4. Axonometric of the repetition of the matrix.

On the first floor, the open space will manage the flow to the hospital, complete the elevated promenade, and give access to a lobby for the theaters.

Each 200-seat theater will have a reduced stage area, its own foyer, bar, sanitary facilities, dressing rooms, with technical and management rooms to be located...

The spatial hypothesis is intended to allow an architectonic and constructive system to emerge from the urban geography and the reiteration of the chosen module. The metropolitan tower becomes a work of architectural, symbolic, and programmatic significance (fig. 2).

A special project in five points of method[1]

1. The unit:

100-seat cinema

The unit is the matrix, the module, the element of the program that must be repeated and stitched together.

In this project, it consists of three horizontal walls, the first two of which are connected by the slope of the cinema's tiers. Two axes intersect perpendicularly. The first, longer axis is located on the intermediate horizontal wall. On either side, it joins a staircase and the upper access level to the cinema. This is the axis of the entrance walkway. The second extends across all levels. It is bounded on either side by two further flights of stairs. The unit is structured around this crossing, allowing it to be covered by a diagonal development of the upper horizontal wall. As a result, solids and voids alternate around the intersection of the two axes (fig. 3 and 4).

2. Assembly:

The foyer

Assembly is "2 by 2". How do you link two units together? The foyer is formed by the assembly and will connect two stacked units. The project proposes a void between the two units to leave a floor free in the superimposition. This will allow us to take advantage of the large upper horizontal wall of the lower unit to set the reference level of the foyer. The space is held by the large horizontal front wall. The assembly allows two units to be neighbors.

1. Project by Gwenaël Clément, 1998-1999, drawings and model further developed for publication.

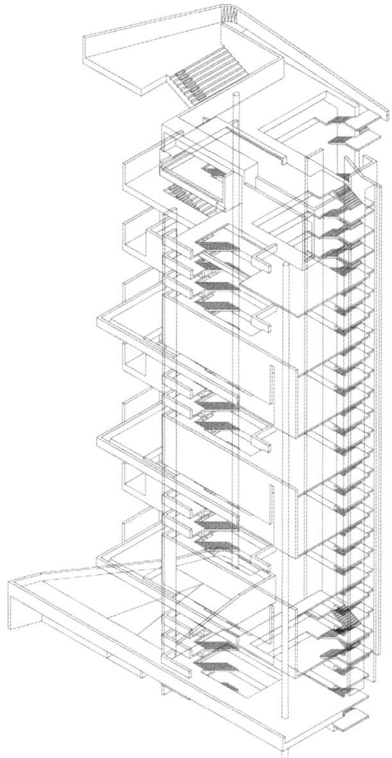

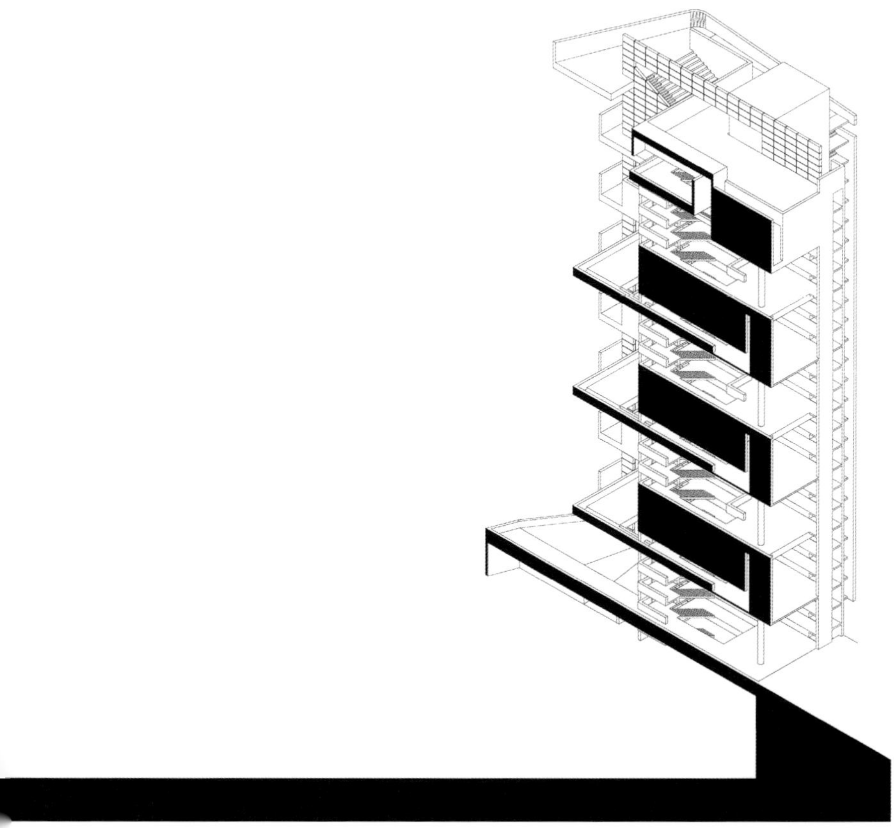

fig. 5. Elevation on the Daumesnil viaduct side.

3. The repetition:
the free interstice

Repetition means measuring and scaling by superimposing 7 units, i.e. 3 assemblies of 2 units + 1. The non-assembled unit raises the question of its positioning, above or below. The choice was made to position it on top, to reflect on the future crowning. Repetition will create a series of interstices, breathing spaces between the different assemblies. Each gap becomes a terrace, a belvedere available at varying heights (fig. 6 to 9).

4. The crowning glory:
Relationship to the sky

The crown offers a silhouette of the project from the outside, and of the city from its raised level. It's a belvedere position. At the crown, a space is designed in the form of a small open-air amphitheater, which provides a stepped view of the surrounding horizon. It's a kind of "exposed" part of the program, a sort of "écorché" offered to the sky.

5. The base:
Relationship to the ground

The base of the metropolitan tower plays a key role in the project's connection to the existing context. In addition to the pedestrian dimension, in the emblematic site of Avenue Daumesnil, the base must provide access both to the tower and to the raised planted promenade. The ascent towards the Coulée verte will begin beyond the tower's right-of-way, so that the beginning of this urban pathway covers and qualifies the entrance to our project. In this way, aspects of two territorial dimensions intersect, one existing, horizontal, beginning here, and the other, vertical, proposing a gradation of public space towards a higher horizon. The very idea of the entrance conveys a landscape dimension, between near and far, between promenade and panorama, between tactile and visual reception (fig. 5).

opposite, fig. 6. 7. 8. & 9. The four sides of the tower, study model (scale 1/200).

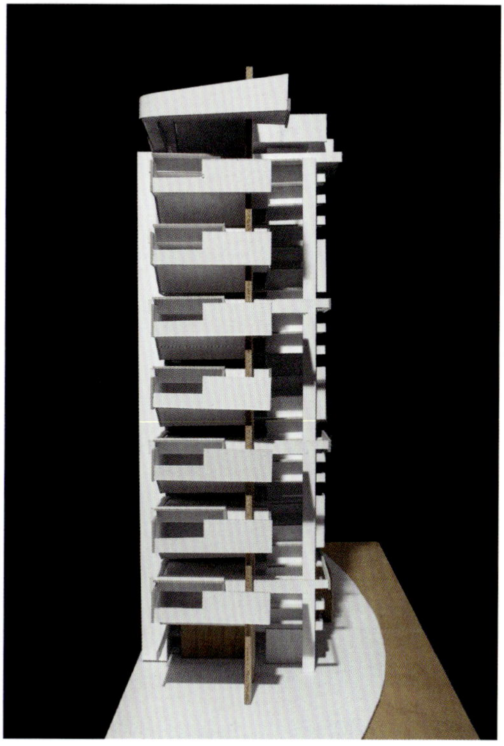

fig. 1. The project as a manipulative experiment, Michel Kagan manipulating student models, 2007–2008.

A Pedagogical Promenade

Nancy Ottaviano

For this article on the pedagogical experience of the Metropolitan Tower, fourteen testimonials from former students[1] of Michel Kagan were collected and linked according to themes shared by each discourse.

Given the length of Michel Kagan's teaching career, it would have been possible to opt for an approach based on a large number of brief, synthetic interviews conducted, for example, in the form of a questionnaire. To avoid the pitfall of an approach that paradoxically risked being reductive, it seemed more pertinent to choose interlocutors according to criteria closer to "elective affinities"[2], taking care to span the entire period[3] during which Michel Kagan had the Metropolitan Tower taught at *the École nationale supérieure de Paris-Belleville.*

Over and above the relatively brief time spent in the studio, all those interviewed had a more in-depth relationship with Michel Kagan: some went on to work in his office, while others shared the precious moments of his study trips. For all of them, this teaching was a key moment in their understanding of architectural concepts and a possible approach to the design process.

Between the threads of free discussion around his pedagogy, recurring themes emerged: his presence, the importance of discovery and manipulative experience, repetition as a tool of composition and as a chain of reiteration. How might we articulate what is still alive today in the practice and minds of this group of architects? How can we build a collective narrative on the pedagogy of teaching the practice of the project?

The posture of architect

The posture of architect that he asserted emerges from the various speeches, tinged

1. Thanks to all those who took time out of their busy schedules, including, in alphabetical order: Gwenaël Clément, Adrien Cosnefroy, Simon El Hage, Alexis Guilhaumaud, Gregory Gouard, Sophie Maurin, Marion Nielsen, Grégoire Oberdoerffer, Aleth Pauphilet, Guillaume Renaud, Guillaume Sprenger, Cédric Thomas and Mathilde Tielman. Thanks also to Nicolas Lancereau for his tribute text.

2. Title of Nathalie Régnier-Kagan's lecture, meeting on May 10, 2010 at ENSA Paris-Belleville and exhibition "Être et transmettre" in tribute to Michel Kagan.

3. From 1998, his first year of teaching at Belleville, to 2009, the year of his death.

with a form of informal transmission: *"He was a man who came freely to the studio"* [A.C.][4]. By positioning himself as an architect, he was addressing future professionals rather than students. *"He said, 'I'm an architect,* [...] *here's what you'll have to live with later on, and here's how you can incorporate these parameters into your project.'"* [G.O.] *Reasoning about a project is a necessity, because the project is a mental construction that needs to be made explicit, yet this discussion also exists in itself: "He wasn't concerned with convincing you or himself, but he was arguing a whole discourse that was more of a universal discourse, for everyone, with which to search."* [C.T.]

As a result, *"he refused to validate a project and approach it only in that way, i.e. to give answers to a student who arrives with questions. We practically left with more questions than when we arrived, but they weren't the same.* [A.G.]; *"More questions because you want to know more, not because you have more difficulties. In fact, all the questions you didn't dare ask yourself afterwards you asked yourself because you knew there was someone opposite you who could help."*[S.E.H.].

The substance of what was up for the taking seemed to emerge indirectly from the accounts gathered from the table discussions between teachers and students based on the proposals brought in from one session to the next. *"There was always criticism of one's own project. There's no such thing as a good project; there were projects. He didn't hesitate to ask other students for their opinion on one of the projects."* [C.T.]; *"He really let the students work with him* [...] *then he created a world of references, but there were never any instructions. It was the opposite of a directed pedagogy; he didn't draw for us."* [A.C.]

Filiation and difference

When the group was formed, models were passed from one to another and manipulated on the spot. Words were exchanged in a supple framework, without a strictly magisterial approach, which in the context of the École de Belleville (formerly UP8), at the end of the '90s, marked a break with the so-called "Uno-style"[5] teaching and was characterized by taking up a strong position with regard to the modern heritage. Michel Kagan's architectural writing has often been identified with the neo-modern movement by critics and architectural historians[6], and his teaching a priori affiliated with that of the Uno group. His singular position, however, seems to lie somewhere between filiation and difference, due on the one hand to his experience in New York and on the other to his various experiences in the schools of architecture in Geneva and Lille. These practices "elsewhere" seem to have given him, at least from the point of view of his students, a singular trait that conveys independence, an autonomous approach, outside the question of the magisterial teaching carried by the Uno current: *"I had friends from Rouen who were also at Belleville but at Uno. We walked together for a while, then compared notes... We realized that with Michel Kagan we had real freedom."* [S.E.H.] *"I'd just left the Uno group, which was very strict and where space was above all functional. So when I arrived at Michel Kagan's studio, there was a feeling of freedom in terms of the plastic side of architecture, of its creation... At the same time, Michel Kagan always put safeguards in place, which were those of the right measure of space, the space necessary for the place to be viable. It was the encounter between a gesture, a sketch, intentions that he didn't direct at all, and these safeguards that helped us structure the tower as the studio progressed."* [G.R.] (fig. 1)

4. Unless otherwise indicated, the quotes are from transcribed interviews, and the interlocutors are referred to by their initials in square brackets.

5. The Uno group was founded by Henri Ciriani in 1978.

6. See for example Jacques Lucan, *France Architecture 1965–1988*, (Milan, Paris: Éditions Electa Moniteur, 1989).

fig. 2. Spatial matrix, Project by Simon El Hage, 2003–2004.

Structure

"From the very first day in the studio, we knew we were going to make a tower, so all we had to do was find out how we were going to do it" [G.R.]. For the teacher, it's a matter of bringing to life the tower that exists virtually in each student, while preserving the sense of discovery that is part of the game, the pleasure of designing. Although their importance varied from one year to the next, a number of sub-exercises punctuated studio time like a flexible canvas supporting the formation of the architectural project.

Each year, students are asked to analyze a tower from the reference list provided in the exercise statement, or sometimes from a spontaneous proposal discussed and validated by the teacher. Although this is a classic approach to building up a database of references for the whole group, it turns out that in some years the results of this exercise were not presented, and when they were, these "case studies" were never compiled in the form of a booklet or made available to the students, as might be the case in other studios at the school. This constituted a "servant" exercise, just as there are "servant" spaces in Louis Kahn's thinking. Drawing on this analogy of "serving" spaces/exercises, we can focus our attention on other, more operative experiences that are more indicative of the truly singular character of the pedagogy propounded by Michel Kagan: the matrix, collage, repetition, beginning and end, the urban figure. The interest and paradox of these exercises is that they placed the students in an attitude of discovery of their own projects, the driving force behind their sense of freedom, their "*gourmandise du projet*" ("intense appetite for the project") [C.T.], even though the exercises recurred, were tried and tested, and in some cases practiced in other teaching contexts.

The matrix

The Metropolitan Tower exercise raises the question of verticality, and this notion initiates reflection through the observation of urban, architectural or artistic examples: *"We first worked on the idea of the vertical city.* [...] *He asked us to research buildings that we found emblematic, whether skyscrapers or detached houses, and which contained verticality and had a kind of radiance"* [G.O.] But also by practicing it: *"There was this work on the vertical itself. In*

fig. 3. The Villa Savoye collage as a tool for appropriating a reference and playing with the notion of scale, Guillaume Sprenger, Grégoire Oberdoerffer, 2008-2009.

other words, we had a model template, which was 5 by 5 and 15 or 20 cm high, and we questioned the relationship between the sky, the ground and the environment in a vertical element. It was very sculptural work." [G.R.] The question of verticality can also be approached in a less direct way: *"He had us make little model cubes, spatial exercises: how to make an open space, a closed space..."* [A.C.] (fig. 2). As a first step in spatial research, it's not uncommon to get students to work on abstract spaces devoid of predefined functions, in which the aim is to establish spatial concepts[7] on the basis of elementary geometric shapes: *"The cubes had no program, at the start it was all about manipulation. How do you transcribe a feeling of verticality into something that wasn't vertical at all in the first place?* [...] *It was quite strange."* [S.E.H.] Here, the Bellevillois background can lead to a certain type of geometric approach, such as *"destruction, deformation of the initial volume"* [S.E.H.], while other interpretations take place in the studio, due in particular to the large number of Erasmus students present: *"Some Italians had cubes of a very classical composition"* [S.E.H.]. Between abstraction and ideality, this exercise exists by and for itself: *"If we really played the game, we really thought about the ideal character of the project, devoid of any context or follow-up. Even if we inevitably lost our "idealism" when we inserted the program and multiplied and repeated everything..."* [A.P.].

Collages of images and models

Many of the students had to work with photomontages: *"He had us do montages with existing buildings to get an idea of the scale of a tower. I superimposed the' villa Savoye' with several orientations, several layouts and several morphologies."* [G.S.] (fig. 3). The graphic approach sometimes varied in scale, in order to perceive the overall scale and to work on a tectonic tower rather than a simple stack of floor levels. It was also a time-saving way of getting students directly involved in fine, complex architecture: they could be asked to work on their matrix from an iconic reference that would become their basic module. The question *"How did the house become a movie theater?"*[8] opens a whole new field of possibilities for designers, as they interrogate the notion of scale. A multitude of approaches are possible in these intellectual gymnastics: using architectural references such as, for example,

7. Tasked with articulating oppositions between open and closed, stable and dynamic, or to search for vertical spaces.

8. Question asked during one of the interviews.

taking a spatial sequence or obviously altering it. Talking about their tower, some said *"I took a sequence from the 'Villa Laroche'"* [G.G.] or *"the module started from a house by Tadao Ando, it was very repetitive. I used it as a starting point".* [G.C.]. As with the cube exercise, it's a question of finding verticality in spaces that don't seem vertical a priori, but this exercise also presents a possible approach for using architectural reference: *"The house was with a very projectual objective, whereas the tower analysis was done to reflect on this (architectural) type in general."* [G.C.]. The idea is to interpret spatial and functional maneuvers in relation to the program of cinemas, known from the start of the studio, and their objective of vertical repetition, a reading that goes beyond the understanding of the reference architecture as such, to find in the project an appropriation rather than a quotation.

Repetition

The initial unity eventually finds its programmatic reasons, pretext and volumetric parti: *"I told you the term performance hall because it could have been theaters [...] that stood one on top of the other. They were cinemas, but not a multiplex. There was a foyer at each of the cinemas."* [M.N.] after which "[there was the] *work on a programmatic unit and then on the vertical repetition of these units with the articulations and the serial effect that this produced, but also the consideration of the scale which, all at once, by the simple fact of repetition was modified."* [A.G.] (fig. 4). The moment of repetition is a key factor in the project's development: *"We didn't put 7 on at once, it was first one on top of the other."* [G.C.] then *"The module had to be repeated 7 times, and then that's when the module could become deformed. Two modules could become one, it was no longer a cube, it became a parallelepiped... well... it became something else. That's when the tower emerged."* [S.E.H.] Repetition is an important factor in the articulation of the part to the whole: *"we were in a complex that unfolded and developed on the basis of this primary matrix, and which tended to make us forget its initial uniqueness. [...] The whole job was to create diagonal dilations within this tower, from one hall to another [...] to create a Piranesian space where the*

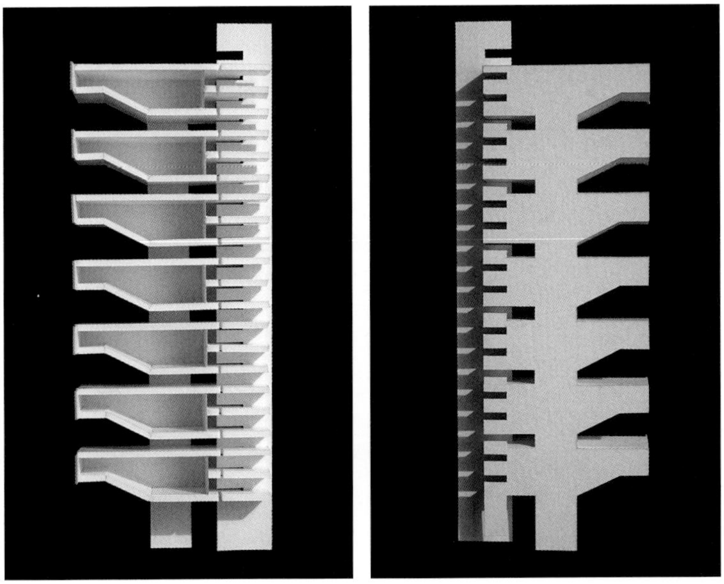

fig. 4. La répétition, study model, Gwenaël Clément, 1998-1999.

fig. 5. Other examples of repetition. Student projects, EAPB 2002-2003.

vertical develops." [G.R.]. What is the nature of repetition? Is it a stacking game, or does it contain pivots and rotations? How can we link the modules together and create a path? The possibilities seem limitless: "*Repetition was not determined. Repetition was a form of invention.*" [G.C.]. This action provided the impetus for several issues, such as "*the structure came with the question of repetition.*" [G.C.] or the architectural promenade with "*the idea that the city went up to each floor and that there was a mini-articulation specific to each room.*" [M.N.]. Moreover, "*to go from light to darkness in a tower is quite something... It's a kind of light well, a tower, you go up into the light, and the higher you go, the more you're in the sky* [...]. *A tower is a kind of inverted skylight, and when we make 7 cinemas they are 'dark rooms', so the question of how the public enters this semi-public room was fundamental, as was the transition from light to darkness*" [C. T.].

Beginning and end

How do you work with these movements and paths? The question of the series always involves its beginning and end, so what is the beginning of the tower, its relationship to the ground, and its end, its relationship to the sky? "*What do we give to the sky, and how do we anchor it to the earth?*" [M.N.]. This question seemed to emerge naturally from observing the objects made by the students: "*When we arrived at the 7 modules and the model was placed on the table, the object engaged this question of the relationship to the ground. They were questions about the very basis of the model.*" [G.C.] (fig. 5). The emblematic site of the exercise was also apt to raise questions about the urban connection, as "*there was a work of articulation between this green corridor that comes from very far away and suddenly turns into a cultural vertical*" [M.N.]. The presence of the Daumesnil viaduct ensured the transition from the urban to the architectural, asking "*how do you build a hall, how do you get people into the building? And at the top, how do you give this tower the impression that it's touching the sky, how do you get the sky into the tower?*" [M.N.] (fig. 6). As a complex project, the subdivision of the *Tour métropolitaine* enabled us to bridge the gap between the functional issues of access and circulation, with their own poetics, and the question of interaction with the landscape and the wider area, while at the same time addressing the tectonic and structural issues of the unitary arrangement of substantial volumes.

The figure

The tool that addresses the unity of the whole is the notion of the "urban figure". While putting up a tower on the Bastille site "*didn't really*

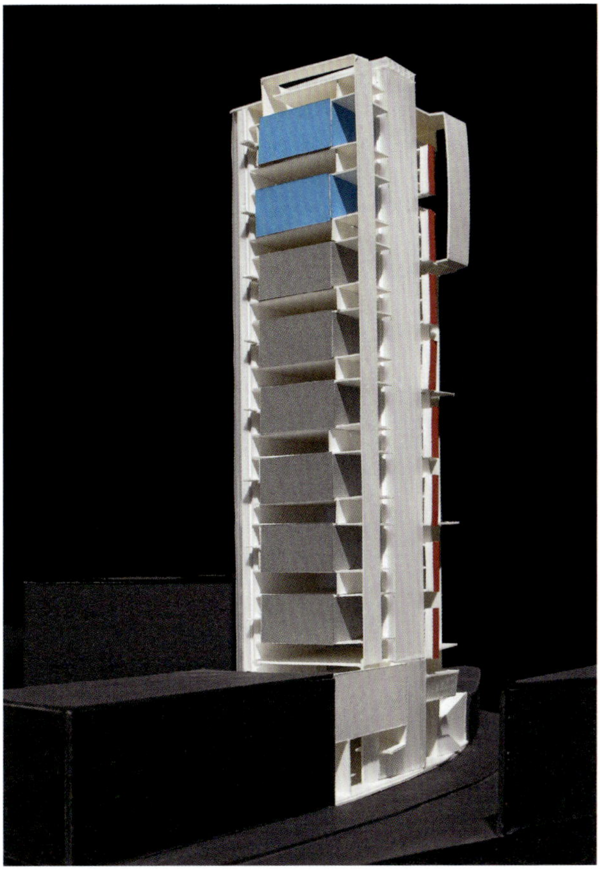

fig. 6. Inserting the project on the site by anchoring it to the Viaduct. Grégory Gouard, 1999–2000.

engage in any polemics about the urban parti" [G.R.], previous semesters spent on other sites brought out the concept of figure more distinctly. We could briefly define this notion as a set of abstract intentions addressed to the context. But this seems insufficient: *"It's mostly spatial… It wasn't formal, it wasn't the beauty of the overall figure, it didn't start from a drawing… It was in-depth, it wasn't just structural or context-dependent either, but it was important nonetheless… It was a match."* [G.S.]. Once again, making a figure involved the manipulation of models: *"He was trying to get us to sum up a set of urban intentions in a form, it was a piece of cardboard, three pieces of cardboard assembled together, and each time he asked us about such and such an angle, a specific fold done in such and such a way, and a particular direction of the line…"* [A.P.]. Abstract by nature— *"The figure is always very abstract to begin with."* [C.T.] —it calls for interpretation, a steady gaze to extract the rules of the game for the project. At the same time, the figure is generated by a free plastic gesture, and later becomes a "contract" with reality: *"At the outset, in the urban figure, the tower didn't have so many constraints, it didn't impose much on us, it gave us a placement and some dimensions in relation to the site…"* [S.M.]. Then, *"if we had used a particular color of cardboard that showed the ground on the site and was raised in the tower, this meant that we were signing a kind of moral contract in the project. Michel Kagan said, 'if you do that, it means that in the project the site will really be the ground that rises up, so you'll have a continuity of materials, etc.' It's not easy, because when you make a figure, you might think it's just a concept, a gesture… but here, the*

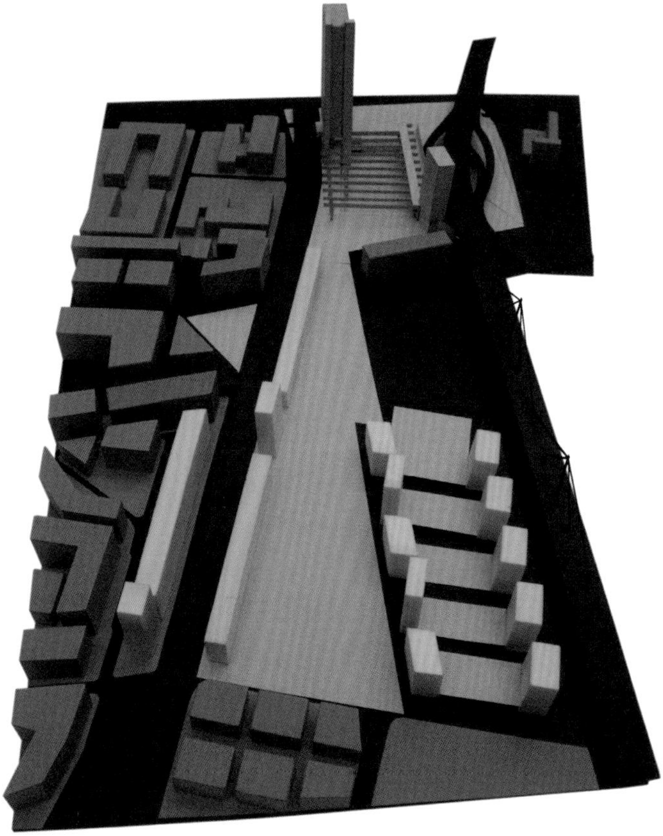

fig. 7. Studio presentation model, Guillaume Springer, Grégoire Oberdörffer, 2006-2009.

gesture was exceeded by what you did with it. It was a kind of moral contract." [G.O.] A contract that *"really had to do with a thousand things: the context, possible regulatory lines, the question of the program, the space, the light and therefore the space, the structure and therefore the space too, the orientation so that the light would bounce off the walls and therefore the structure.* [...] *An opacity became a structure and this structure had a thickness, a materiality"* [C.T.]. The metropolitan tower is therefore as much a conceptual space as it is a place of research into a relationship with the real, existing as much in its parts as in its whole. The order in which the sub-exercises are recounted above only serves the narrative. This sort of zooming-in of the module towards the overall figure does not necessarily correspond to the order in which the exercises are performed in the studio. On the one hand, their chronology has varied from one year to the next, and on the other, there is a perpetual back-and-forth (fig. 7).

Iterations

The theme of repetition is present in the superimposition of modules along a vertical axis, in a desire to compose the tower, but it *"was also present throughout the studio in the fact of redoing the models, redoing the drawings, reexamining the project..."*. [G.R.]. The architectural design process is an iterative one, involving the fine-tuning and holding together of disparate parameters: structure, program, urban placement, orientations can sometimes enter into an equation that the project aims to solve in its own way. *"If we modified this initial module, we modified our parti, so we came back to the figure, and it was a succession of back-and-forths, knowing once again that our constraint was a kind of contract we had with Michel Kagan through our figure."* [G.O.] Architecture is not an exact science. It is not based on calculation, but on an empirical process of constructing a line of reasoning, a "*cosa mentale*". In this way, manipulative experience guides design. In this posture, the model plays an essential role. *"Model, model, model... Cut, paste, place and elevate...We did relatively little drawing compared to other studios. If we didn't have a model, there was no point in coming.* [...] *The renderings were very heterogeneous; some were still at the basic concept stage, but that didn't bother him. The experimentation process was more important."* [A.P.].

A pretext for thought

Despite the presence of engineers throughout the studio, many of the former students expressed doubts as to whether such a project was rooted in reality: *"In reality, I don't think it's possible to make objects like these."* [M.N.] But all seemed to agree that this was not necessarily the most important thing. Indeed, the leitmotif of the studio run by Michel Kagan was more to do with knowing how to ask oneself the relevant questions about one's own project, to learn an internal dialectic vis-à-vis one's production. *"He didn't teach me a method, but he taught me to look for a method, to ask myself what a method could be.* [...] *Instead, you discovered a capacity to reflect, no longer to say, I'm capable of doing that, but to say, I'm capable of arguing my project, of reflecting on my project. To be stronger about my project."* [C.T.] And this is one of the fundamental challenges of architectural education: to train future architects to adopt a critical stance. *"His teaching revealed me as an architect, and continues to do so today in the practice of my profession"* [N.L.], for as he himself says: *"work on projects in a school of architecture is still the best way to learn how to learn."*[9]

9. M. W. Kagan, in Françoise Arnold and Daniel Kling, *Transmettre en architecture*, Paris, Éditions du Moniteur, 2002.

fig. 1. The John Hancock Center in Chicago, designed by SOM between 1965 and 1970, an exemplary structural affirmation of a trussed structure.

Sciences and Techniques in Architecture

Jean-Marc Weill

Preamble

In preparing this text, I kept asking myself what had induced me to take part in teaching science and technology at Michel Kagan's studio on the Metropolitan Tower. I imagine it was simply the desire to illustrate the path that leads from the idea to its implementation—through an examination of technical design, means of manufacture, tools and materials, in order to formulate the "constructive idea" as articulated and implemented by Jean Prouvé in his day. Let's not forget that, in the day-to-day practice of architecture, technical parameters are (all too) often referred to as a category of questions whose terms do not hinge on deliberate choice. And yet, we know that the activity of building appears, on the contrary, in an open field of varied possibilities. Allow me the liberty of saying that solutions must be chosen without any claim that some technical reason provides a sufficient condition (even if it is necessary). The technical solution does not impose itself. It is constructed in the same way as a hypothesis, and its solution appears as its verification. The *Tour métropolitaine* exercise allows for this "freedom of expression" of technical thought—as a structuring element of the project but also a source of the project itself.

Because this technological environment is undergoing profound change in the precise relationship it establishes with its surroundings, Michel Kagan proposed to inscribe the teaching of techniques in a search for meaning, to rethink the place of sciences and techniques in project practice and, by extension, the models used to teach it. In the text that follows, I have assembled notes I wrote down for myself after the sessions and which I have used in recent years as a personal memoir of the exchanges with students that I was trying to problematize.

Structure and materials

As Gordon points out in the preface to his book *Structures and Materials*[1], adequate mechanical properties, such as strength and toughness, rigidity or flexibility, are clearly essential to the existence and survival of all

1. J. E. Gordon, *Structure et matériaux. L'explication mécanique des formes* (Paris: Pour La Science, 1994).

fig. 2. View of the twin towers of World Trade Center in context.

forms of life. This is true for plants, animals, and human beings, and almost all human technological achievements from the Stone Age to the Space Age. Mechanical properties are essential, not secondary, characteristics of biological tissues. Life places special emphasis on robustness and mechanical integrity from tissues, while also demanding lightness and metabolic efficiency. Most plants and animals are highly efficient structures. A large proportion of human structures must also permanently withstand a wide range of mechanical stresses and deserve the name of structure as well.

In materials science, and the study of structures in particular, *"technological innovations and mathematical advances have played their part, but the real difficulties and advances have been of a conceptual nature"*[2]. Humans and animals alike were confronted with certain problems of solid mechanics, even before the advent of structural design. It seems to me that this world of strict technical conquest has now come to an end, particularly in architecture. The work of the construction engineers to whom the Centre Georges Pompidou devoted an exhibition entitled "*The Art of the Engineer*"[3] in 1997 is an important part of the history of 20th-century architecture and includes Eugène Freyssinet, Buckminster Fuller, Torroja, Candela, Berger, Le Ricolais, Lindsay, Rice, and Duchateau. In this exhibition, the engineer's aesthetic was shown for what it is: *"first and foremost an aesthetic of the object in the making, rather than of the object as already made"*[4].

The materiality of architecture

Inventions (innovations) are now not so much about large structures than about local issues, often relating to flow, comfort (at the outer wall), and air control. On the other hand, it is difficult to recognize a strictly technical level of problems in building today. On the contrary, the activity of building appears in an open field of varied possibilities. The technical solution shifts the question, but never solves it. Technical objects are part of an intricate, interconnected context, of which the city is the most obvious manifestation: the interweaving of housing, industry, offices, infrastructure, equipment, and communication networks.

Strictly speaking, technique only exists under the conditions of "all other things being equal". This situation would only be achieved in constructive practice when the distinction between the practice and its model had been erased. Technique for architecture appears as

2. J. E. Gordon, ibid.

3. "L'Art de l'ingénieur. Constructeur, entrepreneur, inventeur" exhibition, Centre Georges Pompidou, June 25-September 29, 1997.

4. Alain Guiheux, *Collection d'architecture du Centre Georges Pompidou* (Paris: Éditions du Centre Georges Pompidou, 1998).

a problem by the very fact that reference to the model, to the norm, is insufficient to achieve the set goal. A technical solution cannot be formulated without reference to a given situation. This knowledge must not be misleading. It is provisional, situational, and strategic[5]. No constructive solution can be given as totally exhaustive. Terms are independent of constraints, materials, and project forms, but also of tools, people, and their institutions.

It should also be noted that the concepts behind technical solutions have become more complex, less articulated, and less clear-cut. The rigor of the Iron Age has become more supple and complex, and gluing is gradually replacing the joint, a nostalgic image of articulation. It's easier to glue than to assemble. Technical thinking adopts fluctuating methods of analysis, manipulated and distorted on purpose. This trend is also encouraged by computer tools that transform calculation into simulation.

By becoming user-friendly, calculation becomes as much a virtual experience as a step-by-step intellectual process. The algorithm behind the program has become more opaque. You have to work your way through the profusion of possible models. This is a new experience: the method of designing a framework lies as much in the way the question is posed as in the method chosen to answer it.

Technical logic no longer produces meaning

The unprecedented trend towards global urbanization we are currently witnessing presents those involved in urban design with new theoretical, technical, and artistic challenges. In a context of very high population density, pressure on land, and ever-increasing pollution, environmental ethics are more than a political commitment or the strict application of good building rules. Like the industrial revolution at the end of the 19th century, they provide an opportunity for the world of architecture to rethink the place of science and technology in the practice of design, and by extension, the models used to teach it.

At construction conferences for architects and engineers, it's always possible to express enthusiasm for materials and, more generally, for structural systems, and to demonstrate that there are structurally convincing solutions for almost every construction project, according to the rules of "logical engineering". And yet, whether in lectures or in project follow-up, there is always the question of the meaning of the choice of a technical device, a question that is not sufficiently addressed as a prerequisite for the development of a technical solution in the architectural project.

Which building materials and techniques are not only technically and logically us able, but also offer the most meaning in the particular context under study? This type of question about meaning is a priori unquantifiable, insofar as the logical aspects to be considered have greatly proliferated and strongly differentiated over the past century. 100 years ago, the choice of materials and construction methods was essentially dictated by the availability of materials, manpower, and know-how. the logic of availability dictated logistics. As a result, different solutions emerged almost naturally on a regional and even local scale and became dominant in their sector. Although project managers still had to decide on the meaning of structure, the choice of materials and techniques was dictated by technical logic and logistics.

In the space of 100 years, the number and availability of artificially produced materials have steadily increased, thanks to the spread of industrial processes and improved transport systems. This was all based on the unlimited availability of highly efficient fossil fuels (oil). The logic of industrial commodity production—centralization, rationalization through mass production, monopoly formation, market domination—has led to the regional domination of

5. Jean-Pierre Séris, *La Technique* (Paris, Presses Universitaires de France, 1994.)

a small number of building materials and techniques. In Europe, the dominant materials are cement-based, reinforced concrete blocks and floors, and industrially produced porous bricks, while North America has seen strong development of wood and wood-derived industrial products.

Industrial logic imposes the dominance of a small number of building materials, just as logistics and technical logic did in the past.

Our modern, post-industrial consumer societies have only recently begun to discover that the logic of the past can lead to painful, even perilous nonsense in the future. Fossil fuel reserves are on the wane, and the carbon cycle, disrupted by the combustion cycle of fossil fuels, is changing the climate, while countless secondary effects are beginning to cost us dearly. Finally, the logic of industrialization, with its principle of the cheapest product and a market without frontiers, is generating unnecessary consumption, unnecessary transport, and a dynamic of financial interests that are spiraling out of control. The production of ethically guided meaning is therefore the starting point for the development of a technical solution in an architectural project today.

Responsible education

While it was possible to select building materials solely on the basis of technical feasibility, market presence and price in the past, in the future, society will need to introduce new criteria to limit further damage. The objectives are already defined: systems for covering needs that consider the notion of cycle, that preserve the fundamental elements of human life, and that serve to restore balance. In addition to the old selection criteria (technology, market, price), new ones will have to be adopted derived on the one hand from the study of environmentally relevant mechanisms—primarily the consumption of fossil fuels and greenhouse gas emissions—and from other social considerations, particularly their regional distribution. To make such "ecological" and "socio-logical"[6] criteria applicable, we need to try to quantify fairly the advantages and disadvantages. Methodological difficulties are heightened when it comes to comparing materials produced by industrial processes with materials produced in nature by biological growth processes.

It is therefore essential to organize the teaching of science and technology in a School of Architecture in such a way as to be "responsible", and to train project managers who are committed to this decisive process of evolution in the field of construction.

It's no longer a matter of training spectators of the development of technical solutions in architecture, but rather committed authors who are also prescribers.

6. These arguments are developed by Professor Wolfgang Winter, from Technische Universität Wien, who is an expert in timber frame design and construction.

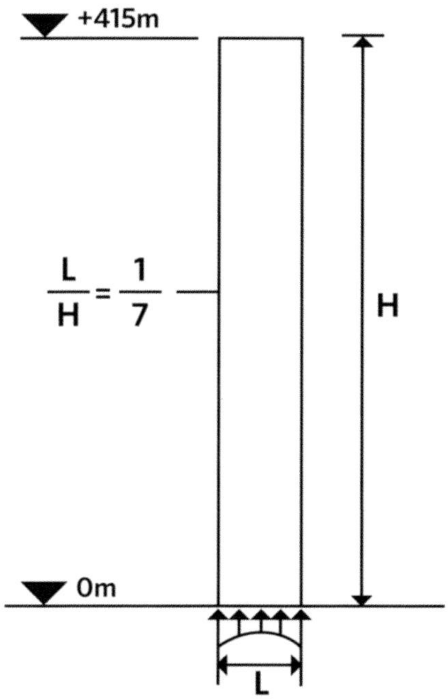

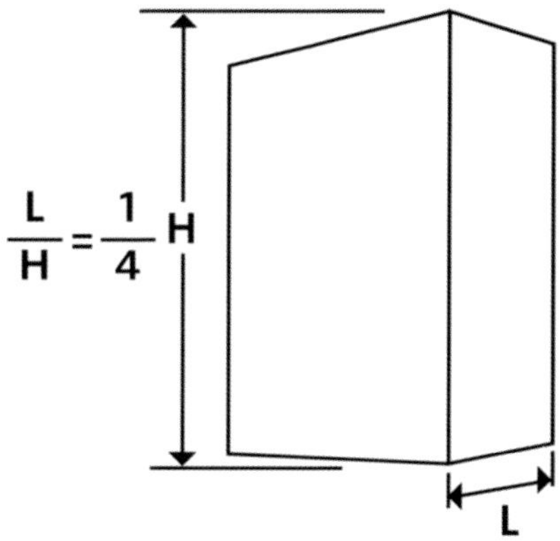

fig. 3. Proportions of the World Trade Center as a reference for the slenderness of a tower.

fig. 4. The usual proportions of a building as a basis for questioning the profile of a tower: through its proportions rather than height as such.

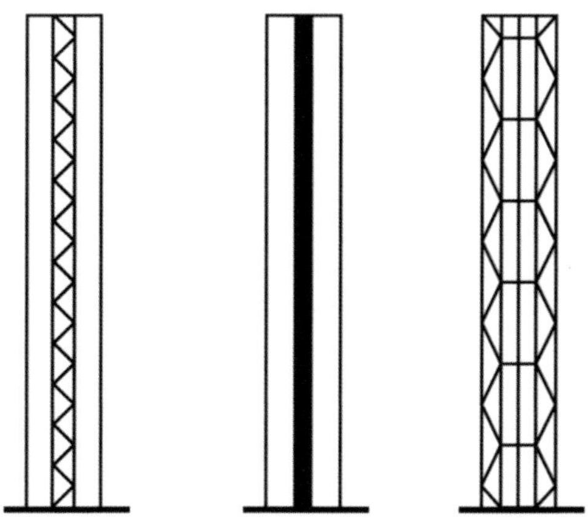

fig. 5. Diagrams of families of braced structural cores.

5a. Lattice central core
5b. Reinforced concrete central core (e.g. Tour Montparnasse)
5c. Tubes with braced walls (e.g. Constructions USA, 1960s)

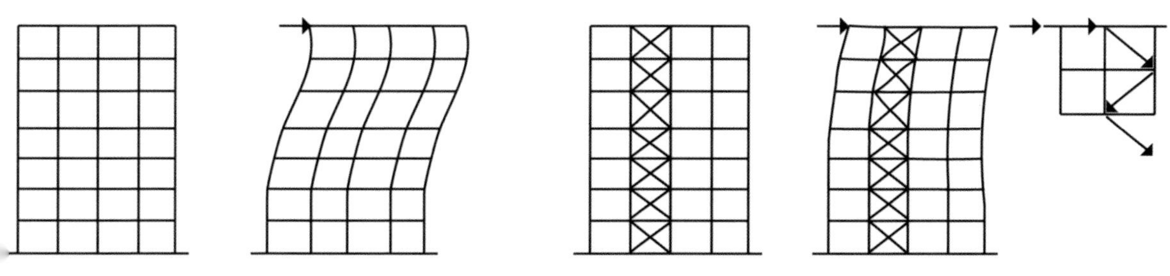

These diagrams are taken from a photocopied handout prepared by J.-M. Weill, accompanying the exercise (EAPB, 2001). Daniel Schodek & Martin Bechthold, *Structures* (Pearson: 2013).

fig. 6. Different behaviors of free-standing and braced frames. braced: frames transform hori-zontal thrust into vertical thrust on the columns concerned.

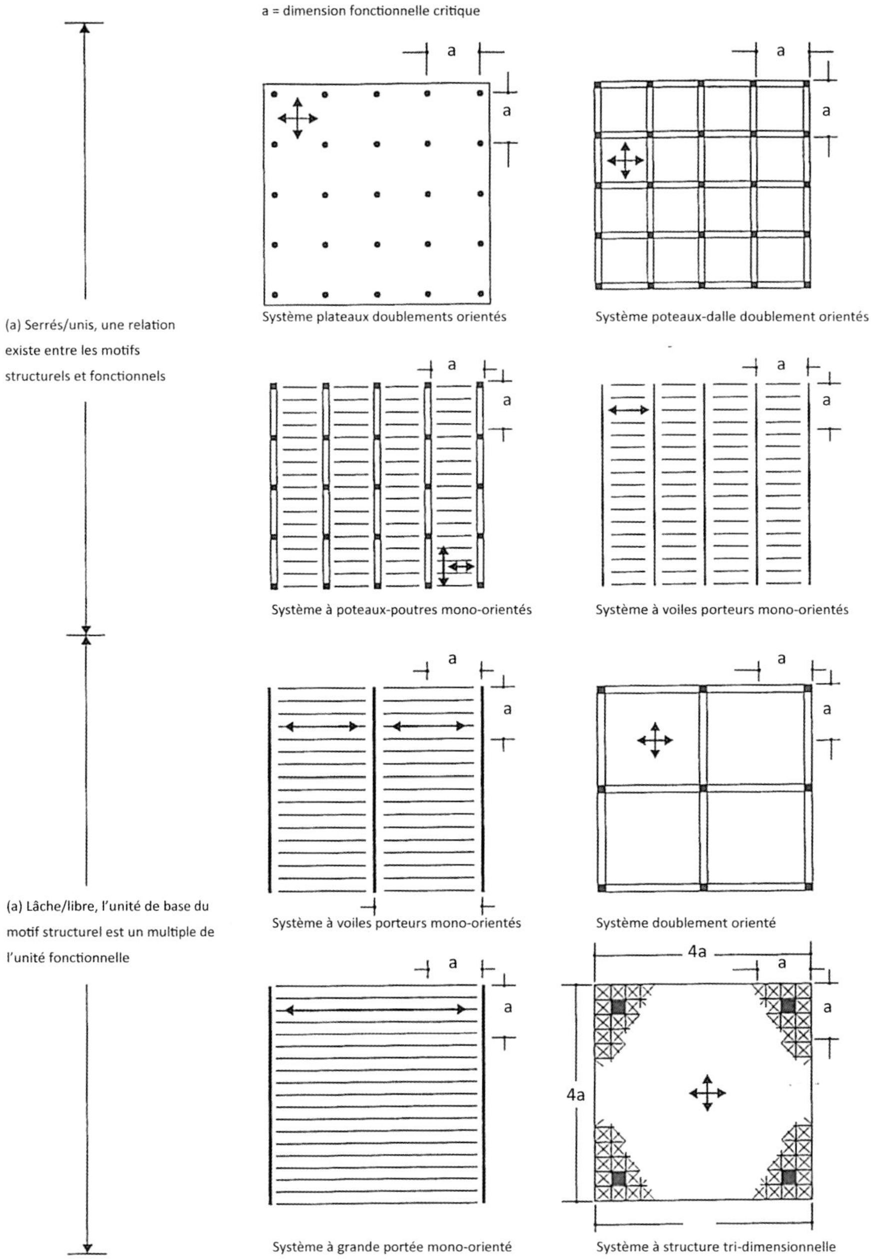

fig. 7. Possible relationships between functional and structural units:
a = critical functional dimension.

a / b / c / d set: (a) Tight / unified relationship exists between structural and functional patterns.

Assembly of set of e / f / g / h: (a) Loose / free: the basic unit of the structural pattern is a multiple of the functional unit.

7a. Two-way slab
7b. two-way post and slab system
7c. One-way post-and-beam system
7d. One-way load-bearing wall system

7e. One-way load-bearing wall system
7f. Two-way system
7g. One-way long-span system
7h. Three-dimensional structural system

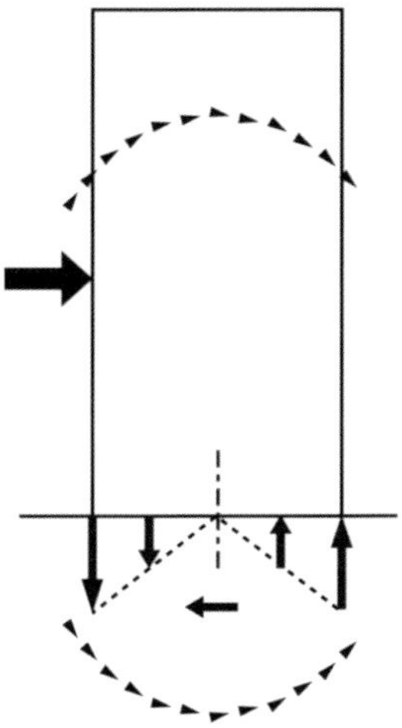

fig. 8. Wind effects, reasons for bracing a high-rise building.

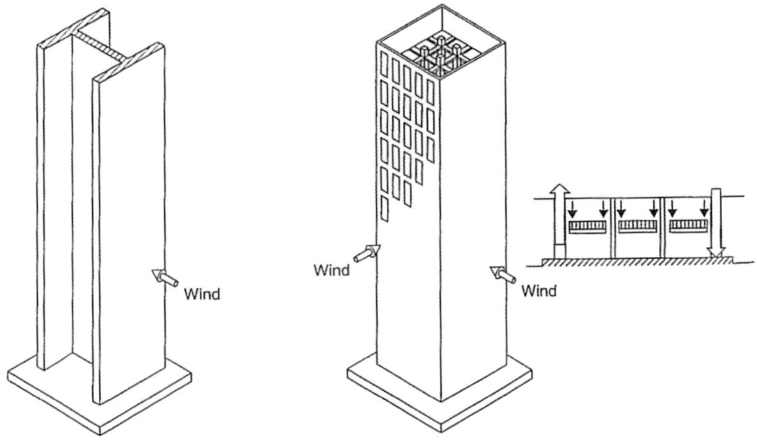

fig. 9. Tower and console beams, an analogy. The exterior supports take up lateral thrusts due to wind (in addition to the building's own weight, the effect of gravity), while the in-terior supports only take up loads due to gravity.

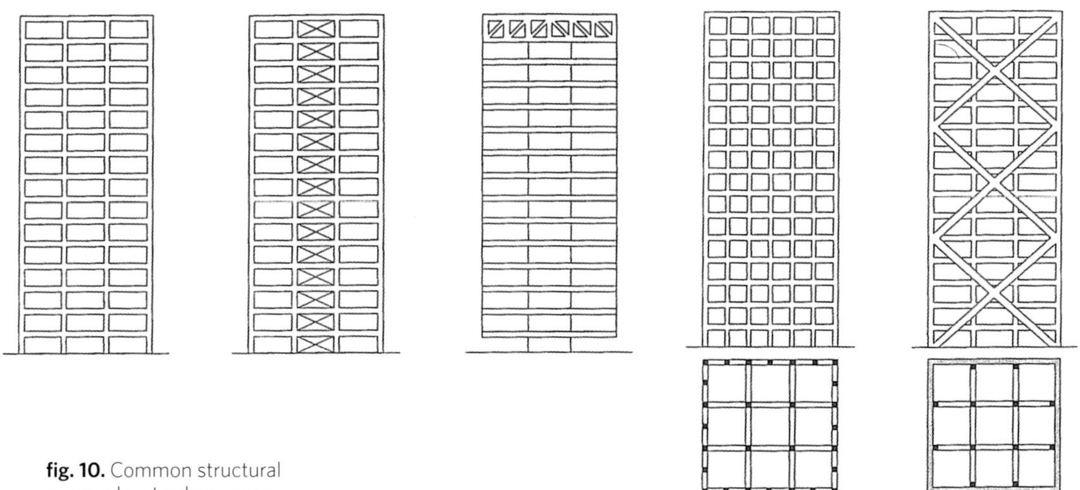

fig. 10. Common structural approaches to skyscraper construction.

10a. Frame, valid for low-rise perimeter, post-and-beam integration represents sufficient inertia
10b. Braced frame
10c. Structure suspended from a reinforced concrete core
10d. Tubular structure
10e. Lattice structure

fig. 1. The New York skyline in 2022.

From Intuition to Theory

Miguel Macian

I have stretched ropes from bell-tower to bell-tower;
garlands from window to window;
chains of gold from star to star,
and I dance.

Arthur Rimbaud[1]

To introduce himself to his students, Michel Kagan used to say that he was first and foremost an architect, which, he added, did not prevent him from also being a teacher. His proven talent as a teacher stemmed in part from the architect's constant questioning of the development of architecture, *cosa mentale* par excellence. For him, architecture, understood as the intellectual elaboration of architectural and physical space, of space arranged and constructed, differs from lazy architecture, which limits itself to its mere external display value and concerned with image—based a weak argument limited to appearance.

It's not enough for architects to come up with a few timely answers; they need to think deeply about every aspect of their work. Projects are the perfect opportunity to try to restring the bow of architectural theory. Architecture is not limited simply to its capacity for rapid seduction; it consists in formulating coherent spaces as precisely as possible. It was this critical questioning that Michel Kagan wished to share with his students, while also openly displaying his profession, which in his mind cannot be conceived without a reflexive return to the critical and theoretical horizon.

The pedagogical laboratory

Michel Kagan was attached to forms and figures of transformation of things and more or less constituted architectural types, for their capacity for regeneration, in particular. For him, the type was an operative concept defined by its structure and motifs, capable of being "exported" in a way, of moving and being responsive to local situations. His project for the Tête-Défense competition in 1984, for example, was a metropolitan tower projected into a context that was the opposite of what he would later develop. It's not surprising to see a tower appear on the slab of La Défense, but it's more interesting to see how it arose from a horizontal system of buildings and public spaces organizing the surrounding slab, a veritable springboard justifying the great height. This experience played a key role in the gestation of this very particular type of building, situated between civil engineering and public space, between architecture and urban planning.

1. *Illuminations*, translation by John Ashbery (New York, W. W. Norton & Company, 2011).

fig. 2. The skyline of San Gimignano, Tuscany, Italy.

The exercises he called "metropolitan tower" and "green grid" testify to the extent to which the architect's critical thinking has contributed to the pedagogy of architectural design. It was in the context of this global reflection that Michel Kagan proposed the subject of the tower to his graduate students, despite the objections it might have aroused as an object derived from theories that had been controversial in Europe, and more particularly in France, at the dawn of the 1970s.

Far from being prejudiced on the subject, he advanced the idea that unprecedented research in this field could not only rehabilitate the tower—a secondary goal in itself — but also foster contemporary reflection on the development of the European city. Michel Kagan was so attached to debating theories that he wished to re-establish the intellectual platform provided by the *Congrès Internationaux d'Architecture Moderne* until the 1960s, as Nathalie Régnier-Kagan recalls[2]. There is no doubt that he could have contributed to the emergence of new forms of the CIAM and revived international theoretical exchanges.

Far from being a figure of speech, Michel Kagan's initial statement to his students corresponded profoundly to his reality as an architect. Not only did he build his projects, but he also developed his positions, his critical reflections and his pedagogical sequences in the same movement, each benefiting from the growth of the others.

A theoretical project?

At the root of the renewed interest in the tower project are several principles that were put forward to the students as guidelines for their own approach to the project. The "metropolitan tower" is not simply a high-rise building: this is not an end in itself. It doesn't simply stack undifferentiated spaces vertically on top of each other, to gain in height: it superimposes buildings and public spaces that are articulated and made legible by the type that constitutes them. From the outset, it has two "instructions for use": rules for internal organization and a mode of action towards the outside world.

As a project of interior organization, the metropolitan tower proposes the extension of an existing public space, to be developed vertically by the addition of the tower. The

2. Colloquium held on May 10th, 2010 at ENSA de Paris-Belleville and *"Être et transmettre"* exhibition in tribute to Michel Kagan.

fig. 3. Hong Kong skyline, China.

public space is linked to a freely accessible vertical extension. The tower offers a series of facilities and their public extensions. As an initial indication, the first version of the tower located near the Bastille opera house, at the end of the *Viaduc des Arts*, featured a complex of superimposed movie theaters. Here, the relationship between the ground and the sky gives rise to variations in the serial arrangement of spaces. Above all, the exercise addresses the question of repetition and its legibility.

The tower is a vertical focus of public use, extending the scope of public spaces around it. Whether part of a significant arrangement of towers or a simple pole modifying its site, it joins the scene of public spaces set high above the membrane of urban fabrics. It takes on the dimension of the horizon and raises the question of the construction of the distant landscape in the European city. How can the siting and addition of a few vertical constructions, depending on morphological or topographical situations, establish this new-scale public space and modify the city's landscape in its distant vision? How can we renew the traditional image of the city and its monumental emergences cutting into the sky above the fortifications? It's a question of reclaiming an idea of interiority, through limits and thresholds constituted in the expanse and apparent indeterminacy of the global metropolis.

We're reminded of medieval towns, and in particular the patrician towers of San Gimignano in Tuscany, which we know made a deep impression on Michel Kagan. The space delimited by the towers, forming a rough crown, constitutes a kind of interiority, superimposed with its own contours on the fortifications and topography (fig. 2).

A tower in context

These initial ideas are complemented by other propositions. The tower is not an isolated, "autistic" object, taking over a landscape and subjecting it to its physical and plastic presence. Nor is it a kind of transgression that should be confined to La Défense or Beaugrenelle—to take Parisian examples—in order to limit its perverse effects.

It must not be monumental. Instead, the superimposition of repeated public spaces results in the layering of scales and practices. The tower raises the question of its own constitution as a type, and the articulated repetition of rooms, lobbies and terraces expresses, in contrast to elevators, shafts and supports, the rhythm

fig. 4. Central Park, New York: in and out of the city.

and internal organization of this particular program.

The tower grows out of the historic horizontal city that provides its various contexts. It is not an opportunistic response to the quest for density, nor a colonizing model capable of absorbing any context with its "bigness". It is the opposite of a generic urban model, such as can be seen on a huge scale in emerging Asian countries (fig. 3).

The aim is to restore possible contexts to the tower considered as a type. Examples of their various modern implementations in a city like Paris are inconclusive, apart from a few well-known examples. It's in the attention to its context that the tower becomes metropolitan, secreted, and implanted in the European city. The metropolitan tower is a contextualized tower—an apparently simple idea, but one that is not self-evident, if we consider the best-known Parisian examples mentioned above. Its vocation is to intervene in existing situations, obviously to transform them, but also to give abandoned spaces, negligible and neglected quantities, a presence and an existence in time and space on the distant horizon.

It goes without saying that the metropolitan tower recycles or updates some of the great utopian dreams of the modern metropolis, vertically accumulating multiple levels of exchange and circulation. In largely the same way, and perhaps even more importantly, it represents an instrument for reclaiming the future—the future of the city and of architecture as it was imagined a century ago, and as it is still imagined in certain parts of the world.

Interior low / Exterior high

As one climbs up the public levels of the metropolitan tower and moves away from the ground of the historic city, the visual field opens up to the horizon, revealing a second, properly visual scale of public space: that of the large expanse. It is, of course, New York, the cubist city par excellence, that fueled

Michel Kagan's vision of the American dream. Curiously, this vision is superimposed on the image of the medieval town of San Gimignano, a European reference point. The cubist city would no longer be governed exclusively by plan and building envelope, but also by three-dimensional volumetric rules.

The terraces of the penthouses and crowns of the neo-Gothic towers over the treetops of Central Park reveal an unexpected perspective: an interiority on a metropolitan scale (fig. 4). The vertical lobbies of the grand hotels that lead to the panoramic bars and restaurants, reinforce this modern optical dream: to be both in the city and able to extract oneself from it—the better to admire it from another point of view: both inside and outside! Within the territory, but outside its physical confines. You get this feeling at the top of the Eiffel Tower as you gaze, fascinated, at the carpet of Haussmannian blocks.

Michel Kagan maintained that two cities are emerging in Europe and superimposing each other: the horizontal city and the vertical city. The first is the city of horizontal extension, as we know it in Europe: a city sedimented by multiple historical imprints and successive settlements; the second is the city of vertical extension, the conquest of height and density. The landscape is organized between the near and the far. This is how it appears to us the first time we see it. Our two cities have different horizons. Once again, some of Tuscany's landscapes remind us of these obvious facts: the undulations of wheat fields stretch into the distance, outlined by alignments of yew trees along a farm road. A mound here or there is crowned by an oak or olive tree and punctuates the picture all the way to the woods descending from the highest peaks. The slopes are steeper than they appear, and tractors struggle to plough the steep hillsides. Towns and villages dot the ridges. Pienza can see Radicofani just over the horizon, the Rocca d'Orcia to the west, Montepulciano and, above all, the magnificent village of Monticchielo in the municipality of Pienza.

Towns are silhouetted against the sky, visible from afar, observing each other, coexisting on the territory, and allowing us to apprehend the reality of the map. They mark out landscape intervals and create the territory we live in, the territory we travel through. Heights give a distant view, which in this case is part of everyday life.

In contrast, the Abbey of San Antimo lies at the bottom of a valley dominated by the village of Castelnuovo: you discover it as you arrive and descend. The near landscape is an interior, and the distant one does not exist. The horizon's playfulness is limitless, and we dream of discovering new urban horizons, new perspectives on familiar cities.

When you go up... you discover another city that, in a nutshell, is what the metropolitan tower is all about.

An architectural object that fabricates the landscape

Michel Kagan's thinking draws on contributions from architects and critics with whom he shares certain affinities. To Sergio Crotti's question "What environments, what measures, what legibilities, what centralities for the contemporary city?", he responds by developing the notion of the threshold in architecture, cities, and landscapes.

"*The threshold is at odds with the amorphous diffusion of the contemporary city. The threshold divides and decides what is included and what is excluded. In the banal landscapes of today, there is a need to create artificial thresholds, themselves created by new centers and by the new places of interest found in the diffuse metropolis* [...]. *Although it is a hierarchical value in a landscape, the threshold enhances the sense of space and legibility between organized and chaotic places. It is space of transition. The threshold is not the point where something ends, but the beginning of its true essence. Mountains, rivers, valleys... like major infrastructures, pre-existing elements—bridges, gates... divide urbanized or natural regions and connect nature to the fragmented urban through thresholds, while at the same time bringing them together and identifying them. The disorientation of the dispersed city forces us to think that the threshold does not divide two worlds endowed with meaning but brings together different scales of urbanized landscape"*[3].

It's hard not to see in these lines the urban challenge posed by the metropolitan tower, a sort of missing link between architecture on the one hand and the cityscape on the other: a form that can shape thresholds and meanings in the urban landscape, or even organize cleavages and arrangements on an urban scale with "minimal" interventions *in situ*. In his texts, Michel Kagan refers to Kenneth Frampton's notion of the "megaform": *"to refer to the potential offered by certain horizontal urban fabrics capable of assuming topographical transformations within the existing metropolitan landscape* [...] *Landscape as infrastructure becomes urban landscape"*[4].

The purpose of the metropolitan tower as invented by Michel Kagan is to propose an urbanism of architecture, as he himself announces in a chapter in which he quotes Paul Ricœur in what appears to be a key to the metropolitan tower: *"how to become modern while preserving one's roots in the same move"*[5].

Texture city / Pole city

Michel Kagan continues: *"The conceptual characteristic of these towers is the desire to seek a subtle 'strong form', to multiply scales, volumes, materials, fragments and continuities. The result is an urban, cubist architectural purity composed of strict dimensional relationships. A real urban presence emerges from the street corners, which produce an ascending volumetric vision, clearly linking the horizontal lower city to the vertical upper city"*[6].

In this ongoing reflection, the dialogue between these two ideas of the city produces parallel correspondences. The low-rise city is the primary, even generic, texture of the European city, made up of more or less open private blocks within the network of streets and public spaces. The metropolitan tower and its vertical public extension, on the other hand, constitute and provoke urban poles anchored on a territorial scale. It is a node linking the fabrics of the lower city. A paradox that is only apparent.

Theoretical intuitions feed into pedagogical work: Michel Kagan proposed, as a complement to "The metropolitan tower", the exercise entitled "Green grid: from open block to urban room". The aim was to respond specifically to the establishment of common city blocks and their assembly. The green grid deals with the constituent texture of the modern mixed-use city. Each islet must integrate the plans for two local facilities. The open block is a kind of "perimeter block" based on the principles of the *Casa Bloc* that Sert, Subirana and Torres Clavé built between 1933 and 1935 on avenue Torras i Bages in Barcelona (fig. 5).

Casa Bloc uses alternating indentations to open up a 170-meter-long block and divide it into at least two open courtyards (fig. 6 to 8). The emphatically social program of this workers' housing complex incorporates what we now call community facilities. The Casa Bloc project brief, dating from 1933,

3. Michel Kagan, "La ville qui s'invente" in *La ville qui s'invente, Actes du séminaire de Rennes, Saint-Jacques-de-la-Lande et Nantes, Corps des architectes-conseils de l'État* (Paris: Thotm éditions, 2008).

4. Michel Kagan, op. cit., 10.

5. Michel Kagan, op. cit., 12. Quote from Paul Ricœur, *Histoire et Vérité* (Paris: Seuil, 1955).

6. Michel Kagan, "La torre metropolitana", *Il Giornale dell'Architettura*, March 2008. See p. 67.

fig. 5. Casa Bloc, period view, Barcelona.

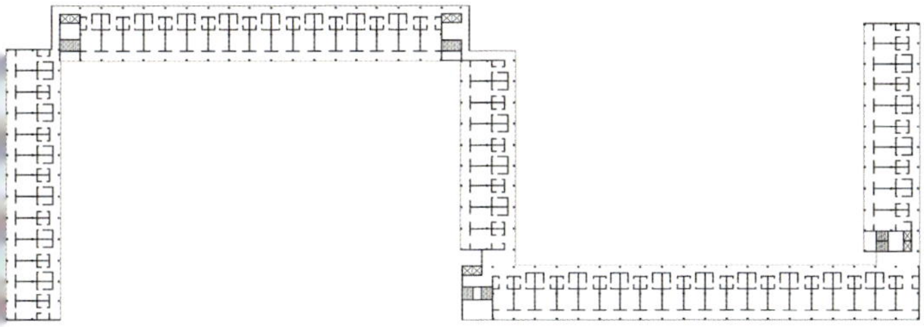

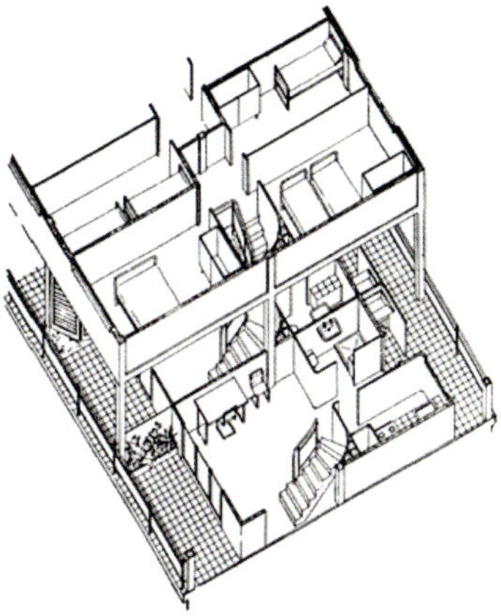

fig. 6. Casa Bloc, photograph of one of the two courtyards today, Barcelona.

fig. 7. Casa Bloc, overall view, Barcelona.

fig. 8. Axonometric view of Casa Bloc housing.

fig. 9. Perspective view of Plan Macià—The New Barcelona, 1931–1939, GATCPAC, Casa Bloc is a full-scale experiment of what might have been.

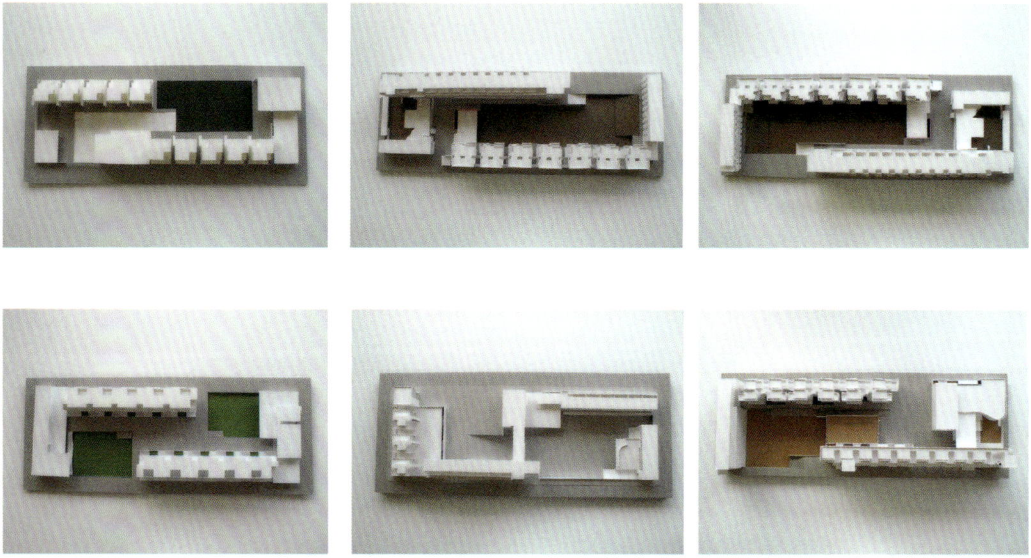

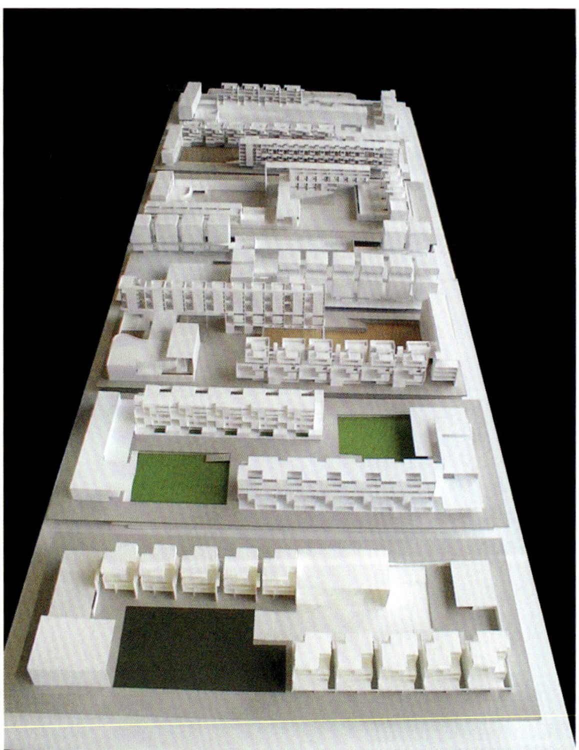

fig. 10 & 11. Student models of the Green Grid exercise, the development of a block based on GATEPAC principles. EAPB, 2002–2003.

states: "*The planned workers' housing complex will be equipped with all the ancillary services that a clearly social orientation requires, such as: bathing establishments, consumer cooperatives, popular libraries, day-care centers, workers' clubs, open spaces for sports, swimming pools, kindergartens with sandboxes and paddling pools. These social intentions do not include a school, as it is located in front of the planned block*"[7]. The brief adds that the density achieved at Casa Bloc is 1,140 inhabitants per hectare.

The Casa Bloc is a full-scale experiment in the urban planning projects carried out by GATCPAC (Grup d'Artistes i Tèchnics Catalans per el Progrés de l'Arquitectura contemporània), in particular the Macià Plan—the new Barcelona, 1931–1938 (fig. 8). In the Macià plan, we find the indentations (*redents*) based on a 400-meter-long grid, corresponding to three Cerda blocks. GATCPAC's architects and urban planners were keen to show the articulation of the contemporary city with the Cerda blocks for the expansion area, the *ensanche*, as well as their proposals for the Cerda blocks of 113 meters plus 20 meters for the street.

For the green grid, no large 400 m × 400 m blocks. In groups of two, the students formulated a project for a city block based on the figure and approximate dimensions of the Casa Bloc. The 185-metre-long block would include two local facilities, the function of which would be decided collectively, and a required number of housing units with a minimum density objective. The types of housing and their open-plan layouts need to be designed to take account of the main sunlight orientations, which requires coordination between the two students responsible for the project (fig. 10 and 11).

The blocks are then assembled to produce a neighborhood according to the internal configurations of each block and on the basis of a project for an oriented territorial grid, the "green grid": "*This term 'green grid', reminiscent of the Chandigarh city plan, in fact develops a theme of mixed use that reaffirms that a complex city, with housing and facilities, both industrial and residential, can take on diverse forms associated with each of the places where it is found. These differences can be managed within an urban thickness; a grid capable of giving a measure to today's diffuse city, containing sufficient density, allowing variations according to the accidents of the topography and the fragments of city to be preserved, modified, and/or consolidated, ensuring real breathing space for these spaces*"[8] (fig. 12).

The purpose of the *redent* construction type is to retain and fix the expansion of the contemporary city in a territorial grid determining the unit of measurement of both its urbanism and its architecture.

As always, this project work is accompanied by a critical analysis, and in the case of the green grid, the aim is to study, in addition to the hypothetical model, examples of housing/equipment mixes, possible figures based on the original figure, as well as intermediate groupings between block and building, such as the assembly of four dwellings in the 12-metre square cubic envelope.

Back to pedagogy

After this overview of the different themes of the metropolitan tower, let's return for a moment to the exercise itself, and observe how Michel Kagan conceived his pedagogy. The work systematically begins with critical analysis, using a precise collective analytical grid.

This is supported by a corpus of references and a bibliography. These are the starting tools. They reinforce the research work by constituting a critical baggage in which the student can freely evolve, and which also has the advantage of combating contemporary amnesia.

7. *2C Construcción de la Ciudad*, 15-16, Barcelona, 1980.

8. Michel Kagan, « La trame verte », teaching program, EAPB, 2008.

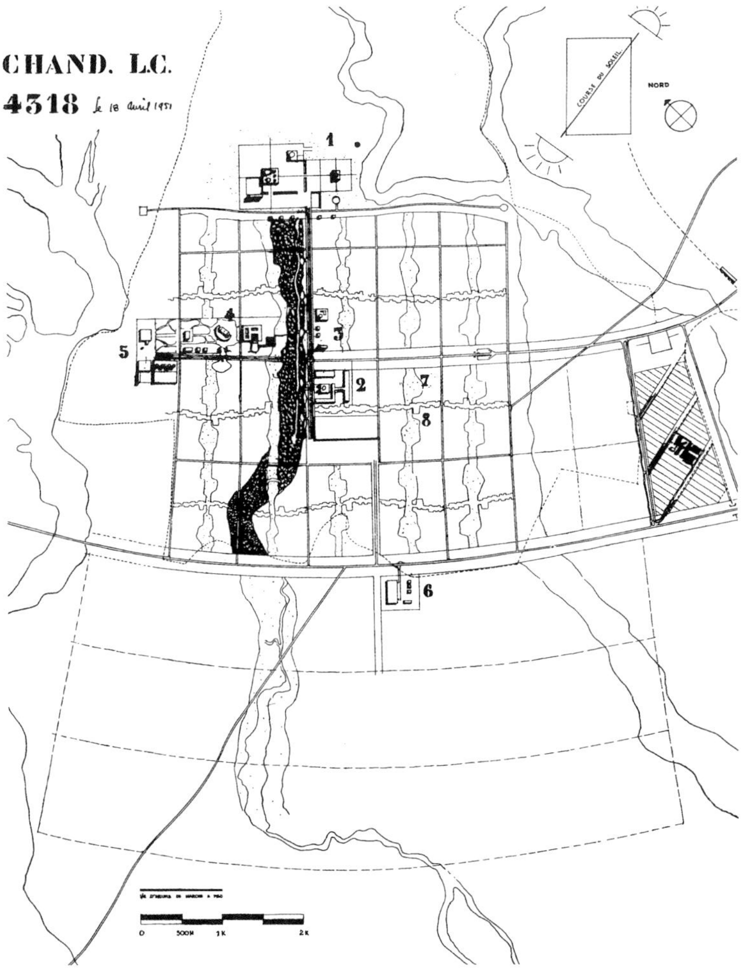

fig. 12. Plan drawing of the city of Chandigarh, Le Corbusier, 1958.

This was followed by research into vertical space, expressed in a variety of modes, from photo montages to experimental model-building. The result is what is presented as a theoretical project.

The final phase of the transformation process consists of confronting the theoretical project with the realities of the site and a program: taking reality into account. The site, its uses, structure, tectonics and dimensions call the theoretical project into question and transform it. The involvement of engineers enables students to examine structural and regulatory issues in greater depth. The major challenge of this phase is to ensure the overall coherence of the project in all its aspects, and in particular the match between the spatial and sensory hypothesis and the concrete project.

These three phases of the student's work can be found to varying degrees in all the exercises proposed by Michel Kagan throughout his career as a teacher.

A contribution: the city in cross-section

In the two complementary exercises on the "green grid" and the "metropolitan tower" proposed by Michel Kagan's studio at the

École d'architecture de Paris-Belleville from 1998–1999 onwards, we can see that the theoretical concerns we have just outlined feed into the construction of the teaching subject. The reflection common to these themes and projects is basically a questioning of the nature of today's urban context, without forgetting, along the way, the achievements of recent decades.

At their root, these exercises propose a kind of method: the cross-section of the building is systematically related to the cross-section of the city. Figures are imposed, modes of composition are suggested. But what is really at stake, and what remains open, is experimenting with how "the point of view of the section" offers the European city a critical and audacious material made up of public spaces conquering the sky. In this respect, the metropolitan tower could well be the lasting, concrete proposal for a European city of the 21st century, an unexpected response to metropolization and its dislocated spaces.

fig. 1. The garden city. Camille Benoit, Leo Demeillers, Raphaël Guerrier, Margaux Kleindiest, Vincent Tissandier, Alexis Zanotta, Ensa PVS, 2019.

A "Vertical Garden City"

Nathalie Régnier-Kagan

> *We should look upon a city as a forest. The streets of this are the roads of that and ought to be entered into the same manner. [...] Let us make the application of this idea, and that the design of our parks serve as a plan for our cities.*
>
> Marc-Antoine Laugier, *An essay on architecture* (1755)

Beyond symbolic gestures, beyond feats of technology, formal prowess, or even financial achievement, the challenge of building high today is primarily an environmental one. The high-rise building is an architectural and urban response to the need to densify large metropolises. Recent legislation addressing the right to light is now at the forefront of regulating construction and is helping increase the amount of open space on the ground. The creation of vast urban parks will be an integral part of the metropolis of the 21st century, to absorb runoff water and promote the growth of vegetation on land surfaces, to increase water retention and reintroduce biodiversity, while meeting the ever-increasing demand for housing. We need to build higher and to reintroduce nature into the city, open up vistas, and offer comfortable, light-filled homes, with cross-ventilated interiors, for as many people as possible.

With this goal in mind, we taught "the metropolitan tower" for almost ten years, from 2013 to 2023, at *Ensa de Paris Val de Seine*, first as an isolated element in the existing city, as initiated by Michel Kagan, then evolving over time to integrate it into a wider context. As Jean Mas points out, experimentation shifted from a "typological" exercise to a "territorial" vision, promoting a *"shared set of high-rise projects, multiplied and juxtaposed with horizontal urban developments, on sites and territories already engaged in major contemporary metropolitan mutations"*[1] (fig. 1).

Why build tall?

Skyscrapers are necessary for several reasons: rising land prices, population growth, and the tendency of business districts to concentrate. In terms of vocabulary, we need to distinguish between "skyscrapers", which originated in North America and refer to multifunctional buildings over 100 m in height, including offices, hotels, shops, restaurants and housing, and European "towers", which usually have a specific function, and have sometimes acquired a tourist vocation (like the Eiffel Tower). In French, they can mean residential buildings as well as office towers. French regulations define a high-rise building (IGH — *Immeuble à grande hauteur*) as being 28 m or higher if it is open to the public, and 50 m or higher if it is a residential building,

1. See Jean Mas, p. 207.

fig. 2. Shanghai skyline, 2017.

and 200 m or higher if it is a very tall building (ITGH — *Immeuble à très grande hauteur*). It's not just a question of size, but also of proportion: a 12-storey building can feel like a high-rise in certain contexts, depending on a particular proportion or "slenderness". While the construction of high-rise buildings was almost exclusively part of the North American urban landscape until the beginning of the 20th century, to serve the image of a company, today it is widespread almost everywhere in the world, including the major European capitals. From the '90s onwards, competition for height a global phenomenon, particularly in China (fig. 2) and the Arab emirates. In 2009, a real leap forward was made, with the completion of the Burj Dubai culminating at 828 m, shattering all records. Towers of over 1,000 m in height are currently being planned in Dubai and China, serving the economic interests and influence of the states[2].

In Europe, towers are no longer a taboo subject: they must be integrated into the existing historic city. It's like a signpost punctuating an avenue, a district. It's part of the urban fabric, part of a desire for urban transformation to revitalize a district and the image of a city. The tower can be conceived as part of an urban whole, capable of offering public spaces, or it can remain attached to the contours of a plot of land[3]. In the European imagination, the high-rise building evokes the office block rather than the family home and domesticity. As some authors participating in current European debates and controversies around questions of respect for built heritage and the "desirable skyline"[4] point out, in the current context of land scarcity, even if the density of high-rise complexes is not necessarily higher than that of a Haussmann district, to avoid urban sprawl and the mobility that it requires, to create the city based on proximity, high-rise construction could be the means not only to densify, but also to free up natural soil.

But the fact remains that, in Europe as elsewhere, examples of high-rise buildings with genuine architectural qualities are few and far between. The speculative frenzy of cities, the desire to attract investors, along with technical complexity, increasingly stringent regulations, and rising construction costs all relegate architecture to the sidelines: urban quality is often sacrificed to the imperatives of profitability. The construction of high-rise buildings

2. Clarisse Didelon, "Une course vers le ciel: mondialisation et diffusion spatio-temporelle des gratte-ciel", *M@ppemonde*, 2010.

3. Ingrid Taillandier, Olivier Namias, Jean-François Pousse (eds), *L'invention de la tour européenne*, (Paris: Pavillon de l'Arsenal, A. & J. Picard, 2009).

4. Manuel Appert, "Politique du skyline. Shard et le débat sur les tours à Londres", *Métropolitiques*, September 2011, 12.

fig. 3. Bois-le-Prêtre Tower, Paris, Frédéric Druot, Anne Lacaton and Jean-Philippe Vassal architects.

is more a matter of business than architecture. Yet examples of remarkable high-rise buildings do exist, and most of the great masters of 20th-century architecture have tackled this type of architecture, from Frank Lloyd Wright with the Price Tower, to Mies van der Rohe with the Lake Shore Drive Apartments. Today, opposing "modernity" and "historic preservation" is no longer a sufficient argument: the recognition of the heritage value of certain towers has become a reality, accentuated by environmental concerns, which favor the conservation and rehabilitation of existing buildings[5]. We urgently need to develop a genuine culture of high-rise building, with its expert models. As Jean-Louis Violeau concludes in his sociological study, conducted with Monique Eleb, of two high-rise districts, in Bagnolet and the 20th arrondissement of Paris: *"There's something absurd about being for or against high-rise buildings"*[6]. Indeed, it's a topical issue: learning how to transform this bulky, energy-guzzling existing heritage into environmentally-friendly buildings is becoming a matter of urgency. The renovation of the *Tour Bois-le-Prêtre* in 2010 by architects Frederic Druot (fig. 3), Anne Lacaton and Jean-Philippe Vassal is a remarkable example. Choosing reconversion over destruction, this transformation, focusing on housing quality and resident comfort, shows how to intelligently transform a run-of-the-mill social housing building located along the Paris ring road, while in bringing more daylight and improving its thermal and acoustic performance: *"Never demolish, never cut out or replace, always add, transform, use"* is their credo, which has met with worldwide recognition.

The endless city

At the time of the yellow vests and urban protests in France, it became clear that we needed to rethink life in the metropolis and finally consider decentralization and proximity, social mix and its uses. The city of tomorrow is the "polycentric" city with all its facilities and services, to provide urban environments on a human scale, prioritizing alternative forms of mobility, decongesting public transport, and deconcentrating historic centers[7]. In challenging periods, it's time to draw lessons from the past, and revisit archetypes. The notion of "city" calls for a form of autonomy: a city within the city. The historical ideal of the garden city, born at the end of

5. Catherine Sabbah, "Tours et retours", in *L'invention de la tour européenne*, op cit.

6. Jean-Louis Violeau, "Les tours, nouveaux villages", in *L'invention de la tour européenne, op. cit.*

7. Carlos Moreno and Pierre Veltz, "La ville du quart d'heure: voie à suivre ou mirage idéologique ?", *Forum Vies Mobiles*, April 7, 2022.

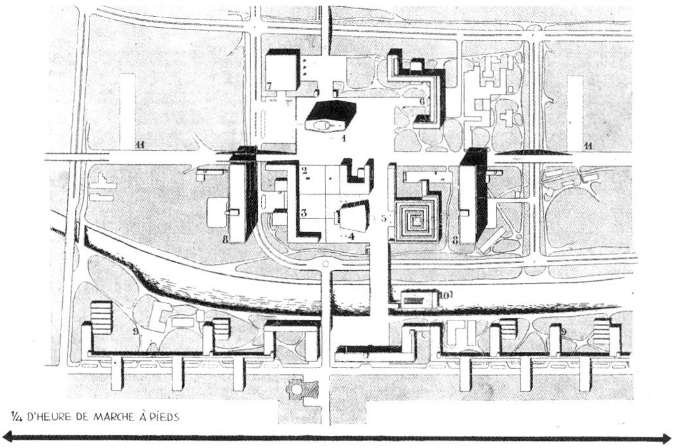

fig. 4. Le Corbusier, Immeuble-villas, a building of 120 superposed villas, 1922.

fig. 5. Le Corbusier, the civic centre of Saint-Dié, 1945.

the 19th century in England under the influence of Ebenezer Howard, was a response to the need to preserve the environment in the face of the galloping industrialization and exponential growth of cities, with the famous example of Hampstead, a highly sought-after London district whose garden city, designed by R. Unwin and B. Parker, was developed at the beginning of the 20th century up to the Second World War, to house workers and the middle class. The idea was to combine the advantages of the city with those of the countryside, while offering residents a degree of autonomy through the creation of vegetable gardens and public services. Unlike large housing estates, the garden city is characterized by high-quality landscaping, attention to detail, constructive economy through repetition, a mix of functions, and architecture that adapts to its context, to local craftsmanship, and to the vernacular.

As early as 1922, Le Corbusier, who had already tackled the design of a garden city in Saint Nicolas d'Aliermont and in Saintes, was thinking about a utopian city: "a contemporary city of three million inhabitants", in which individual and collective housing models would coexist. What he proposed was a more "modern", more space-efficient way of thinking about urban planning than the garden city: the "immeuble-villa" model (fig. 4), i.e., the repetition of superimposed individual houses, with an exterior extension for each dwelling in a single living unit (of which the Esprit Nouveau pavilion would be the prototype presented at the Exposition des Arts Décoratifs in 1925). The influence of the American "apartment hotel" model formulated by the Groupe d'habitation franco-américaine was well known, as Pierre-Alain Croset has shown[8]. Le Corbusier continued to develop this theme after the Second World War, in his research initiated with Ascoral[9],

8. Pierre-Alain Croset, "Les origines d'un type." In *Le Corbusier, une encyclopédie* (Paris: Centre Georges Pompidou, 1987), quoted in Jean-Louis Cohen "Le Corbusier observateur de la ville américaine." In *Le Corbusier: la ville, l'urbanisme* (Paris: Les rencontres de la Fondation Le Corbusier, 1995).

which he disseminated in *"Les trois établissements humains"*[10], and *"Manière de penser l'urbanisme"*[11] in 1946. Peripheral housing estates gave concrete form to the "horizontal garden city", while "housing units" close to the center, together with public buildings and office skyscrapers, formed what he would call the "vertical garden city" (fig. 5). The *"unités d'habitation"* housing units, the centerpieces of this new urbanism, were to be served by a hierarchical network of roads, while the "interior street" would allow exchange and community living in the buildings, based on the family unit and offering a mix of services as needed to give everyone the opportunity to *"cultivate their body and mind"*[12]. In a visionary manner, he stated: *"Walking around the city in the middle of parks, or devoting one, two or three hours a day to distant mechanical transport... the answer seems to emerge that the man of the machinist civilization will walk around inside his redeveloped city"*[13].

fig. 6. The vertical promenade, Thomas Dietert, Ensa PVS, 2018.

This concept prefigures the idea of the "15-Minute City": At the time, it was already a response to sustainable development objectives, giving new relevance to the issue of density and high-rise construction. To escape the sprawl of the "endless city", we need to conquer the sky. Based on this premise, at the Ecole de Paris Val de Seine, we proposed that projects revisit the question of the "vertical garden city," as a counterpoint to the "horizontal garden city". This approach intrinsically contains a strong theme linked to a careful vision of land, attentive to both land use opportunities and avoiding the systematic sealing of its surface. The aim is to explore how to live, work, and relax in a high-rise building, how to use distribution spaces on a daily basis to encourage exchanges, and how to offer outdoor spaces and plant structures in the tower. The tower should be seen as part of the city in the sky, a kind of vertical urbanism. High-rise construction in specific metropolitan areas seems appropriate, so that the city is no longer an endless continuum, a *"Città diffusa"* as Bernardo Secchi describes it[14], but rather to mark a place, a city entrance, a square... It's a question of conceiving the vertical city, with all its aspects of social and cultural life. The project invents the possibility of creating not just "interior streets", but genuine "vertical streets" (fig. 6), i.e. common spaces linking the levels together, offering outdoor spaces within the tower, making the roof an accessible place, open to residents with specific programs. As Jean Mas explains, in the project exercise, the program is *"the pretext for a typological reflection based on the search for the essential reasons for the morphogenesis of a vertical architectural project for the city and its public space, in a project for a reinvented 'urban landscape'."*[15]

9. Assemblée de Constructeurs pour une Rénovation Architecturale [assembly of constructors for a renewal of architecture] (1942).

10. Le Corbusier, *Les trois établissements humains*, (Paris: Éditions de Minuit, 1968).

11. Le Corbusier, *Manière de penser l'urbanisme* (Paris: Gonthier, 1972).

12. Op. cit.

13. Op. cit.

14. Bernardo Secchi, *Première leçon d'urbanisme*, (Marseille: Parenthèses, 2006)

15. See Jean Mas, p. 207.

"Ethically" inhabiting the world

Building a high-rise is both a technical and architectural issue. But it's also a question of ethics: how can we meet economic imperatives without sacrificing architectural and constructive quality? In the design process we have set up at Paris-Val de Seine, following the method initiated by Michel Kagan, we establish a back-and-forth between a "theoretical" and abstract approach, based on project culture, and a "plastic" understanding of the landscape, tied to a sense of contemporary architectural and urban space, with its poetics, its functional and constructive rationality. Our research is based on the repetition of a matrix that generates space, a structural and distributive principle, a relationship to the ground, and a relationship to the sky. Theoretical synthesis is developed from this preliminary work, which is then confronted with the real site (fig. 7). Working with models enables students to discover how space works, to experiment with paper folding, and to understand the importance of three-dimensional representation in developing a hypothesis or "urban figure"[16]

16. This concept of "figure" has been developed in the teachings of Henri Ciriani and the Uno group.

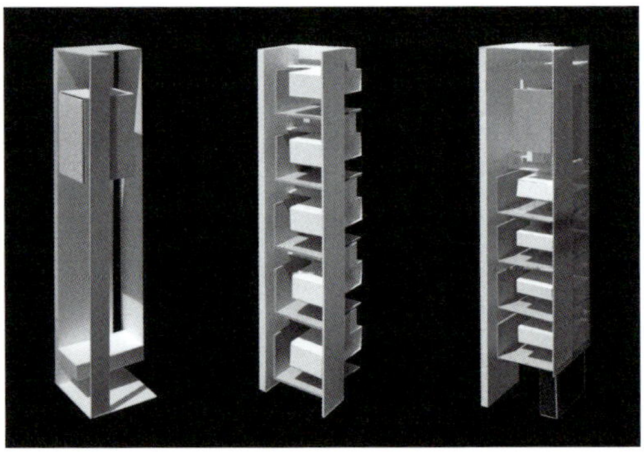

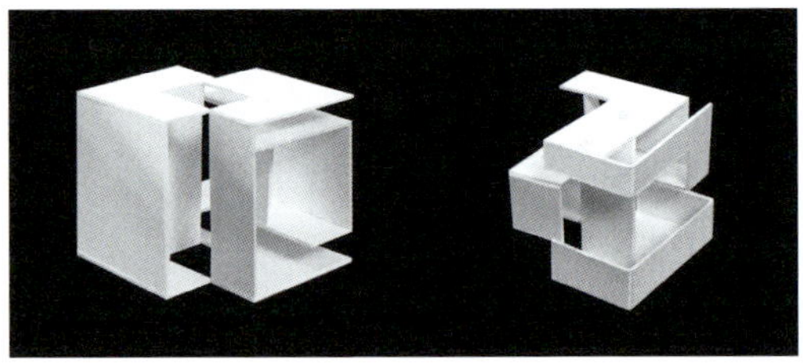

fig. 7a. Theoretical model, François Nahory, Ensa PVS, 2013.

fig. 7b. Module, Marie Prel, Ensa PVS, 2018.

fig. 8 Mixed-used programs

a & b. Victoire Bergey, Antoine Kubik, Sacha Luisada, Ensa PVS, 2019.
c. Raphaël Guerrier, Ensa PVS, 2019.

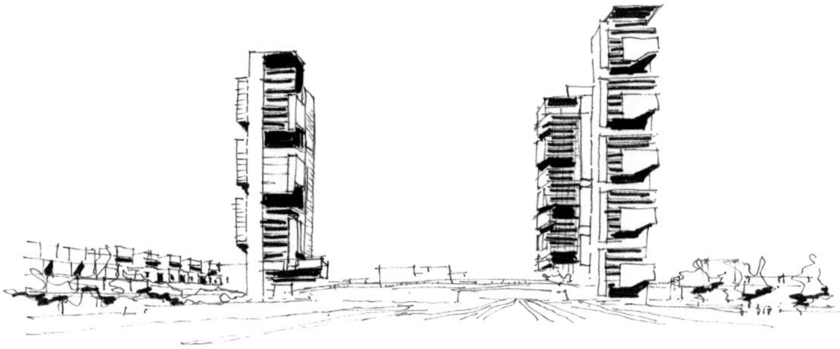

fig. 9. Melissa Dyminat, Ensa PVS, 2018.

fig. 10. Vincent Tissandier, Ensa PVS, 2019.

that is not a formal whim, but a detailed understanding of the relationships that the constituent elements of a project can establish with its environment: it's a question of placing "the first opacities" on the site.

Our concerns as teachers at Paris-Val de Seine have been integrated into the formulation of the project: questions of safety, structural dimensioning and environmental issues are explicitly addressed. The "Metropolitan Tower" is not intended to be a structural feat: it is not meant to exceed 100 m in height. It is multifunctional, and can contain public programs such as cinemas and restaurants, as well as "social condensers" such as those envisaged by Michel Kagan in the 11th arrondissement of Paris, near Place de la Bastille. In the Masséna-Bruneseau district in the 13th arrondissement, we have developed mixed-use programs, mainly for universities, superimposing lecture theaters, libraries, workshops, classrooms, offices and student accommodation. In our most recent experiments, in Boulogne Billancourt and Ivry sur Seine in particular, we have focused on residential research, mixing housing and mixed-use programs such as sports halls, restaurants and crèches, with particular attention paid to questions of floor heights, intermediate halls, the interiority of common spaces, their external extensions and the possible greening of upper levels (fig. 8). The "transversal" contributions of teachers from other disciplines were essential: structural engineers Bruno Person and Bruno Thomas, to facilitate dimensioning and structural choices, and Pierre Vincent for digital representation. This technical knowledge was complemented by the arrival of a landscape architect in our team: Giovanna Marinoni, enabling us to take a more concrete approach to greenery.

The importance of a common language

In this project, the choice of structure is essential and makes it possible to envisage the scalability of spaces and uses, by associating various functions: sports halls, swimming pools, restaurants, exhibitions, cinemas... for a transitional lifestyle, offering all the advantages of the horizontal city, on a restricted floor area. The techniques used to build a tower are not just a matter of calculating ductwork, elevators, load drops and wind resistance. It's also a question of physical presence, reacting to the site, its geography, climate, and solar orientation. Ecological considerations were taken into account in the layout of the buildings, to avoid cast shadows, to take advantage of solar gain, reduce water consumption, ventilate and light all spaces naturally, reinforce solar protection and recycle materials. We favored a "bioclimatic" approach by designing less hermetic,

fig. 10a. & 10b. Insertion in the context Bruneseau Nord: view and model. Paul Pelletier, ENSA Paris-Val de Seine, 2013.

more porous envelopes[17]. More than any other building, a high-rise establishes a territorial relationship with the city's distant landscape, but also with its immediate surroundings: its location has profound consequences for the evolution of a neighborhood. The latest towers in Paris are striking examples of this.

We saw the tower as a continuation of the existing city, rather than as an additional element of "congestion", or as a "Bigness"[18]. The theory of a "generic" city with no particular quality or identity is not our intent: on the contrary, we have sought to establish a relationship with place. When designing a high-rise building, digital tools are used more than ever to assess the impact of a construction on the existing urban fabric: 3D modeling is important for structural issues, fire safety, urban integration, the representation of interior spaces and natural light. Nevertheless, the physical model remains fundamental to research: it is an effective control tool for understanding the relevance of a layout, but also an effective means of learning and design, which we have always encouraged. The human eye and hand are often the best judges. (fig. 9)

We practiced this teaching approach at Ensa Paris Val de Seine, with several architects and teachers who shared our convictions, within the A-Ito field of study[19]. This combination of teachers within a School of Architecture that has almost 300 tenured professors and 2,000 students, has proven indispensable for training students in a coherent, progressive approach that achieves the desired results. The training of our undergraduates should enable us to tackle the complexity of such subjects. This teaching has evolved according to the different contexts studied, the programs envisaged, and also by the teachers who have supervised it: in the early years with Jean-Michel Veillerot, then Thomas Heuzé, Jean Mas, Pierre-André Comte, and finally with Laurent Beaudouin. These multiple collaborations enabled me to enrich the initial pedagogical proposal, and to approach it from a variety of angles. With Jean-Michel Veillerot, we focused on the contextual aspect (fig. 10): the importance of the relationship to the ground, the integration of a Tower into the continuity of an urban context, the consideration of standard dimensions, the reversal of the horizontal to the vertical... Thomas Heuzé and Dominique Pinon

17. Ken Yeang, *The green skyscraper* (Munich: Prestel Verlag, 2003), and *Reinventing the skyscraper*, (NYC: Mc Graw Hill, 1995).

18. Rem Koolhaas, Bruce Mau, *S, M, L XL* (New York: The Monacelli Press, 1995).

19. A-Ito : Architectures—Laboratoire des Territoires Ouverts, Area of Study founded in 2015 at EnsaPVS.

brought a demanding eye to bear on the tower's constructive and ecological aspects, right down to the details of the envelope. With Jean-Mas, we insisted on the structural rationality of the tower in relation to its spatial composition. With Pierre-André Comte, we renewed the architectural references. And finally, with Laurent Beaudouin, this teaching was enriched, on the one hand, by the importance given to interior spaces, their natural light, their materiality, while on the other hand, by exploring the fantastic possibilities of three-dimensional urbanism: how to connect several towers horizontally, at different heights (fig. 12). However, this research differed from the "utopian explorations" of Archigram and Peter Cook, by giving primacy to spaces, less subject to structural research, in a pursuit of urban integration and scale.

The Park City

In order to better articulate the Tower project in relation to its urban context, the project's pedagogy was further enriched when a highly fruitful collaboration with Jean-Michel Veillerot and Thomas Heuzé was set up within the A-Ito field of study. We transformed the "Metropolitan Tower" into the "Vertical Garden City" with Laurent Beaudouin, as a counterpoint to the teaching of horizontal urbanism: "arborescence and canopy"[20], to create a city-landscape for dense housing that develops horizontally. This approach is part of a project logic that stems not only from research on the villa building, but also from Team X's work on the "mat building" concept, and in the continuity of Anglo-Saxon research[21]. This collaboration has strengthened the relationship with the ground at the foot of the towers, giving them a more human scale and a link with the surrounding neighborhoods. The ground freed up by the towers opens up new urban possibilities: it can become public space, squares, shared gardens, land for urban agriculture—green spaces for the benefit of all, right in the heart of the city, to create the Park City (fig. 11). The garden itself is part of the project: it is the subject of a design, in association with an in-depth landscape study in continuity with

20. Design studio project taught by Jean-Michel Veillerot and Thomas Heuze in Master 1, since 2015.

21. See: Mark Swenarton, *Cook's Camden, the making of Modern Housing* (London: Lund Humphries, 2017).

fig. 11. Raphaël Guerrier, Margaux Kleindiest, Ensa PVS, 2019.

fig. 12. Twin towers, Cecile Achard, Eudes Cazaunau, Ensa PVS, 2018.

fig. 13. Paul Rudolph, The Colonnade Condominums.

the built environment. Students from each group work in teams to develop spatial correspondences between horizontal and vertical housing typologies, to create a coherent urban project.

These experiments were carried out in well-defined urban contexts: first, in the "Seine Rive-Gauche" district of Paris's 13th arrondissement, within the "Masséna-Bruneseau" urban project designed by the Ateliers Lion and SEMAPA, which is currently developing an urban design of towers, near the Ecole de Paris-Val de Seine, then in the town of Ivry; there, we studied the site around the "Parc des Cormailles", to either side of the railroad tracks coming from the Gare d'Austerlitz, and close to the remarkable housing built in the 1970s by architects Renée Gailloustet and Serge Renaudie, pioneers of providing space for plants, terraces, and patios in their architecture. The structuralist approach of our teaching, combining spatial structure, constructive structures and plastic structure to create formal coherence, went hand in hand with in-depth urban reflection, so as not to create a rupture with the old town.

Hanging gardens

The idea of integrating plants into buildings was developed in South-East Asia, to compensate for the loss of a relationship with nature and the lack of outdoor spaces in dense metropolitan cities, and to provide natural ventilation and cooling in these tropical climates as well. Examples of towers built in the '70s, such as Charles Correa's Kanchanjunga apartments in Bombay, or Paul Rudolf's Colonnade Condominums in Singapore[22] (fig. 13), as well as more recent experiments such as Woha's Newton Suites in Singapore (2007), have shown the possibilities of creating real outdoor green spaces in high-rise buildings[23]. Taking account of wind and rain, and offering gardens on shared terraces, enables residents to meet up and rediscover the feeling of living in a village. The idea here is not to use "greenwashing" as a colored filter for our views, or to superficially "green" buildings, but to imagine real interior gardens, intermediate spaces between the outside and the inside, in the heights between floors, which the inhabitants themselves can green, like the hanging gardens of Babylon, to create places where it's good to live high up.

In the contemporary context of climate transition, all urban forms must be called into question. The vertical urbanism of high-rise buildings remains unavoidable in major metropolises: it's up to us architects to promote architecture that is humane, harmonious and responsible. We need to design eco-friendly towers to accommodate people in a more virtuous way, in comfortable, naturally ventilated, and daylit homes with large, planted outdoor spaces. It's about going beyond hubris and gigantism to define the new urban rules of tomorrow's equitable city.

22. Sacha Kagan, "L'échelle de l'habiter dans la Tour" (master's thesis, ENSA Paris Val-de-Seine, February 2023, supervised by Emmanuelle Sarrazin).

23. Annette Gigon, Mike Guyer, Felix Jerusalem, eds., *Residential Towers* (Zürich: Gta verlag, 2016).

Project Notebook II

‹esearch on Verticality

François Nahory, Ensa PVS, 2013.

ˈheoretical Model

2. Assembling modules, Margaux Kleindienst, Ensa PVS, 2019.

ˌite Registration

. and 3b. Urban banks, Ivry, Camille De Labbey, Kevin Laurent, Pedro Pereira, Hayder Hamid, Joanna Souraya, Nicolas Regnard, ısa PVS, 2022.

Intermediate Module

4a. and 4b. Research on the intermediate hall: maquette and perspective, Leo Demeillers, Ensa PVS, 2019.

Mixed-use Programs

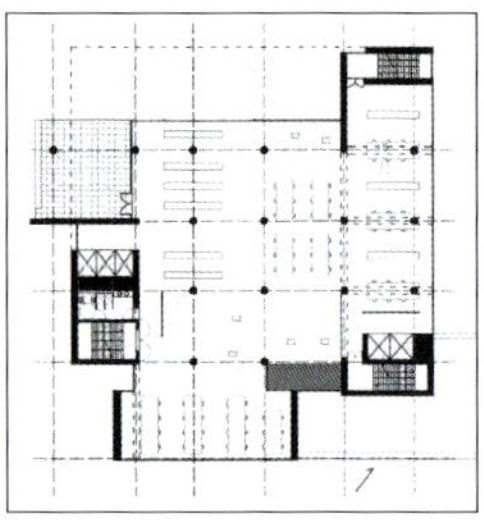

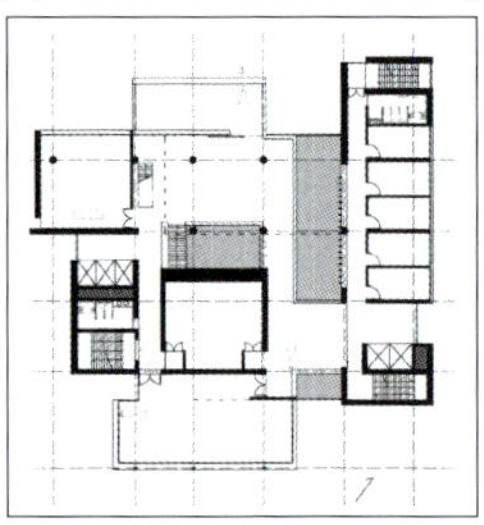

5a. and 5b. Interiority of common spaces: plans and views, Raphaël Guerrier et Margaux Kleindienst, Ensa PVS, 2019.

6. Overlapping functions and spaces, Alexandre Laurent, Ensa PVS 2019.

Relationship to the Ground / to the Sky

7a. and 7b. Victoire Bergey, Antoine Kubik, Sacha Luisada, ENSA PVS, 2019.

.iving High

8a., 8b., 8c. and 8d. Emma Dufour, Ensa PVS, 2022.

uspended Garden

A suspended greenhouse, Théo de la Presles, Ensa PVS, 2019.

. The tower as a vertical extention of the city, Mathilde Shaal, sa PVS, 2017.

arden-City

. and 11b. "High-line d'Ivry" Tom Debaye, Emma Dufour, Samia Filali Aoual, Paloma Rodriguez, Ensa PVS, 2022.

Studio Atmosphere

12. Jean-Michel Veillerot, Nathalie Régnier-Kagan. **13.** Henri Ciriani, Nathalie Régnier-Kagan, Laurent Beaudouin and students, 2018 **14.** Victoire Bergey, Antoine Kubik, Sacha Luisada with Bruno Person. **15.** Mélissa Dyminat. **16.** Raphaël Guerrier, Margaux Kleindies Leo Demeillers, Vincent Tissandier. **17.** Margaux Kleindiest with Laurent Beaudouin. **18.** Laurianne Chiri and Simon Valero with Hen Ciriani. **19.** Meritt Bucholz. **20.** Bruno Thomas, Simon Rodriguez, Clément Péqueux, Laurent Beaudouin, Pascal Hofstein.

Structures-Envelope

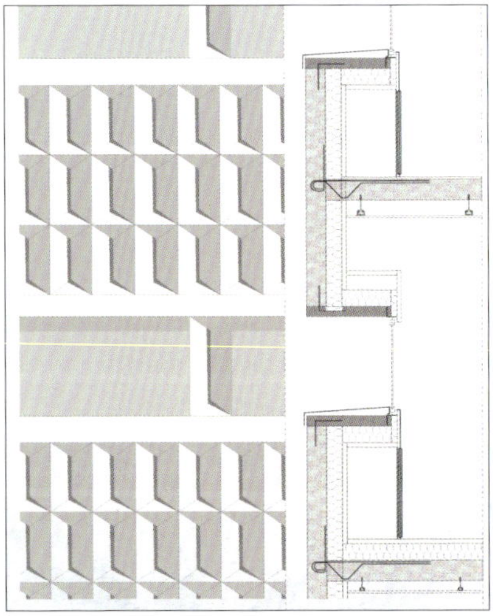

21. Model, Irina Vilmus, Ensa PVS, 2015.

22. Detail elevation and section, Marie Prel, Ensa PVS, 2018.

Twin Towers

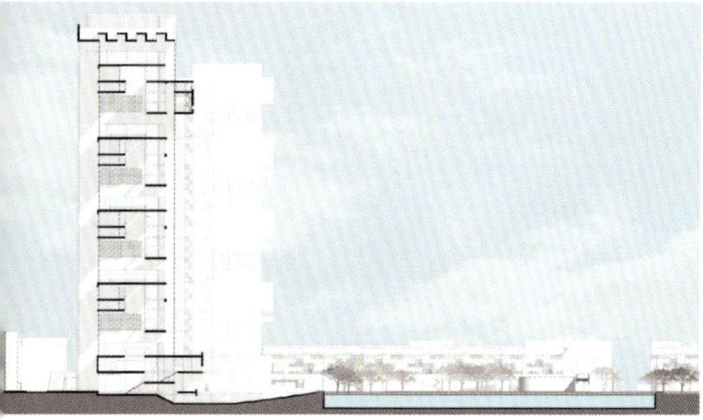

23. Raphaël Guerrier et Margaux Kleindienst, 2019. **24.** Solene Duplessis et Felicia de la Tullaye.

Final Model

25a. and 25b. Emma Collet, Thomas Diettert. **26.** Victoire Bergey, Antoine Kubik, Sacha Luisada.

"Arborescence and Canopy"

The "Arborescence et Canopée" project is designed to create a landscape of horizontal housing opposite the "Tour Métropolitaine". By bringing together projects for towers and flat roofs, "Ville-Parc", or the city-landscape or inhabited park, allows for powerful relationships with the environment and natural elements. This research is in line with projects that have emerged from research into "Mat-Buildings", buildings in the form of tablecloths, and their reinterpretations of the "Immeuble-Villa", of which this would be the flat projection. The "Canopée" refers to the top of a layer of vegetation, a horizon line in relation to the sky, establishing a fifth façade, a territory inhabited by planted terraces and hanging gardens, while the "Arborescence" conjures up the image of the branches of a tree in three dimensions. This form of growth questions the notion of boundaries and harmonious integration with the landscape. The space freed up beneath this suspended habitat, above the natural ground, can be used for public facilities and tertiary activities.

Jean-Michel Veillerot

27. Ladin Yacizi, ENSA PVS, 2023.

3 / Sharing the Project

fig. 1. Stepped building: The New City (*La Città Nuova*)
Antonio Sant'Elia, 1914.

Mental Structure, Constructive Structure[1]

Jean Mas

Babel

In the film *Metropolis*, shot by Fritz Lang during the Weimar Republic and inspired by Antonio Sant'Elia's futuristic megalopolis, with its immense and monolithic skyscrapers (fig. 1), one scene tells the story of the Tower of Babel: its purpose, its construction, and finally, its demise. A strange dialogue evokes the incomprehension between the hand and the head.

What's striking about the myth of Babel is the relationship between the human desire to raise the tower "to heaven" and the loss of the meaning of the original universal language. The tower is the cause of the confusion and multiplicity of languages among the peoples "scattered over the face of the earth".

A more recent film, Babel, directed by Alejandro González Iñárritu in 2006, also refers to the myth of the tower, drawing on the difficulties encountered by human beings in communicating, despite all being united by the same humanity. This myth of Babel, the founding myth of otherness itself—linked to the multiplicity of languages and incommunicability—must undoubtedly be reread with greater attention paid to the writing, beyond glosses and descriptions: Babel is first and foremost a city—the city, Babylon—and it is in its midst that men build a tower, the two are linked.

The city is a melting pot of humanity. The tower has no other purpose than to serve the enterprise of building the city.

If Babel is mentioned here, it is because it only recently occurred to me that, in tackling the unprecedented subject of the *metropolitan tower,* Michel Kagan undoubtedly saw in it the central cultural reference capable of posing head-on and in its structural dimension the question of the universality of architectural language, and of associating it with the question of the *meaning* of urban form.

In the form of personal pedagogical syncretism that Michel Kagan has developed over the years from the reinterpretation and "mixture" of many of his own references (Uno, Bauhaus, Cooper Union, Columbia, among others), the

1. Exchanges between the Versailles and Belleville schools of architecture in the 2004-2005 and 2005-2006 academic years between Michel Kagan (ENSAPB) with engineers Pierre Bismuth and Marc Saluden on one hand, and Jean Mas and Nathalie Régnier-Kagan (ENSAV) with engineer Jean-Pierre Laute on the other.

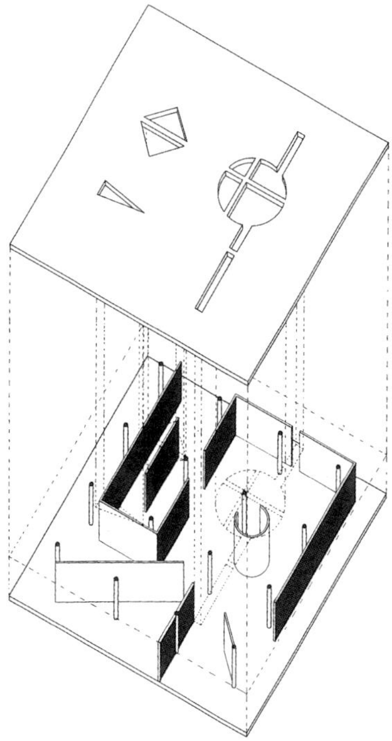

fig. 2. The nine square grid exercise, student project, Geneva School of Architecture.

primary hypothesis is thus stated: architecture is structured like a language.

Command of a language is a particular form of "understanding": the Metropolitan Tower's pedagogical project, in contrast to the myth of Babel, is intended as a sign of the need for and faith in a universal language to be rediscovered in the field of architecture.

A project like none before

Few architecture schools anywhere in the world—with the possible exception of some schools in Asia—still include high-rise architecture in their curricula, and it's clear that—in addition to the myth of Babel—the program suffers from a disreputable reputation linked to more or less well-founded criticism of the urban-destroying and often business-oriented nature of this type of nonetheless important building. French citizens are fascinated to see these towers in Asian and North American metropolises, especially in New York, but the vast majority of them nonetheless continue to reject high-rise construction in France, particularly in Paris.

Michel Kagan initiated reflection on the subject of the metropolitan tower quite early on and developed it on the strength of his teaching experience, particularly in North America, before setting it up at Paris-Belleville as soon as he arrived at the School.

Then, in the early 2000s, Nathalie Régnier-Kagan and engineer Jean-Pierre Laute and I introduced a Master's course on the Tower at the *École Nationale Supérieure d'Architecture de Versailles*, a school that since the 1980s has been marked by in-depth work on the historic city and urban planning in general. Our students, unprepared by the academic curriculum at Versailles for the particular problems of the exercise, were lucky enough to work for a semester in parallel with a group of students from Paris-Belleville, supervised by Michel Kagan.

The results of this shared teaching between the two schools were remarkable in every way. Beyond the quality of the projects and the exchanges between the groups of students and teachers, it was more the discovery of the incredible pedagogical power of this exercise (new to me at the time) that I found fascinating. I was already familiar with Michel Kagan's pedagogy, having taught with him for several years in Geneva. A pedagogy marked in particular in the first cycle by the notion of successive thematic exercises: the nine squares (fig. 2), the magic box (fig. 4), the spatialized image (fig. 3), the cube, the minimum-maximum house..., articulated as so many elements in the learning of an architectural language that builds up in the student over the course of the exercises through the acquisition of a grammar, a syntax, a specific vocabulary leading ultimately to a comprehension specific to each individual in the field of architectural know-how.

fig. 3. The spatialized image exercise, student projects, Geneva School of Architecture.

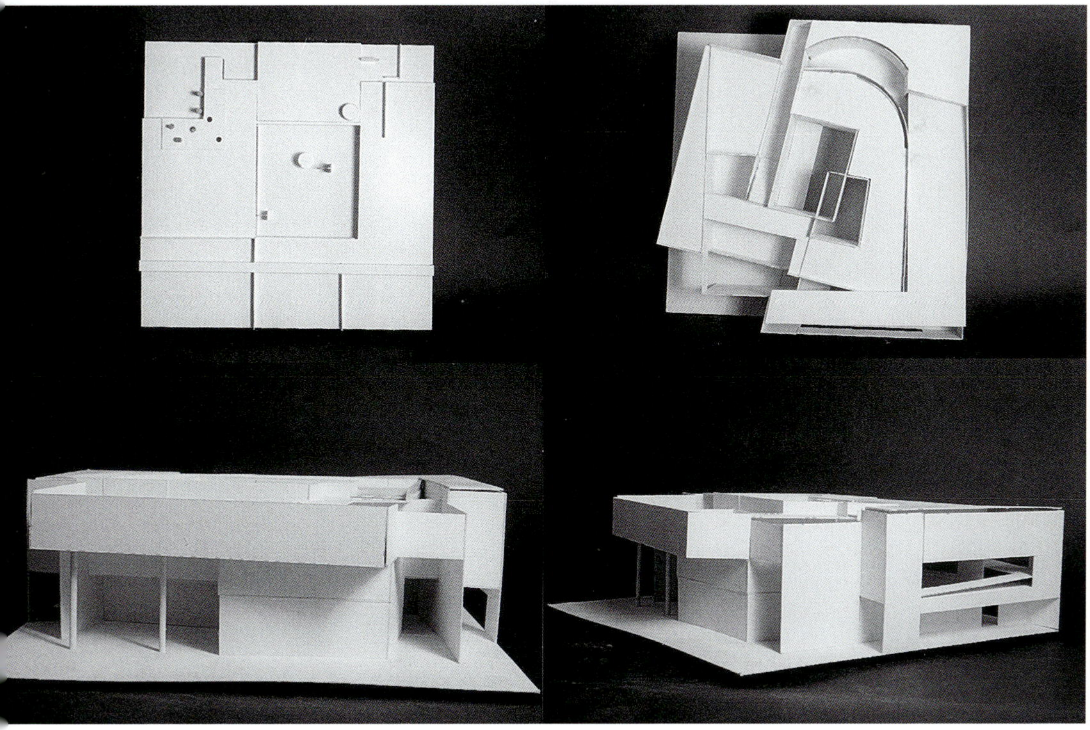

fig. 4. The magic box exercise, student projects, Geneva School of Architecture.

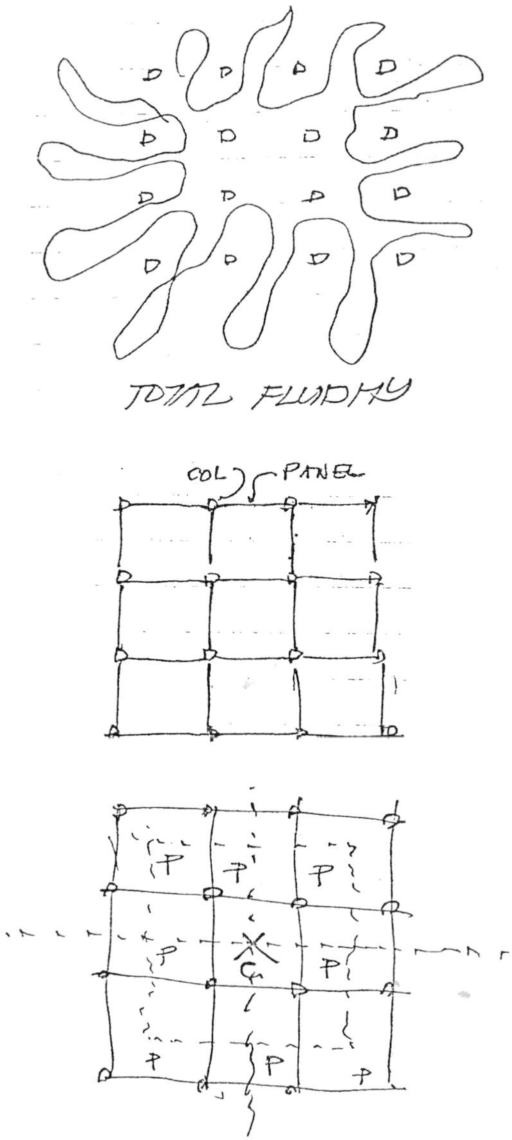

fig. 5. John Hejduk, sketch "the nine square problem", Cooper Union.

A language of its own

Michel Kagan was undoubtedly able to deepen his pedagogical roots by working alongside John Hejduk[2] and his distinctive teaching at New York's Cooper Union in the '80s (fig. 5). If reference is made here to a language specific to architecture, it is to insist once again on the structural—or structuralist—dimension of Michel Kagan's pedagogical approach, of which the metropolitan tower exercise is, in my view, the most accomplished synthesis and the richest in meaning for students in their studio project work.

In Ferdinand de Saussure's course on general linguistics: *"every language (is) like a system in which each of the elements is definable only by the relations of equivalence or opposition that it maintains with the others, this set of relations forming the structure..."*[3]

Michel Kagan shared with those who taught with him his constant quest to get as close as possible to the idea of a certain form of structure in architectural knowledge, and to the very notion of structure in particular. In a multi-scale, interlocking project (like the Russian "matryoshka" doll), several specific types of structure of different orders, articulated by reciprocal relations of opposition or equivalence, must necessarily "come together" at the final stage of the project, to bring out the mental structure of the building. This structure carries the overall meaning of an architectural form that can only "stand tall" if everything in it expresses this construction from within, in the very depth of the project's spatial incarnation.

In the same vein, the student can only "stand upright" in the field of architectural knowledge if his or her pedagogical learning has structured this idiosyncratic knowledge as a personal language of architecture, specific to the understanding of a spatiality whose meaning can then be shared by others.

In the pedagogical process of the Tower project, five essential forms of structuration are involved for the student:

— structuring based on the near and distant context: relationship to the territory, to the

2. John Hejduk, *Mask of Medusa* (New York: Rizzoli International Publications, 1989).

3. Ferdinand de Saussure, *Cours de linguistique générale* (Paris: Payot, 1916).

nearby city, to the ground, to the sky, as an urban sign, for escapes, signaling, frontality... (fig. 6a, 6b, 6c)

— structuring based on the redefinition of the program and its spatial transcription, ordered as a vertically assembled type according to particular modes.

— structuring based on access spaces and general distribution (halls, sky lobbies, elevators, escalators), intrinsically associated with particular modes of vertical typological repetition: simple superposition, rotation, inversion, opposition...

— constructive structuring, in its ability to transcend spatial arrangements and implement the evidence of stability (stability of form / stability of the whole)

— finally, the structuring effect of spatial devices, articulations, and the particular use of light.

It took me some time, I confess, to discern at the outset what the Tower exercise had to do with the other pedagogical exercises in the curriculum that Michel Kagan had been patiently developing over the years, due to the unusual scale of the project, which quickly led to the prejudice that the tower is an architectural type apart, unclassifiable in the order of prototypical buildings from which the discipline of

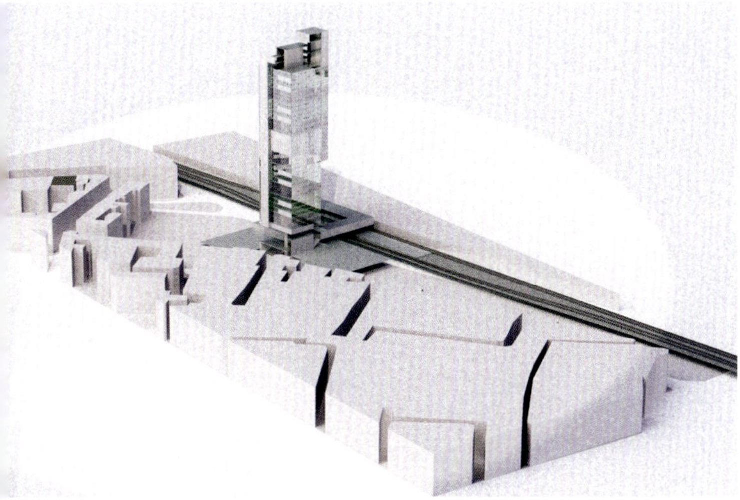

fig. 6a. Axonometric view of the tower and its relationship to the tracks it serves, Clamart project, Virginie Pernot, ENSA Versailles 2004–2005.

fig. 6b. Perspective view of the tower, volumes, relationship to the ground, relationship to the sky, Clamart project, Virginie Pernot, ENSA Versailles 2004–2005.

fig. 6c. Chloé Wawrzyniak project, Seine Riverfront, ENSA Versailles 2005–2006.

fig. 7. The matrix on a cubic base and its repetition, Fanny Dohen, ENSA Versailles 2005-2006.

fig. 8. Placing opacities, repetition, and solid-void alternation, Laurent Bariat, ENSA Versailles 2005-2006.

architecture has always been taught, whether from classical treatises or modern manifestos. At the time, I saw in this unprecedented exercise the audacity of taking on a difficult subject, linking it to the doctrinal upheaval provoked in the last century by the birth of vertical metropolises (Metropolitan Highrise), and seizing the opportunity to go beyond the rationalist syntax of the modern masters by renewing the question of vertical spatiality in the European cultural context of the urban project.

Genesis of the form

It was only when Michel Kagan showed us the striking drawing of Raimund Abraham's project for the Times Square competition in New York in 1984 that I understood how directly the Tower exercise was linked to the question of the genesis of architectural and urban form, to its meaning, and how it brought into play several of his personal pedagogical resources:

— work on the *type and its rational repetitions*, here accentuated in the vertical dimension and specific scale of a very particular type (a multiple type composed of the assembly of several sub-types) in the tower model, initially dimensioned on the elementary shape of a 25-metre cube.
— work on *elementary forms* (fig. 7)
— work on the *mental structure* (the preliminary figure), calling from the outset for several orders of intuitive structuring destined to merge in the future project, and bringing into play the question of hypotheses, then the validation of devices, and the realization of their meaning at the end of the exercise.

— work on *vertical public space*, here interior and exterior, associated with the concept of the *architectural promenade*, developed here in height and based on a model of a vertically practiced street.
— work on the question of *superimposed scales* (matryoshkas) and the measurement of these differentiated scales.
— work on determining the right place for (structuring) and *significant opacities* in the project. (fig. 8)
— finally, work on *lifting up and lightness*, inseparable from work on any tower and often materialized by the device of *folding*.

Territorial integration

The Tour métropolitaine exercise targets a number of sites in Paris, including the Bastille (at the end of the "Coulée verte"), the Porte Maillot (on the major historic East/West axis, bordering the Boulevard périphérique) as well as the Île Seguin (in the meander of the river).

Here, we can see the importance of the territorial nature of the exercise, and the profound relationship between the horizontal axes and networks that partition the city's ground and the need for vertical emergence as the culmination of this horizontal energy projected into the sky. Beyond its sign and anchoring effect, the Tower's origins lie in the upturn of structural lines expressed in the reference ground of the lower town (fig. 9).

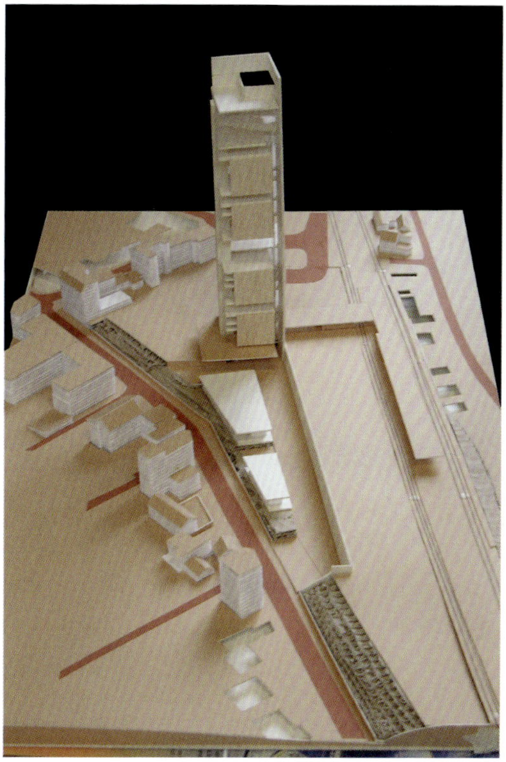

fig. 9. Territorial Inscription and relation to the urban ground. Emanuela Marinska, project in Clamart, ENSA Versailles 2004–2005.

The pretext of program

From a pedagogical point of view, since the teaching method specific to this project involves a theoretical approach and is intended to lead to significant typological work, the Tower exercise is marked by the need to avoid at least two major difficulties inherent to its theme, and therefore necessarily to its program.

The exercise is based on the intention of treating each space in the project with the same intensity of use and the same spatial qualities, without sacrificing any of them on the altar of a repetition that would only be initiated by financial rationality, and therefore could not be part of a realistic approach that could have led to two major pedagogical fallacies:

— on the one hand, to avoid structuring the project around the quasi-planetary programmatic model of the Anglo-Saxon high-rise and its two codified versions: speculative skyscraper / corporate skyscraper, both of which, with a few variations, are marked by a situation of extreme land pressure (exorbitant value of land ownership), leading inevitably to a project of maximum development of floor areas multiplied according to a principle of vertical extrusion as generated both by the constructive structure (the core, the central structural nucleus) and by the distributive structure (the elevators).

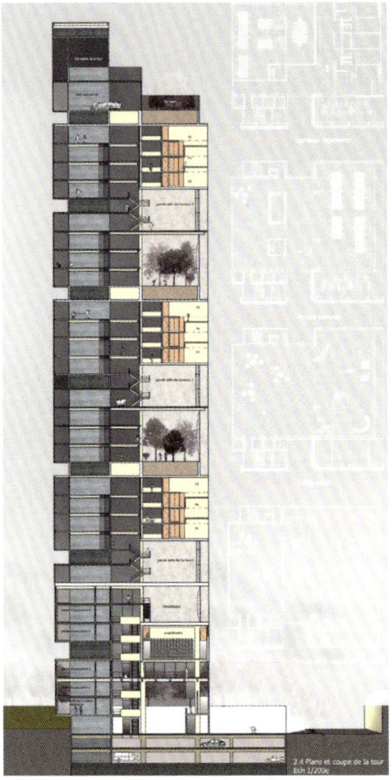

fig. 10. & 11. Circulation and the vertical articulation of modules, Florian Foucault and Florian Mathieu, EAV 2004-2005.

— on the other hand, to avoid structuring the project as an object of urban design focused on the out-of-scale formal work of a sculptural mega-form whose rationale is based solely on its external plastic effect, without any of the inner reasons mentioned above.

Michel Kagan's intention was to stand in stark contrast to the quasi-planetary model of the Anglo-Saxon speculative private tower, extruded over dozens of repetitive, standardized floors and devoid of any quality of use (topped by penthouses signifying the places of power at its summit alone), but also to the tower as urban design object, whose morphogenesis is structured solely by the relationship maintained by the exterior envelope with its context.

Each student is therefore asked to reinterpret a program with a public dimension, bearing within itself the contingency of a major spatial development on the scale of a 25-meter megatype articulated in its specific mode of vertical repetition. (fig. 11)

Taking up R. Abraham's idea for the Time Square competition, the initial program was based on the superimposition of cinema theatres (Metropolis...), which allowed for a major development of distribution spaces and their articulation in the height of the tower, but also the installation of the structural opacities that the darkness required in the theatres naturally justified.

Other programs, always with a public vocation, were tried out, such as the vertical promenade museum, and mixed office-housing programs were also explored, always implementing a strong structuring of the vertical architectural promenade through the meeting and distribution spaces of the tower, here thought of as a vertical urban island reinterpreting the themes of the street, the square, the residential building or even the urban park, here lifted into the sky.

Beyond the "typological" exercise of a single tower at the outset, the contingency of a pedagogical exploration of a project on a more assertive "territorial" scale became apparent over time, as part of an inter-reactive and shared composition of tower projects multiplied and juxtaposed by students on sites and territories already historically involved in the major contemporary metropolitan transformations we are experiencing.

In an educational project in which the original concept of the "Metropolitan Tower" has been able to evolve into the very concept of a possible "vertical European city", that of "living high up", a project that we have been able to undertake in recent years in Paris—Val de Seine with Nathalie Régnier-Kagan, and subsequently with Laurent Beaudouin.

In the final stages of this project, we emphasised the goal of creating a "vertical garden city", a reinterpretation—beyond Babel—of another mythical construction, that of the "Hanging Gardens" of Babylon: by proposing this unprecedented urban "figure" capable of reclaiming, through height, the right metropolitan density now being sought, necessarily articulated at a territorial level around de-carbonised transport networks, in a new balance between the dense city and the nature of the metropolis, where the freeing up of land undertaken here makes it possible to rediscover, on a large scale, the natural space (the great urban "Park", like Central Park) essential to urban life, and indispensable to the positive perception of the high density of this form of "vertical" City by its inhabitants (fig. 12a, 12b).

The programmatic question, here set in its urban dimension of a strong and necessary vertical mix, is in the exercise only the pretext, as we can see, for an archetypal and typological reflection based on a search for the essential reasons for the morphogenesis of a vertical architectural project for the City and its public space, in a reinvented "Urban Landscape" project.

Over and above the issues of non-standard scale and disproportion, which, through a magnifying effect, make all the particular problems of the project process even more obvious, the Metropolitan Tower exercise essentially re-interrogates the project at all scales, at the end of the student's curriculum.

fig. 12a. & 12b. "Jardins de L'Arche" Towers (Swing), nightview and sketch, Atelier 2/3/4/, Paris, 2018.

Contrary to the myth of Babel, the modern archetype of the tower is no longer the cause of the confusion of languages and the hermeticism of discourse that makes communication between people impossible: architecture speaks, the project stands upright in the city.

Understanding is at work.

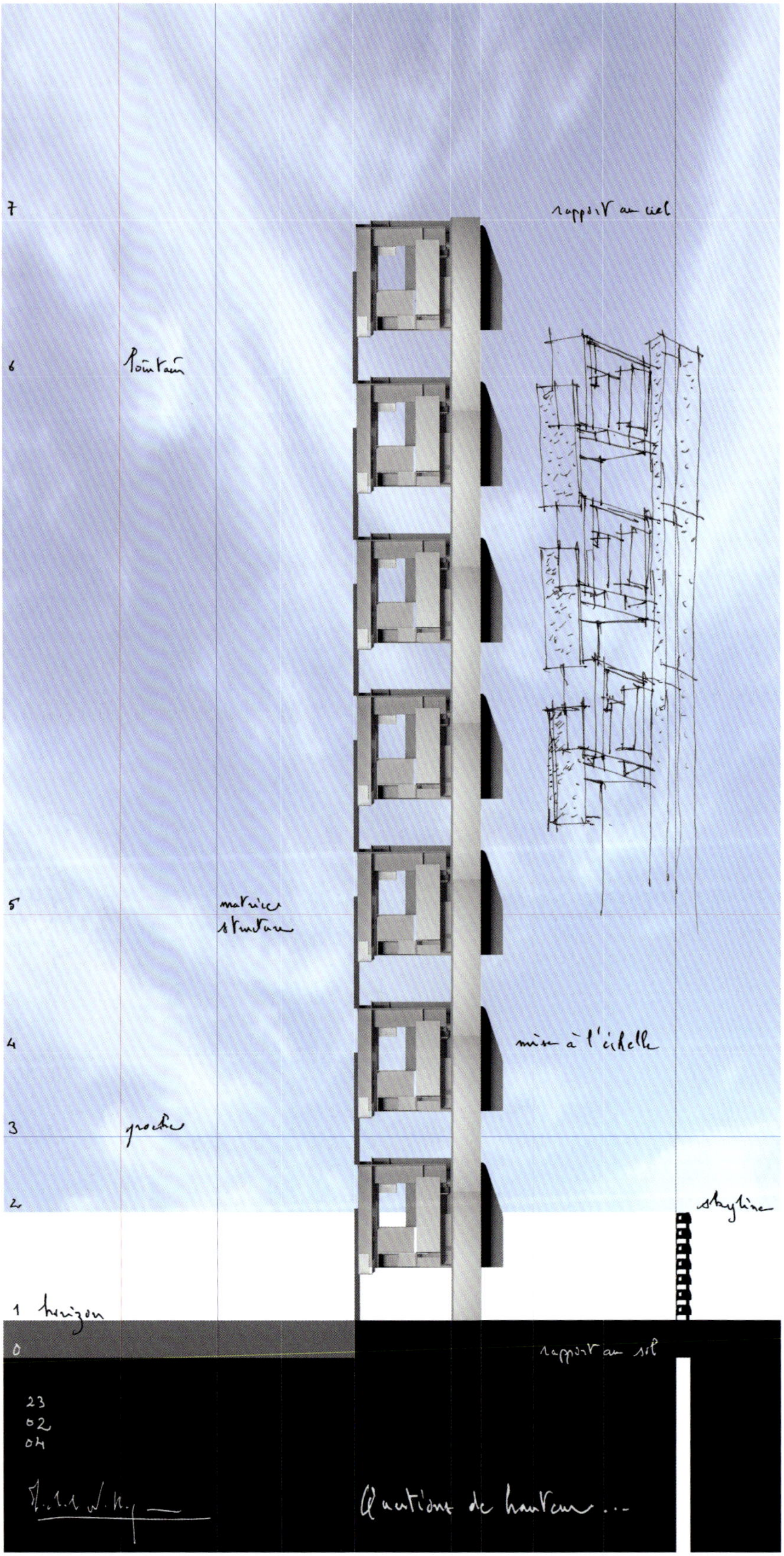
rapport au ciel
7
6
lointain
5
matrice
structure
4
mise à l'échelle
3
proche
2
skyline
1
horizon
0
rapport au sol
23
02
04
Questions de hauteur ...

A Tall Building in an Urban Zone: From Cimbéton to Trophée Béton

Norbert Laurent

Michel Kagan's passion and commitment to architecture extended far beyond his work and teaching. As a professor at the *École nationale supérieure de Paris-Belleville*, he developed a thought-provoking and pedagogical approach to the issue of metropolitan towers, which has spread far beyond the academic world through the positions he took on contemporary towers in a variety of contexts.

As part of the preparations for the seventh 2004–2005 session of the "*Bétons, matière d'architecture*" competition, Michel Kagan was one of the personalities invited by Cimbéton to take part in the advisory committee, whose debates are designed to establish the theme and subject for consideration by architecture and engineering school students. During the discussions at the first meeting, Michel Kagan presented and explained the method and pedagogy of the "Metropolitan Tower" exercise he had assigned to his project group and suggested that it provided food for thought for the theme of the upcoming competition. A number of participants agreed, believing that the question of high-rise buildings was a forward-looking and interesting one for students to ponder. It should be borne in mind, however, that at the time, the subject of towers had negative connotations for a significant number of people. The issue of building densification in urban areas was not a topical one, and there were no plans yet to rebuild high-rise buildings in Paris, or in certain regional metropolises. The advisory committee's discussions therefore focused on the merits of such a theme and its potential to attract students. Over the course of the discussions, Michel Kagan argued his initial point by referring to numerous examples of American towers, as well as examples of towers built in the Netherlands, Germany, and Asia. I can't recount here all the arguments exchanged between the participants, but I have fond memories of high quality, fascinating debates to which Michel Kagan brought all his culture and the refinement of his thinking. At the end of its two meetings, the Advisory Committee unanimously and enthusiastically proposed the theme of high-rise construction for the seventh 2004–2005 session of the "*Bétons, matière d'architecture*" competition.

fig. 1. Sketch by Michel Kagan, Cimbéton competition poster, 2004.

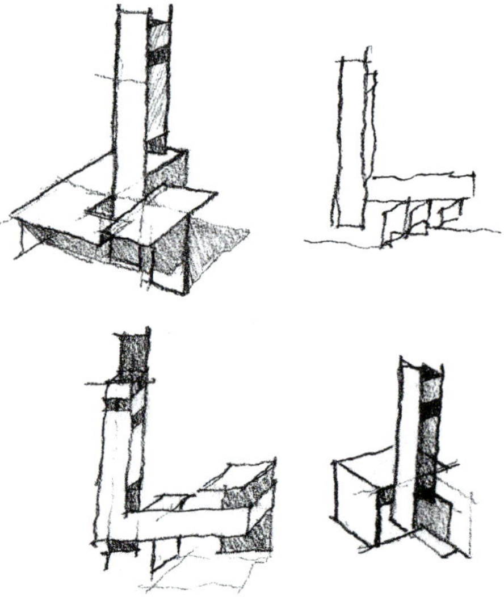

fig. 2. Project by Anne-Lise Verlyck, developed for the Cimbéton competition from studio work, honorable mention EAV 2005.

fig. 3. Study sketch, project by Nicolas Lancereau. ENSAPB 2004-2005.

Michel Kagan's contribution to this session of the Cimbéton competition was not limited to his participation on the advisory committee. At the request of Mr. Roland Dallemagne (Cimbéton), the competition commissioner, he designed and produced the illustration for the competition's launch poster. The image can also be found on the cover of the brochure presenting the theme, subject and rules of the consultation, as well as on the cover of the results brochure. This image shows the virtuosity and precision of Michel Kagan's drawing, which expresses the conceptual and prospective challenges of the competition's theme (fig. 1).

Through the themes of urban density and high-rise construction, the aim of the competition was to encourage students to reflect on the contribution of high-rise buildings to urban redevelopment, with a view to sustainable urban version. The question of urban density was raised, in particular by questioning the notion of qualified density. Density is not in itself a negative factor, but it needs to be modulated and made acceptable to residents, depending on the context. In certain circumstances, tall buildings can be useful, creating a sense of urban centrality, or even contributing to a better ecological balance. The symbolic dimension and aesthetics of the high-rise building were also proposed for the students' consideration. From the evolution of its significance in the city to the invention of new architectural forms, made possible by innovative materials and new technologies, a vast field of exploration was open to designers (fig. 2 and 3). The same applied to programming, by inviting competitors to study the relationship between a relevant programmatic mix and the development of a form of urban living at height. The projects submitted at the end of the consultation showed that the theme of "A tall building in an urban area", despite its complexity, had captured the imagination of the participants. At the three proposed sites in Clamart, Grenoble, and Rennes, almost all the projects

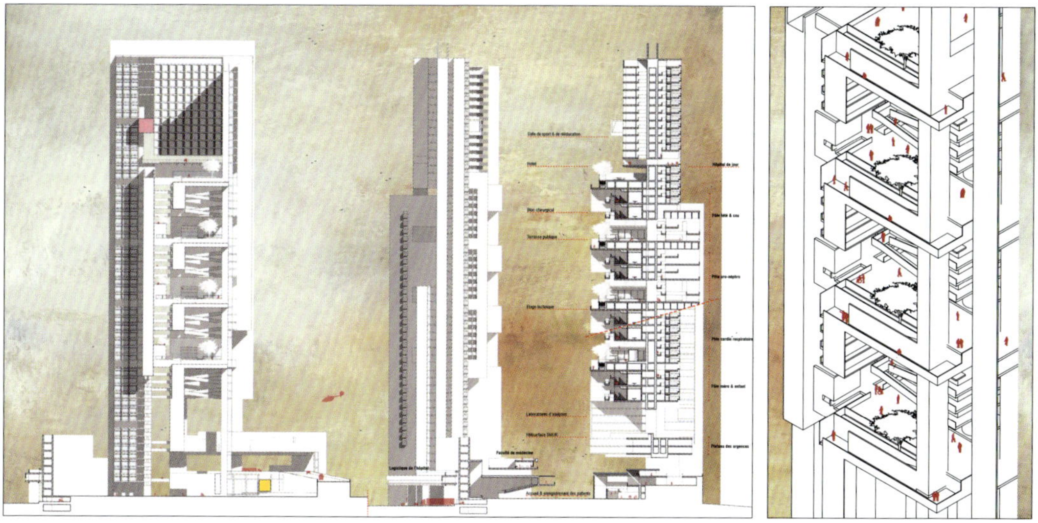

fig. 4. "La Ville debout", final-year project by Russell Jagger. ENSA Normandie 2015. Honorable mention Trophée Béton competition 2016.

had departed from the classic high-rise models, and proposed, with great creative imagination, veritable pieces of the vertical city.

At the end of this evocation, I am reminded of Le Corbusier's phrase: "*Pleine main j'ai reçu—Pleine main je donne*" ("Full hand I receive—Full hand I give"). Michel Kagan's work as an architect, teacher and educator of architecture is a vibrant testimony to this epigram.

Trophée Béton

The Trophée Béton competition, organised by the associations Bétocib, CIMbéton and the Fondation École Française du Béton, under the patronage of the French Ministry of Culture and Communication, replaced the CIMbéton competition in 2012. The aim of the competition is to showcase young graduates of architecture schools, sponsor them and give them visibility at the start of their professional lives. It invites future architects to consider the aesthetic, technical and environmental qualities of concrete. It awards prizes to final-year projects whose architecture and constructive performance highlight the use of concrete: architect-engineer teams are encouraged to work together. The jury is made up of architects and engineers, as well as a representative of each partner, with one guest from abroad. For the first three years of its existence, the jury was chaired successively by Paul Chemetov, Emmanuelle Colboc and Nasrine Seraji. The fourth edition, in 2016, was chaired by Nathalie Régnier-Kagan.

The project by Russel Jagger, a young graduate of the School of Architecture of Rouen, was one of the projects singled out. It took a fresh look at the issue of the tower in the city and the idea of the Vertical City. The challenge was an experimental one, involving thinking about how to articulate the complex programme of a hospital in a vertical space (fig. 4).

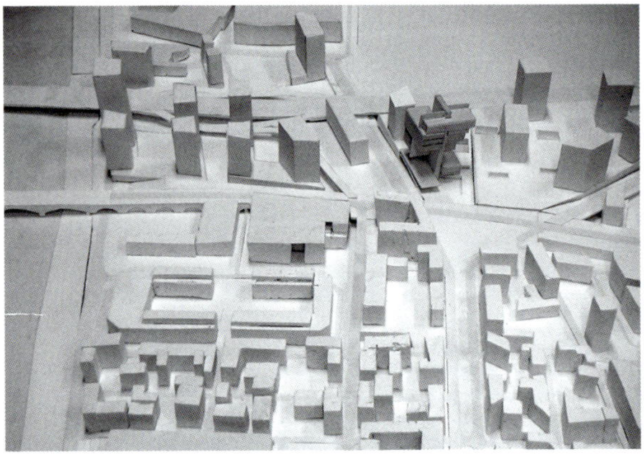

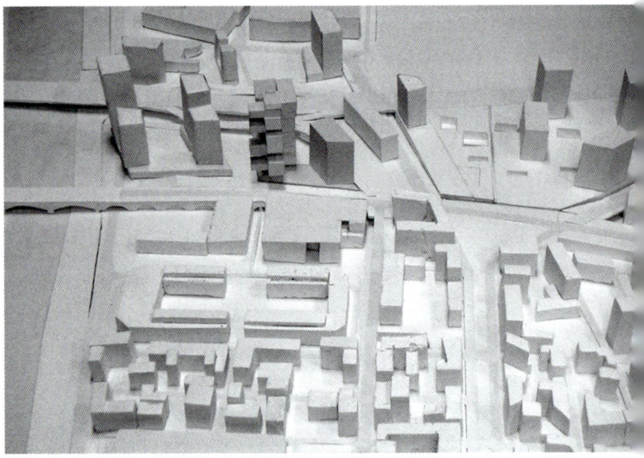

fig. 1. Student interim review at the Politecnico di Torino, 2008.

fig. 2a. & 2b. Study models inserted into the site Massena-Bruneseau, 2007–2008.

Designing an Innovative Structure for a European Tower

Pierre-Alain Croset

I had been familiar with Michel Kagan's pedagogical work on the theme of "the metropolitan tower" for some years and was very keen to experiment with a similar approach with our students at Politecnico di Torino. The opportunity arose in the form of a multidisciplinary design studio entitled "Structures and Constructive Form", which I had been running since 2003 with structures professor Paolo Napoli. The pedagogical challenges of this 14-week design studio, within the new master's degree entitled "Architecture and Construction", include verifying how structural choices condition architectural form, and offering students not only methodological and conceptual instruments, but also computational and calculation tools to fully master structural design (fig. 1). Students are asked to develop an architectural project based on a given structural typology. This collaborative design approach, in which architects and structural engineers teach together, is conceived to highlight the importance of teamwork in designing complex buildings.

With Paolo Napoli, we wanted to experiment with a deep beams structure that would radically rethink high-rise architecture. In a "traditional" high-rise, the volume is defined by the envelope, which is in principle continuous, enclosing the floors supported by the structural core. A deep beams structure challenges the relationship between core, floors and envelope: the tower is conceived as a superposition of self-supporting cantilevered volumes assembled around one or more cores. Our concept was inspired by William Lescaze's famous design for New York's MoMA, conceived in 1931 (fig. 3), in which exhibition spaces were stacked in staggered rows to guarantee zenithal lighting for all rooms. We also wanted the exceptional character of the structure, and therefore the consequent architectural form, to be justified by a highly public program (sports facilities). The choice of site was linked to the current debate in Paris on high-rise construction: the ZAC Masséna-Bruneseau, according to the urban project defined by Yves Lion (fig. 4), envisaged a dense fabric of 50-metre-high buildings, complemented by a series of high-rise towers, up to 200 meters high. Our students' projects had to take these urban planning guidelines into account, and each student had to find a precise location for his or her tower, 100 to 120 metres high, while seeking

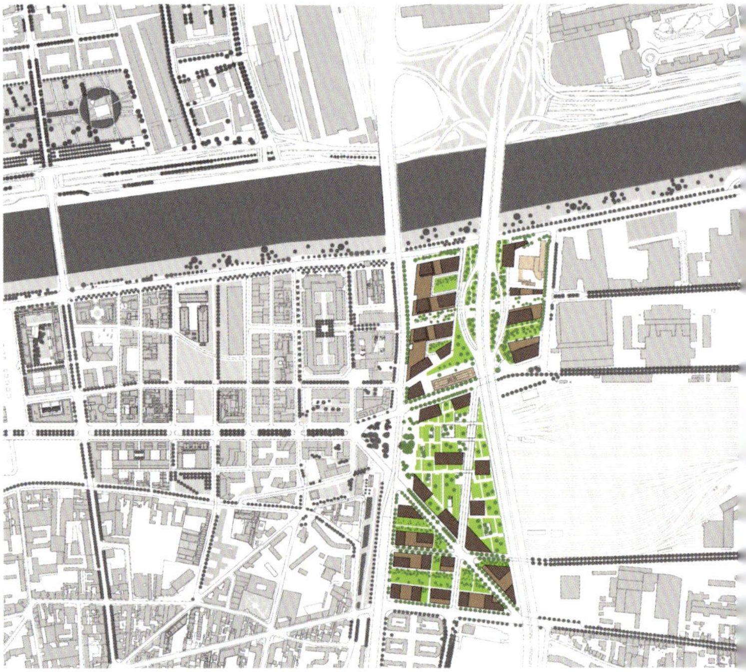

fig. 3. William Lescaze's design for MoMA, New York, 1931.

fig. 4. Yves Lion project for the Masséna-Bruneseau site, Paris 13th, 2006.

to take advantage of the most remarkable features of the site: the views over the Seine and central Paris, the long perspective of the Avenue de France, the symbolic boundary of the *Boulevard Périphérique* (fig. 2a and 2b).

Our design studio was organized into three phases of work. In the first phase—lasting 4 weeks—the theoretical principles of deep beams structures were taught intensively, in parallel with an initial exploration, using cardboard models, of the architectural form generated by the superimposition of cantilevered volumes. The aim of this formal exploration was not only to concretely verify the structural principles set out by the theory, but also to reason about the notion of balance—both in the sense of the static equilibrium of the tower's overall form, and in the sense of harmony between the various volumes making up the whole. The second phase—5 weeks — began with a trip to Paris to get to know the project site and visit a series of significant towers (Front de Seine, La Défense, Tour Albert). As each student had already acquired the basics needed to design a complete tower project, they had to choose a precise site within Yves Lion's urban plan and develop the tower at 1/500 and 1/200 scales. This work phase ended with an intermediate submission and a collective review of the projects. During the third phase—5 weeks — the structural project was developed, with calculation of the general equilibrium, and the dimensioning of the most heavily loaded deep beams. The more significant construction details were then developed, in particular for the facade cladding. The final review of the projects took into consideration both the expressive qualities of the architectural form, in relation to the characteristics of the urban site, and the control of the tower's structural choices and constructive aspects. Discussions with Michel Kagan and his students at the *École d'architecture de Paris-Belleville* developed over 2007 and 2008, following the decision to work on the same site in the ZAC Masséna–Bruneseau. Our discussions focused on the urban values of the "metropolitan tower": to what extent can a tower, as an exceptional and typically "modern" architectural object, contribute to urban re-generation? Can it establish a meaningful relationship with the context? To further this debate, a seminar was organized with Nathalie Régnier-Kagan at the École d'Architecture de Paris Val-de-Seine (October 13, 2008), inviting Éric Lapierre, Jacques Ferrier and Jean Mas to present their tower projects. It was important for our students to be directly involved in the Parisian debate on high-rise construction, and to be able to exchange their experiences with students from Paris-Belleville. These exchanges continued during Michel Kagan's trip to Turin with his students (16-18 December, 2008) (fig. 5) to take part in the final review in our design studio, and to present our students with their own project hypotheses in the form of an intermediate submission. This confrontation between different teaching methods was highly stimulating for our students, and I took part in the final review of the Paris-Belleville students' projects in February 2009. Our design studio required students to produce an architectural project in a single semester, studied in detail in terms of its structural and constructive components, and this obliged them to limit their thinking about the urban project, and therefore to accept as such the master plan defined by Yves Lion. Michel Kagan's teaching method was more radical in its questioning of the already-defined urban project, forcing students to think about an urban composition for the entire site that emphasized the public vocation of the ZAC Masséna–Bruneseau. While our students' projects focused primarily on defining the architectural object and its interaction with a context considered unchangeable (fig. 8a, 8b and 9), the Paris-Belleville students' projects proposed genuine urban "visions", insofar as the "metropolitan tower" project was to be at the same time the design of its context.

Epilogue

Michel Kagan made me discover all the architectural and educational interest of the theme of the "metropolitan tower", but also the critical issues of an architectural typology that I wrongly judged as necessarily "out of scale" within the dense fabric of the European city.

fig. 5. Michel Kagan at the jury of the Croset-Napoli design studio, Turin, December 18, 2008.

fig. 6. Project by Maria El Tabib for Rijeka, Politecnico di Milano, 2022-2023.

fig. 7a. & 7b. Project by Ekaterine Meskhi and Ani Periashvilli for Rijeka, Politecnico di Milano, 2022-2023.

fig. 8a. & 8b. Project by Manuele Mandrile, Politecnico di Torino, 2007-2008.

fig. 9. Project by Davide Pallaro and Elisa Valpreda, 2008-2009.

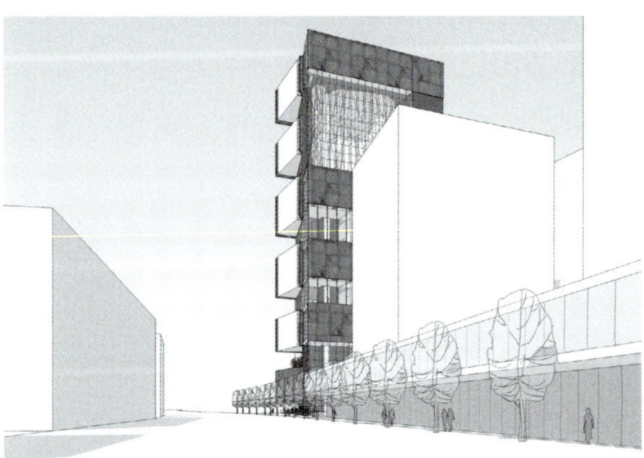

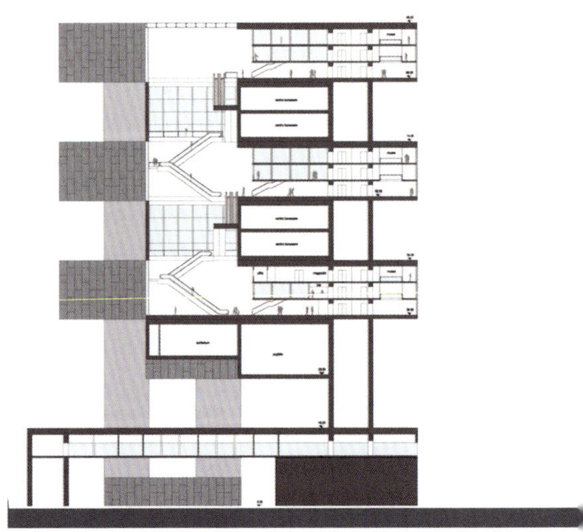

fig. 10. Collage by Maria El Tabib.

fig. 11. Collage by Ekaterine Meskhi and Ani Periashvilli 2023.

The architectural results of our students' best projects were surprising to me. Composed spatially as a montage of large volumes, and not as the traditional superposition of floors, the tower with a deep beam structure offers the image of a vertical "urban composition", which has real squares and hanging gardens suspended at different levels, which constitute new forms of public spaces.

I returned to the "metropolitan tower" exercise more than ten years later, following my transfer to the Politecnico di Milano, as a design studio of the Master's degree in architecture and urban design. To encourage the strong demand for social exchanges which followed the pandemic crisis of 2020–2021, the idea of a vertical assemblage of urban functions was enriched with the principle of mixing cultural functions (library, theater, gallery of art) and sports, with the aim of creating a "social condenser", inspired by the SESC (Serviço Social do Comércio) programs in São Paulo. This new program made it possible to renew the structural typology, to the extent that the different volumes containing the activities have greatly diversified in terms of dimensions, distribution, and use. At the heart of the design work remained determining the significant relationship between the tower and the urban context. The best proposals for the cities of Split (2021–2022) and Rijeka (2022–2023), along the Croatian coast, demonstrate that the tower can strongly enhance an urban context still marked by traces of the recent industrial past, but also constitute a strong landmark in the landscape which manifests the primacy of the public and collective value of architecture.

fig. 1. Milan skyline from the Duomo roof.

Metropolitan Towers as Urban Infrastructures

Elena Fontanella

I was lucky enough to attend Michel Kagan's architectural design studios in the academic year 2007/08, when I studied at the *École Nationale Supérieure d'Architecture de Paris Belleville* as part of the Erasmus programme. Relations between the School of Architecture of *Politecnico di Milano* and ENSA-Paris Belleville had been established for some time in this period, through the workshops organised in Bergamo (LIPAU – *Laboratorio Internazionale di Progettazione Architettonica e Urbana*) by the group of lecturers and researchers coordinated by Sergio Crotti, and in the Bachelor's degree course in the design studio taught by Ilaria Valente in the third year. From the academic year 2005/06 onwards, the design topic of her course was a tower in the Milanese fabric of the Bicocca district: a portion of the university campus developed upwards. The programme included student accommodation and services, and was an opportunity to link the fabrics divided by the railway at the Milano-Greco Pirelli station.

Un cahier à pages blanches

Every year, Michel Kagan led two design studios in Belleville: one in the first semester and one in the second, as well as a course on architectural theory. That year, the studio devoted to the *tour métropolitaine* (metropolitan tower) was the focus of the spring semester.

In the first phase, students had to explore different stages of articulation of the tower, and particularly its relationship with the ground and the sky, with the fine-tuning of a principle of spatial definition, repetition and variation. It was only at this point that the site came into play, with the need for a *mise en échelle* (scaling) that dealt with the measurements, the solids and the voids, the structuring and rising elements of each context.

The plot siding the beginning of the *promenade plantée,* Place de la Bastille (11e), and in Place Clichy (18e) were the two sites of reference that year. The choice was free and had to be motivated. Together with the site, there was the programme: seven stacked cinemas, as in Raimund Abraham's well-known project for Times Square in New York.

In the meeting phase between the definition of the spatial principle of the tower and the chosen context, as in the previous and following phases, the manipulation of several study maquettes was fundamental. A large collective maquette of the project site extended to its surroundings was kept in the middle of the classroom: a veritable tool for verifying the *mise à l'échelle*, as well as the relationship to the site. The maquette of the tower was constantly updated and verified in the collective model: white the first, grey the second, so that it was as neutral as possible. We were invited to make simple, quick but effective study models: "*sketch a model*" was Michel Kagan's recurring instruction: the ability to represent the project concept quickly in three dimensions was just as important as knowing how to represent it through sketches on paper, and more precisely on a *cahier à pages blanches* (a blank-page notebook). Each filled page would thus in itself be a small project: the absence of lines and squares as a condition for learning to manage and structure the space on the sheet. The importance of controlling the project through maquettes, on different scales, emerged constantly in his teaching. This was crucial throughout the entire design process, at all stages: not just for the final presentation. For the exams, all the models that were significant for the design development were shown together with the final model: the room was full of white maquettes, which were used perhaps more than the drawings on the boards during the project presentation.

The height, the width of the base, the layout on the ground and top floors, the development of the body of the building: no data were assigned a priori but rather constructed in continuous research that was initially autonomous and then referred to the place, and to the urban fabric of reference.

The tower as infrastructure

This dialectical relationship between project and context was a fundamental element in the design of the metropolitan tower: it is through the project itself that it is possible to provide answers to places awaiting a project. Each project was required to provide a solution to these urban nodes that were as significant for their location as they were lacking solutions from a spatial point of view. This is the case of the plot near the starting point of the *promenade plantée* in the Place de la Bastille. In this case, the metropolitan tower becomes an opportunity to develop a public piece of the city, even with a small fragment of available land: it allows us to look out over the surrounding fabric and at the same time to become a landmark, as well as a reference point for the *promenade plantée* itself, which extends for several kilometres from the heart of Paris to its most peripheral areas. The conquest of verticality, has no choice but to adopt a dialectical relationship with the load-bearing structure: structural and spatial principle feed each other, until they finally coincide. The metropolitan tower, therefore, finds its place in relation to its setting: it accommodates a non-residential programme of spaces for the community, it multiplies the public space by developing it both upwards and internally. It represents a landmark in the contemporary city and is an opportunity to provide solutions to urban nodes in need of new design: from this perspective, it can be considered a veritable urban infrastructure.

The design exercise started by Michel Kagan at the Belleville School of Architecture and renewed by Nathalie Régnier-Kagan at the School in Val-de-Seine, addresses issues of great relevance in current times. Indeed, European cities are going through a transition from a process of growth through the extension of its fabrics to growth on top of the existing fabric: by transformation, densification and replacement. From this perspective, where specific different characteristics emerge for each urban fabric, careful intervention on metropolitan towers limits the footprint on the ground, frees up public space and increases services and spaces for local communities at height: this offers great potential, distancing towers from being just a tool for real estate speculation.

fig. 1a., 1b. & 1c. Studio Kagan, final review with Nikos Ktenàs, 2007–2008.

A case study: a cultural and sports hub in Split

This was the background for the Architectural Design Studio held in the academic year 2021/22 with Pierre-Alain Croset at the School of Architecture of Politecnico di Milano (Master of Science in Architecture and Urban Design). Organised as a 'collaborative class' with Roger Riewe and his students from the Institute of Architecture Technology at the Technical University of Graz, the studio was devoted to the design of a hybrid building integrating cultural functions and sports facilities in a vertical composition. In the aftermath of the COVID-19 pandemic, we have in fact witnessed an increasing demand for places for social gatherings, with a particular focus on intergenerational activities and fostering the coexistence of cultural activities and physical well-being. The post-pandemic cultural and sport hub was conceived as a possible response to these growing needs, particularly in peripheral contexts marked by a prevalent residential monofunctionality and absence of community spaces. The reference context was the city of Split, and specifically the Split3 district, which is extremely interesting both for the reasons behind the settlement and for its architecture. However,

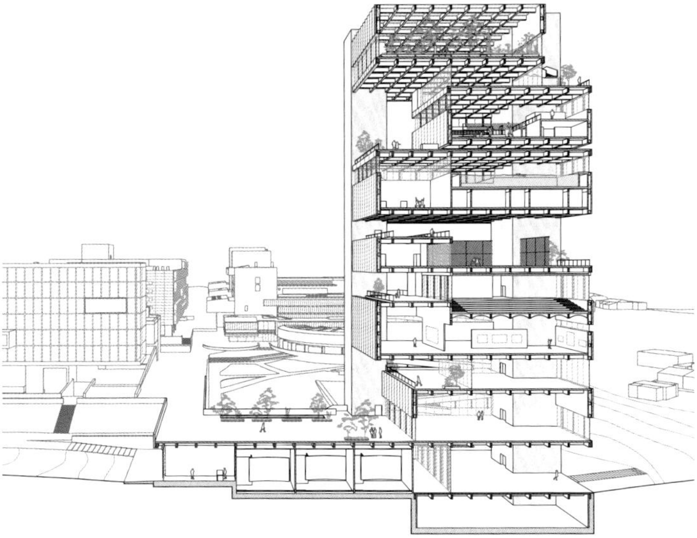

fig. 2. Project by Alina Kim for a cultural and sports hub in Split, Politecnico di Milano, 2021–2022.

fig. 3. Project by Emanuel Sanchez for a cultural and sports hub in Split, Politecnico di Milano, 2021–2022.

today the district needs new spaces for the large local community: hence the identification of three areas in which to experiment the design of a vertically-developed social condenser. The programme for this cultural and sports hub was finalised in relation to the presence of the university, the entry into the city of a major road connecting with the surrounding metropolitan region, and as a reference for the southern part of the district, towards the coast. The organisation of a mixed programme combining sports and cultural functions in a predominantly residential neighborhood demonstrates how tall buildings in the existing urban fabric can be an effective tool for urban regeneration and rethinking of spatial relations. Standing out against the skyline, the tower is a visual landmark: a reference point for the life of the neighborhood and beyond. The organisation of the spaces according to a vertical composition takes public and collective spaces upwards, defining from time to time the different thresholds of transition between public and private. The body of the tower, where the principle of spatial organisation is developed in accordance with a consistent principle of structural definition, includes different degrees of porosity, with public or semi-public spaces at height. Last but not least, the top of the tower offers public users a view of the urban landscape from a new perspective, far from the elitist condition embodied by American penthouses.

Learning about complexity

The teaching of the metropolitan tower is therefore extremely relevant for various reasons. The cases mentioned here, together with the many presented in this volume, allow us to identify the characteristics that make it a building of great interest, not only as a teaching exercise for training young architects, but a real opportunity for the transformation of contemporary urban contexts. In the first place, it enables us to intervene on small plots and to develop programmes multiply vertically public or collective spaces, while controlling the transition from public to semi-public to private. The attachment to the ground of each building is of crucial importance, and this becomes even more significant where the building's footprint on the ground allows us to rethink spatial relations at height in the city, connecting different levels where present (as in the case of Split), or to give access to underground or semi-underground spaces, especially where there is public transport infrastructure, but not only.

The complexity of an urban block is thus given a vertical dimension, ensuring higher quality of densification and consequent intensification of spatial relations that are affecting European cities: the metropolitan tower is unrelated to speculative logic. This is confirmed by its finding, in accordance with current regulations, the right place, dimension and proportion in relation to the surrounding area and its rising elements. Not least, the metropolitan tower represents an important tool for building on the already built environment, both where demolition and reconstruction are foreseen, and in cases where modifying and therefore manipulating existing buildings is preferred. It is an opportunity, in any case, to rewrite the urban palimpsest starting from precise interventions capable of significant impact on their surroundings. Designing in increasingly stratified settings, full of roads and buildings, is a skill that will be necessary among the future generations of architects, who are currently being trained in the Schools of Architecture.

Urban Architectures between Paris, Milan, and Bergamo

Ilaria Valente

Urban architecture(s): This was the subject of our discussions with Michel Kagan during our exchanges between universities[1]. In the course of the international seminars organized by the International Architecture and Urban Design Workshop for almost sixteen years in Bergamo[2]. as a member of the scientific committee, Michel Kagan distinguished himself by his enthusiastic and valuable contributions. These encounters between several generations of architects and teachers from Italian and European schools of architecture consolidated and deepened regular and intense relations. Michel Kagan also participated in the Politecnico di Milano's post-graduate Master's and Doctorate in Architectural and Urban Design, and was also a member of its scientific committee.

In 2006, with Nathalie Régnier-Kagan, he organized internships at the École de Paris-Belleville—as part of a "second-level master's program" for doctoral students in Milan and for our post-graduate students, on the theme of the transformation of the Ile Seguin. He also collaborated on master's theses in Milan on the same subject. In parallel, they subsequently developed the themes of the Bergamo workshop in the context of teaching the project in France. Discussion of the urban project was deepened through reviews in Paris and Versailles, with Sergio Crotti, Andrea Gritti, Nathalie Régnier-Kagan and Jean Mas. Some of our students also came to study in Paris Belleville as part of the "Erasmus" exchanges.

An intersection of points of view

The cross-referencing we were able to do between the lectures given on his work and the critiques and discussions on the students' projects highlighted the coherence with which Michel Kagan linked the teaching and practice of architectural design. I'm convinced of the importance of his ethical stance in his thinking and work as an architect and teacher. In it, he asserted an "attitude of resistance" in the practice of architectural

1. Ilaria Valente is a professor at Politecnico di Milano, see appendix "Contributing authors".

2. *Laboratori Internazionali di Progettazione Architettonica e Urbana* (LIPAU), Politecnico di Milano, Municipality of Bergamo, directed by Sergio Crotti and Roberto Spagnolo.

fig. 1. Piazza Vecchia, Bergamo.

fig. 2. Jean Mas, Michel Kagan, Nathalie Régnier-Kagan, with the students in front of Casa del Fascio, Terragni in 2002.

fig. 3. Jury at a workshop in Bergamo, with Sergio Crotti 2002-2003.

design, thereby to defend the civic content and purpose of architecture, and to block the trends in architectural production associated with both the logic of the market and the processes of mediatization that characterize our times. With great attention and a critical sense, he considered the conditions of transformation and loss of identity of the contemporary city, whose scales, forms, and materials he had repeatedly analyzed. He often deplored the lack of a "vision of the city of the 21st century"[3] It was important for him to question the search for a new identity for the contemporary city, and how architecture could claim a role and legitimacy in the construction of places in which the community could once again recognize itself.

In Milan, the research that characterized the Italian school after the Second World War was devoted to describing and interpreting the forms of the city and urban places, as fundamental instruments and integral parts of the architectural project. From the 1960s onwards, the essential contribution of the Italian school was to consider the city no longer as a coherent whole, but as a fabrication "in parts", with its particular places embodied in "urban architecture". In the Italian approach, we can distinguish two main points of view regarding how to interpret the relationship between project and place. After the idealist approach of Saverio Muratori, who introduced the techniques of typological description to the urban fabric of Venice and linked the morphology of the city to the typology of the buildings, two theoretical hypotheses were clearly formulated. On the one hand, a more static conception that refers to the idea of a crystallized and idealized memory, according to Aldo Rossi's[4] position fueled by the reading of texts by French historians and geographers such as Marcel Poëte or Pierre Lavedan. On the other hand, another line of research was characterized by the major influence of structuralist thought, which led to an idea of site and habitat rather than that of a fabric of stratifications and transformations. This was the position favored by Vittorio Gregotti and summarized in his book *Il territorio dell'architettura*[5], as well as a

3. Michel Kagan, *Parti pris: les espaces modernes sont les lieux modernes*. Conférences Paris d'architectes, (Paris: Pavillon de l'Arsenal, 1996).

4. Aldo Rossi, *L'Architettura della Città* (Venice: Marsilio, 1966), english translation by D. Ghirardo, J. Okman, *The Architecture of the City* (Cambridge: MIT Press, 1984).

fig. 4. Piazza Vecchia, Bergamo.

series of studies developed in the 1960s by his students at the Milan School: Sergio Crotti and Emilio Battisti. Sergio Crotti pursued this direction with rigor and originality for thirty years at the Politecnico di Milano. The themes of the dynamic stratification of urban forms and the possibility of interpreting them through architectural design, developed in Milan and Bergamo with Sergio Crotti, Roberto Spagnolo and others, are those that we are still pursuing today in our doctorate program.

This was our point of contact with Michel Kagan, in a field that brought together different architects in the European milieu, as Ignasi de Solà Morales rightly pointed out, attributing the definition of the "urban project" to a set of studies and projects carried out by Vittorio Gregotti, Alvaro Siza, Rafael Moneo, etc.. This research established urban traces as working material for projects, in contrast to the "generic city" and self-reference to the architecture of the "ideal object", which is part of a decontextualized practice of architectural work.

Italophilie

Michel Kagan's "italophilie", in the meaning introduced by Jean-Louis Cohen, was evoked during a tribute[6] to him at the *École d'architecture de Paris-Belleville*. His interests in Italian architectural culture have been of different kinds and have matured over time: his discovery of Terragni's work in his student days, his interest in the architectural milieu gravitating around the magazine Casabella in the Nineties, and our subsequent academic exchanges. This critical attitude, inherited from the generation born in the '50s, spread throughout European schools of architecture in the '70s, a period during which the reading and discussion of Aldo Rossi's *L'architettura della città* and the research of the Italian school gained recognition in both Europe and the United States. This parallel milieu of

5. Vittorio Gregotti, *Il territorio dell'Architettura*; (Milan: Feltrinelli, 1966).

6. Colloquium held on May 10th, 2010 at ENSA de Paris-Belleville and *"Être et transmettre"* exhibition in tribute to Michel Kagan.

fig. 5. Aerial view of the city of Bergamo, showing the two project sites.

references, and his training with Henri Ciriani, are the deep roots of Michel Kagan's work, in which the project and the architectural work are presented as a synthesis of knowledge of urban facts. His projects are always precisely defined in terms of their relationship to the site and their "scaling". His way of revealing the characteristics of a place through architecture has always been an effective position between continuity and transformation; similarly, his definition of architectural form is a critical transcription of his quest for modernity. In his work, Michel Kagan has always sought to define "modernity" in relation to "contemporaneity", paying close attention to our roots with the aim of building an architecture that would be the expression of a common heritage, of a "new civilization". His contribution to the symposium marking the fiftieth anniversary of the CIAM in Bergamo in 1999, held at the Palazzo della Ragione in Piazza Vecchia (fig. 1 and 4), is also worth mentioning.

From this perspective, Michel Kagan's relationship with the work of Giuseppe Terragni, and his ability to build "urban architectures" as something more than a mere "shaping in a context", is demonstrative of a work attentive to the measure of the urban fabric, to the variations and complexities of its components in contemporary environments. This was certainly an essential message for his students, a major contribution to the development of an ethic to educate new generations of architects (fig. 2). In his critiques and discussions of projects, Michel Kagan had the extraordinary ability to give the key to the architectural interpretation of a place, and to shift the student's point of view to help him better understand and define the objectives and content of his project.

fig. 6. Bergamo 2003-2004, Sant'Agostino Gate.

fig. 7. Bergamo 2002-2003, Sant'Alessandro Gate.

It seems that the crucial common thread in our research has been to consider the project as a "theoretical practice", an action that reconsiders the a priori separation between architectural theory and practice. The effort to develop the foundations of a new urban identity through the architectural project constitutes an experiment in theoretical position-taking. The link between project theory and practice has long been a subject of debate in our doctoral studies. It was this aspect of our research that interested Michel Kagan in the Bergamo laboratory and led him to work with us to build significant experiments in the domain of "urban architecture", within the framework of the doctorate and post-graduate study.

Urban projects for Bergamo and Paris

The projects we shared with Michel Kagan were the confrontation between modern architecture and the historic city in Bergamo, and in Paris, the transformation of industrial wasteland on the Île Seguin, after the demolition of the former Renault factories.

In the case of Bergamo, the themes developed in the LIPAU 16th and 17th editions[7] Seminar were then developed by students from the Paris-Belleville and Versailles schools, under the guidance of Michel Kagan, Jean Mas, Nathalie Régnier-Kagan and Jean-Pierre Laute, and presented successively to international final juries at Versailles and the École de Belleville (fig. 2 and 10).

The projects for the Île Seguin were developed between 2005 and 2006: in September 2005 in the "Atelier de Projet Architectural et Urbain Européen", organized by Michel Kagan and Nathalie Régnier-Kagan at the École de Belleville, for post-graduate Master's students at the Politecnico di Milano; and in Master's theses prepared in Milan within a diploma laboratory on the theme of the Île Seguin. This was the period when the reconstruction of the Ile Seguin was at the heart of the Parisian debate, with an architectural competition aimed at transforming the island.

7. Lipau XVI *"Modern Architecture, Ancient City"* in 2002, Lipau XVII *"Infrastructure Architecture for the Ancient City"* in 2003.

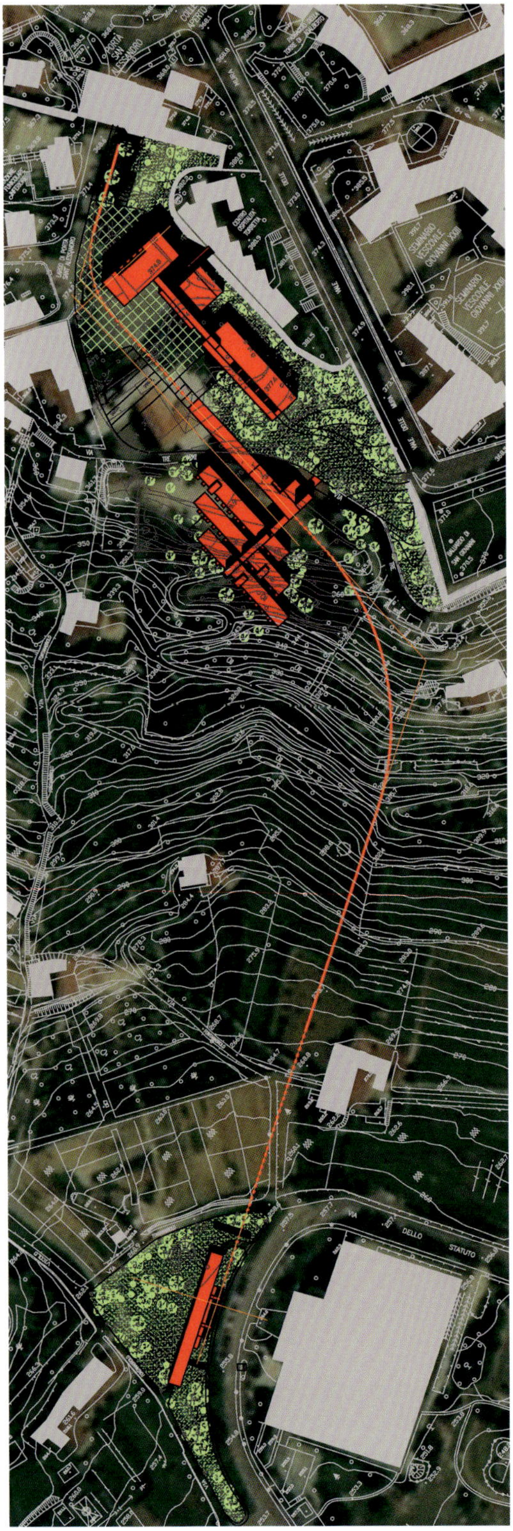

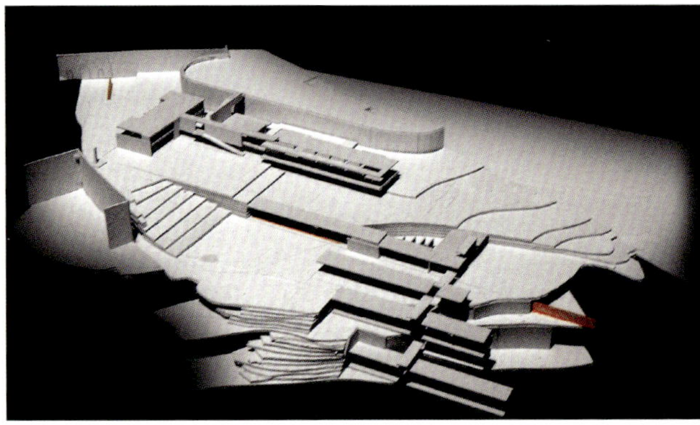

fig. 8 & 9. Project by Xuemei Shao, EAPB, 2002–2003.

fig. 10. Jury at École d'architecture de Versailles, 2002–2003, in the picture, Michel Kagan, Andrea Gritti, Sergio Crotti and Nathalie Régnier-Kagan.

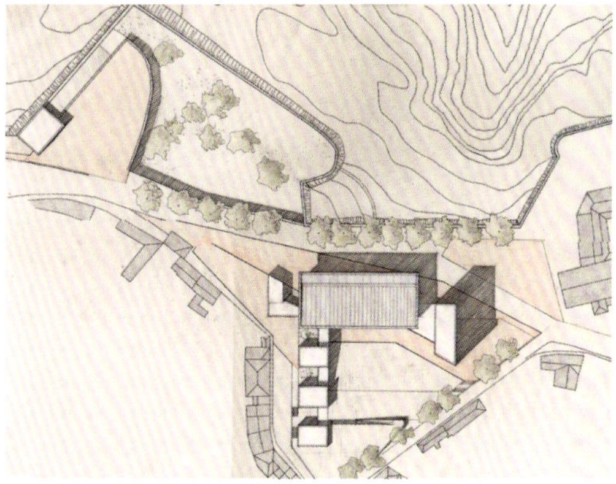

fig. 11. Project by Clément Blanchet, EAV 2003–2004.

The aim was to reorganize the city's boundaries, but on two very different scales. In the case of Bergamo, the city's historical stratification was seen as an "inner" boundary (fig. 5, 6 and 7), while in the case of the Île Seguin, it was an "outer" boundary—of the city of Paris. Among the common themes were the relationship with extraordinary urban landscapes characterized by distinctive topography and the need to consider the relationship between near and far. There was also a need to reflect on the shape of public spaces in the contemporary city, whose dimensions are sometimes altered by interference with the landscape.

In addition, we wanted to expose the students to different types of historical traces. In Bergamo, the ramparts of the Venetian fortifications, the ancient city gates, and the entrances to the upper town made up a system of infrastructures. Their architectural definition is recognizable in the technical forms specific to different periods of the city's construction. It is a system in which the built is built upon the built, where the definition of public space is the outcome of a learned practice, In addition, we wanted to expose students to different types of historical traces. In Bergamo, the ramparts of the Venetian fortifications, the ancient city gates and the entrances to the upper town made up a system of infrastructures. Their architectural definition is recognizable in the technical forms specific to the different periods of the city's construction. A system in which the built is built on the built, where the definition of public space is elaborated in a learned practice, in which contemporary forms and uses are linked above all to the tourist and cultural accessibility of urban space (fig. 8 and 9). The projects developed by the French students in winter enabled them to delve deeper into issues that were only partially addressed in the Bergamo summer workshop (fig. 11). The way in which Michel Kagan worked with his students on architectural sequences, emphasizing the relationship between light and shadow, the tectonics of intervention, was expressed through skillful work on the ground.

fig. 12. Project by Manuela Festa, Andrea Oldani, Ju Sik Yang, International Ph.D. Summer School 2008 - Politecnico di Milano.

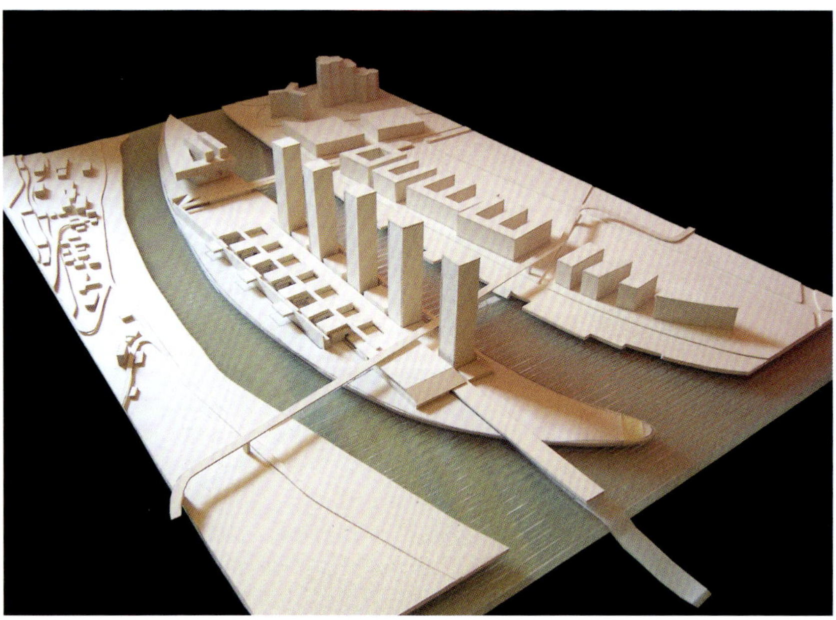

fig. 13. Project by Elena Leggeri, Politecnico di Milano and ENSA Paris-Belleville workshop, 2005.

In the case of the Île Seguin, it was necessary to confront the choice, already largely completed, of demolishing the Renault factories, erasing in one fell swoop the historic traces of the city, and posing the problem of "re-naturalizing" an urban terrain that had become completely artificial. The Île Seguin was an "island-building". In developing the project, Michel Kagan was highly critical of the official projects submitted for the competition, as well as of the idea of rebuilding the entire island as an ordinary city district, with the simulation of an urban front built on the periphery, as the facade of a "Potemkin city". In his view, it was necessary to work on the restitution of a large open space, in keeping with the urban landscape and the great dimensions of the city of Paris. In a very short space of time, he and the Milan master's students developed a project strategy based on the transformation of the ground, working essentially on the "section cut". In the process of formulating the diploma theses in Milan, I extended one of his particularly interesting ideas, which was to consider the history of urban transformations without ignoring their phases, forms and imprints. In one of his hypotheses, Michel Kagan had suggested the theme of the metropolitan tower as the measuring element of urban relationships and the system of green spaces (fig. 12 and 13).

Collaboration with Michel Kagan opened up important avenues for us in design and the teaching of architecture. He gave us an example of patient research and coherent teaching for both architects and students who were lucky enough to meet and work with him.

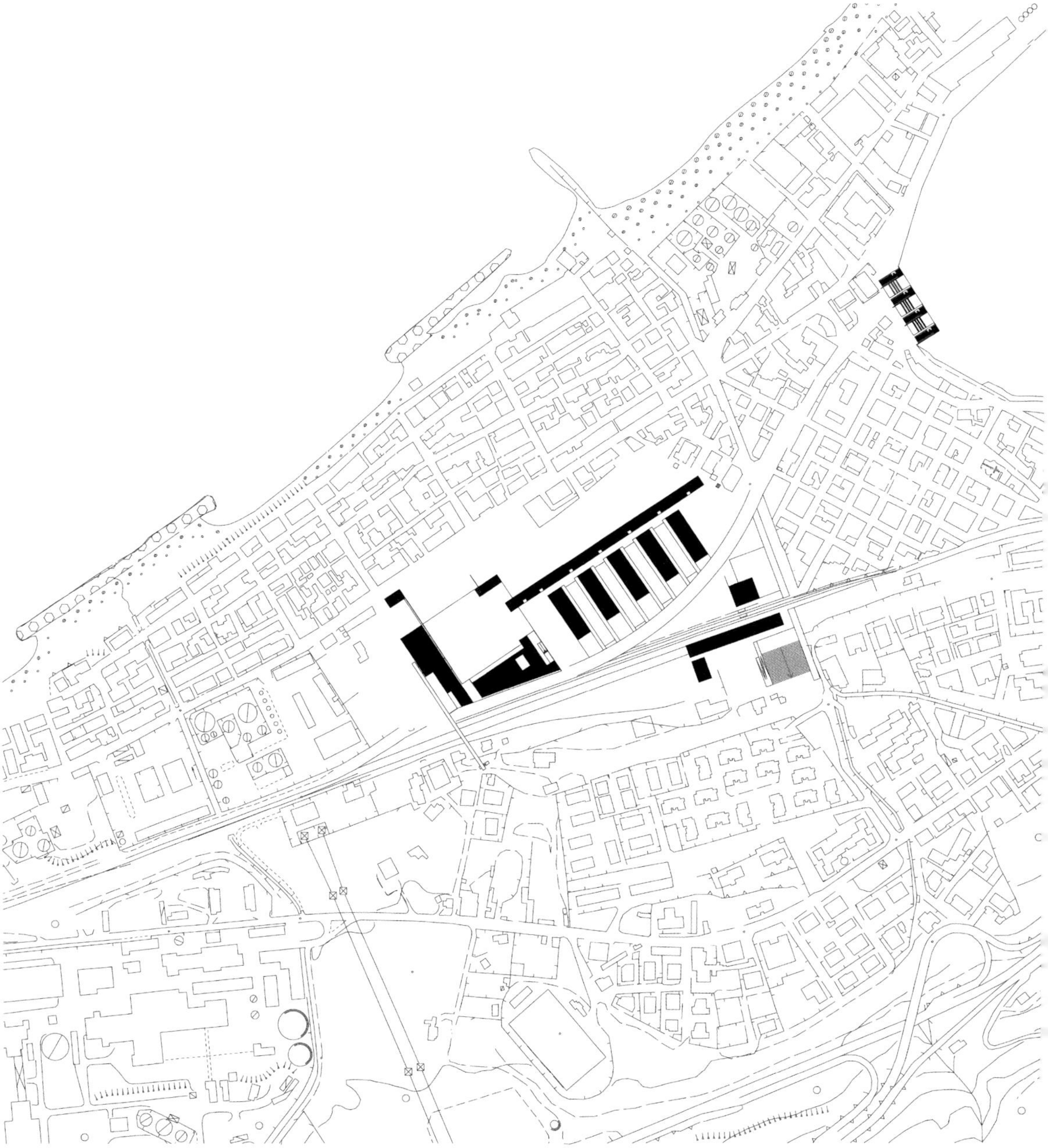

fig. 1. Mass plan of the proposed intervention under the direction of M. Kagan, going beyond the original framework: a territorial scale from Vibo Marina to Vibo Valentia.

Laboratories of Architecture: from Vibo Valentia to Athens

Hervé Dubois

In 2003, Laura Termes and Franco Purini asked Michel Kagan and five Greek, German, Italian, and Spanish architect-teachers to work with a group of fifteen European students for a fortnight, as part of the International Architecture Laboratory, set up by the University of Reggio di Calabria. The chosen subject of study was to be the town of Vibo Valencia, located on the steep west coast of the Calabria region.

The groups of Michel Kagan, Nikos Kténas and Marcello Panzarella were assigned the area of Vibo Marina, a largely self-built agglomeration around an industrial zone located on the coast a few kilometers below the historic town.

Vibo Valencia, maritime city[1]

Three working areas were defined: the port, the residential blocks, and the largely disused industrial zone at the heart of the urban scheme designated to Michel Kagan. In contrast with other workshops, such as those in Bergamo, where pedagogical support consisted in guiding the students' individual research, here Michel Kagan had the opportunity to involve the "*corsisti*" in his own architectural and urban concerns, through a proposal whose objectives, typological, and formal options he would control.

The Vibo Marina industrial zone is located in the center of the urban area and represents the heart of the seafront city. To ensure the pertinence of his approach, Michel Kagan had to look beyond the area he had been allocated, to find the appropriate scale defining the city's relationship with its territory (fig. 1 and 2).

In order to correctly define the intervention zone, made up of a collection of both abandoned buildings and workshops still in use, an

1. Since 1991, Michel Kagan has regularly taken part in summer seminars in Italy, mainly in Bergamo (see article p. 225) at the invitation of Sergio Crotti, where for fifteen years he was a leading figure alongside Pasquale Culotta, Franco Purini, Aurelio Galfetti, Ferran Sagara and Gonzalo Byrne. These meetings were followed by a series of workshops in Vibo Valentia, Italy, during which Hervé Dubois, Nikos Ktenas and Michel Kagan were invited to share their teaching methods dedicated to urban projects in the city, where young architects worked on problematic sites, leading to the long-term creation of a veritable atlas of projects informing the municipality's urban considerations.

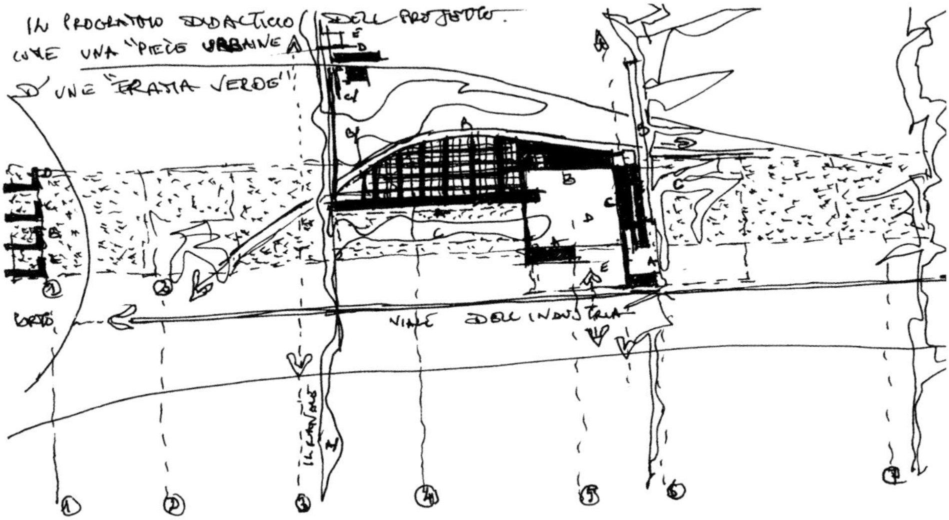

fig. 2. Intentions for the Vibo Marina industrial zone. Sketch by M. Kagan.

initial identification of the city's territorial limits was undertaken: to the East—towards the hill and the railroad line; to the West—towards the sea and the Pennello district, a dense urban sector made up of self-built dwellings; and to the North—the port area shared by industrial and tourist activities (fig. 3).

The need to "take the measure" of the city led the team to extend the project's footprint to the entire coastal zone, locating the most prominent part of the intervention on the harbor, where four towers, scaled to be visible from the open sea as well as from the historic center of the upper town, would serve as Vibo Marina's new territorial landmark (fig. 4 and 5).

These would then form a counterpoint to the *Italcementi* factory that emerges prominently from the urban profile to the South and maintain an intense relationship with the entire territorial context, constituting an important landmark by virtue of their scale and significance (fig. 6).

Erected on a large horizontal plinth that will house the municipal aquarium in direct contact with the sea, they face the port. Each is assigned to a specific function. One houses the new town hall; another the harbor master's office; yet another is meant for a large hotel in anticipation of an increase in tourist activity. The last is to house a cultural center and offices.

The proposal also calls for the transformation of the existing railway station into a new building designed in close relationship with the system of canals, characteristic of the Tyrrhenian Calabrian coast, which run through the town to return run-off water to the sea.

These canals, organized as nature parks, are intended to reveal the presence of nature within the city, demonstrating the necessary relationship between the mountains and the sea.

Considering the unauthorized status of the Penello residential area built on the public seafront, the project involves the creation of a new area for residential use and local services only. The characteristics and quality of the proposed housing should encourage a significant proportion of the population to relocate and to initiate a process of abandonment of illegal

fig. 3. A built-up front on the harbor, sketch by Michel Kagan.

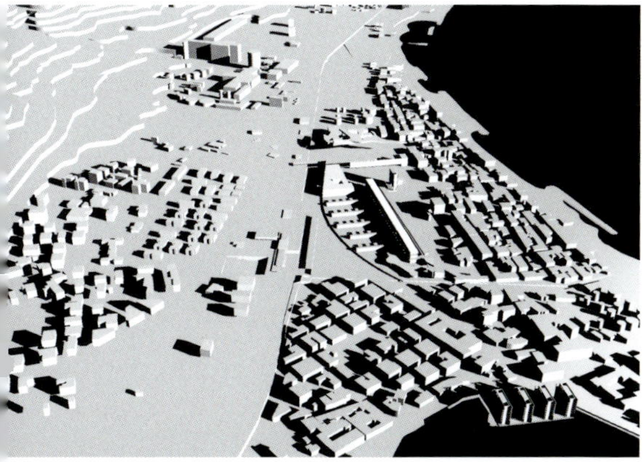

fig. 4. Layout of towers perpendicular to the skyline and coastal limit.

fig. 5. Researching the territorial limits of the site and the project.

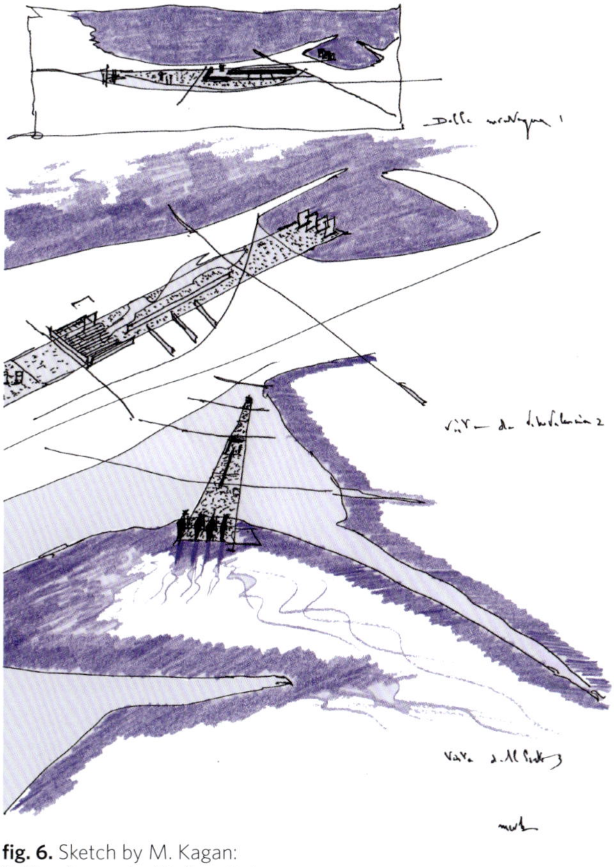

fig. 6. Sketch by M. Kagan: linking the port with the city's mainland districts.

housing areas that would enable all the residents of Vibo Marina to reclaim their beaches in the long run.

The proposed residential area is made up of a long linear building of housing units that follows the axis of the road towards the port, dividing the intervention area into two parts: the first consisting of a large urban courtyard open towards the Penello district and the sea, the other composed of a system of patio houses, in homage to Adalberto Libéra, positioned perpendicular to the main building, whose duplex housing units evoke Le Corbusier's *immeuble villa*.

This housing complex culminates in a large, square, and raised plaza that embodies the civic heart of the neighborhood. The public space is defined by buildings positioned to establish its spatial coordinates. In the eastern corner, the library sets the vertical dimension,

fig. 7. Topographical relationship between the Acropolis and Lycabettus Hill.

fig. 8. Athens, urban insertion plan for Lycabettus Hill.

fig. 9. Working atmosphere during the workshop in Athens.

while two horizontal public buildings define the edges of the area.

The development of such a project would necessarily be more complex and organic. But what emerges clearly from these brief observations is the desire to combine contemporary architecture's search for new public spaces with the questions raised by the reinterpretation and requalification of industrial wastelands, with the precise objective of bringing out the necessary latent correlations, beyond the obvious dialectical oppositions.

Athens beyond history[2]

Modern Athens is a capital / metropolis characterized by the whiteness of its urban fabric, open to the sea to the south, contained by a ring of hills, and made up of neighborhoods on a human scale, like large, adjoining villages. Lycabettus Hill, the rocky outcrop at the center of this landscape, represents a unique opportunity to escape the city's interlacing streets and discover a magnificent vista over the Acropolis, Piraeus, the Aegean Sea, and the dimension of the city as a whole, in its relationship to the land. (fig. 7 and 8) Located in the northeast of the city, this mountain is a piece of nature, embedded in the urban fabric, like a wild Greek island emerging from the urban grid, the integrity of which has underpinned the city's identity since its origins.

Intervening in Lycabettus, therefore, could not mean creating a new Acropolis (i.e. a high city). On the contrary, the importance of the hill as a dominant, wooded counterpoint to the expanse of the built-up capital became an urban axiom that the students' project had to confirm (fig. 9). At its summit, the church of Agios Georgios is the very definition of a typical Greek landmark, the culmination of a climb through the fragrant pine forest, with a panoramic view over the urban expanse. A hemicycle-shaped theater sits delicately against the ridge in a unique situation, set into the hollow of the hill and facing the modern city: a light metallic structure, it barely touches the ground that has simply been stabilized and levelled to accommodate it.

2. Almost six years later, Nikos Kténas invited Michel Kagan, Nathalie Régnier-Kagan and Hervé Dubois for a similar didactic experiment in Athens in July, 2009. This time, the other group leaders were Manuel Aires Mateus, Antonello Monaco, Valter Tronchin & Andrea Scascia, Antonio Tejedor & Mercedes Linares, Bruno Messina and Nikos Ktenas respectively. The chosen sites were located in the center of Athens, close to the neoclassical triangle. The Kagan team chose to work on Lycabettus Hill.

fig. 10. Model of the student proposal.

fig. 11. Michel Kagan and Nathalie Régnier-Kagan at the Athens workshop.

The aim of the workshop was to devise a series of actions designed to enhance this "already there" in its relationship with the contemporary city.

To preserve the integrity of this site, the project aimed to establish, through a detailed analysis of what already exists, the value of the existing elements on the hillside, and their potential for sensitive development, like so many "acupuncture points". The aim was not to build a city or a district, but to create landscape architecture, or "land art" (fig. 10 and 11).

The search for a relationship with the neighboring districts according to the 4 cardinal points was the first of the founding themes: it took shape by highlighting significant places of attachment to the urban fabric whose qualities we chose to reinforce:

— the departure point of the funicular railway: buildings and public space are redefined and linked to the site of the former Athens reservoir, which collected run-off water from the hill.

— The natural canyon opposite to the north-east, an extension of the stadium district, itself awaiting urban redefinition, through which it is proposed to establish access to the plateau.

— Voulgaroctonou street to the north and Ploutarthou street to the south, whose course is interrupted by the hill, will be linked across the plateau by extending the "lovers' promenade" winding through the pine forest over the ridge, in the style of the famous Pikionis path (fig. 12 and 13).

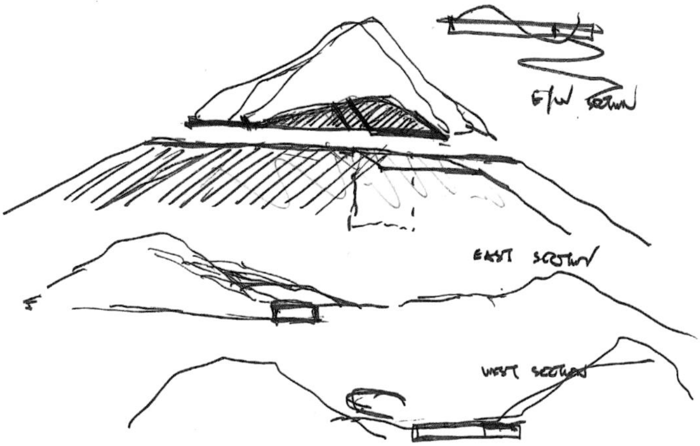

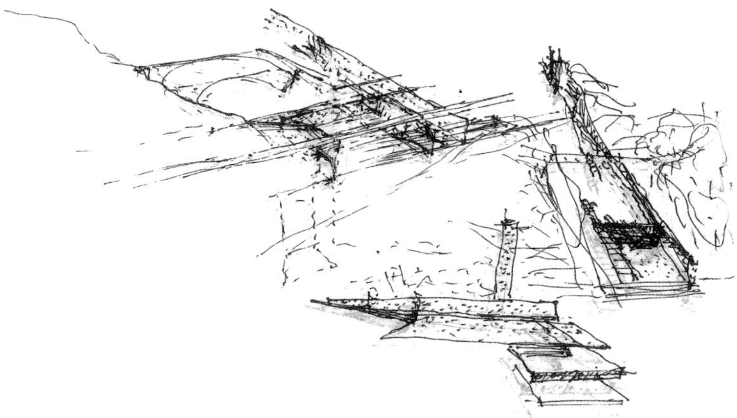

fig. 12. & 13. Sketches by Michel Kagan. A reference line establishes a direction in the landscape.

A second theme is developed at the summit: an accompaniment to the crest of the hill by a north-east/south-west line extending the natural canyon to the north, oriented towards the Acropolis and the sea. The geography of a place can conceal latent geometries. This line, both in plan and cross-section, establishes a reference, a ground level between the two hilltops. It provides an opportunity to link the northern districts to the historic center, through successive elements of use and pathway, like a common thread: the ascent into the canyon, the theater, the built esplanade, the belvedere facing the city and the sea, the promenade towards the city... It becomes the support for the layout and the watershed. It contains the land, limits the terrace and imprints its direction on the landscape.

A terrace surface was formed by filling in the hollow between the two knobs, to accommodate the current theater: the purpose of this fill has been to define a plane suitable for human activities. The aim of the project is to take advantage of this level, to define an esplanade above, and hypogeum architecture below, taking advantage of the slope to receive light and frame views, at the crossroads of the two perpendicular crossings of the hill. It is proposed that this observatory house a research and project center on the city of Athens, as a modern, silent echo of the Acropolis, the birthplace of democracy.

fig. 1. Michel Kagan, facing the sunset.

Open Dialogue

Nikos Ktenas

Since ancient times, the journey itself has taken on more importance than the destination, as the intellect is enriched by new experiences that can sometimes alter the very notion of arrival. The driving principle behind the "absolute of travel" has always been linked, from the outset to the need to interpret in order to create thought. Ithaca represents the esoteric goal of every traveler.

This journey begins in Vibo Valentia, in southern Italy. It was here that our first meeting with Michel Kagan took place, facing the Mediterranean (fig. 1), on those ancient traces of Greece, and it was here, through the definition of two urban projects, each reflected in the water mirror of the small port of Vibo Marina, that we found our first common ground. Michel Kagan's four towers created a link between the new residential district and the sea, rethinking the relationship with the land and rewriting the geography, while our tower project marked a new entrance to the district and at the same time resized the historic sector.

The first leg of this journey concluded with the promise of new encounters redefining what I had envisioned for my itinerary. A change of destination that had perhaps already been predestined.

The next stages took place in Paris, where, invited by Michel Kagan to take part in the juries for his students' projects, our points of affinity were confirmed: the focus was to be on the "metropolitan tower", an architectural concept inseparable from place and territory. The invention of the tower as an architectural challenge that houses multiple functions to meet the demands of contemporary society seems to me the only plausible response to the contemporary city, where huge suburbs have degraded into generic agglomerations with no identity on the brink of collapse.

The inertia and alienation of these mega-cities are destroying the traditional European city, depriving its center of the defining value that distinguished it until the last century. In recent years, investigations into the diffuse city, into non-places conceived as new gathering spaces, and the transposition of the city as an analogical metaphor for communication networks, have all failed for lack of any obvious objectives.

fig. 2. Jury at ENSA Paris-Belleville, 2008. Fung Tat Wai, J. Zaffaroni, M. Kagan, N. Ktenas.

fig. 3. Aurelio Galfetti in conference at his home in Paros.

fig. 4. End of workshop in Paros, July 2009.

By merely analyzing the metropolis, we do not provide ourselves with the means to solve the problem of "habitat", despite the fact that these very conditions are already written into the age-old stratifications of these places. Today, the world has become a single neighborhood without a territory inscribed in a "global objective", Marshall Mc Luhan's Global Village[1] devoid of physical and historical reference points. In today's cities, monuments have lost their meaning in the face of waning centrality, where we can no longer see the difference between urban challenges and fabric.

This is the answer that the "metropolitan tower" is intended to give by defining a new "polarity network", a kind of hypertext written on the existing city as a new order capable of restoring identity to places.

To address these requirements, the "tower" must take root in the forgotten parts of the city, in the unresolved places, in the interrupted territories of the contemporary megalopolis. In defining these "new spaces of the contemporary", we must first and foremost look for the anchoring point, because only the exact position of the architectural object can give substance to the writing of new stories and engage in a dialogue with the geography of the territory. Place and its privileged relationship with the territory represent the essential point of affinity between my own architectural research and Michel Kagan's.

Our search for analogies continued in a new encounter, this time in Athens, which strangely brings us back to our starting point, once again facing the Mediterranean, the birthplace of architectural history to which all architects return (fig. 3 and 4).

In Athens, in the company of Nathalie and Hervé Dubois, Michel Kagan chose the location for the project before defining the theme. Here, geography is omnipresent, and architecture must inevitably live up to it. Preference was given to Lycabettus Hill, the city's highest hill, visible from all sides.

The choice of location allows the project to express the founding values of this heritage, rewritten with a new language,

1. Herbert Marshall McLuhan (1911-1980) was a Canadian philosopher, sociologist, professor of English literature, and communication theorist. He was one of the founders of contemporary media studies. McLuhan is best known for his formulation of the phrase "The medium is the message", as well as for his use of the term "global village": See: Herbert Marshall McLuhan, and Bruce R. Powers, *The Global Village, Transformations in World Life and Media in the 21st Century*. (New York: Oxford University Press, 1989).

in the footsteps of the city's history and, of course, its geography. The project is articulated around three themes: the relationship of Lycabettus Hill to the horizontal urban fabric, rewriting the relationship with the Acropolis by tracing a horizontal line reordering the morphology of the hill, and construction of a terrace at the summit creating an observation point on the geography of the territory.

A meticulous intervention, concerned with preserving heritage while focusing instead on rewriting the relationships between urban sectors in Athens.

This dialogue remains open every time I walk from Saint Isidore to Saint George on Lycabettus Hill...

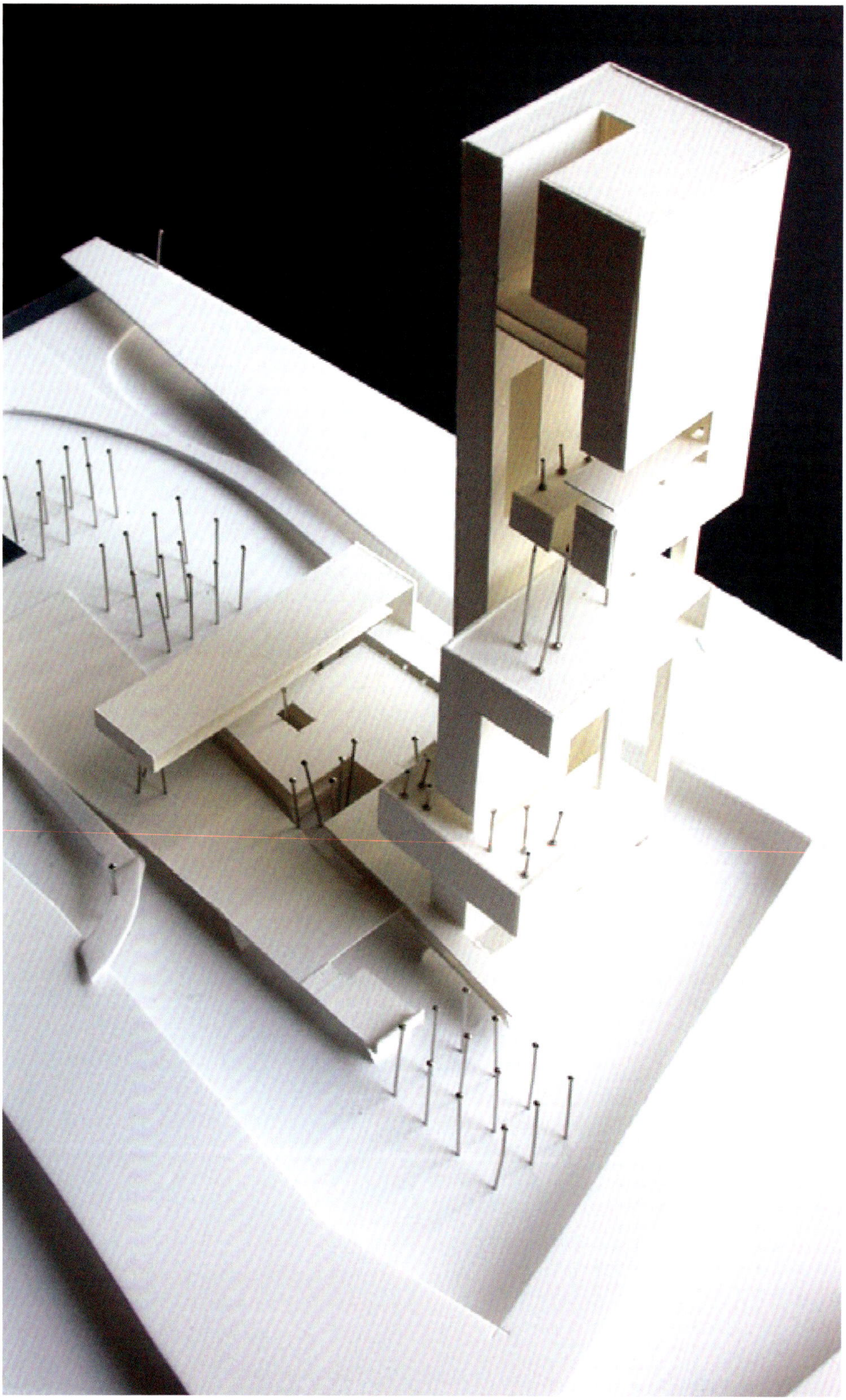

fig. 1. Project by Lee Yun Ho, Kim Joo Mi and Cédric Thomas, High Density Urban Residence workshop, 2006.

The Standing City[1]

Laurent Salomon

The construction of the World City is underway. This City is the scene of an economic and social transformation, whose future outcome is anyone's guess. In this politically uncertain and economically fragile context, a network of megacities is developing on the four corners of the world, according to roughly similar rules, often extrapolated from the North American city model. The latter was imagined following a long sequence of mutations, from Hippodamos of Miletus to the new towns of Louis XIV, via the models of the Italian Renaissance. This is how Western culture evolved, spreading to Asia, South America, and Africa. Today, this evolutionary process applies to societies that are either theoretically democratic or theoretically open to liberal economic concepts. What characterizes the state of this new "World City" most profoundly is its extreme dependence on "land value". This situation makes "speculation" one of the first rules conditioning its shaping—an economic notion whose intrinsic corollary is density. By a happy coincidence, and in contrast to the pejorative aspect of the term "speculation", the notion of sustainable development opportunely attributes an ecological value to this density. It was previously equally decried by the hygienist critique at the end of the industrial revolution as by the more anthropological approaches of the sociology of the great postwar acceleration. From a more architectural point of view, the most literal representation of density is undoubtedly verticality, a morphological feature that resonates strongly in the collective unconscious. As William Curtis puts it: *"the Tower is plutocracy meeting phallocracy"*[2]. But this shortcut, while striking, waters down the Tower's genealogy, both for its virtues and for the avatars with which history has alternately cast it in the past. It also avoids the etymology, the origin of this name intended for fortifications, which alludes as much to the circle (*torus*) as to protect (*tutare*), both terms affirming its warlike essence, but neither

1. Workshop 2004 / 2007: Sakhu (Seoul-Korea) and Paris-Belleville (Paris-France) schools of architecture. Sakhu: Professors Lee Eun-Seok and Jeong Jae-Heon—Paris-Belleville: Professor Laurent Salomon—Guest professor: Michel Kagan.

2. William J.R. Curtis, "Plutocracy and Phallocracies: the skyscraper and the virtual city," in *Critical Perspectives on recent Architecture* lecture series at the SFA (June 8, 2007).

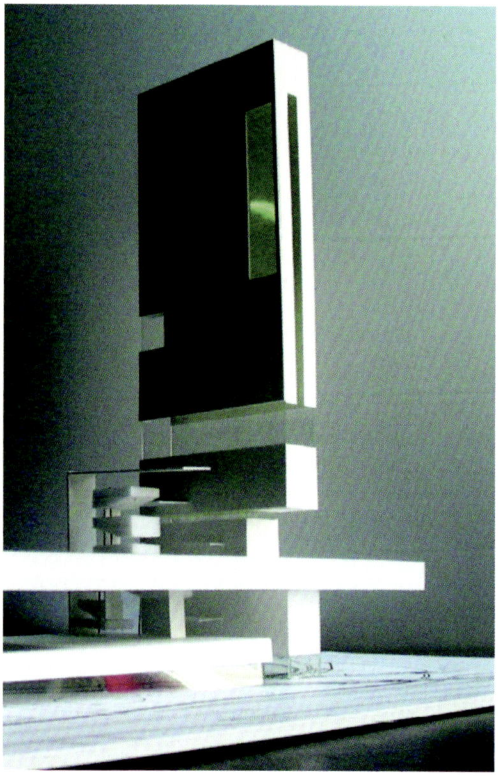

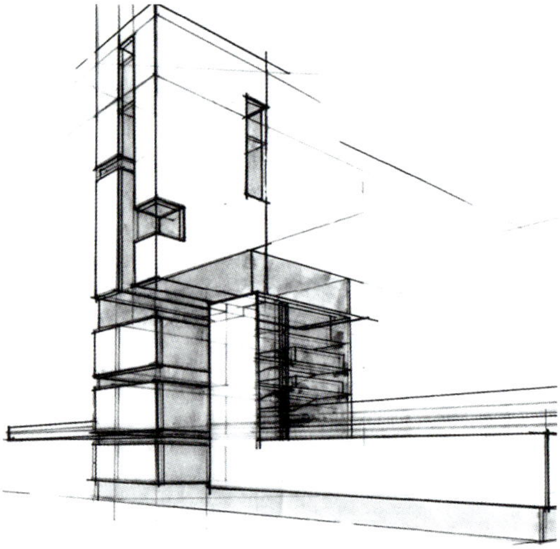

fig. 2. Project by Song Kyu Nam, Im Mi Young and César Vabre, "Les yeux ouverts vers Paris", University Tower workshop, 2005.

introduces the notion of verticality that dominates today.

Beyond these debates, which involve semantics, history, economics and politics, and no doubt because of them, the tower remains an architectural issue that receives little attention. And yet, from the point of view of both architect and educator, verticality is just one of the many "conditions of architecture". It is therefore a prospective subject like any other, enabling architects to resolve certain design issues, or helping students to come to terms with complex constraints combining structure, circulation, and urban presence. It is also a means of addressing the question of the city on less conventional grounds. Verticality itself is not extra-urban or anti-urban, but, if architecture is to incorporate the city as material, it must also address its capacity to ensure the continuity of the public space established on the ground. By its very nature, this continuity threatens its perimeter, and more often than not it is excluded from architecture's core by convention... at least until now. From all this, it is possible to deduce that, unless the Tower is envisaged as a matrix of public space, its verticality generates objects that do not correspond to the public potential of the European city model, a conspicuous situation that can easily be verified wherever it is implemented, in each of its various expressions, from Macao to Hong Kong, from Shanghai to Hô-Chi-Minh-City, in Europe or the Americas (North or South), everywhere, in the so-called emerging world, as well as in those contexts that are still in search of visibility.

Based on these findings, a workshop on "The Standing City" was organized for the years from 2004 through 2007, between the Sakhu (Seoul, Korea) and Paris-Belleville

fig. 3. Project by Lee Yun Ho, Kim Joo Mi and Cédric Thomas, High Density Urban Residence workshop, 2006.

fig. 4. Project by Kang Ho Suk and Lee Seo Joo "Interactive City ", workshop Business Center and Hotel, 2007.

(Paris, France) schools of architecture[3]. For four consecutive years, the teaching team— and the various groups of students it brought together—confronted the question of Urban Verticality. This notion includes a vertical public space for the new territory of the World City, combining qualities acquired in the old models of the horizontal city with the possible conquest of the horizon. A permanent territorial presence on the horizon puts the entirety of the urban into perspective, brings the urban horizon into resonance with the natural horizon, and rediscovers the special relationship between the city as an accomplished form and geography in the pre-modern urban world, irrespective of the actual completion of the form itself.

Drawing on his many years of experience teaching the "Metropolitan Tower", Michel Kagan took on this adventure as part of a pedagogical practice of international exchange with which he is very familiar, in which students of different nationalities work in groups around ideas developed collectively during lively brainstorming sessions. The ideas that emerge from these meetings are always inspired by the discovery—for the

3. See: Lee Eun-Seok, Lee Kwan-Seok, Jeong Jae-Heon, and Cho Dae-Hee, eds., *Vertical City of Paris, Architectural Design Workshop, Sakhu et EAP Belleville, 2005, 2006, 2007* (Seoul: PixelHouse, 2008); Lee Eun-Seok, Lee Kwan-Seok, Jeong Jae-Heon, and Laurent Salomon, eds., *Vertical City of Paris, Architectural Design Workshop, Sakhu et EAP Belleville, 2008, 2009, 2010* (Seoul: PixelHouse, 2010).

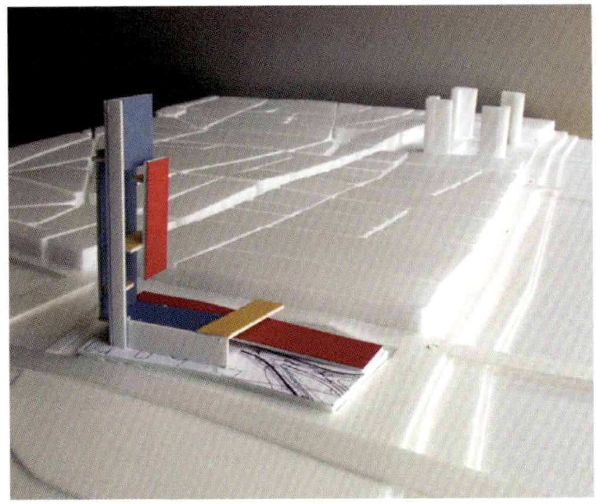

fig. 5. Project by Koo Hee Jeong, Jeon Jo Young and Julien Corbin, High Density Urban Residence workshop, 2006.

fig. 6. Project by Lee Dong Hoon and Hong Jong Hwa, "Vertical Plaza", workshop University Tower, 2005.

Korean students—of Paris, a city that is horizontal in essence. In this city, where very subject of verticality seems like a criticism, the predominant feeling of students discovering it is admiration for the aesthetic coherence of the historic city, the richness of its public spaces, and the conviviality of their uses. Café terraces don't exist in Korea. This contrast between the proposed subject and the urban qualities—which it may seem to criticize—enhances the explanation of the notion of the "Standing City" and elucidates its objectives.

While the Korean students have an almost instinctive knowledge of the Tower as a type of building, they quickly become aware, through contrast and the culture shock that gripped them, of the lack of urbanity of those tall constructions that are familiar to them. Conversely, the French students understood the problem of verticality more easily with the help of their Korean colleagues who were trained in it. They were all enthusiastic about the idea of instantly marrying type and problem. This is an essential cog in a pedagogical process in which the main obstacle to student production is the limited time available. The resulting projects in the workshops were therefore the fruit of exceptionally rapid work, which could only be carried out through collective production, and in the full awareness that the proposals that emerged is would be more the architectural delineation of a clear theme than the resolution of all the problems it raises (fig. 1 to 8).

The complex play of programming / shaping, the underlying question of structure, the nagging question of distribution—and therefore safety—all these elements for consideration were compressed into the proposals and led the students to surpass themselves, both conceptually and in terms of reading the context. The multi-functional program involved

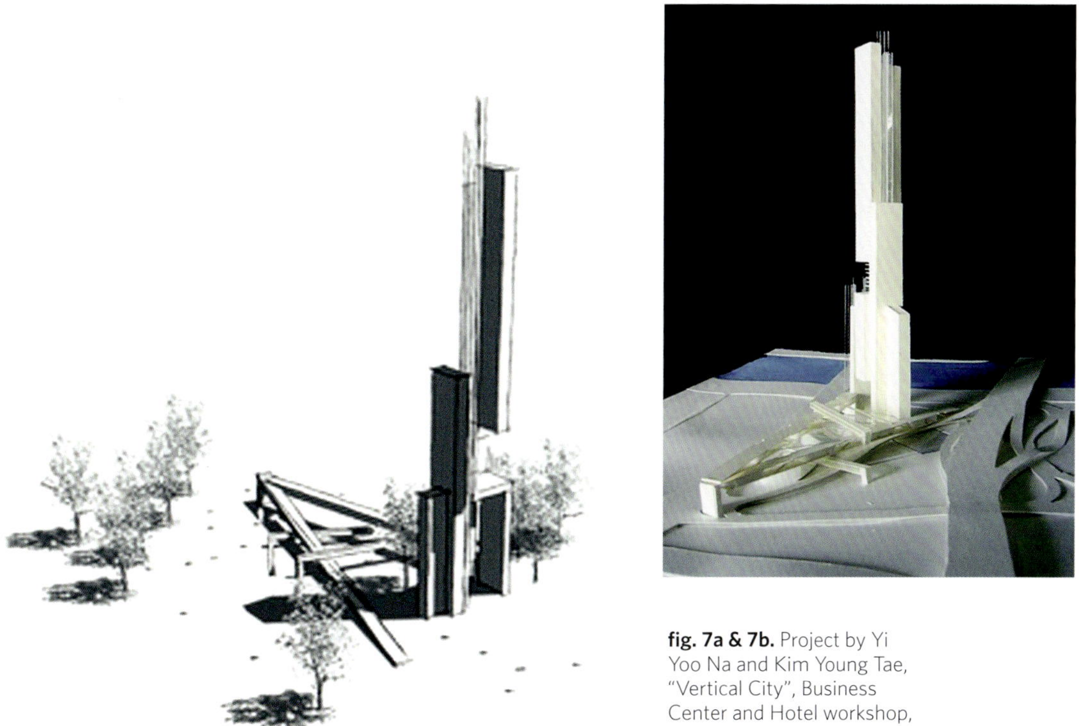

fig. 7a & 7b. Project by Yi Yoo Na and Kim Young Tae, "Vertical City", Business Center and Hotel workshop, 2007.

the extension of the Seine-Rive Gauche university facilities: student residences, lecture halls and amphitheaters, the library, sports facilities, and catering. The site chosen for this adventure is the land between the south-east ring road and boulevard Masséna, in the section between quai Panhard & Levassor and rue Bruneseau, opposite a project designed by Michel Kagan for the Parcs et Jardins de la Ville de Paris in 1990[4]. The layout included the need to design for a continuity of use under the various structures, to facilitate relations between the various university sites, both with the city center and with the suburbs.

Not only does the subject matter of this project-based experiment inspire the creativity of the students, but it also demonstrates that architecture can be endlessly revitalized if the creative impulse is "shared space".

This renewal is nourished by culture, and the result, as Luigi Snozzi puts it, is that "nothing needs to be invented, everything needs to be reinvented"[5]. This work on the vertical dimension is addressed in the light of the demands of urban culture to nourish the height of all these previous inventions, is the opposite of the amnesia that justifies media-driven architectural production, concentrating most of its research on the outer envelope of space, a layer that is certainly necessary, but is far from constituting the whole of a thought on inhabited space. Whether as a link between interior and exterior, or as the main instrument of separation and isolation, this skin is confronted in a Tower with the problems of wind and vertigo, which prevent it from fulfilling many of its original functions. If the city we want is one of interfaces and exchanges of all

4. See the documentation of the sites at the beginning of Part 2.

5. One of seventeen basic teaching aphorisms of Luigi Snozzi, architect and professor of architecture.

fig. 8. Project by Lee Jae Min, Choe Woo Lin, Choe Hyeon Yeong, Pauline Raurt, "Urban gateway", workshop Inner city, new city hall, 2008.

kinds, where people become aware of their belonging to a group, of their dependence on others, and of the infinite empathy they should feel for them, this means that, in a Tower, the place of articulation between it and the city lies in an "in-between" to be invented.

To a certain extent, this workshop represents a research project that goes "against the grain" of current trends, enabling students to build their own identities by situating their work outside the "fashion" obsessions that often lead them to convey ideas whose underlying ideologies they don't fully understand, and which do not serve their long-term interests, but rather instrumentalize them in the service of a "market" that expects no intellectual autonomy from them.

In this game of demystifying contemporary issues, reallocating meanings, and metaphorically requalifying architectural production—nourished by philosophical and societal intentions—the presence of Michel Kagan and the clarity of his analyses and criticisms reinforced the work of the teaching team in charge of the daily supervision of these multicultural groups, who were given just ten days to work out their proposals. His teaching experience in relation to high-rise public buildings helped to maintain focus one of the major interests of architecture, which is to nourish society with utopia, a responsibility shared beyond friendship and common convictions.

Three years after this pedagogical work, in 2011, with Judith Rotbart, we had the opportunity to take part in a competition in the city of Busan, South Korea, for a 450,000 m^2 project, comprising 1,500 homes and a shopping centre. We were lucky enough to win the competition against teams from KPF and SOM. Located at the arrival of cruise ships from Japan, we named it 'Ocean Gate' to accompany both its conceptual process and its morphology.

fig. 9. International competition, "Ocean Gate", first prize, Busan, South Korea 2011, project by Judith Rotbart and Laurent Salomon, Jean-Marc Weill, structural engineer.

fig. 10. Drawing by Laurent Salomon.

In contrast to the student productions, we emphasized the structural inventiveness of the towers, which made it possible both to simplify the relationship with the ground and to propose major communal spaces distributed within the structure. This project, studied with the engineer Jean-Marc Weill, was based on the solution of a hollow-core tower proposed by Jean Prouvé for the Ministry of Éducation at La Défense, on the outskirts of Paris, which was never built. Due to a dispute between the city and the developer, the project was only partially realized, but here are the images from the competition.

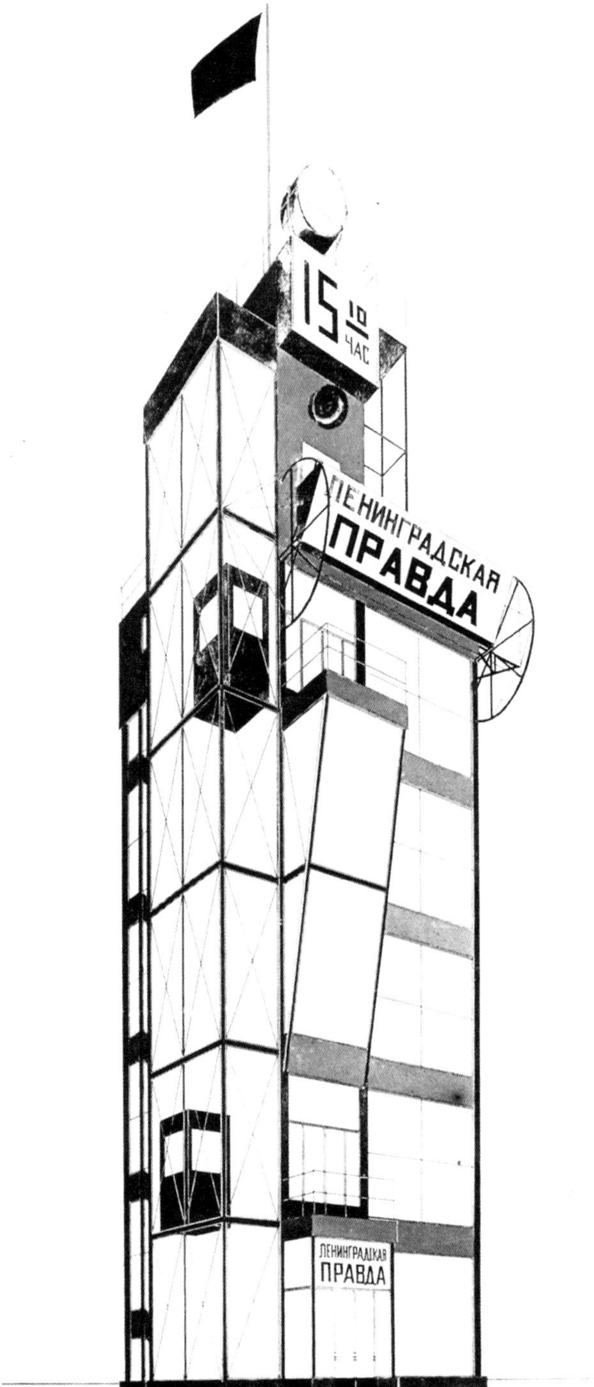

fig. 1. Design for the Pravda building, Vesnin Brothers, Moscow, 1923.

The Air of Modernity

Georges Adamczyk and François Giraldeau

According to Rémi Hess and Gabriele Weigand, Henri Lefebvre liked to declare that "Man's work is himself". In the case of our friend Michel Kagan, this is hardly an exaggeration. It's quite true! In this testimonial, we'll try to put into a Québécois context, and to some extent a New York context as well, the ties that the two of us and numerous colleagues and students forged with Michel Kagan over the years. We will evoke the architectural theme of the Tower as a significant moment in this unique encounter with Michel Kagan, the architect and educator, a man of reason and feeling, qualities he displayed in abundance in his profession, in his teaching, and in his friendships.

Our first contacts with Michel Kagan date back to his time in New York (1981–1984). With the benefit of hindsight, it is tempting to compare the intellectual relations between New York and Montreal in the 1980s with those of the 1940s. Although each was a minor episode in cultural history in general, let alone for the story of modernity in Quebec, it must be recognized that things would certainly not have been the same without the presence of Jacques Maritain, Fernand Léger, André Breton and, of course, Père Couturier, in New York and Montreal. The 1980s were no longer a time of exile, but of distance, transatlantic exchanges, fertile oases, and unfinished modern projects. And let's face it, these New York contacts would prove seminal for the revival of architectural education in Quebec.

Let's recall, for a moment, some recent events: In the late 1960s, the École des Beaux-arts de Montréal became part of the new Université du Québec à Montréal (UQAM), often compared to the Université de Vincennes of the time. In this effervescent environment, in the wake of the 1967 World's Fair, and in a society in the midst of the Quiet Revolution—overwhelmed by the events of October '70 and the forthcoming referendums for national independence—a small group of young professors, practitioners of architecture and design, founded a new educational program in environmental design whose ambition was to extend, in Quebec, the pedagogical experiments of the modern period in Europe and the USA. This initiative was heavily influenced by a strict functionalism, driven by radical political movements. When this approach ran out of steam, the program quickly turned in circles.

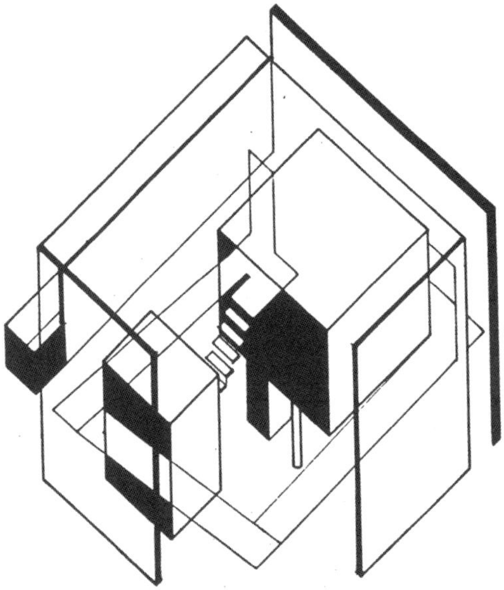
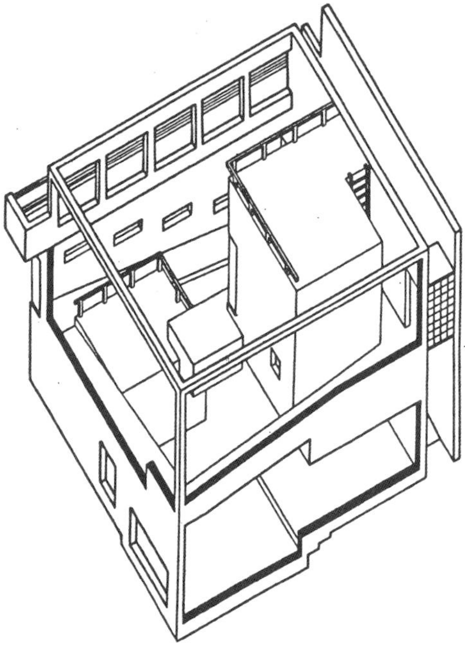

fig. 2a & 2b. Yves Rouleau's cube project, Design and habitat workshop, University of Québec at Montréal, 1982.

The teaching of architectural design, heavily instrumentalized by objectives external to our disciplines, had become something of an afterthought.

In the early 1980s, when François Giraldeau was a young teacher, we had just discovered Kenneth Frampton's new publications; especially his *Critical History of Modern Architecture* and his texts exploring the links between architecture and the political thought of Hannah Arendt. Our first exchange with him, in New York, dates back to 1981. Frampton's generosity is proverbial, and his commitment to peripheral causes like ours is exemplary. In February 1982, he agreed to take part in a round-table discussion in Montreal on the 1979 CCI travelling exhibition *Architecture in Germany 1900–1933*, for which Jean-Louis Cohen was the scientific advisor, presented at the UQAM gallery. At this meeting, Frampton recommended a young architect who had arrived in New York the previous year. He had studied with Henri E. Ciriani, whose work Frampton appreciated, and was assisting him in his comparative analysis course, as well as being a studio instructor at Columbia University's Graduate School of Architecture and Planning.

While a few of us were helping to re-establish a form of architectural education that encouraged the pleasure of design, a summer school called Design International was created at UQAM. The aim was to offer students and recent graduates intensive week-long workshops, led by guests from all over the world. In 1982, Michel Kagan was on the inaugural list of those invited to teach. He returned to Montreal in 1983 to take part in the international colloquium that France Vanlaethem and Georges Adamczyk had organized with Kenneth Frampton. The colloquium, entitled *Architecture et Identité culturelle*, modernité et tradition, brought together, among others, AlbertoSartoris, Alvaro Siza, Rogelio Salmona, Harry Wolf, Jacques Gubler, Douglas Cardinal and Michel Kagan. At the time, Michel Kagan, who was in his thirties, told us little about his work, although his competition projects already demonstrated the strength of his social and aesthetic position, as well as his mastery of his discipline. His lectures were mainly devoted to presenting the projects and achievements of his elders, particularly Henri Ciriani, Edith Girard, Yves Lion and Christian Devillers. We get to know Michel Kagan, his commitment, his demands and tenacity, and his pleasure in teaching.

Michel Kagan's first workshop at the UQAM School of Design focused on the theme of the cube, as set out by the Villa in Carthage (1927–1930). This workshop was given to students new to architecture, and for many, like Yves Rouleau, it was to be foundational. (fig. 2a and 2b) Not only did they discover architecture, but also Purism, if we accept this title as "a term that allows us to express in an intelligible word the characteristic of the modern spirit", as proposed by Ozenfant and Jeanneret, in *Après le cubisme* (October 1918). In this context, the students discovered the exceptional passion of a teacher, a passion that would not waver, at the schools that would later welcome Michel Kagan—no matter which and no matter where. Yves Rouleau and his colleague at the time, Alain Archambault, were both students of Henri Ciriani at Belleville shortly afterwards. Today, they teach at UQAM's School of Design.

It must be said that this question of the modern spirit is not an innocent one in Québec. If grain silos were a reference point for avant-garde architects in Europe, they were also, from the 1920s onwards, a new subject for Québécois painters. In a way, they represent the threshold crossed towards abstraction. This young, rebellious, and ambitious modernity was soon to be overwhelmed by darkness. In this country, as architect Marcel Parizeau said in the '40s, "we avoid difficulties and never question principles". For French-speaking students of architecture, the teachings of the moderns, and of Le Corbusier in particular, did not reappear until the late 1970s, when the winds of freedom were blowing once again.

While the *Presence of the Past* settled its accounts with the future at Venice in 1980, it was against this polemical backdrop of modernity that the exhibition and publication project *Nouvelles directions de l'architecture moderne, France / USA*, curated and written by Kenneth Frampton and Michel Kagan, saw the light of day in 1985. Over forty architects took part. The Columbia School's *PRECIS* magazine would regularly publish the projects of students Michel Kagan tutored with Michael Mostoller. The theme of the Tower contributed to the evolution of Columbia's four-types program, and for Michel Kagan, it would become a real question of architecture and urban planning.

It's worth recalling that in the early eighties, the housing studio offered to Master of Architecture students was one of the great strengths of Columbia's program. It brought together the school's most committed teachers, and from the outset, Michel Kagan's cultural and academic background put him at ease. The proposed typologies in this studio are the Carpet Type, the Superblock Type, the Mews Block and the Perimeter Block, this last type being dear to Kenneth Frampton for its ability to resist context. Like Frampton, Kagan was called upon to teach this position using the four models, although he nevertheless liked to put forward the idea of an "open perimeter", for which the tower would act as a key operator, part starting point, part pivot.

High-rise buildings are not always appreciated, even in New York. Speaking of the four typologies, Richard Plunz wrote the following in the first issue of *PRECIS*, in 1979:

"The choice of housing types is intended to challenge the norms governing standards of practice in New York City over many past decades. All of these types are variants on low-rise themes. They express the rejection of the high-rise model in New York City at the present time, when it seems that not a single community—except the most favored or the most

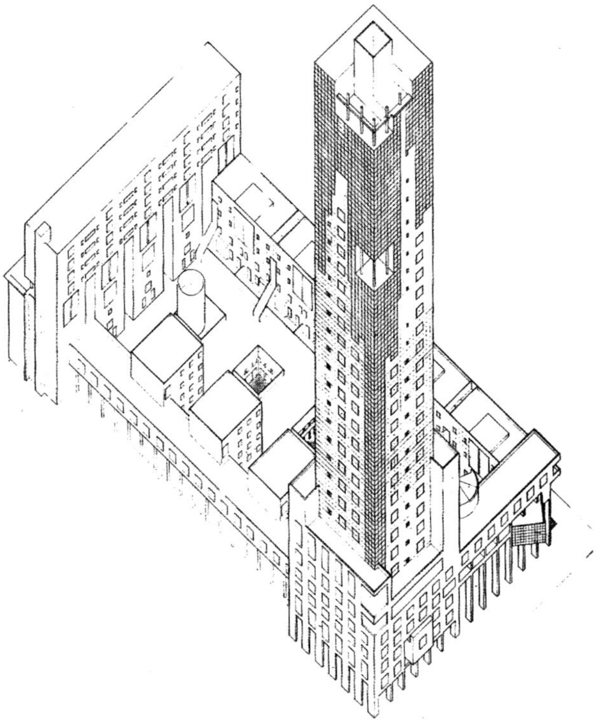

fig. 3. Project by Colin Cathcart and Keith Hone, Single Room Occupancy High-Rise Housing, Columbia University, 1981.

fig. 4. Project by Theodore Krueger and Peter Pfau, Mixed-Use Tower Community, Columbus Circle, New York City, Columbia University, 1982.

deprived—is advancing high-rise projects. These current attitudes are the culmination of a skepticism that predates even Jane Jacobs' West Village struggles of the early 1960s"[1].

In subsequent issues, Michael Mostoller published "The Tall Building Urbanistically Considered" (*PRECIS* 3, 1981), an article featuring the work of a non-studio housing workshop entitled "Mixed-Use High-Rise Building", and "Urban Housing for the Eighties: The High-Rise Block with Common Services" (*PRECIS* 4, 1983). In 1981, Mostoller and Kagan conducted a housing workshop together, on the theme of "Single Room Occupancy High-Rise Housing", and in 1982, on a "Mixed-Use Tower Community", located at either of Central Park's corners along the western edge. In both cases, the proposals articulated a perimeter block and tower. *PRECIS* 4 and *PRECIS* 5 (1984) featured student projects by Cathcart / Hone, Dickey / Loomis, Goldblum / Strum and Krueger / Pfau (fig. 3 and 4), more than half of whom would join Studio 7, Michel Kagan's architectural practice studio, in New York during these years.

In all of this, Michel Kagan contributed his uncommon strengths, interests, and skills,

1. Richard Plunz, "Introduction", *PRECIS, Volume 1, The Street, the House and the Garden*, (Spring 1979): 3; also published as: Richard Plunz, "The Four Typologies", *Lotus International* 27, "Architecture in the American university" (Cornell, Cooper Union, Columbia, 1980): 107.

including his expertise in space, form, the design of a good home, habitability, light, the history of the avant-garde and the question of "social condensers". A real contribution, and a counterpoint to the prevailing post-modernism or incipient intellectualism. And all around him, were Kenneth Frampton, of course, Michael Schwarting and Henry Smith-Miller, long-time colleagues of Richard Meier and of Michel Kagan at Columbia, Steven Holl, also a colleague, and his *Pamphlet Architecture*, Diller/Scofidio and Art on the Beach, the IAUS, Revisions, the study group in which he participated, John Hejduk and the Cooper Union, the American "new directions", Raimund Abraham,... and New York.

By the summer of 1986, Michel Kagan had moved back to Paris and came to Montreal for the third time to take part in the Design International summer school. With François Giraldeau, who had just returned from Columbia, he proposed the theme of the tower, or more precisely, the rehabilitation of an existing tower, an opportunity to move away from the New York tower and to revisit constructivist proposals (fig. 1). In a rather conservative cultural context, dominated by the protection of the Victorian city after the colonial one, rehabilitating a tower was a challenge that students enthusiastically embraced. (fig. 5, 6, 7 and 8) In 1987, our colleague Börkur Bergmann and I launched SILO magazine, an "irregular monthly" as Pascal Quintard Hofstein so aptly put it. In it, we published the projects for the tower projects, under the title "*Jouer la tour*" ("Playing the Tower"). Here, we quote from our SILO magazine presentation (fig. 9 and 10).

fig. 5. Project by R. Arpin, C. Gosselin, M.A. Letarte: Alternation.

fig. 6. Project by M. Gamache, P. St-Laurent, Marc-André Tellier: Private-public "clip".

fig. 7. Project by G. Bérubé, A. Giroux, Simon Coquoz: Verticality placed horizontally.

fig. 8. Project by Josée Bérubé, R. Daoust, G. Gagnon: Spatial cross.

An urban tower[2]

As part of the UQAM Design Department's summer session on International Design, the "Design and City" workshop explored the theme of urbanity through the design of a building whose function and location have a strong urban character.
In contrast to previous experiments, where a void (missing tooth or corner plot) was chosen as the location for a small facility (cultural center, community center), the 1986 workshop invited participants to reflect on an existing building, a high-rise apartment building located downtown.
The project involved transforming the building at 175 West Sherbrooke Street, in Montreal, to give it a truly urban dimension (fig. 9). This important course of action involved:

1. Reconsidering its monofunctional character *by transforming the base of the building and making use of the adjacent parking spaces to include facilities and services: a small auditorium, an exhibition space, and, if required, a small retail outlet. It was also meant to introduce a public space at the top of the tower, that could include a café-restaurant, and possibly updating the housing typology by adding "lofts", duplexes, etc., to the tower.*

2. Developing its formal potential*, by seeking to hone its expressive plastic qualities (rhythm, mass, movement, and their semantic relationships), while respecting the "constructivist" character of the building,. The week-long workshop brought together students and recent graduates from UQAM, Université de Montréal and McGill University.*

Relevance of the tower:

Why propose the study of an existing high-rise building for pedagogical purposes?

Existing buildings *can be used to promote practices such as rehabilitation and to qualify what is already there, in relation to the city's current needs. But why is it that structures from the 1960s, which preservationists claim are degrading the urban environment, tend to be excluded from such concerns?*

The tower, *as a constitutive typology of contemporary urban centers, opens the way to experimentation with themes that are rarely explored locally, including the "cubist" character of the modern city, the tower in its articulation with the urban system, and the high-rise structure as a factor in enriching the urban landscape, in relation to verticality and horizontality, near and far.*

Finally, considering ***housing*** *as the starting point for an intervention involving public functions reminds us that the complex relations between the private and the public in today's city cannot be satisfied with the separations called for in the conventional practice of "zoning".*

There are many reasons that this should stimulate greater interest in contemporary forms of urban architecture in Montreal, such as tower architecture. This schematic presentation outlines aspects of a framework for reflection that the "Design and the City" workshop was only able to sketch out.

> From a general point of view:

The character of the North American city
Objects and surfaces in the architectural definition of the city; the role of the tower at different urban scales.

> From a specific point of view:

The urban tower
Private functions and public vocation: roofs and ground floors as urban spaces defining an architectural promenade.
Apartment typologies and social needs: anonymity and recognition as a phenomenon of urban culture in a metropolitan context.
Tower as object and urban form: typological and sociological consequences of the tower as a component of the traditional city block.

> From a local perspective:

Sherbrooke Street
Spatial definition of the downtown edge: the "houses" and "towers" of Sherbrooke Street. Metropolitan networks and utilities: Sherbrooke Street versus traditional thoroughfares and shopping malls.

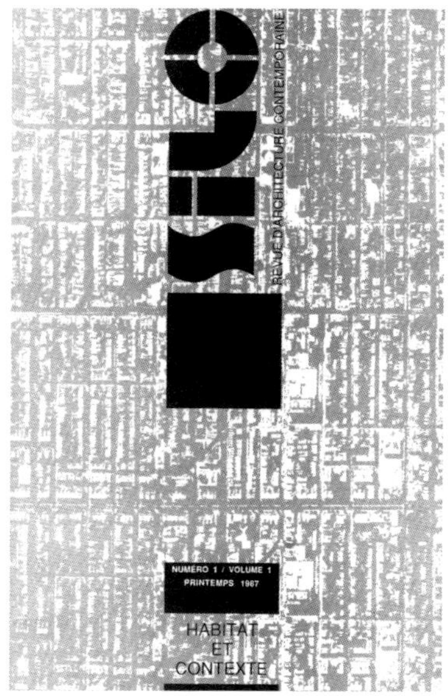

fig. 9. The tower in its context.

fig. 10. SILO magazine cover.

All this requires some clarification. The existing tower is the starting point. Work on form dominates: with the same keywords, hierarchy, geometry. As a catalyst, the form carries the programmatic content, the development of which remains, in a single week, at the sketch stage (private/public, housing types, etc.).

The process unfolds between abstraction, observation, intention, and path.

Despite the embryonic state of the projects, Michel Kagan was particularly keen that they should translate into tangible images: small plastic objects with the capacity to condense and evoke, for each student, the various questions and reflections undertaken over the course of the workshop, and to act as generators of ideas and future projects (fig. 11 to 14).

Among these considerations was the cubist character of the American city (didn't he also sometimes say "the cubist city"?) Michel Kagan often came back to this in the studio with his students, and during walks around Montreal. At the time, it was more a matter of observation, something to see, to think about, to let simmer. It was also referred to in *New Directions in Modern Architecture* of 1985, in connection with Raimund Abraham's tower project and, more generally, *"the tower-function and the urban type that the skyscraper can become in a city like New York, where, unlike the horizontal homogeneity of European cities, a cubist dimension and vision of the city become evident"*[3]. So, it was with curiosity and interest that, some ten years later, we learned more about his thinking.

2. "Jouer la tour", *SILO 1, Habitat et contexte*, (Montreal: Studio Cube/UQAM, 1987), 29-31.

3. Kenneth Frampton and Michel Kagan, *Nouvelles directions de l'architecture moderne* (Paris, Milan: Electa Moniteur, 1985). (English version: New York: Rizzoli Intl Publishers, 1985)

   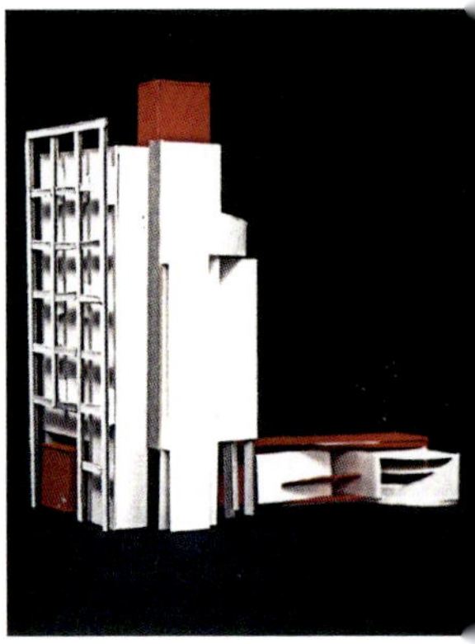

fig. 11. Project by R. Arpin, C. Gosselin, M.A. Letarte: Alternation.

fig. 12. Project by G. Bérubé, A. Giroux, Simon Coquoz: Verticality place horizontally.

fig. 13. Project by M. Gamache, P. St-Laurent, Marc-André Tellier: Private-public "clip".

fig. 14. Project by Josée Bérubé, R. Daoust, G. Gagnon: Spatial cross.

In his *Parti pris: Les espaces modernes sont les lieux modernes*[4] (1996), no explicit reference is made to the cubist dimension of the city, other than to return to the theme of the New York perimeter block, saying that *"it creates, more than a facade on the street, a real volume, a 'cubist' island, which emerges to take advantage of views and orientations"*.

Nevertheless, this mature text sets out in depth his position on the city—ethical and political as much as disciplinary. One of its cornerstones is undoubtedly to be found in his successive reflections on the "cubist" question. He would say, for example, of the architectural promenade that it is *"a social link in a democratic, relational architecture: it's the aesthetic question of modern contextuality. We need to let buildings breathe and fight against the culture of congestion* [...]. *The architectural promenade is an effective way of being in space, a 'will for space' that engenders the idea of possession through vision"*[5].

We also appreciate the importance Michel Kagan came to attach to the question of the city's "predictability", which he saw as a core task for architects of his generation. *"To predict,"* he says, *"you have to understand. Before you can understand, you must observe. Knowing how to observe is already an act of creation. We architects have a 'geometric' eye"*[6].

If we accept this as the definition of a generative path of knowledge, and remember his words and silences, we can better understand Michel Kagan's approach in the mid-1980s: observe, observe to understand, teach others to observe, project, understand by proposing projects.

The educational challenge posed by the metropolitan tower as an architectural type continues to this day, taking various forms under the guidance of a new generation of teachers.

4. Michel Kagan, *Parti pris: Les espaces modernes sont les lieux modernes*. Conférences Paris d'architectes (Paris: Pavillon de l'Arsenal, 1996): 26.

5. Michel Kagan, op. cit.: 23.

6. Michel Kagan, op. cit.: 19.

fig. 15. Atelier Manon Asselin, École d'Architecture, Université de Montréal.

At the School of Architecture at the Université de Montréal, for example, Manon Asselin (fig. 15), co-founder of Atelier Tag, is working with her students on the question of materiality, introducing the use of aluminum, a material that has marked the skyline of the city of Montreal since the construction of the cruciform tower at Place Ville-Marie designed by Henri N. Cobb and Ieoh Ming Pei (1958–1962) (fig. 16).

In Canada, as in many cities around the world, Toronto, Vancouver and Montreal are growing vertically. In Toronto alone, since the beginning of the century, 67 towers have been built, 31 are under construction and 59 are planned, according to Radio Canada in 2020. Learning from Kagan's *Tour Métroplitaine* is more and more urgent.

fig. 16. Place Ville Marie, Montreal, 1962, Pei Cobb Freed & Partners.

4 / The Project in Practice

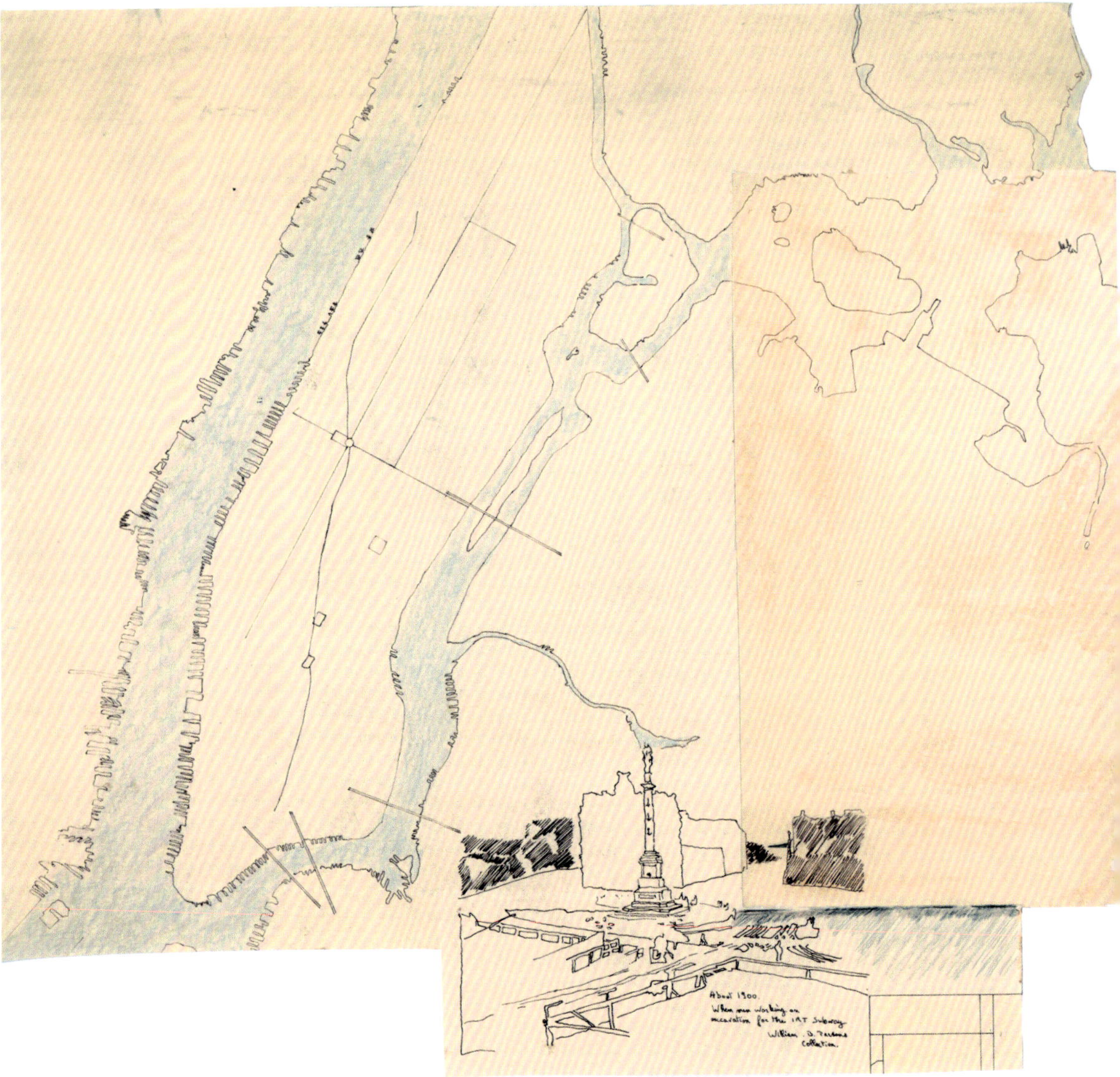

fig. 1. Sketch of Columbus Circle, New York. Michel Kagan, 1982.

The New York Years 1981–1986[1]

John A. Loomis

In 1981 Michel Kagan was awarded the coveted Villa Medici *hors les murs* prize, a French government scholarship that allowed the recipient to pursue individual architectural research abroad. Unlike recipients before him who typically chose to go to Rome, Kagan chose to go to New York. As he put it, *"I was interested in the structural urban parameters of New York, the city of contemporaneity, as opposed to those parameters of Rome, or any other European city."*[2] (fig. 1). As a part of his course of study, he was invited by Kenneth Frampton to conduct research and teach and at the Graduate School of Architecture, Preservation, and Planning at Columbia University. Frampton had been on the jury for the Alberti Prize, which Kagan won along with Bernard Desmoulins in 1978. Frampton was impressed with the talent and vision of the young Kagan.

Leaving the artistic grandeur of Paris for the energetic grandeur of New York City, Michel Kagan arrived in Manhattan in the fall of 1981 and began teaching at Columbia that same term (fig. 2). At this time postmodernism was at the peak of its reign, and Columbia was a hotbed of architectural debate between those advocating postmodern style and those defending the Modernist program. Robert A. M. Stern and Kenneth Frampton were the leading poles around which the debate orbited. Added to the mix were Claus Herdeg and other second generation Cornell school advocates of a renewed input of history and typology into architectural design practice. Romaldo Giurgola contributed a modern vision, informed by history, acquired from his apprenticeship to Louis Kahn. And there were many others representing variations of these tendencies.

Outside the context of Columbia, New York was emerging from the leftover economic malaise of the late seventies as well as from the shock of John Lennon's assassination the previous year. This was a period of rising economic activity, junk bonds, cocaine, and a vibrant art scene where artists like Laurie Anderson and David Byrne crossed

1. Text written in collaboration with Studio 7 architects Colin Cathcart and Peter Pfau.

2. Pentti Kareoja, Interview of Michel Kagan, in Michel Kagan, *Pro architect* 47, (Seoul: Archiworld, 2008).

from the galleries to the clubs, active scenes of both creativity and hedonism. Jenny Holzer's and Tibor Kalman's creative works confronted the wreckage of Reaganism. New York City was a rich locus for learning and experimentation that drew Columbia students away from the classroom. In the early part of the eighties, before Phillip Johnson's *coup d'etat*, the IAUS was in full flower with exhibitions like Rem Koolhaas' *Delirious New York*, a robust public lecture series, innovative design education programs, and a platform for new critical thinking about urbanism.

To this context Michel Kagan brought the European, Parisian urban experience, informed by the principles of Le Corbusier and a rigorous modernist formation at U.P.8 where under the mentorship of Henri Ciriani geometry was embraced as the predominant intellectual tool, the "instrumentalization of rules"[3] for architectural design. Geometry, and the orthogonal grid in three dimensions, were activated by the frame, and here Michel Kagan also looked to Giuseppe Terragni's work. One of the urban goals of architecture was to create a *pièce urbaine*, a place of urbanity, not unlike Hanna Arendt's[4] place of public appearance. The *pièce urbaine*, was conceived as a strategic catalyst that could influence the greater urban fabric. Taking all this to Columbia University at the height of postmodernism's influence, Michel Kagan stated *"My role was to provide another architecture, an architecture of relations and serenity, an alternative to the historical kitsch of the times."*[5] He also brought an interest in the

fig. 2. View of New York, the cubist city. Photo Michel Kagan, 1982.

3. Ibid.

4. Hannah Arendt, *The Human Condition* (Chicago: University of Chicago Press, 1958).

5. Pentti Kareoja, Interview of Michel Kagan, op. cit.

prismatic materiality of light, a "search for splendid luminosity"[6] as Richard Ingersoll so aptly puts it. And above all he brought a true compassion for people and an intense passion for the craft of architecture.

Beyond the formal, Michel Kagan also had an in-depth working knowledge of multi-housing design which he shared with his students in a surprisingly matter of fact way. No doubt his time working with Henri Ciriani and his passion for Le Corbusier contributed to this intuitive understanding of the issues. To discussions about distribution and possible layouts, he answered with an encyclopedic understanding of the collective housing history.

For Michel Kagan, teaching was research, and an important activity related to practice. Teaching and practice formed a critical dialectic that informed each other and operated at opposite scales. Apart from the macro, urban research, he also attended to the micro and achieved small architectural gems such as the upper east side Filine beauty salon. The two most important architectural projects, both competitions, of the New York years were The Peak, Hong Kong (1982) and Tête La Défence, Paris (1984). They were the work of Studio 7 which included Brigitte de Kosmi as well as Columbia students: Colin Cathcart, Ted Krueger, Peter Pfau, Faye Sueltz and myself (fig. 3). Kenneth Frampton served as a discrete advisor and friendly *eminence grise*. Kagan called his competition sketches 'research', and his teammates remember his patient narration of the collaborative design process: "Look to the image!". Studio 7 was a dialectic synthesis of his teaching and practice.

Studio 7's first project, the international competition for The Peak in Hong Kong was for an international conference center located high on a splendid escarpment site with panoramic views of the city and harbor below. An axis was deployed perpendicular to the slope of the hill as the primary organizer. It generated an architectural promenade that was also built out as a three-dimensional frame that contained major programmatic components. Gently cradling the promenade frame were two graceful curves, one developed as a residential block, the other as an esplanade balcony/retaining wall. Like cupped hands they also acknowledged the formal organic nature of the landscape. The conference center was both an object in the landscape and landscape itself. And the opposing

6. Richard Ingersoll, "The work of Michel Kagan: a gift of luminosity", in Michel Kagan, *Pro architect* 47, Seoul, Oct. 2008.

fig. 3. The members of Studio 7 in their atelier, 1983. From left to right: Michel Kagan, Ted Krueger, Colin Cathcart, John Loomis, Peter Pfau, John Frishman, Jeff Bacon.

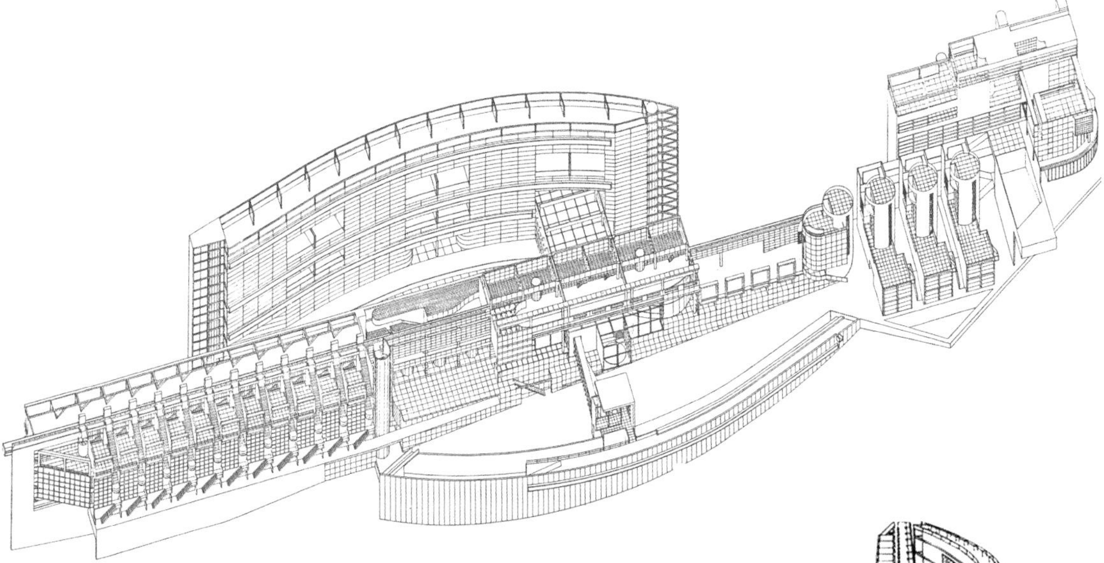

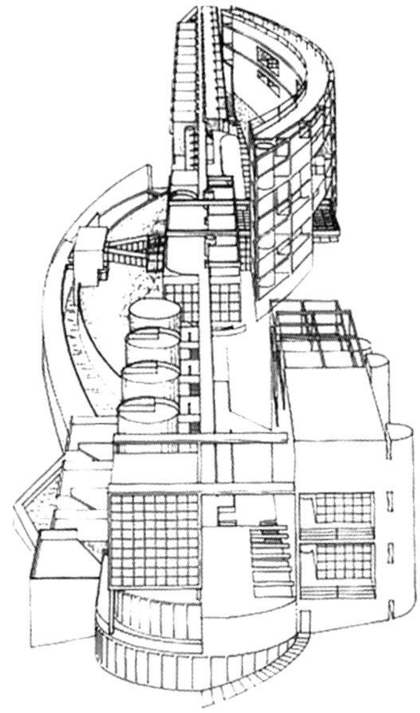

Peak, Hong Kong, Studio 7

fig. 4. Bird's eye view along the main axis.

fig. 5. Overall axonometric view: an urban set-piece.

fig. 6. Massing plan

fig. 7. Explanatory diagrams of the plan.

7a. Distribution of the masses
7b. Unifying framework
7c. Proportions and composition
7d. Framework and circulations

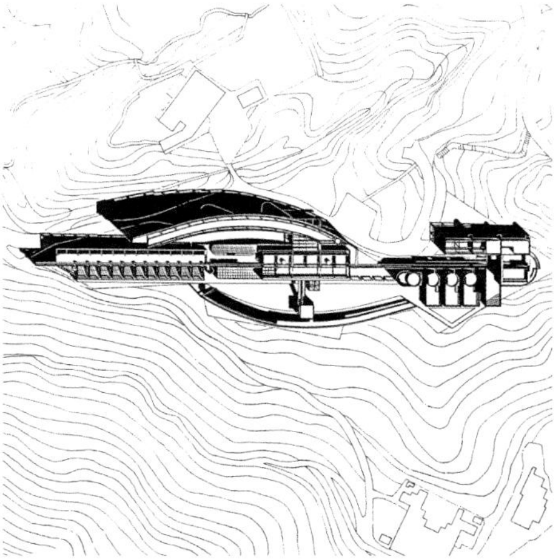

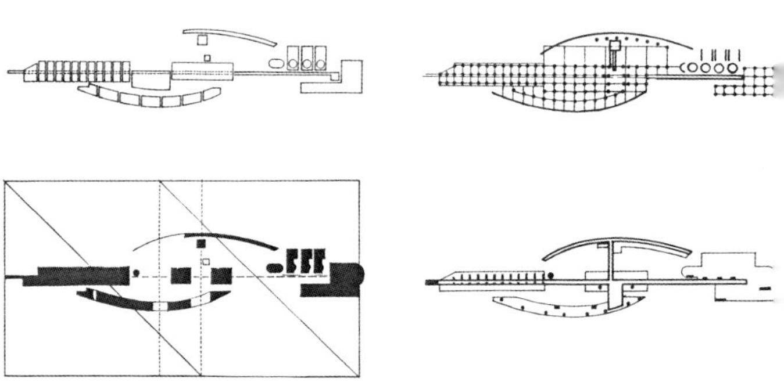

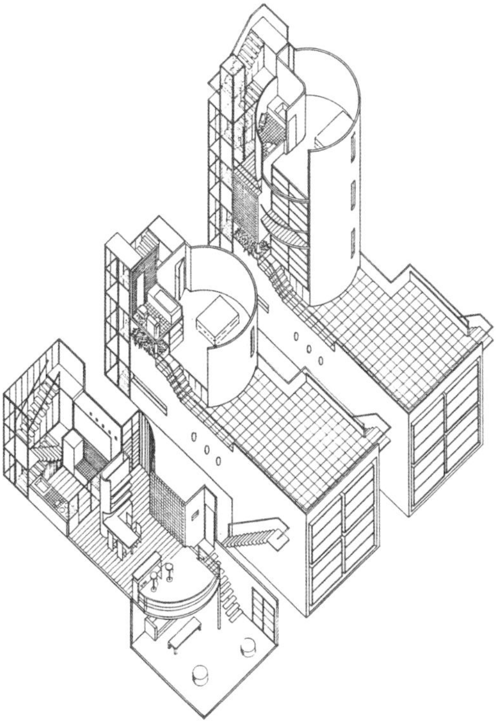

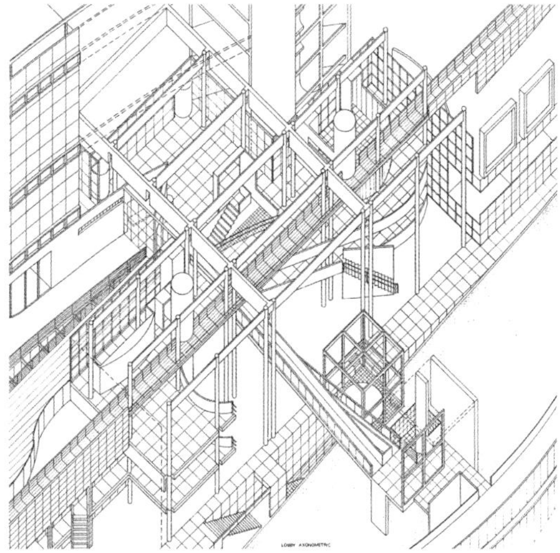

fig. 8. Axonometric view of the town houses.

fig. 9. Detailed axonometric view of a three-dimensional grid.

curved forms spoke of a yin-yang relationship and the interaction of East and West. Despite the brilliance of the project, the competition was won by Zaha Hadid.

Following up on momentum of The Peak, Studio 7 embarked on another international competition, this for one of the *grands projets* of President François Mitterand, the Tête la Défense project in Paris. This site was located at the extreme end of the long axis that originates between the two wings of the Palais du Louvre and continues on the Champs Elysees then through the Arc de Triomphe and beyond. Here the challenge was not so much as to how to address the axis but how to create a place, a *piece urbaine*, in the unfortunate placelessness of the uninspired modern La Défense commercial development. The Studio 7 project openly defied much of the competition rules and site restrictions and created a project as polemic. The project design captured and raised a length of the axis, flanked it by program on both sides, creating both a *piece urbaine* and an architectural promenade on the otherwise featureless 'parvis', outside the boundaries of the competition site. The project was decidedly not an object building and certainly not an icon, but rather a poetic programmatic proposition, a strategic whole that was much greater than the sum of the parts that honored the infinite projection of the monumental historic axis. Such a polemic ignored the unspoken political exigencies of the program, and as such was designed not to win. Nevertheless, it received an honorable mention.

Despite the collective operations of Studio 7 and the outstanding significant contributions made by its different members, punctuated by moments of communal culinary conviviality, it must be acknowledged that Michel Kagan was the undisputed design leader. His vision and geometric rigor provided guidance for both projects. And in both projects, Kenneth Frampton's thoughtful critique was

fig. 10. Perspective view of Tête Défense project.

a quiet keel that kept the sailing smoothly on course.

Michel Kagan taught at Columbia through 1984, following which he was a guest professor at other universities in the U.S. and Canada. Nevertheless, New York remained his locus of operations and his relationship with the city and with Frampton had a profound influence on his formation during his fruitful five-year period abroad after which, in 1986 he returned to establish his architectural practice and life in Paris.

What did those five New York years mean to his formation and how should they be evaluated?

"New York interested me as uniquely opposed to the European city," he wrote *"There is no dominant conventional streetscape, in most cases the four facades are visible from all sides. This cubistic vision of the city contrasts with the European and Haussmannian city and conveyed to me the meaning of the verticality of the skyline with the horizontality of the urban fabric."*[7] This was an important lesson. Moreover, for Kagan, the blocks of New York opened up the possibilities of transparency through structure, seeing through otherwise hermetic facades into sculpted functionally defined forms, with circulation and housing units silhouetted against lighted courts. The social housing of Le Corbusier pulled apart by the playfulness of Manhattan.

Not only did Michel Kagan learn directly from New York City. He learned from the amazing, accomplished people who lived and passed through there. He related meeting and getting to know Tadao Ando, Mario Botta, Fumihiko Maki, Richard Meier, Max Bond and Donald Judd among many others. He also learned from his students and colleagues. The U.S. was much more favorably disposed to postmodernism than France,

7. Pentti Kareoja, Interview of Michel Kagan, *op. cit.*

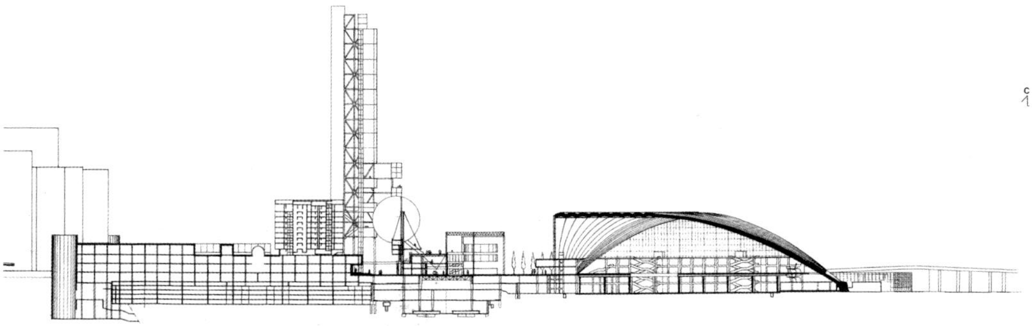

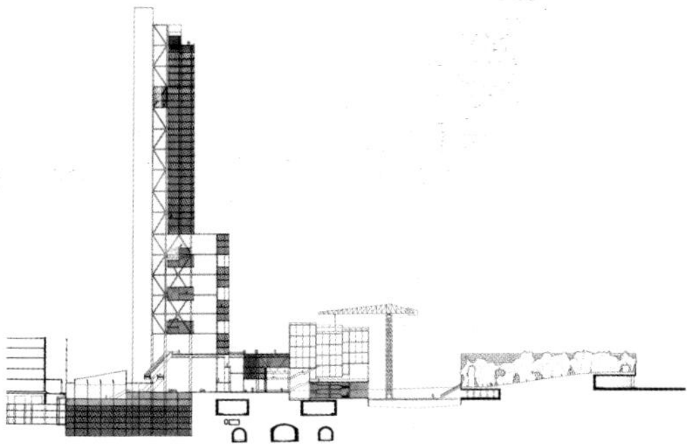

fig. 11. East-west section overlooking the CNIT, Tête Défense.

fig. 12. Longitudinal section along the axis of the project towards the CNIT, Tête Défense.

and often Columbia was apologetic at best toward modernism, quite the opposite of his passionate embrace and poetic practice of modernist language. He talked about feeling a bit lonely at times with his position, his belief in the social program, and his interest in the poetics of light, structure, and spatiality. His participation in the ongoing debates regarding postmodernism and modernism honed and refined his critical intellectual thought and discourse. Also, in his intellectual development, his close relationship with Kenneth Frampton is notable, and Kagan later related that he learned first-hand about the concepts of an architecture of resistance and critical regionalism from his relationship with Frampton. One of the fruits of this relationship was *Nouvelles directions de l'architecture moderne*[8], which the two co-authored.

It would appear that Kenneth Frampton and above all the powerful urbanity of Manhattan were the two strongest influences acquired from Michel Kagan's New York sojourn. He liked to point out that the 2028 blocks of New York City were laid out in 1804, the same year that Napoleon was crowned emperor. What a contrast in scale, what a contrast between the New World and the old Europe, what a contrast between a view towards the future, and another turned towards the past! For him, the New World provided an antithesis to the thesis of Europe, and the dialectic between the two resulted in a luminous synthesis that enriched Kagan's work throughout the subsequent years.

8. Kenneth Frampton and Michel Kagan, *Nouvelles directions de l'architecture moderne*, op. cit.

fig. 1. Panoramic view of Seoul, South Korea.

On Verticality in the Korean Project

Jae-Heon Jeong

When I was a student in Paris 20 years ago, while driving along the ring road around the city, I was struck by a magnificent building, white and very elegant: the Cité Technique et Administrative de la Ville de Paris. It was a real architectural and emotional shock. That's when I decided to go and see Michel Kagan and worked in his agency from 1991 to 1992.

A special bond

Korea is a small country a long way from France. And yet, a special bond has been established between this country and Michel Kagan, first because in ten years, he has designed four projects for Korea: two cultural centers and two housing projects[1]; And second, because he has reached an audience through Korean magazines. A monograph has been devoted to him, setting out his process and projects in detail as well[2].

A modern tradition

A tradition of modern architecture has existed in Korea ever since Kim Joong Eop[3], a former associate of Le Corbusier, perpetuated the ideals of this modern and generous culture, which is vital to Korean society. Admiration for Le Corbusier, as well as for Henri Ciriani and Michel Kagan, was promulgated by the many students trained at the Paris-Belleville School of Architecture, who helped spread these ideas. Michel Kagan's abstract, rational, and refined architecture met the Koreans' need for modernity and sophistication.

1. Ilsan Cultural Centre, 2002; Masan Cultural Centre, 2004; Heonin Village, 2006; Osan Urban Project, 2008

2. "Michel Kagan", *Pro architect* 47, (Seoul: Archiworld, 2008).

3. Kim Joong-Eop (1922–1988): a renowned Korean architect and professor, who worked with Le Corbusier in 1952–1956, building the French Embassy and Jeju University in South Korea.

The Korean context

Korea's geographical, historical, and cultural context is very different from the European one (fig. 1). On the one hand, 70% of Korea's topography is made up of small and medium-sized mountains. This means that any building site generally must deal with an uneven topography. Secondly, the scale of a Korean city is much larger than that of a European city. From the width of thoroughfares to the size of blocks, plots, and buildings, everything is larger than in France, and the verticality of the buildings is quite natural, given the scarcity of space and the high population density of South Korea since the division of the country.

fig. 2. Cultural center in Ilsan, 2002.

fig. 3. Perspective view, Masan Cultural Center, 2004.

These three Korean peculiarities—uneven topography, large-scale programs, and verticality—have helped shape a new context, and in all three of these dominant contexts, Michel Kagan has confirmed his talent as an architect.

Cultural center in Ilsan

Ilsan is a town near Seoul. The center consists of two parts: the first is a complex of halls including an opera house, a theater, a rehearsal hall and a cinema. The second includes a public library, and a sports complex comprising several gymnasiums. By installing a horizontal elevated figure in the landscape (fig. 2), Michel Kagan achieves several objectives: on the one hand, he gives unity to this group of halls of different sizes and programs. On the other, he creates a gateway to the mountain, wel-coming the public into a protected space open to both the city and nature. The 120 m length of this horizontal line is a simple gesture that conveys the large scale of the facil-ity. His project was ranked first by the jury but was subsequently downgraded by the design-build procedure.

Masan Cultural Center

This modest center includes a large Italian-style theater, a small square theater and a museum dedicated to the memory of the students who were victims of the March 15 crackdown. It is located at the foot of a steep hill, facing the main traffic artery. Once again, Michel Kagan developed the idea of a raised horizontal surface that would accommodate the museum (fig. 3), form a front along the traffic axis, and open up access to an inward looking outdoor space, located between the two theaters, the true heart of the project, open to both the city and nature. Here, too, the promenade continues towards the mountain, or towards an open-air amphitheater on the sloping roof of the Italian-style theater, which responds in counterpoint to the slope of the mountain.

The village of Heonin near Seoul

The program includes 40 single-family homes and 260 apartments. Located in natural surroundings, the project features a varied typology of single-family and multi-family dwellings. Michel Kagan proposed two types of layouts: a flexible one that follows the curved limits of the land, and a rigid one along a double north-south and east-west axis (fig. 4). Single-family dwellings are mainly located on the periphery, while the central zone is occupied by multi-family dwellings (fig. 5 and 6). The "archipelago" concept used here corresponds to the scattering of small units in a natural environment. The project, entitled "haute couture housing", was intended as a sensitive response to the brief, through a modern reinterpretation of the space of the traditional house, in harmony with nature. Kagan liked to say that *"The typologies we can propose in Korea must take the scales of traditional housing, from the house to the block into account. We need to invent intermediate scales, proposing a certain density to avoid urban sprawl, with rational urban planning capable of taking the environment into account. For this reason, it seems particularly interesting to revisit the question of the 'garden city', whether vertical or horizontal. Reconsidering the typology of the traditional Korean patio house, in line with new lifestyles and construction systems, is a way of reinventing contemporary Korean housing, on a 'human scale'"*[4]. Ranked second in the architectural competition, behind Robert A. M. Stern's classical project, Michel Kagan's design was much appreciated by the client, who subsequently invited him to redesign the entire Osan district.

1,500 apartments

For Michel Kagan, *"the tower is an urban and social condenser, in which the mixed-use program is a response to the need to densify the contemporary city, as an alternative to the diffuse city. It represents an opportunity to intervene in historic centers, to renew the heart of old cities, to create public spaces. The metropolitan tower is both a support and a force for transforming the city. It responds to the*

4. Jae-Heon Jeong, «Discussion with Michel Kagan on the question of contemporary housing in Korea», Seoul, *ANC Architecture and Culture*, no. 300, (May 2006).

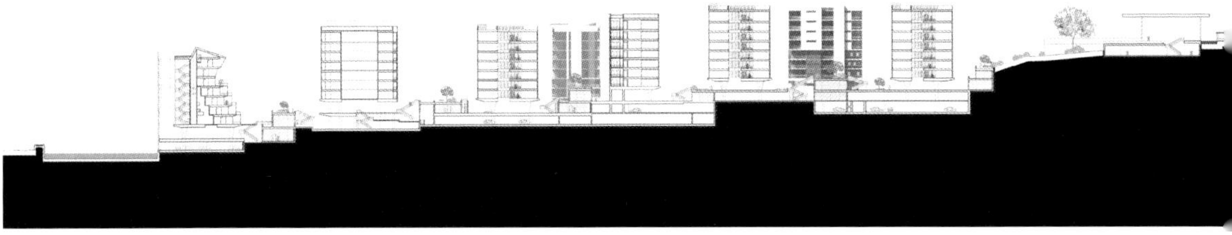

fig. 4. Cross-section, Heonin village, 2006.

fig. 5. Perspective view, Heonin village, 2006.

fig. 6. Project model, Heonin village.

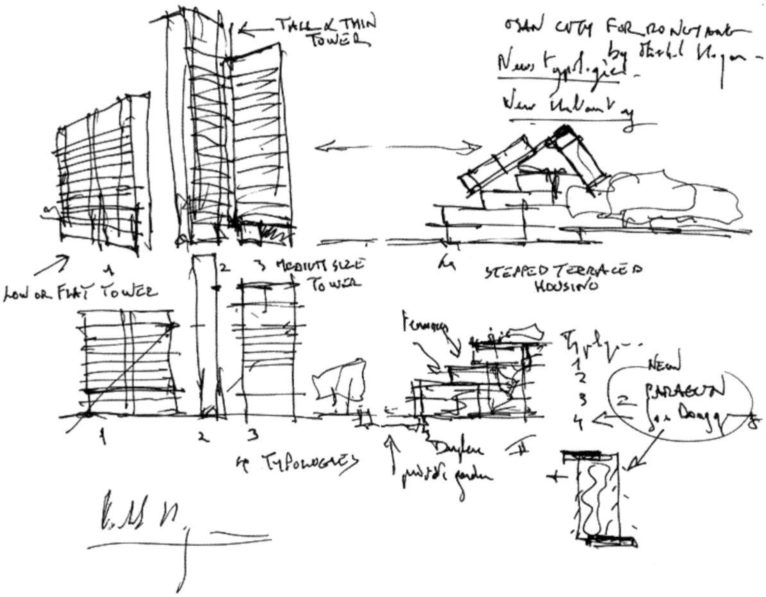

fig. 7. Research sketch for the Osan Paragon project, Michel Kagan, 2008.

goals of a sustainable environment by giving a new dimension to the issue of density and the vertical development of cities. Building vertically in a specific urban area is appropriate to mark a place, an urban event, a city entrance, a square... The condensation of elements along a vertical axis provokes a cross-sectional relationship between the horizontal and the vertical. Viewpoints between near and far create a duality between the regional scale of the city, in relation to the urban fabric, and modify the fabric by asserting a new urban potentiality"[5].

Michel Kagan had never previously obtained the opportunity to work on such a large, dense project. He was thus confronted with the urban question of large scale and verticality (fig. 8). The herringbone layout of the towers enabled him to optimize the orientation of the residential units to the southeast and southwest, and to avoid having any towers face each other, in order to keep the site open at its largest dimensions, i.e. the diagonals (fig. 7, 9 and 10). To get the full measure of the site, Michel Kagan compared it with his New York references for the towers, and with Paris for the central green space he proposed.

Over the course of his design studies, he progressively defined and shielded the large central green space with a continuous, terraced, linear building, a reference to Le Corbusier's Durand housing estate in Algiers. The function of this low belt of terraced housing, facing the river or the park, was also to address the issue of human scale and the approach to towers up to 36 stories high. It links them all together to control their spatial scale and make them safe to approach on foot. The towers are therefore not isolated objects, but the vertical extensions of a looping horizontal figure. The spatial experience of verticality is, therefore, experienced in relation to horizontality.

The scale of the towers is both tempered by a horizontal division of the facades into multi-story modules, giving an intermediate scale, and heightened by the finesse of the opaque parts of the gable walls. Michel

5. Jae-Heon Jeong, "Discussion with Michel Kagan..." op. cit.

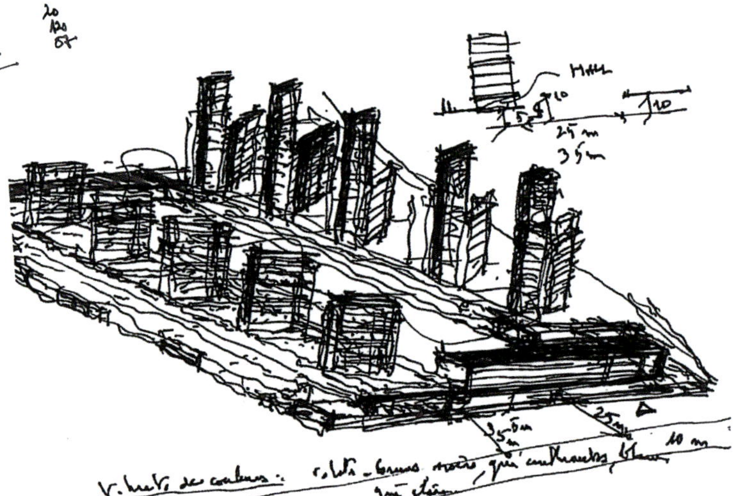

fig. 8. View of the Osan City project site, 2008.

fig. 9. & 10. Research sketch for Cité Osan, view of a tower, Michel Kagan, 2007

Kagan's mastery of this gigantic project was exceptional, but the project was temporarily interrupted due to a change in urban regulations and was not continued after his death.

Michel Kagan's contribution

Michel Kagan addressed the very essence of architecture: the value of space as a fundamental notion of architecture. Employing an elementary architectural language of planes and lines, and an abundant, refined spatial imagination, he created spaces of unique visual and sensual quality, light, airy, bathed in the whiteness and clarity of light.

His notion of space was always open, either through the light, through the view to another space or to the landscape, through an improbable extension or expansion, or through multiple uses that go beyond the program. The universe he has left us is in perpetual relationship with an elsewhere, near or far. He put humanity back at the center of this open space, offering sensations, emotions, and the means to read, understand and situate oneself in this artificial structure that is architecture, between city and nature. It is this humanist task that we take to heart, this path that he has outlined for us.

fig. 1. View of the Montparnasse Tower from Montmartre, sketch by Michel Kagan, 1998.

Theoretical Practice

Nathalie Régnier-Kagan

"From the surface city of the 18th century to the network city of the 20th century, the city in the making is a city in three dimensions: (height, width, and depth). It is horizontal and vertical, with its social and economic history and its anthropo-geographical territory. It is the 'integral city', a city whose strategy and program form the basis of a new democracy, that of equality of urban conditions,"[1] as Michel Kagan put it at the *Architectes Conseils* seminar in Rennes in 2006.

Michel Kagan often spoke of his "theoretical practice". He defined his thinking as deriving from his "project culture"— his experiences moving from one project to the next. But that didn't mean going from one idea to another. *"There is no greater pleasure than that of constancy..."*[2] he said in a 1996 lecture at the Pavillon de l'Arsenal. Some have criticized him for writing too little. He replied that his generation was considered "silent", in contrast to the "talkative" generation of the 1970s... His research, reflections and reading notes were compiled in black notebooks (fig. 1 and 2), filled with sketches and notes, which always found expression in his projects, as well as in his teaching. His drawings were not intended to please. He gave them a utilitarian value, to express a synthetic vision of the project, a spatial conception, a tectonic articulation, a geometry. His formal intuitions took shape in his design work and found a didactic dimension in his pedagogical experiments. Although he condemned the written word for its own sake (the self-referential "scholarly criticism" that says nothing essential) Michel Kagan wished more recently to devote more time to writing, to publications, to fix and transmit his thinking.

The theme of the metropolitan tower is a key research topic that he explored in his teaching, first in Montreal in 1986, then at the École d'architecture de Paris-Belleville, from 1998 to 2009. His New York years were the crucible of his theoretical reflection: projects for major international architectural competitions, the rare concrete realizations, and teaching at Columbia University were the opportunities to develop a real dialectical

1. Michel Kagan, "La ville qui s'invente" in *La ville qui s'invente, Actes du séminaire de Rennes, Saint-Jacques-de-la-Lande et Nantes, Corps des architectes-conseils de l'État* (Paris: Thotm éditions, 2008).

2. Michel Kagan, *Parti pris: Les espaces modernes sont les lieux modernes.* Conférences Paris d'architectes (Paris: Pavillon de l'Arsenal, 1996).

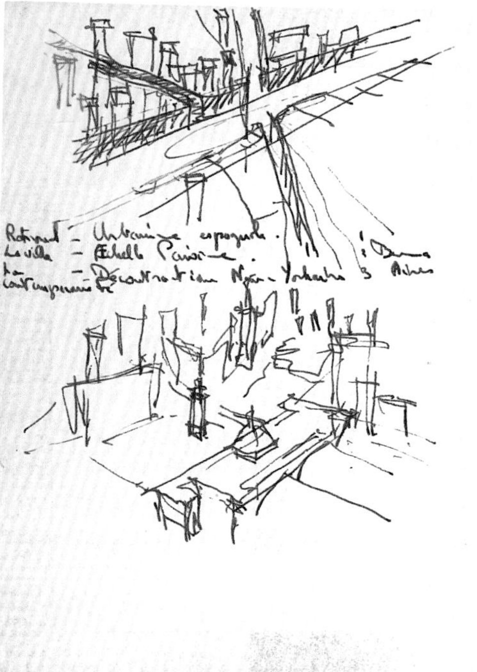

fig. 2. Buenos Aires, sketch by Michel Kagan, 1985 (See p. 44).

thinking, nourished by a deep architectural culture. These American years prolonged his training as an architect, before his immersion in practice. This time allowed him to assert his ideas and attitudes.

Michel Kagan's interest in the metropolitan tower was not in building a tower at any price for the sake of expediency, but in designing the "cubist" city, the three-dimensional city. The projects described here are part of this research. The theme of great height, or the vertical object, is not a goal *per se*. The aim is to develop the conditions for a revisited city, with a democratic vision and a strong relationship to landscape and topography: the vertical extension of the city, as a counterpoint to its horizontal extension.

Tête Défense

His involvement with towers began with an entry for the Tête Défense competition project in 1984—a project mentioned by the jury—which he designed with the Studio 7 team, "a team of architects from the 4 corners of the earth"[3]. The project aimed to physically rebuild the historic axis, by introducing a promenade-bridge a dozen meters above the slab. This long access platform, almost 600 metres in length, stretches out in front of the forecourt beyond the limits of the site. As a counterpoint to this linear "pontoon", which integrates both the CNIT and the Quatre Temps shopping center and distributes the various "cubes" destined for the Carrefour International de la Communication, the designers proposed a 177 m high, 12 m thick "flagship building" at the far end of the site, dedicated to ministerial offices. The building, like a prow, opens, orients, and energizes the main axis to the inner suburbs, well beyond the allotted site. The entire project was designed around a pre-existing 9 m grid on most of the lower levels, in a dynamic

3. Odile Fillion, "Michel Kagan, portrait," *Architecture Intérieure Cree* 211 (april-may 1986).

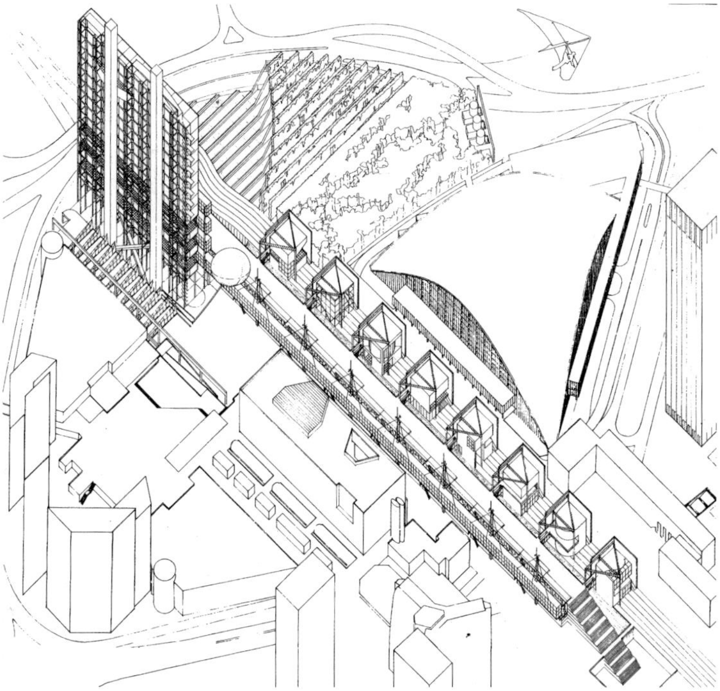

fig. 3. Axonometry of the Tête Défense competition, project by Studio 7, 1984.

relationship with the Nobel Tower and the CNIT, avoiding the heaviness of a frontal approach to the Champs Élysées axis. It was presented as an "urban piece" with the ability to glue together disparate existing elements and new constructions. The project's axonometry (fig. 3) is reminiscent of certain utopian drawings by Russian Constructivists, published in El Lissitsky's *Russia: an architecture for world revolution*[4].

The premises of the metropolitan tower are all there: the relationship created by cutting from the horizontal to the vertical, the repetition of an elementary module, the geometric understanding of a context, the symbolic presence in abstraction, the dynamic conception of space, the relationship between near and far.

European grid

Michel Kagan's first Parisian commission, the last part of which was completed just after his death, should be seen as the catalyst for his ideas: the Cité Technique et Administrative de la Ville de Paris, combined with student housing in the 13th arrondissement, was built over a period of more than twenty years. After several years during which he built almost nothing, while architects of his generation had already completed their first projects, he finally had an opportunity to express himself on the scale of the real city. This building embodies the idea of the "perimeter block", and of a city conceived in 3 dimensions (fig. 4).

The project originated from an initial study in 1987 for a possible development of the area, a derelict plot of land resulting from the construction of the Paris ring road interchange. It is located in the hollow of an on-ramp, below the boulevard on the banks of the Seine, the last Parisian Island to be rejected as being "outside the walls". The site's particular location, within a discontinuous urban fabric, made traditional urbanization impossible. Like a geography of the fringe, which would interact with a chaotic environment to form a

4. El Lissitzky, *Russia: an architecture for world revolution.* (1930; repr. London: Lund Humphries, MIT, 1970).

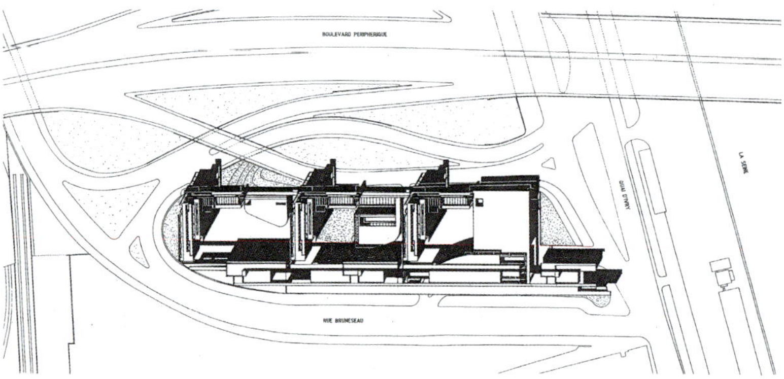

fig. 4. View of the Cité Technique et Administrative from the Périphérique, 1991.

fig. 5. Sketch of the possible block extention, 1991.

fig. 6. Cité Technique et Administrative block, first sketches, Michel Kagan, 1987.

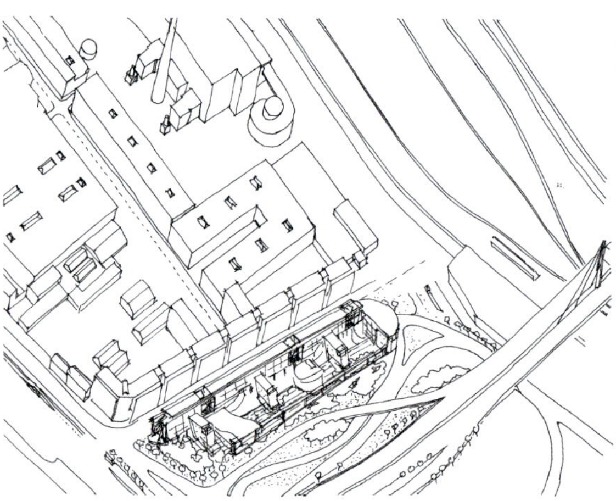

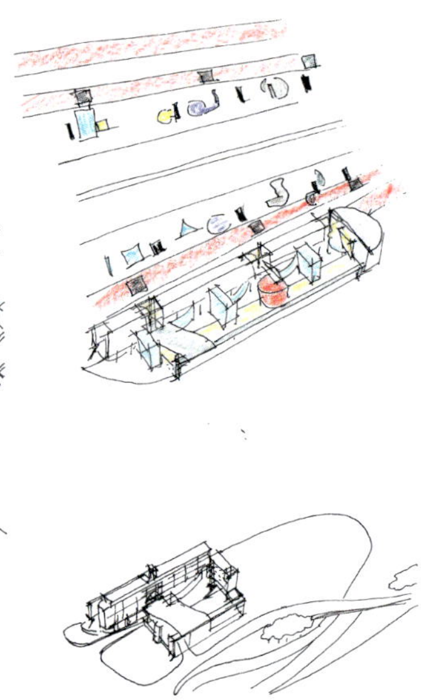

fig. 7. Tower of the Cité Technique et Administrative, 1991.

fig. 8. Courtyard façade of the tower, 1991.

contemporary islet according to a new urban grid, the project defines an assertive frontage on Rue Bruneseau, parallel to the ring road, punctuated by perpendicular "tower" buildings, and framing a series of enclosed courtyards or gardens—a theoretical sketch for a metropolitan architecture (fig. 5): Here, Michel Kagan elaborates the idea of a "European grid", underpinned by the linear conception of an American-style "parkway". The drawing (fig. 6) may also recall some of John Hejduk's projects.

Completed in 1991, the Cité Technique et Administrative de la Ville de Paris is a fragment of this system, a "matrix" that can be repeated. It is based on the dialectic of object and structure: the prominent office "tower" (fig. 7) pinches the ring road perpendicularly, and forms a square with a horizontal, linear building along the ring road. To give the building a presence and dignity, Michel Kagan created a protected perimeter, with garages and workshops, that creates a sense of interiority, like an enclave in this chaotic universe. He then raised the small, 33 m-high tower on stilts, perpendicular to the ring road, to capture views and engage in dialogue with the surrounding buildings. Engineers and administrative staff are housed here, while technicians work in horizontal buildings. The large, curved roof unites and shelters the parallel workshop and garage volumes. On the highway side, the tower is screened with sunshades and glass brick panels. On the courtyard side, the concrete wall widens to illuminate the functional exchanges between interior and exterior (fig. 8). Between tower and slab, the service courtyard articulates the spaces of this city in miniature. The complexity of the details—cantilevers, openwork or draped canopies—contributes to the building's scale and the relationship between near and far. The design is rigorous and precise, the formal ease is not gratuitous. It is at the service of potential uses.

The final element of this "phalanstery", the student residence, completes the architecture of the complex, along the rue Bruneseau, "consolidating the urban fabric". its purpose is to requalify the street. A horizontal building planned from the outset of the project, set against the backdrop of the

fig. 9. View from rue Bruneseau of the 100 students and young workers' dwellings, 2010.

ring road (fig. 10), balances the existing office tower. First sketched in 1987 as an industrial hotel, then as an artists' studio for which planning permission was granted in 1994, in 2005 a residential program for students and young employees was finally submitted, and completed in 2010, contributing to the urban mix of the Seine-Rive-Gauche district and its major university programs.

The edifice is a building that addresses the territory of the ring road: a linear building raised more than11 m from the ground, to escape the presence of the Brigades building along the street, it is punctuated by a series of *pilotis*. The 100 student apartments, spread over 4 levels, are distributed on either side of a central corridor and face either north, offering panoramic views over the Paris landscape, or south toward Ivry. They are structured by a 5.85 m grid of dividing walls, whose loads are taken up by two monumental beams almost 100 m long, which contain a technical gallery, in the style of Le Corbusier's Swiss Pavilion. The building is anchored to the ground at the corner of Rue Bruneseau and Quai d'Ivry, with the main hall, staff quarters, a study room, and a recreation area opening onto a semi-sunken patio.

The facades are in light-grey concrete divided up into identical square modules, alternating the solids and voids of the glazed bays and wooden shutters. The north facade is smooth, while the south facade features concrete and wood *brise-soleil* elements, punctuated according to the structural grid (fig. 9). The space beneath the *pilotis* is an opportunity to create a vast covered area open to the street, containing a suspended gallery and a monumental ramp in raw concrete, allowing the building to be walked around in a loop. Like the Roman basilica, it's a place where citizens can meet and talk under a roof, a place

fig. 10. Cité Technique et Administrative and its extension.

of urbanity, a plastic space that reveals the essence of the context, that creates it. The fire escapes are part of this urban-scale architectural promenade.

This building complex was both Michel Kagan's first and last project. It embodies the three main components of his work: the architectural promenade, the thick façade, and the importance given to structural expression. Here again, as at Tête Défense, the use of the vertical provides a landmark in the urban fabric, as a counterpoint to the horizontal; the tower is never an isolated object but is anchored and extended in the ground of the city, a full participant in the landscape. In his latest building, Michel Kagan employs his architectural language without superfluous gestures. The materiality of the building has become more concrete: the structural rationality, the tectonics of the façade elements, compose a mathematical harmony...

A number of competition projects, such as the medical and educational center in Bouffemont in 2000, the competition for the Liben harbor docks in Prague in 2002, the project for a new fine arts museum in Lausanne in 2004 (fig. 12), or the competition for the Pelikan district in Hanover in 2008 (fig. 11), all bear witness to this desire to address the design of a vertical element. But was in the last Korean project that Michel Kagan tackled the specific issue of designing a metropolitan tower.

Osan Paragon

The first "metropolitan towers" to be commissioned, Osan Paragon is an urban project on the scale of the city of Seoul: an entire district of 1,500 housing units. The project was not created ex nihilo: it grew out of an

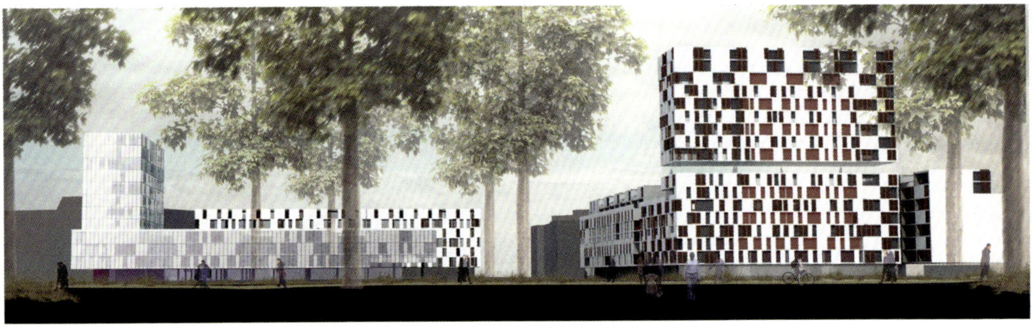

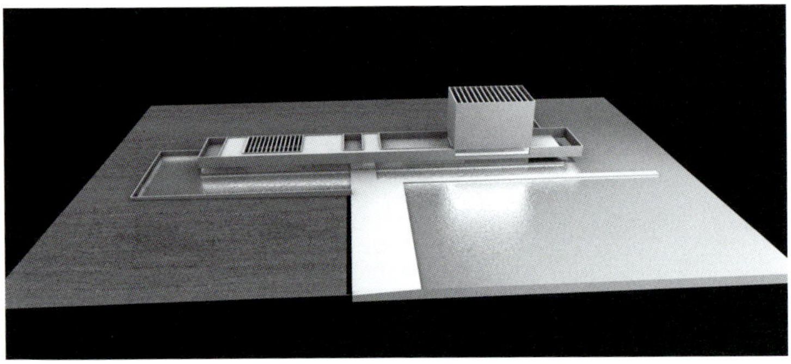

fig. 11. Pelikan district project in Hanover, 2008.

fig. 12. Museum of Fine Arts project, Lausanne, 2004.

initial master plan proposed by the Kunwan design office, which the developer wished to improve. The project, still at the schematic design stage, is a reflection on the capacity of vertical urbanism to create public spaces that can be held together and identified: it is an urban enclave consisting of a rectangular park that unites all the towers, in reference to Central Park in New York, or the gardens of the Palais-Royal in Paris (fig. 13). A change in urban regulations interrupted the process. Michel Kagan's death left the project unfinished...

The project site benefits from an exceptional location: it is situated along a 500-meter stretch of the Osan river. Its banks have recently become a new pedestrian walkway, below the existing road which was to be completely redeveloped. The site was therefore a major attraction, with significant potential for public spaces. This reclamation of the banks of the Osan River was to profoundly change the organization of the town center, which was to move towards the river to benefit from leisure and natural spaces yet to be defined. The presence of the Osan River was meant to give future residents direct access to those banks, for sports, walking or contemplation.

There is no city model without a clear relationship with nature. The view of the river, the calm it provides, its eternal presence, the burble of water and its reflections, are an inexhaustible source of pleasure, which was meant to be an integral part of the project (fig. 14). For this reason, the "feng-shui" and the need for the buildings to face due south were adapted to this specific situation. The urban figure and many of the buildings were therefore oriented towards the south-west, in order to identify this new district, the "Osan Paragon", by its relationship to the river, and not simply by a number on a gable. A large, rectangular, and very dense park was integrated into the heart of the project, and delimited by low, terraced buildings facing the river (fig. 17). Here again, the vertical springs from a horizontal anchor.

In a spirit of democracy, the apartments, both large and small, are arranged according to the same basic typology that determines the shape of the towers. The large apartments are placed in the foreground, opening directly onto the Osan River, but also onto distant landscapes and wooded hills. Each of these dwellings has three orientations: not only do they enjoy a panoramic view of the water to the south-west, but also a view of the trees in the inner park to the south-east, while offering complementary views towards the city of Osan. Alternating with lower-rise buildings, the overall plan features an intermediate scale of small towers more reminiscent of townhouses than high-rise buildings. The incrementally increasing heights of the buildings mean that those in the background, overlooking the inner park, also benefit from views of the river through the openings between the towers.

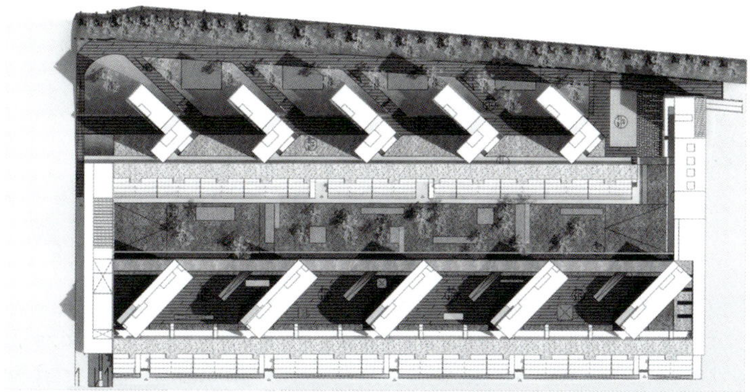

fig. 13. Masterplan, Osan Paragon project, Seoul, 2008.

fig. 14. Night view, Osan Paragon project, Seoul, 2008.

fig. 15. Study sketch, Michel Kagan, Osan Paragon project, Seoul, 2008.

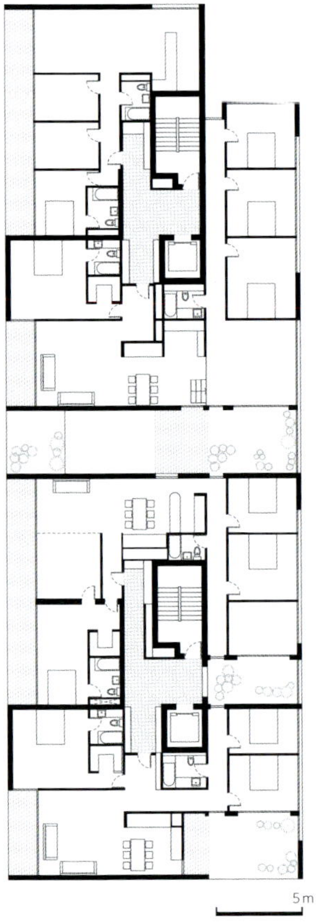

fig. 16. Plan of a current floor, sketch stage, Osan Paragon project, Seoul, 2008.

Megaform as urban landscape[5]

Michel Kagan has often quoted this text by Kenneth Frampton in his discussion of the Metropolitan Tower. It highlights *"the need to operate topographical transformation in terms of landscape, rather than through the independent aestheticization of a single building"*[6]. Although Frampton emphasizes the horizontal aspect of "megaforms" such as Le Corbusier's Obus plan, this concept can also be applied to the metropolitan tower. Raymond Hood's Rockefeller Center in New York is a most refined example, a city in miniature, asserting *"the plastic continuity of its forms to the point of being almost legible as a geological metaphor"*[7].

"Today's megalopolis is growing exponentially: "the new infrastructures have led to a chain of mutations, inducing a different kind of architecture"[8]. In these globalized contexts, Rem Koolhaas proposes another kind of response: "Bigness", characterized by its independence from context, by its higher and deeper dimensions, by an obvious

relationship to individual expressionism, both in style and in the glorification of the isolated building—rendering obsolete problems of composition, proportion, or scale. Michel Kagan always opposed the idea of relational architecture to this approach; He liked to speak of an "architecture of relationship", based on consideration of context, through abstraction rather than mimicry, on respect for human scale, through repetition and measurement, on the relationship between near and far, entailing a certain "harmony" of form, in the musical sense of the term, based on balance rather than symmetry, rhythm rather than assembly or collage, the use of a common language rather than individual expressionism, and rationalism with a capacity for evolution over time. He cites the example of Alvaro Siza in Evora, as an "urbanism of modification"[9] that is not inscribed in a defined time, and leaves open the possibilities of new changes. *"Place is therefore the primary material of urbanism, without which the city does not exist"*[10]...

fig. 17. Terraced buildings, Osan Paragon project, Seoul, 2008.

It seems that in the end, our perception of verticality also depends on the way we look at things: a street in Montmartre can become a vertical space in a quasi-cubist vision (fig. 18)... The metropolitan tower is ultimately an investigation into measure as opposed to excess. Michel Kagan defined the three requirements for a good building: *"the first is to adapt to its site, to make it resonate; the second is to offer a symbolic presence,*

5. Kenneth Frampton, *Megaform as urban landscape. Raoul Wallenberg Lecture.* (New York: University of Michigan A. Alfred Taubman College of Architecture + Urban Planning, 1999).

6. Ibid.

7. Ibid.

8. Rem Koolhaas, "Bigness or the Problem of Large" in *S, M, L, XL* (New York: Monacelli Press, 1995).

9. Michel Kagan, "La ville qui s'invente", op. cit.

10. Ibid.

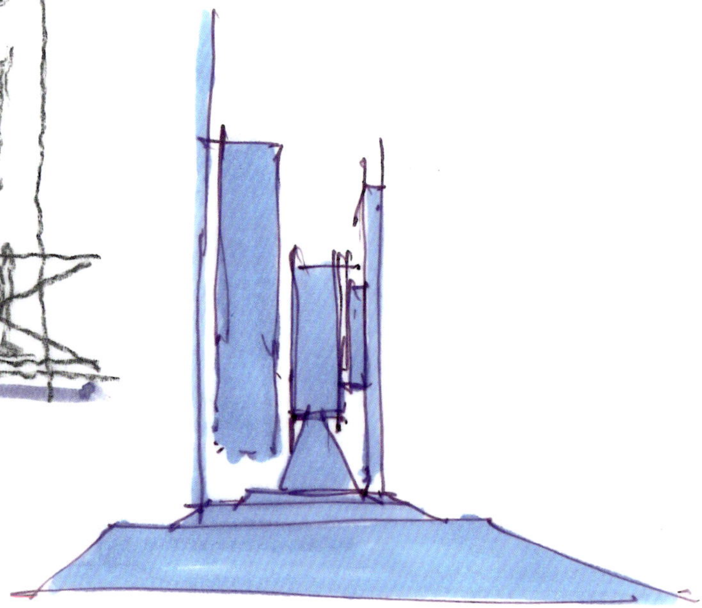

which is an abstract dimension, not an allegorical one; and the third is to be representative of a type. If this type doesn't exist, then it must be invented"[11]. The metropolitan tower is part of this objective.

When he spoke of his "theoretical practice", Michel Kagan wanted to show how his projects and his teaching were intimately linked; and how his existential experience and his artistic experience were as well. He was always convinced that a good building cannot be just a sum of good ideas; that a strong theoretical position is not enough to produce a beautiful building: it's a toolbox, useful for the project, but not a guarantee of the quality of a construction, nor of the success of a work... There can be no architectural creation without a physical and sensitive understanding of specific places. Rules are necessary, but not sufficient. Truth is not an absolute but must be sought through contradiction and dialogue. It is the spirit of this man of culture that I wanted to convey in this book...

fig. 18. Perspective sketch of streets in Montmartre, study by Michel Kagan for the exhibition "Paris côté cours", Pavillon de l'Arsenal, Paris, 1997.

11. Michel Kagan, *Parti pris : les espaces modernes sont les lieux modernes*, op. cit.

Postscript: Bruneseau Nord

After Michel Kagan's death, my fight to save the Cité Technique et Administrative de la Ville de Paris began. In 2011, the urban project by Ateliers Lion for SEMAPA, the developer of the area, had evolved, proposing a massive square tower set on the Cité Technique et Administrative, crushing part of the building (fig. 19). Partial demolition would have denatured the building and undermined its integrity. While I'm not opposed to the need for densification—Michel Kagan had already explored the possibility of extending the zone (fig. 5 and 20)—I went on a crusade against this project, which filled every urban gap and whose design denied any relationship to the existing buildings.

After writing to the City of Paris several times and taking advice, I began to apply to the Ministry of Culture and the Direction Régionale des Affaires Culturelles for protection. A number of key figures supported me in my efforts, in particular the historian Kenneth Frampton, Jacques Toubon, former mayor of the 13th arrondissement and former Minister of Culture, who had inaugurated the building, the historian Jean-Louis Cohen, the architect and town planner Christian Devillers, and the journalist and critic François Chaslin, Agnès Vince, then Deputy Director of the Heritage Department, and various institutions, including the Board of Governors of the Paris Val de Seine School of Architecture, the French Academy of Architecture, the French Society of Architects, numerous architects, professors and academics...

I finally got SEMAPA to entrust us with a feasibility study in 2015, to look at the possibility of building a Tower on the plot while preserving the existing building. We complied with the specifications in terms of surface area, and proposed a "lamellar" tower facing the Seine, along the quays, in line with the existing structures, respecting the visual axes and geometry of the site, and creating a "green corridor" along the ring road, on the former "non aedificandi" zone. (fig. 21). The proposal was accepted (in part) by Yves Lion and SEMAPA. With the *"Inventer Bruneseau"* call for projects, the City of Paris set about developing its own land, with a programme for 90,000 m² of floor space, including two towers 100 m and 180 m high. The competition was launched with this feasibility as an

fig. 19. Urban project for Masséna-Bruneseau, Ateliers Lion, 2011.

appendix to the specifications. Subsequently, four teams of developers and architects[12] were invited to take part in the competition: the architectural teams were selected from among the most prominent international architects. I was on the jury but I didn't take part in selecting the teams, and didn't vote for the winning project.

The speculative madness that reigned pushed the teams to build on the smallest m2 of land, without any breathing space and almost without any green space all along the ring road, without taking into account what was already there. The projects proposed luxury housing around the ring road, while ignoring the area's industrial environment. The winning "*Nouvel R*" project (fig. 22), a far cry from the kind of urban planning that concerns local residents, proposed housing facing the Seine, with no particular typological thought given to solar orientation, and no relationship with the context; temporary occupation of the Cité Technique et Administrative premises was proposed while the towers were being built, using the transitional urban planning method that has been practiced for several years in Paris, and dialogue with the architects was difficult...

At the Paris Council meeting in October 2021, a political coalition led by the Ecologists enabled a strong majority to oppose the sale of the land, which was essential for the construction of the first 100 m Tower: this vote scuppered the whole project. *"At a time of climate change and the drafting of the new bioclimatic PLU, the project ticked all the wrong boxes"*[13]: extremely dense construction along

12. Names of the four teams invited to compete: 1.BNP Paribas, Vinci Immobilier, Emerige, Cie de Phalsbourg / Porzamparc, MAD, Xtu, Carlo Ratti; 2. Unibail Rodamco, Sogeprom, Kaufman & Broad / Heatherwick, L. Gothmeh, D. Vaniche, Brénac & Gonzales; 3. Bouygues Immobilier, Novaxia / Big, Lan, NP2F; 4. Les nouveaux constructeurs, AG Real Estate, Icade, Nexity / Youssef Thomé, Hardel et Le Bihan, D. Adjaye, Buzzo et Spinelli.

13. Bernard Landau, "Le projet de tours dans Bruneseau nord va être remis à plat ! L'occasion enfin, d'un projet bioclimatique intercommunal ?", *La Seine n'est pas à vendre*, Lettre n°5, (February 2022).

fig. 20. Research by Michel Kagan, 2008.

fig. 21. Feasibility of siting a tower, sketch by Nathalie Régnier-Kagan, 2015.

fig. 22. Nouvel R project, 2020.

fig. 23. Cité Technique et Administrative, view from the roof of Hotel Berlier's building.

the ring road on a polluted site, lack of green spaces, shadows cast on homes, excavation of thousands of m^3 of earth replaced by colossal foundations in a flood zone, etc.

The Cité Technique et Administrative was awarded the "Remarkable Contemporary Architecture" label on 30 May 2022, the culmination of a number of initiatives. The article "Defending contemporary architectural heritage in Paris"[14], signed by Paul Chemetov, Jean-Louis Cohen and myself, and co-signed by more than a hundred architects, professors, journalists and personalities from all over the world, had a huge impact on the Parisian architectural scene. In the end, the City of Paris decided to abandon the *"Nouvel R"* project and to keep the Cité Technique et Administrative as part of its heritage and in use by the Highways and Parks and Gardens departments. Renovation is not yet scheduled, and the building is now covered in tags (fig. 23). The densification of this plot is now again under study, so the story is not over...

14. Letter written on the initiative of Bernard Landau, published in *Le Moniteur, D'Architecture, Domus International*, in October 2020, reported by *Télérama, Chroniques de l'architecture*.

Architectural Coincidences[1]

Sergio Crotti

Strangely enough, I got to know Michel Kagan's indomitable energy even before I got to know him in person that. We first met at the Geneva School of Architecture, where he was teaching. I stopped at the threshold of his classroom and listened to him chatting with his students and assistants. In the years after that, he visited the Faculty of Architecture in Milan, and the LIPAU in Bergamo in particular—which was also attended by Nathalie Régnier-Kagan and some of his close friends such as Hervé Dubois, Cyril Faivre or Jean Mas and others, and I was lucky enough to come into contact with the intelligence, culture, and talent that created the contagious aura emanating from his person. He himself invited me here to the École de Paris-Belleville and the École de Versailles, as well as to several Parisian events. After this long-standing relationship, the emotion of his absence today makes it difficult to distinguish between the memories of these personal relationships and the intellectual friendship he considered inseparable. In untying this knot within his school, how can we fail to devote ourselves to the duty of delivering my testimony as well as that of the many colleagues—from Milan or elsewhere—who also had the good fortune to admire the content of his thought and work.

It's hard not to appreciate the virtuous anomaly that enabled him as a teacher, to propose himself not as a "man of the school" in the academic sense, but as a militant architect. On the other hand, as an architect, he became a "man of research" and a teacher of great stature, because he was also a "man of discipline". He cultivated architecture

1. This text is a transcript of Sergio Crotti's speech at the Colloquium held on May 10, 2010, at ENSA Paris Belleville and the exhibition "Être et transmettre" in tribute to Michel Kagan.

as a specific knowledge, a knowledge sustained by the rigor of a very ancient ancestry, in the name of which he fought as much against the arbitrariness of architectural staging, as in favor of the demonstrable necessity of "habitat forms": "there" where nothing is superfluous, where everything stems from the power of inscribing reality "by design."

His thinking came from a distance to go the distance. It passed through the present. For him, architectural design was a radically projective act. He was acutely aware that pre-figurative anticipation brings with it a spatiality that modifies the living environment in a forward-looking way. This is why he condemned the aberrant situations resulting from architectural interventions that produced "new urbanisms without coherence". To this, he opposed a "return to the fundamentals" and, in this perspective, without any taint of historicism, he took as his starting point "the most advanced disciplinary consciousness", as one French philosopher put it. It took up and continued the legacy of the Modern, the last cultural stage in the reconstitution of the new status of architecture, reintegrating the spatial, social, and productive components of the built environment. Far from merely formalist replicas of modernism, Michel Kagan's intellectual acuity recognized, on the contrary, the very laboratory of a "state of crisis" which, in the truly phenomenological sense of the term, has become an intrinsic component of the architectural profession. Aware of the irreversibility of this state of affairs, his lucid aim was to rebuild the meaning of architecture in all its dialectical force. Following a course of such clarity, he strove to achieve a crystalline coincidence of the logical, ethical. and aesthetic contents that are the true origins of architecture. This "co-incidence" perhaps dispensed a sparkle of utopia that illuminated his thinking, coming directly from the "passionate attraction" of which Fourier spoke.

These recurring themes informed many of our exchanges. They underpinned his steadfast defense of the milestones of architectural work whose demands he shared. His unequivocal cultural choice led him to an uncompromising assertion of the reasons for architecture, linked to the founding sources of a specific knowledge to which he bore witness by renewing it. He rejected the "tragic insouciance" of the false avant-gardes of the recent decades, which, in pretending to infringe the infringed, have inexorably turned into rearguards subject to the clichés of multinational production of pseudo-architectural media images—profoundly removed from any disciplinary content. He was an authentic witness to his times, armed with the courage to plunge his projectual visions into the crucible of all its wrenching tensions.

He fascinated us with his insightful analysis every time, which he conveyed through an extraordinary capacity for synthesis, both in theoretical reasoning, and in applied demonstration. His stratigraphic vision, which penetrated the depths of things to reveal their underlying matrices, revealed the structure of the diffuse suburban magma that surrounds us. He knew how to bring out magnificent architectural crystallizations, with the precise contours that Gio Ponti wanted. On today's upheaved chessboard of architectural and urban space, he moved his pieces according to the skillful play of a theoretical, methodological and operational syncretism of project data. He achieved a virtuous fusion of "esprit de géométrie" (geometric spirit) and "esprit de finesse", (spirit of finesse) rereading French traditional references through the prism of open-mindedness and international culture. And yet, although he spoke of them ardently, he nonetheless commented on them with a certain restraint. He assimilated them deeply, to the point of making them part of his self-construction. Although he was endowed with astonishing artistic talent, these works were nonetheless devoid of any formal self-representational complacency. His creations are, after all, "mental constructions", before they become "material constructions". Perhaps this is where Michel Kagan teaches us that architecture needs architects.

Firm in his principles, attentive to others, he openly enjoyed discussion about architecture; and according to my discussions with him, he accepted the hypothesis that architecture outlives itself by metamorphosis within the genetic inscriptions of its deepest layers. We agreed on other points, not only that the architectural and the urban are inseparably linked to each other, but also on the existence of internal boundaries that arise in the course of their transformations. We shared the same interest in the generative nuclei of a new form of habitat that is not superimposed from the outside but is produced from within metropolitan extensions, as an aggregation process of a new "multipolar city", which he called an "archipelago city", made up of "selected parts of the megalopolis" that he raised as a banner in the face of "aberrant situations" in order to excoriate the disorientation of the "dispersed city", as he put it.

What remains and will remain in our memory of Michel Kagan's strong personality, in addition to his excellence as an architect and teacher, is above all his moral integrity, intellectual loyalty and civil courage, as well as his faith, tenacity, enthusiasm, and irony—all gifts of a rare soul. When one of my young assistants, seduced and fascinated by his intelligence, asked him about his cultural, professional, political, and religious affiliations, Michel Kagan replied with a simple, disarming smile: "Well, yes, I'm all that, but... I'm a free man! This luminous statement of freedom, which suited him in the most absolute of ways, remains engraved in my very spirit.

Contributing Authors

Michel W. Kagan

Michel Kagan, architect and professor, passed away prematurely on December 27, 2009. The creator of luminous architecture and a teacher with a fascinating international career, he was a major figure in a school of thought that grew out of the Modern Movement, in search of harmony between invention and permanence. For Michel Kagan, thinking did not mean adhering to this or that doctrine, but maintaining a constant dialogue with oneself, being "two in one".

Michel Kagan was born in Paris in 1953 and studied architecture at UP7 – Grand Palais. He graduated as a DPLG architect in 1979 with Henri Ciriani, and held a diploma in Arts-Sciences-Lettres, Thorlet Prize from the Académie Française. He was awarded the Alberti Prize in 1977, the "Albums de la Jeune Architecture" in 1981, the "Villa Médicis hors les murs" scholarship in 1981; he was nominated for the Mies van der Rohe European Architecture Prize in 1990 and 1992, the "Prix de la Première Œuvre" in 1991, and Le Moniteur's "Prix de l'Équerre d'Argent" in 1992. In 1991, he was awarded the First International Prize at the Buenos Aires Architecture Biennal for the Cité Technique et Administrative de la Ville de Paris, and the Silver Medal of the Académie d'Architecture in 1997 for his work. In 2006, he was awarded the "Pyramide d'or", the annual grand prize of the developers and contractors federation of France, for his apartment building built in Rennes in 2005. Three of his projects—the Cité Technique et Administrative, the student residence and the Cité d'Artistes—have been awarded the "Remarkable Contemporary Architecture" label in 2022 by the Regional Directorate of Cultural Affairs (DRAC).

Until 2009, Michel Kagan was a professor at the École d'architecture de Paris-Belleville, consulting architect for the French Ministry of Public Works, and a member of the Board of Directors of the Le Corbusier Foundation His career as an architect and teacher began in the United States, at Columbia University in New York, where he taught from 1981 to 1984, and where carried out his first projects. He subsequently held visiting professorships at the Université du Québec in Montréal (1982–1983–1986), École d'architecture of the Université de Montréal (2003), Syracuse University in New York (1986), and the University of Toronto's Study Abroad Program (1984–1988). In 1985, he curated and co-authored with Kenneth Frampton an exhibition and book entitled *New Directions in Modern Architecture*. Upon returning to France in 1986, he taught at the École d'architecture de Genève from 1989 to 1994, at the École d'architecture de Lille from 1994 to 1998, and at the Ensa Paris-Belleville from 1998 to 2009.

His practice was founded in Paris in 1987, dedicated to the design and construction of public buildings, schools, university buildings, administrative centers and multi-family housing. In collaboration since 1992 with Nathalie Régnier-Kagan architect, the firm has taken part in numerous national and international architectural competitions and is also developing a business in renovation and interior architecture, private homes, stores and apartment renovations.

Nathalie Régnier-Kagan

Born in La Rochelle in 1961, Nathalie Régnier-Kagan graduated as a DPLG architect from the École d'architecture de Paris-Belleville in 1989, and obtained a DEA (post-graduate diploma) in "Architectural and urban design" from the Université Paris 8 – Institut Français d'Urbanisme in 1994. She has been an honorary member of RIAS since 2011, and a full member of the Académie d'Architecture since 2016. She received a special mention in the "Women Architects" prize in 2015.

After working for Richard Meier & Partners in New York in 1990, then for Pierre Riboulet in Paris from 1991 to 1992 as a project manager, she entered architectural competitions on her own behalf, and built single-family homes and renovations in Charente-Maritime. She subsequently went into partnership with Michel Kagan from 1992, until his death in 2009. Today, she is managing director of the company, continuing the work begun with Michel Kagan. Since 2009, the agency has continued to enter and win competitions and has completed public facilities, housing and renovations in France and abroad.

Alongside her work as a practicing architect, she taught architectural and urban project theory and design as a senior lecturer at national architecture schools since 1994 (Rennes from 1994 to 1997, Versailles from 1997 to 2007, Paris-Val de Seine since 2007). She created a Master 1 course within the A-Ito Research and Study Area on the theme of the "Metropolitan Tower" with Jean-Michel Veillerot, Jean Mas, then with Laurent Beaudouin—a course that later evolved into the issue of the "Vertical Garden City" and the "Park City".

She has published numerous articles in the architecture magazines *Construction Moderne* and *Le Moniteur*, as well as a monograph: *Kagan architectures 1986–2016* published by AAM-Anteprima. She is currently an associate member of the EVCAU research laboratory.

Christian Hubert

is an architectural designer, writer, and translator. He is a Belgian citizen and a longtime resident of the United States. He was born in Washington DC in 1948, where his father was posted as the military attaché to the Belgian embassy. While French was his native language, his entire education has been in English. Christian Hubert holds a B.A. degree in European History from Columbia University and a Masters of Architecture from the Harvard Graduate School of Design. During the 1980's, he taught at the Institute for Architecture and Urban Studies in New York, where he was elected to the fellowship, translated articles for *October* and *Oppositions*. He taught courses at Columbia and crossed paths with Michel Kagan during that time.

Christian Hubert also maintains an architectural design practice and has designed residences for artists and collectors as well as exhibition installations, most notably the "American Century" exhibition at the Whitney Museum of 1999-2000, that contained over 700 artworks in the Breuer building. His residential projects for the artist David Salle were widely published. He also worked on projects in Greece, including residences in the Cyclades, and the renovation of a building in

Athens for the Deste Foundation. He continues to teach and to translate texts on art and architecture, including several recent books and catalogue essays by Jean-Louis Cohen.

> ***In alphabetical order:***

Georges Adamczyk

Georges Adamczyk, born in Paris in 1943, is a professor at the École d'architecture of the Université de Montréal, where he was director from June 1999 to June 2007. He was a professor at the Université du Québec in Montréal from 1977 to 1999. In 1983, with Kenneth Frampton and France Vanlaethem, he organized the colloquium Architecture and Cultural Identity. A researcher at the LEAP (Laboratoire d'étude de l'architecture potentielle), he is also a critic and exhibition curator.

Laurent Beaudouin

Laurent Beaudouin is an architect and teacher. He founded his own practice in 1980, immediately after graduating from the École d'architecture de Nancy. He was joined in 1987 by Emmanuelle Beaudouin, also a graduate of the École d'architecture de Nancy. Together, they have completed a large number of public buildings throughout France. In 2023, they were awarded the Équerre d'Argent for the Grasse Multimedia Library. They have also designed homes, houses, furniture and objects. On an urban scale, they worked on downtown Montreuil between 1992 and 2013.

Laurent Beaudouin began teaching as an assistant to Christian de Porzamparc in 1984 at Nanterre, after spending the year of 1983 in New York at the Cooper Union, with John Hejduk. He taught with Henri Ciriani and the Uno group from 1986 at Ensa Paris-Belleville, then at Ensa Nancy, and finally at Ensa Paris - Val de Seine.

Laurent Beaudouin was a member of *AMC magazine* in the 1980s; he has written several collections of interviews, notably with Henri Ciriani and Alvaro Siza.

Henri Bresler

Henri Bresler, born in Marseille in 1942, is an honorary professor at the Ensa Paris-Belleville, in the "Ville, transports et territoires" doctoral school, and a researcher at the IPRAUS laboratory (Belleville).

Henri Bresler has been involved in teaching since 1972, during which time he supervised "project" studios and taught courses in architectural history and theory. He has taught in Paris, in the provinces, and, for several years, at the Institut d'Architecture de l'Université de Genève.

He has published articles and contributions in numerous collective works, exhibition catalogs and reviews. He is the author of various studies and publications on architecture and urban planning, often with a forward-looking approach (Front de Seine, Entrepôt Macdonald...).

He is called on as an expert for educational missions; exhibitions (Centre Pompidou, Bercy-village, Pavillon de l'Arsenal); architectural and urban planning competitions; and to conduct studies for the Atelier Parisien d'Urbanisme, SAGEP, SEMEA 15 and ParisNordEst. Henri Bresler is an associate architect with SARL ACTOM Architecture in Sophia-Antipolis.

Catherine Carpentier

Catherine Carpentier was born in Poitiers in 1971 and graduated as an architect in 1997, for which she studied the themes of theater in the city and Le Corbusier's skyscrapers. Fascinated by theater, she decided in 2000 to do a DEA (post-graduate diploma) on *Maisons de la Culture* in the Theater and Performing Arts department at Université Paris X. At the same time, her professional experiences took her from Michel Kagan's agency to that of Emmanuelle Colboc, who welcomed her as an associate in 2010. In 2008, she attended the Urban Planning Chair at the Conservatoire National des Arts et Métiers, which opened the door to teaching for her, as she regularly worked as a visiting lecturer. In 2019, she joined the Architecture Department of Société du Grand

Paris, which is responsible for ensuring the architectural quality of the 68 future stations that will make up the Grand Paris Express.

Gwenaël Clément

Born in Valenciennes in 1975, Gwenaël Clément graduated from Ensa Paris-Belleville in 2007 with a DPLG diploma under the supervision of Michel Kagan on the theme of "an architect's house in Moebius space". He has been a partner at CD Architects since 2003. In 2005, he was awarded the prize for first work for the Jean Moulin nursery school in Samer. Assistant to Michel Kagan in 2003 for the "La trame verte" studio, he has also collaborated with Michel Kagan Architecture et Associés on various projects and competitions, including the Islan Cultural Center in Korea. Since September 2010, he has been a temporary project lecturer with Pascal Hofstein at the Ensa Paris-La Villette. Gwenaël Clément passed away on May 1, 2020.

Henri Ciriani

Born on December 30, 1936, in Lima (Peru), Henri Ciriani is a Peruvian architect of Italian origin, and was naturalized French in 1976. He studied at the Faculty of Architecture of the Universidad Nacional de Ingenieria (UNI) between 1954 and 1960 and went on to become a teacher (1962–1964) and architect, in public workshops, of the urban ensembles of Matute and San Felipe. He then taught at the École des Beaux-Arts de Paris: UP7 from 1969 to 1977, UP8 from 1977 to 1984, where he founded the UNO group in 1978, and at the École d'architecture de Paris-Belleville from 1984 to 2002. Since 2009, he has directed a post-graduate program at the UPC Faculty of Architecture in Lima.

From 1968 to 1982, he was a member of the AUA, where he joined forces with M. Corajoud and B. Huidobro. He has been an independent architect since 1977. He was awarded the Grand Prix National d'Architecture and the Équerre d'Argent in 1983, the Palmarès de l'Habitat in 1988, the Arnold Brunner Memorial Prize in 1997, the Exàgono de Oro 2000 and the Doctor Honoris Causa de la UNI in 2008. He was awarded the Chevalier de la Légion d'Honneur in 1997, the Médaille d'Or de l'Académie d'Architecture in 2012, and the Grand Prix d'Architecture de l'Académie des Beaux-Arts in 2021.

Pierre-Alain Croset

Pierre-Alain Croset, born in Geneva in 1957, is an architect and critic. He graduated in 1982 in École Polytechnique Fédérale de Lausanne (EPFL). As Assistant editor of the international magazine *Casabella* from 1982 to 1996 under the direction of Vittorio Gregotti, he published many critical works on modern and contemporary architecture. From 1985 to 1993 he was a collaborator of Luigi Snozzi at EPFL and in his office of Locarno. From 1995 he has worked as a professional architect in Brescia, where he founded his architectural firm with Chiara Rovetta. He was a visiting professor at the Columbia University (New York) in 1994, and in 1997 he won the position of full professor for architecture at the TU Graz. From 2002 to 2015 he was professor for architectural and urban design at the Politecnico di Torino, and from 2015 to 2018 he was professor of architecture and Head of the Department of Architecture at Xi'an Jiatong-Liverpool University in Suzhou, China. He is currently a full professor in architectural and urban design at the Politecnico di Milano.

Sergio Crotti

Born in Bergamo, Italy, in 1938, Sergio Crotti studied architecture at the Politecnico di Milano, graduating in 1963. His work is published in numerous international journals and monographs. As member of the editorial boards of journals such as *Casabella*, *Edilizia Moderna*, *Frames*, *Cahiers de l'art et de la Ville* and *Politecnico*, he is author of numerous articles and essays on architecture, urban issues and intervention strategies in the process of urban change, published in various books and thematic collections. He has also authored monographs on contemporary architects. Full professor at the Politecnico di Milano since 1970, he was awarded wirh the Chair of Architecture and Urban Design in the Department of Architecture in 1980 and has directed the Doctorate in Architecture and Urban Design since 1995. He was director of LIPAU workshops—Laboratori Internazionali di Progettazione Architettonica e Urbana (International Workshops in Architectural and Urban Design)—between 1995 and 2007.

Hervé Dubois

Born in 1960 in Neuilly-sur-Seine, Hervé Dubois studied at UP8 and graduated from the École d'architecture de Paris-Belleville. In 1983, he founded the Philtre studio with E. Georges, C. Faivre, C. Massin and L. Tournié, which won the "Albums de la Jeune architecture" award in 1990, the call for young architects from the City of Paris the same year, and was selected in the final phase of the competition for the Mont-Beuvray museum in 1991. He mainly designed residential buildings, notably in the Citroën, Bercy and Masséna ZAC (concerted development zones) in Paris. He has teamed up with M. Macian and S. Ramseyer within the DMR agency and a member of the Rad EEIG in partnership with Italian and Spanish agencies. From 1990 to 1993, he taught at the École d'architecture de Genève in M. Kagan's team, then from 1994 to 2007 at the École d'architecture de Lille. A tenured professor since 2002, since 2007 he has taught at Ensa Marseille and Ensa Paris - Val de Seine. He regularly takes part in international seminars in Bergamo, Athens and Piacenza, and has been a guest lecturer at Politecnico di Milano since 2003. Since 2007, he has been consulting architect for the Indre department.

Elena Fontanella

Born in Milan in 1984, Elena Fontanella graduated in Architecture in 2009 with a project for the transformation of Tolbiac-Chevaleret district in Paris (directed by Sergio Crotti) at the Politecnico di Milano. There, she also obtained her Ph.D. in Architectural and Urban Design in 2014, with a thesis on the topic of modification of existing buildings and fabrics, directed by Ilaria Valente. She attended in 2007–2008, Michel Kagan's architectural project studios (master 2), as part of the Erasmus programme at Ensa Paris-Belleville. She is currently a researcher in Architectural and Urban Composition at the Department of Architecture and Urban Studies, where she is carrying out a research project on the architecture of motorway infrastructures, under the direction of Andrea Gritti. She has been teaching at the Politecnico di Milano, since 2015, initially as a lecturer (with Corinna Morandi, Nikos Ktenàs and Pierre-Alain Croset), and as assistant professor in an architectural design studio since 2022.

Kenneth Frampton

Born in 1930 in the United Kingdom, Kenneth Frampton is an architect, critic and Professor Emeritus at the Graduate School of Architecture and Planning at Columbia University in New York. Trained at the Architectural Association in London, he became editor of the English magazine *Architectural Design* (1962–1965). after practicing for many years in England and Israel. He has taught at numerous institutions, including the Royal College of Art (1961–1964), Princeton University (1966–1971), ETH in Zurich, EPFL in Lausanne, the Academy of Architecture in Mendrisio, and the Berlage Institute in the Netherlands.

He is the author of *Modern Architecture and the Critical Present* (1980), *Studies in Tectonic Culture* (1995), *American Masterworks* (1995), *Le Corbusier* (2001), *Labour, Work & Architecture* (2005), and *The Other Modern Movement, Architecture: 1920–1970*, (2021), as well as a fifth edition of *Modern Architecture: a critical History* (2020), He has received numerous awards, including the Golden Lion for Lifetime Achievement at the Venice Architecture Biennale in 2021.

François Giraldeau

François Giraldeau, born in 1953 in Montreal, has been a professor at the School of Design of the Université du Québec à Montréal (UQAM) since 1980. He is a graduate of Columbia University in New York, where he spent time in the early 1980s. His research focuses on the pedagogy and history of architectural education in Quebec. With Börkur Bergmann and Georges Adamczyk, he founded the Studio-Cube laboratory at UQAM, a research-creation workshop on architectural modernity, as well as the journal *Silo*.

Édith Girard

Born in 1949 in Soisy-sous-Montmorency (Val d'Oise), Édith Girard held a degree in architecture from UP8 (now Ensa Paris-Belleville), which she obtained in 1974. In 1977, together with Olivier Girard, Laurent Israël, Patrick Germe and others, she set up a research studio in the warehouses on the Quai de la Loire in Paris. She was a professor at the École d'architecture de Paris-Belleville since 1977 and, with Henri Ciriani, helped found the Uno group; she was also a visiting professor at the Berlage Institute in Holland, the Université de Montréal and UQAM in Canada, the University of Maryland (USA), the Alaba School (Beirut, Lebanon), the Shibaura Institute of Tokyo (Japan), and the Pilot University in Bogotá (Colombia). She built numerous social housing complexes and public facilities, and was awarded the Équerre d'argent prize in 1985 for the 111-unit Quai de la Loire project in Paris. In 2007, she was awarded the insignia of Chevalier dans l'Ordre national de la Légion d'Honneur. Édith Girard passed away on September 6, 2014.

Pascal Hofstein

Pascal Hofstein, born in Paris in 1957, is a DPLG architect who lives and works in Paris. He has taught at Columbia University and the New York Institute of Technology, after completing his studies at the IAUS in New York. He graduated from the École d'architecture de Paris-La Villette in 1982 and was an associate teacher at the École d'architecture de Lille with Michel Kagan, École d'architecture de Rouen, then Paris-Belleville with the Groupe UNO. Since 2006, he has been a tenured professor at the Ensa Paris-La Villette. Since returning to France in 1998, Atelier Pascal Hofstein has built a number of public facilities, including the École Anne Franck in Les Molières (1998), La Maison de la Communauté de Communes in Cattenom (2006), and the Foyer de l'Enfance in Sucy-en-Brie with D. Paysage (2008). The Atelier is currently working on the delivery of several public buildings of varying scales. A study on vertical space called "TBTWIN" is currently underway.

Jae-Heon Jeong

Jeong Jae-Heon, born in Kunoui, Korea, in 1963, studied architecture at Sungkyungkwan University and the Ensa Paris-Belleville, France. He joined Michel Kagan's Paris office in 1991. He opened his own architectural practice in 1998 and teaches at Kyung Hee University. He won the Seoul City Architecture Award in 2005 for the Zeroone Design Center, the Korean Institute of Architects Award in 2006 for the Woori Hospital and the Gyeonggi-do Architectural Award in 2009 for the Dongbaek House. His built work includes the Dumulmeori House, an apartment building in Donggeom-ri, Jaundang in Jeonju and the Yiin Design Center in Busan.

Nikos Ktenàs

Born in Piraeus, Greece, in 1960, Nikos Ktenàs obtained a degree in architecture from Cornell University (Ithaca, NY) in 1983, after studying at New York University, Columbia University,

London and Cooper Union (New York). He taught from 1985 to 1993 at the École Polytechnique Fédérale de Lausanne with Luigi Snozzi, from 2005 to 2013 at the Mendrisio Academy of Architecture and from 2014 to 2022 at the AUIC of the Politecnico di Milano. He opened his own architectural practice in Lugano, Switzerland, in 1987, and in Athens in 1993. His work has been widely recognized and published in many national and international journals; he was shortlisted for the Mies van der Rohe Award in 2001 and 2003, and has taken part in exhibitions including the NAI (Netherlands Architecture Institute) in Rotterdam in 1998, the Pavillon de l'Arsenal in Paris in 1999, the 7th Venice Architecture Biennale in 2000, and the Cesare Cattaneo archive at Cernobbio in Comes in 2002. In 2008, he was awarded the Hellenic Institute of Architecture Prize for his work. He died on July 13, 2022.

Norbert Laurent

Norbert Laurent, born in Paris in 1956, is a DPLG architect with a Certificate of Advanced Studies from the École nationale des Ponts et Chaussées, specializing in Regional and Urban Planning. He has been a freelance architect in Paris since 1988. His main projects are new-build or extension/rehabilitation projects for schools and housing. He has taught in architecture schools since 1992, first at the École d'architecture de Paris-Tolbiac, then at Ensa Paris-La Villette and Ensa Paris-Val de Seine until 2023. He devotes part of his time to the dissemination of architecture, as editor-in-chief of *Construction Moderne* magazine and through the publication of thematic and monographic works.

John Loomis

John A. Loomis, born 1951 in Fresno, California, is a FAIA architect, author, and professor at San José State University in California. He is a former director of CyArk, a non-profit organization that applies geospatial technologies to World Heritage Sites. He practiced architecture in New York with Studio 7, with Mitchell Giurgola Architects, then with Kiss Cathcart Architects; he has taught architecture at the City College of New York, the California College of Art, and Stanford University. His work has appeared in journals such as *Design Book Review*, *Casabella*, *Harvard Design Magazine* and *Architectural Record*. He has also been a visiting fellow at the Getty Research Institute and a Loeb Fellow at Harvard University.

Miguel Macian

Miguel Macian, born in Paris in 1957, graduated as a DPLG architect from École d'architecture de Toulouse in 1985 and obtained a DEA in Paris in 1999. He was awarded tenure at Ensa Nantes in 2003, and has been a lecturer in design at Ensa Paris-Belleville since 2012. After working as an assistant to Michel Kagan at the École d'architecture de Genève from 1991 to 1994, he accompanied Kagan when he took up a post at the École d'architecture Lille from 1994 to 1997, and Ensa Paris-Belleville in 1999. On these occasions, he was involved in teaching both the metropolitan tower and the green grid. He has worked as a project manager in association with Sébastien Ramseyer.

Jean Mas

Jean Mas, architect, was born in 1954 in Casablanca. He is one of the six founding partners of the Paris-based Ateliers 2/3/4/ agency, which develops major projects in the fields of architecture, urban planning and landscape design. His initial training as an architect with Henri Ciriani at UP8 was followed by work with Richard Meier's firm in New York in the 1980s.

Jean Mas won the "*Albums de la Jeune architecture*" prize in 1985 and exhibited at the IFA in 1990 for the exhibition of 40 architects under 40.

He taught at the École d'architecture de Genève with Michel Kagan in 1991, then at the

École d'architecture de Paris-Villemin, and at the École d'architecture de Versailles. He is now an emeritus lecturer at the Ensa Paris-Val de Seine.

As a lecturer at the EVCAU laboratory, he was co-founder of the A-Ito (Architecture/Laboratoire des Territoires Ouverts) Master's program at Paris – Val de Seine. One of its manifesto's essential elements is that theoretical project practice is central to teaching, and points to the urgent need to place research at the heart of project activity.

Jean Mas' projects have been exhibited on numerous occasions in France and abroad, including at the IFA, the Pavillon de l'Arsenal, the Venice Biennale, the Maison de l'Architecture and the Galerie de l'Architecture in Paris.

From 1991 to 1994, he was a consultant architect to the French Ministry of Public Works and Housing and has been a full member of the Académie d'Architecture since 2018.

Jean Mas has written and published numerous texts (notably in the magazines *Faces/Archiscopie/Moniteur/Construction Moderne/Archistorm,* and monographs (Meier/Kagan) on architectural projects or teaching, and regularly gives lectures in Schools of Architecture or at conferences in France and abroad.

Nancy Ottaviano

Born in 1981 in France, Nancy Ottaviano is a licensed architect (HMONP) and graduated with a research distinction from Ensa Paris-Belleville in 2008, where she completed her final project under the supervision of Michel Kagan. She worked at Michel Kagan Architecture and Associates agency in 2009 and later co-curated the exhibition "*Être & transmettre*" with Nathalie Régnier-Kagan. Holding a doctorate in spatial planning and urbanism since 2017, she completed her thesis within the Laboratory of Architecture Anthropology (UMR 7218 Lavue, EnsaPLV). Since 2008, she has been developing her practice, combining academic research in the humanities and social sciences with operational projects through the association Quatorze and the agency Quidam, which she co-founded in 2019 and where she is a partner.

Laurent Salomon

Laurent Salomon, born in 1954 in Drancy, graduated as a DPLG architect from École des Beaux-arts de Paris UP7 in 1979. After 3 years with the Atelier Public d'Architecture de la ville de Chambéry, in 1983 he founded Architectes Associés, a group of architects working mainly on the restructuring of urban peripheries. In 1988, he founded his own studio, initially working on the rehabilitation of the most deprived neighborhoods. Since 1995, he has been active in Korea, China and Germany. Laurent Salomon was also a member of the Corps des architectes-conseils de l'État from 1995 to 1999. He taught at Ensa Paris-Belleville from 1982 to 2014, then from 2014 to 2022 at Ensa Normandie, where he is now Professor Emeritus. He has been Visiting Professor at the AUIC of the Politecnico di Milano since 2015. President of the French Society of Architects from 1992 to 1996, then from 2004 to 2008, he is the author of numerous articles, has given many conferences in France and abroad (Germany, China, Korea, Ecuador, Spain, Italy, Japan, Mexico, Peru), and has taken part in several international cultural events, including the Venice Architecture Biennial in 1996, the Quito Architecture Biennial in 2003 and the 1st Shanghai Architecture Biennial in 2016. He was named Chevalier de l'Ordre des Arts et Lettres for his work and Chevalier de l'Ordre des Palmes Académiques for his teaching career in 2022.

Ilaria Valente

Born in Milan in 1958, and holding a Ph.D. in Architectural Composition (1992—IUAV Venice), Ilaria Valente is a Full Professor of Architectural and Urban Design at the Department of Architecture and Urban Studies (DAStU).

She is Vice Rector for International Affairs, Delegate and Responsible of the project NEWBAUHAUS@POLIMI, and the

Vice-President of the European Association for Architectural Education—EAAE.

At the Politecnico di Milano she was the Dean of the School of Architecture and Society (2012–2015) and the School of Architecture Urban Planning Construction Engineering (2016–2021). From 2020 to 2021, she has been the President of the Conferenza Universitaria Italiana di Architettura (Italian University Architecture Conference, the National Association of the Schools of Architecture).

Valente has collaborated with international and national research institutions, and public administrations. Her research is devoted to theory, tools, and design methods, with particular attention to the architecture of open and public spaces, studies on urban morphology and architectural typology, and the shape of infrastructures in contemporary territories.

Architectural and urban regeneration in the marginal fabrics and fragile territories are the focus of her research in recent years, particularly in recovering abandoned or underutilized public buildings, artefacts, and infrastructure networks.

Jean-Michel Veillerot

Born in 1957, Jean-Michel Veillerot graduated as a DPLG architect from Ensa Versailles in 1981. He became assistant to Édith Girard, then Laurent Israël and Michel Corajoud. In 1990, he founded the CITA architecture firm with Lucas Meister, Pascal Lefebvre, Léo Legendre, Jean-Luc Boursignon and Denis Cronier.

He began teaching at Ensa Versailles in 1993. In 2008, he joined Ensa Paris - Val de Seine and the "A-Ito" Master's program. He teaches "The Metropolitan Tower" with Nathalie Régnier-Kagan, then "Arborescence and Canopy" with Thomas Heuzé, and finally "Ville Parc" with Nathalie Régnier-Kagan, Laurent Beaudouin and Thomas Heuzé.

Jean-Marc Weill

Jean-Marc Weill, born in 1964 in Metz, is an architect and civil engineer by training. After graduating from the École d'architecture de Nancy in 1989, he studied engineering at Harvard University in the USA in 1990 and at the Conservatoire National des Arts et Métiers in Paris in 1995. He has taught at the École d'architecture de Paris-Belleville, as well as at the École d'architecture de Rouen. He is currently Professor of Science and Techniques for Architecture at the Ensa Paris-Est in Marne-la-Vallée, and Visiting Professor at the Faculté de l'Aménagement of the Université de Montréal, while continuing to work as an engineer in structural and envelope design.

Bibliography

Books on metropolitan towers

Alofsin, Anthony. *Prairie skyscraper. Frank Lloyd Wright's Price Tower*. New York: Rizzoli, 2005.

Alvarez Garretta, Ariadna. *Skyscrapers*. Barcelona: Atrium Group, 2002.

Baudrillard, Jean. *Amérique*. Paris: Grasset, 1986.

Bresler, Henri, and Isabelle Genyk. *Le Front de Seine, histoire prospective*. Paris: Semea XV, 2003.

Campi, Mario. *Skyscrapers. An Architectural Type of Modern Urbanism*. Basel: Birkhäuser, 2000.

Ciriani, Henri, and Laurent Beaudouin. *Vivre haut, méditation en paroles et dessins*. Paris: Archibooks, 2011.

Cohen, Jean-Louis. *Scènes de la vie future. L'architecture européenne et la tentation de l'Amérique 1893–1960*. Paris: Flammarion, 1995.

Cohen, Jean-Louis, and Hubert Damisch, eds. *Américanisme et modernité. L'idéal américain dans l'architecture*. Paris: EHESS-Flammarion, 1993.

Davis, Mike, "Sand, Fear and Money in Dubai". In Davis, M., Monk D.B., *Evil paradises: dreamworlds of neoliberalism*. New York: New Press, 2007.

Davis, Mike. *City of Quartz: Excavating the Future in Los Angeles*. New York: Verso, 1997.

De Magistris, Alessandro. *Ivan Leonidov 1902–1959*. Milano: Electa, 2009.

Dunnett, James, and Gavin Stamp. *Goldfinger Ernö: Works I*. London: Architectural Association, 1983.

El Lissitzky. *Russia: an architecture for world revolution*. 1930. Reprint, London: Lund Humphries, MIT, 1970.

Ferrier, Jacques. *Making of Phare & Hypergreen towers*. Paris: ante prima AAM éditions, 2007.

Ferris, Jean. *Architectural visions, the drawings of Hugh Ferriss*. New York: Whitney Library of Design, 1980.

Ferriss, Hugh. *The Metropolis of Tomorrow*. New York: Washburn, 1929.

Firley, Éric, Julie Gimbal, and Philippe Honnorat. *La tour et la ville, manuel de la grande hauteur*. Marseille: Parenthèses, 2011.

Frampton, Kenneth. *Megaform as urban landscape. Raoul Wallenberg Lecture*. (New York: University of Michigan A. Alfred Taubman College of Architecture + Urban Planning, 1999).

Gigon, Annette, Mike Guyer, and Jeru Felix, eds. *Residential Towers*. Zurich: gta verlag, 2016.

Herselle Krinsky, Carol. *Rockefeller Center*. Oxford, London, New York: 1978.

Hill, John. *Skyscraper. Vom Tribune Tower in Chicago zum Burj Khalifa in Dubai*. Munchen: Deutsche Verlags-Anstalt, 2017.

Jacobs, Jane. *The Death and Life of Great American Cities*. New York: Random House, 1961.

Koolhaas, Rem. *Delirious New York. A retroactive manifesto for Manhattan New York*. 1978. Reprint, New York: The Monacelli Press, 1994.

Koolhaas, Rem, and Bruce Mau. *S, M, L, XL: small, medium, large, extra-large*. New York: The Monacelli Press, 1995.

Le Corbusier. *When the Cathedrals where White*. 1937. Reprint, New York, Toronto, London: McGraw-Hill Book Company, 1947.

Lipman, Jonathan. *Frank Lloyd Wright and the Johnson Wax Building*. New York: Rizzoli, 1986.

Marchand, Bruno, *Habiter en hauteur. Traditions organiques: des tours de La Borde (1961–1968) de Frédéric Brugger aux réalisations contemporaines.* Gollion: inFolio, 2013.

Mendelsohn, Eric. *Amerika*. 1926. Reprint, Paris: Les Éditions du Demi-cercle, 1992.

Paquot, Thierry. *La folie des hauteurs. Critique du gratte-ciel*. Gollion: Infolio, 2017.

Richard Plunz, *A History of Housing in New York City*. New York: Columbia University Press, 1992.

Sullivan, Louis. *The Public Papers*. Chicago: Chicago University Press, 1988. translated in French by Christophe Guillouët, Pour un art du gratte-ciel, ed. Allia, Paris, 2015.

Taillandier, Ingrid, Olivier Namias, and Jean-François Pousse, eds. *L'invention de la tour européenne*. Paris: Éd. du Pavillon de l'Arsenal-Picard, 2009.

Yeang, Ken. *The Green Skyscraper: The Basis for Designing Sustainable Intensive Buildings*. London: Prestel Pub, 2000.

Yeang, Ken. *Reinventing the skyscraper*. New York: Graw Hill, 1995.

Willis, Carol. *Form follows finance. Skyscrapers and skylines in New York and Chicago*. New York: Princeton Architectural Press, 1995.

Articles, magazines on metropolitan towers

Appert, Manuel. "Politique du skyline. Shard et le débat sur les tours à Londres." *Métropolitiques* 12 (September 2011).

Bresler, Henri, and Genyk Isabelle, "Paris Front de Seine, un patrimoine en devenir," *AMC* 146 (October 2004): 96-103.

Campo Baeza, Alberto, "Mil razones para una torre," *Arquitectura* 320 (1999): 24-27.

Chaslin, François, "Hauteurs de Paris." In *Surélévations. Conversations urbaines*, edited by Bruno Marchand and Christophe Joud, 182-207. Gollion: inFolio, 2018.

Cooke, Catherine, "Chernikov fantasy and construction," *Architectural Design profile* 55 (1984).

Criticat 1 (January 2008), 56-63.

Devillers, Christian, "La tour d'horizon," *L'Architecture d'Aujourd'hui* 282, (1992):128-133.

Didelon, Clarisse. "Une course vers le ciel: mondialisation et diffusion spatio-temporelle des gratte-ciel," *M@ppemonde* 99 (2010).

Siza, Alvaro, "Torre en Manhattan/Tower in Manhattan," *El Croquis* 215/216 (2022): 318-341.

Vernes, Michel, "Le gratte-ciel toujours recommencé," *Archi Crée* 211 (April-May 1986), 74-93.

▪

Hubert, Christian, and Shapiro Lindsay Stamm, "*William Lescaze*," *Catalogue 16 IAUS*. New York: Rizzoli, 1982.

Quilici, Vieri, and S. O. Khan-Magomedov, "*Ivan Leonidov*," *Catalogue 8 IAUS*. New York: Rizzoli, 1981.

Stern, Robert A. M, and Thomas P. Catalano, "*Raymond M. Hood*," *Catalogue 15 IAUS*. New York: Rizzoli, 1982.

▪

"New York in White and Grey," *L'Architecture d'Aujourd'hui* 86 (1976).

"Jacob Chernikhov and his architectural fantasies," *Process architecture* 26 (1981).

"Quartiers de gratte-ciel," *Urbanisme* 204 (October-November 1984).

"Tours en questions," *Techniques et Architecture* 471 (April-May 2004).

Teaching the vertical design

Bovati, Marco, and Andrea Di Franco, eds. *Edifici Alti e Paesaggio. Progetti, strategie, ricerche per la città-contemporanea*. Santarcangelo di Romagna: Maggioli Editore, 2009.

Eun-Seok, Lee, Lee Kwan-Seok, Jeong Jae-Heon, amd Cho Dae-Hee (eds). *Vertical City of Paris, Architectural Design Workshop, Sakhu et EAP Belleville, 2005, 2006, 2007*. Séoul: Éditions PixelHouse, 2008.

Eun-Seok, Lee, Lee Kwan-Seok, Jeong Jae-Heon, and Laurent Salomon (eds). *Vertical City of Paris, Architectural Design Workshop, Sakhu et EAP Belleville, 2008, 2009, 2010*. Séoul: Éditions PixelHouse, 2010.

Giraldeau, François. "Jouer la tour." *SILO 1, Habitat et context*, Montréal: Studio Cube/ UQAM (Printemps 1987): 29-31.

Thermes, Laura, Marco Mannino, and Laura Marino, eds. *Il progetto dell'esistente – Paesaggi urbani e paesaggio costiero in Calabria – Ripensare Vibo Valentia*. Laboratorio Internationale d'Architettura, Universita degli Studio mediterranea di Reggio Calabria, Facolta di Architettura di Vibo Valentia: Iiriti Editore, 2003.

Weijen, Wang, ed. *Vertical fabric: density in landscape*. Faculty of Architecture, University of Hong-Kong: Design folio, 2018.

Students thesis

Billault, Sébastien. "De l'évolution de la tour: vers l'exostructure." Mémoire de diplôme, ENSA Paris Val de Seine, 2012. Sous la direction de Bruno Person.

Carpentier, Catherine. "Les gratte-ciel de Le Corbusier, de la ville contemporaine (1922) à l'ONU (1947)." Mémoire de diplôme, ENSA de Paris-Belleville, 1997. Sous la direction de Marie-Jeanne Dumont.

Dassonville, Gaston. "Gratte-ciel: structures et évolution." Mémoire de diplôme, ENSA Paris Val de Seine, 2014. Sous la direction de Bruno Person.

Kagan, Sacha. "L'Échelle de l'Habiter dans la Tour. La pièce extérieure en hauteur de Charles Correa et de Paul Rudolph." Mémoire de diplôme, ENSA Paris Val de Seine, 2023. Sous la direction de Emmanuelle Sarrazin.

Malcorpi James. *« La tour écologique : solution pour les villes denses ? l'exemple de Paris »* Mémoire de diplôme, Ensa Paris Belleville, 2005. Sous la direction de Michel Kagan.

Quinton, Jean-Christophe. "*New York, les coulisses d'un gratte-ciel*." Mémoire de diplôme, ENSA Paris-Belleville, 2000. Sous la direction de Henri Ciriani.

General bibliography, or quoted in this book

Abraham, Raimund. Interview by Carlos Brillembourg. *Bomb* 77, Octobre 2001.

Arendt, Hannah. *The Human Condition*. Chicago: University of Chicago Press, 1958.

Arnold, Françoise, and Daniel Cling. *Transmettre en architecture*. Paris: Éditions du Moniteur, 2002.

Baudrillard, Jean, and Jean Nouvel. *Les objets singuliers*. Paris: Éditions Calmann-Lévy, 2000.

Berstein, Serge, and Pierre Milza. *Histoire du vingtième siècle. 1. La guerre et la reconstruction 1939–1953.* Paris: Hatier, 1985.

Bonillo, Jean-Lucien and Gérard Monnier, eds. *La Méditerranée de Le Corbusier.* Aix-Marseille: Université de Provence, 1991.

Chaslin, François. *Deux conversations avec Rem Koolhaas*. Paris: Sens et Tonka, 2001.

Chipperfield, David. *Theoretical Pratice*. London: Artemis, 1994.

Colquhoun, Alan. *Essais critiques: architecture moderne et changement historique*. 1981. Reprint, Paris: Mardaga, 1985.

Croset, Pierre-Alain, *Architecture comme modification*, École Polytechnique Fédérale de Lausanne, Chaire du Professeur Luigi Snozzi, 1987

Crotti, Sergio. *Figure architettoniche. Soglia*. Milano: edizioni Unicopli, 2000.

Debord, Guy. *La société du spectacle*. Paris: Buchet-Chastel, 1967.

Devillers, Christian. "Sur l'histoire et l'analyse architecturale, Lettre à Françoise Choay." In *Les Cahiers de la recherche architecturale. L'histoire, approches et connections* 26, 95-103. Marseille: Éditions Parenthèses, 1990.

Frampton, Kenneth, "Frontality versus rotation." In *Five Architects: Eisenman, Graves, Gwathmey, Hejduk, Meier,* 9-13. New York: Oxford University Press, 1975.

Frampton, Kenneth. *Modern Architecture. A Critical History.* 1980. Reprint, London: Thames and Hudson, 2020.

Gailliot, Jean-Hubert, and Sylvie Martigny. "Être éditeur, au-delà des modes." *Libération*, September 30, 1999.

Gordon, James E. *Structure et matériaux. L'explication mécanique des forms*. Paris: Pour La Science, 1993.

Gregotti, Vittorio. *Il territorio dell'Architettura*, Milan: Feltrinelli, 1966.

Gregotti, Vittorio. *Inside Architecture*. 1991. Reprint, New York: MIT Press, 1996.

Gregotti, Vittorio, "Modificazione," *Casabella* 498-499 (January-February 1984), 2-7.

Guiheux, Alain. *Collection d'architecture du Centre Georges Pompidou*. Paris: Éditions du Centre Georges Pompidou, 1998.

Hejduk, John. *Mask of Medusa*. New York: Rizzoli International Publications, 1989.

Kahn, Louis. *Conversations with students*. New York: Architecture at Rice, Princeton Architectural Press, 1969.

Kandinsky, Vassily. *Point-ligne-plan, pour une grammaire des formes*. Paris: Denoël/Gonthier, 1970.

Koolhaas, Rem. *Conversations with students*. New York: Architecture at Rice, Princeton Architectural Press, 1996.

Kundera, Milan. *L'art du roman*. Paris: Folio, 1995.

Le Corbusier. *Vers une architecture*. 1923. Reprint, Paris: Vincent Fréal, 1958.

Le Corbusier. *Urbanisme*. 1925. Reprint, Paris: Flammarion, 1994.

Le Corbusier. *Précisions sur un état présent de l'architecture et de l'urbanisme*. 1930. Reprint, Paris: Altamira Éditions, 1994.

Le Corbusier. *Manière de penser l'urbanisme*. 1946. Paris: Gonthier, 1972.

Le Corbusier. *Le Modulor*. 1950. Reprint, Paris: Éditions Architecture d'Aujourd'hui, 1983.

Le Corbusier. *Entretiens avec les étudiants des écoles d'architecture*. Paris: Minuit, 1957.

Le Corbusier. *Les Trois établissements humains*. Paris: Éditions de Minuit, 1968

Le Corbusier. *Œuvres complètes*. Zürich: Éd. d'Architecture Artémis, 1967.

Lhote, André. *Traité de la figure*. Paris: éditions Floury, 1950.

Lucan, Jacques, ed. *Le Corbusier, une encyclopédie*. Paris: Centre Georges Pompidou, 1987

Lucan, Jacques, and Bruno Marchand. *Matière d'art, l'architecture en Suisse*. Bâle: Birkhäuser, 2009.

Lucan, Jacques, and Bruno Marchand, eds. *Steinmann Martin, Forme forte. Écrits/Schriften 1972–2002.* Bâle: Birkhäuser, 2003.

Marshall McLuhan, Herbert, and Bruce R. Powers. *The Global Village. Transformations in World Life and Media in the 21st Century.* New York: Oxford University Press, 1989.

Plunz, Richard. "The Four Typologies." *Lotus International* 27, "Architecture in the American university: Cornell, Cooper Union, Columbia" (1980): 106-126.

Plunz, Richard. "Introduction." In *PRECIS*, Volume 1, "The Street, the House and the Garden," Spring 1979.

Plunz, Richard. *Habiter New York*. 1980. Reprint, Bruxelles: Pierre Mardaga, 1982.

Ricœur, Paul. *Histoire et vérité*. Paris: Le Seuil, 1955.

Rimbaud, Arthur. *Illuminations*, translated by John Ashbery. New York: W. W. Norton & Co, 2011.

Aldo Rossi, *L'Architettura della Città*, Venice: Marsilio, 1966. *The Architecture of the*

City, translation by D. Ghirardo, J. Okman Cambridge: MIT Press, 1984.

Rowe, Colin. *The Mathematics of the Ideal Villa and Other Essays*. Cambridge: MIT Press, 1976.

Rowe, Colin, and Fred Koetter. *Collage City*. Cambridge: MIT Press, 1978.

Rowe, Colin, and Robert Slutsky. *Transparency. Literal and Phenomenal*. 1964. Reprint, Basel: Birkhäuser, 1997.

Sallenave, Danièle, "La trahison des clercs," in *Le Monde*, 3 février 1989.

Sartre, Jean-Paul. *Situations philosophiques*. Paris: Gallimard, 1990.

Secchi, Bernardo. *Première leçon d'urbanisme*. 2000. Reprint, Marseille: Parenthèses, 2006.

Séris, Jean-Pierre. *La Technique*. Paris: Presses Universitaires de France, 1994.

Steiner, George, *Lessons of the masters. Charles Eliot Norton lectures 2001–2002*. Cambridge: Harvard University Press, 2003.

Stravinsky, Igor. *Poétique musicale sous forme de six leçons*. 1970. Reprint, Paris: Harmoniques Flammarion, 2000.

Tanizaki, Junichirō. *Éloge de l'ombre*. 1977. Reprint, Paris: Publications Orientalistes de France, 1998.

Thoreau, Henry David. *Walden or Life in the Woods*. 1854.

Turner, Paul V. *La formation de Le Corbusier*. Paris: Macula Architecture, 1987.

Writings by Michel Kagan

Frampton, Kenneth, and Kagan, Michel. *Nouvelles directions de l'architecture moderne*. Paris, Milan: Electa Moniteur, 1985. (English version: New directions in modern architecture, New York: Rizzoli Intl Publishers, 1985)

Kagan, Michel. *Parti pris: Les espaces modernes sont les lieux modernes*. Conférences Paris d'architectes. Paris: Pavillon de l'Arsenal, 1996.

Kagan, Michel, ed. *Hommage à Eugène Claudius-Petit, fondateur du corps des architectes-conseils de l'État*. Paris: Thotm éditions, 2007.

Kagan, Michel, ed. *La ville qui s'invente, Actes du séminaire de Rennes, Saint-Jacques-de-la-Lande et Nantes, Corps des architectes-conseils de l'État*. Paris: Thotm éditions, 2008.

Kagan, Michel. *Pro Architect* 47. Séoul: Archiworld, 2008.

Kagan, Michel. "La torre metropolitana," *Giornale dell'Architettura* 60 (March 2008): 21.

Writings about Michel Kagan

Cohen, Jean-Louis, "Sull'architettura di Michel Kagan." *Casabella* 818 (ottobre 2012): 44-45.

Croset, Pierre-Alain, and Silvia Milesi, "Residenza per studenti e giovani lavoratori, Parigi. Michel Kagan e Nathalie Régnier. L'ultima opera." *Casabella* 818 (ottobre 2012): 36-43.

Fillion, Odile, "Michel Kagan, portrait." *Architecture Intérieure Cree* 211 (avril-mai 1986): 128-135.

Frampton, Kenneth, "Cité d'artistes e Cité technique a Parigi di Michel W. Kagan. Microcosmi e pièces urbaines." *Casabella* 594 (October 1992): 54-67.

Jeong, Jae Hean, "Michel Kagan." *Architecture and culture* 300 (May 2006): 100-155.

Ingersoll, Richard, "The work of Michel Kagan: a gift of luminosity." *Architecture and culture* 300 (May 2006): 102-105.

Purini, Franco, "La construction de l'architecture entre talent et idées. Considérations sur l'œuvre de Michel Kagan." *Le visiteur* 17 (November 2011): 117-122.

Régnier-Kagan, Nathalie, ed. *Kagan Architectures 1986–2016*. Paris: AAM Ante Prima Editions, 2016.

Salomon, Laurent, "Michel Kagan: une architecture polyptique." *Le visiteur* 17 (November 2011): 105-115.

Image Credits

The Shadow of the Vertical
fig. 1., 2. and 3. Student photos, École d'architecture de Paris-Belleville.
fig. 4. Drawing Michel Kagan, Michel Kagan and Laurent Salomon diploma.
fig. 5., 6. Photos © J. M. Monthiers for M. Kagan Architecture & Ass.
fig. 7. Student photos, École d'architecture de Genève, projects of Corrado Alberi, Isabelle Claden, Liliana Collazos, François Dulon, Frédéric Floquet, Alain Gonin, François Guex, Astrid Hajrullahu, Éric Hugel, Ali Imanof, Annamaria Larghi, Gezim Pacarizi, Cinzia Rapetto, Raphaelle Sestranetz.
fig. 8. Project photo Sandra Parvu, EAG.
fig. 9. to 13. Student photos, École d'architecture de Lille.
fig. 14. Notes and sketch, M. Kagan.
fig. 15 to 19. Students photos and drawings, Ensa PVS.

High-Rise Form in the Continuity of the City
Courtesy of Amy Gill, SOM Journal.
fig. 1., 7. and 8. © MoMA. A & D Mies van der Rohe Archive.
fig. 2. Photo © Chicago Architectural Photographing Company (Henry Fuermann). Source: Bush-Brown A., *Louis Sullivan*, George Braziller, 1960.
fig. 3. Source: H. Morrison, *Louis Sullivan: Prophet of Modern Architecture.* W.W. Norton & Company, 1998.
fig. 4. Photo © Thomas Airviews. Source: S. Giedion, *Space, Time and Architecture,* Harvard University Press, 1962.
fig. 5. Source: H. Ferriss, *The Metropolis of Tomorrow,* Ives Washburn, 1929.
fig. 6., 9., 10., 11. and 12. Skidmore, Owings and Merrill Archive.
fig. 13. and 14. Drawing Jacques Lambert in *L'Illustration*, 1922, n° 4. Source: G. Fanelli and R. Gargiani, *Auguste Perret,* Laterza, 1991.
fig. 15. Source: S. Maffioletti (dir.), BBPR, Zanichelli Ed., 1994.
fig. 16. © Fondation Le Corbusier / Adagp.
fig. 17. Source: J. Silvetti (ed.), *Amancio Williams,* Rizzoli, 1987.
fig. 18. Drawing Louis Kahn. Source: *The Louis Kahn Archive: Personal Drawings, Buildings and Projects, 1966,* Garland Publishing, 1987.
fig. 19a. Photo © Ian Lambot. Source: P. Jodidio, *Sir Norman Foster,* Taschen, 1997.
fig. 19b. Photo © Ian Lambot. Source: *Norman Foster Works Vol. 2,* Prestel, 2005.
fig. 20a. and 20b. Photo © Ian Lambot. Source: *Norman Foster Works Vol. 4,* Prestel, 2005.

The Skyscraper According to Le Corbusier
Courtesy of Fondation Le Corbusier
fig. 1. to 7. and 9. Drawings, model photo © FLC / Adagp.
fig. 8. Sketch Le Corbusier, © FLC / Adagp, annoté par Michel Kagan.

Vertical Horizon
Avec l'aimable autorisation de Raimund Abraham
fig. 1. to 5. Drawings, model photo and sketch, © Raimund Abraham.
fig. 6. Photo: N. Régnier-Kagan.
fig. 7. Anonymous sketch. Source: R. Koolhaas, *Delirious New York*, Oxford University Press, 1978.
fig. 8-9. Source: *Abstract 87-88*, Columbia University, N.Y.
fig. 10. & 11. Students photos and drawings, Ensa PLV.

European Towers versus High-Rise Buildings
fig. 1. and 5a. Photos © Paul Tierney for FKL architects.
fig. 2., 8a. and 13. Photos © Luuk Kramer fotografie, Amsterdam for Claus en Kaan Architecten.
fig. 3., 7a., 7b. and 7c. Photos © Brandsberg-Dahls Arkitekter.
fig. 4. and 6a. Photos © Stephan Lucas for Beckmann N'Thépé.
fig. 5b. et 5c. Drawings © FKL architects.
fig. 6b. Drawings © Beckmann N'Thépé.
fig. 8b. Photo © Marcus Bassler for Claus en Kaan Architecten.

Discovering Architecture
fig. 1. to 5., 7., 10., 12., 14. Photos N. Régnier-Kagan.
fig. 6. Photo G. Sprenger.
fig. 8. Photo T. Tarpley. Source: tarpreport.blogspot.com
fig. 9. Source: commons.wikimedia.org
fig. 11. : Photo G. Oberdorfer.
fig. 13. : Photo M. Kagan.

Travel Notebook I
p. 84. Photos N. Régnier-Kagan.
p. 85. Photos N. Régnier-Kagan, 432 Park Av.: E. Beaudouin
p. 87., 88. M. Kagan, G. Sprenger, G. Oberdorfer and © Tom Harris Courtesy Studio Gang.
p. 89. Photos M. Kagan.

Travel Notebook II
p. 90. Amsterdam, Basel, Barcelona : Photos N. Régnier-Kagan. Barcelona skyline : Wikipedia.
p. 91. Berlin, Copenhagen, Frankfurt : Photos N. Régnier-Kagan.
p. 92. Göteborg: Photo Ulf Celander © Malmström & Erdström. Lisbon, Porto. London: Photos N. Régnier-Kagan.
London (last): Photo L. Beaudouin.
p. 93. Marseille, Milan, Paris, Rotterdam, Photos N. Régnier-Kagan.

Singular Towers
fig. 1a., 1b. Photos © Michael Moran.
fig. 1c. to 1f. Drawings © Tod Williams Billie Tsien Architects, New-York.
fig. 2a. and 2b. Photos © Scott Frances / OTTO / Agence A.
fig. 2c. and 2d. Drawings © Richard Meier and Partners.
fig. 3a., 3e. and 3f. Photos © James Steinkamp, Steinkamp Photography.
fig. 3b. to 3d. Drawings © Perkins+Wills.
fig. 4a to 4d. Drawings © Herzog & de Meuron
fig. 4e. Photo: Alexico Group, 2016.
fig. 4f. Photo: Kidfly182, 2022.
fig. 5a. Photos E. Beaudouin.
fig. 5b.-5c. Photos N. Régnier-Kagan.
fig. 5d.-5h. Drawing © Alvaro Siza

A Theoretical Exercise
fig. 1. Drawing, diplôme J.-C. Quinton, EAPB.
fig. 2. Photos 2, 5,6, 7, 8 : Cédric Thomas, EAPB. Photos 1, 3, 4: Daiga Busmane, École d'arch. de Versailles.
fig. 3. Students models photos EAPB.

Project Notebook I
pp. 107-115. Photos and students drawings, EAPB, EAV.
pp. 109-111. Photos Hélène Orlati, EAV.

A Few Tower References
fig. 1. Drawing © Henri Ciriani
fig. 2. Photos: © Charles Correa Foundation
fig. 3. to 5. and 8. Photos N. Régnier-Kagan
fig. 6. Drawing El Lissitzky, *Russia: an architecture for world revolution*, Lund Humphries, MIT, 1970.
fig. 7. Photos Ford Foundation
fig. 9. Photo: Library of Congress. https://www.loc.gov/item/2023676885/ @ Paul Rudolph Foundation
fig. 10. Source: A. Alofsin, *Prairie skyscraper...*, Price Tower Arts Center, Rizzoli, 2005.
fig. 11. Drawing: © E. & L. Beaudouin.
fig. 12. Photo: © WOHA architects
fig. 13. Photo: Andreas Praefcke, wikimedia.org CC BY 3.0 © Norman Foster
fig. 14. Photo: © P. Mendes da Rocha, casa de arquitettura.

The Parisian Context
fig. 1., 6., 7., 9., 12 & 13. Drawings and Photos M. Kagan Architecture & Ass.
fig. 2. Photo: Roberto Casati, wikimedia.org, CC NC BY SA.
fig. 3-5., 8., 10., 11., 14. & 15 Photos N. Régnier-Kagan.

A Site, a Program
fig. 1. to 5. Drawings © Gwenaël Clément.
fig. 6. to 9. Photos © Hervé Abbadie for M. Kagan Architecture & Ass.

A Pedagogical Promenade
fig. 1. Student photos, EAPB.
fig. 2. Photo S. El Hage, EAPB
fig. 3. and 7. Photomontage: G. Sprenger and G. Oberdorfer.
fig. 4. Photo maquette: G. Clément, EAPB.
fig. 5. Student photos, EAPB.
fig. 6. Photos © H. Abbadie for M. Kagan Architecture & Ass.

Sciences and Techniques in Architecture
fig. 1. and 2. Photos N. Régnier-Kagan.
fig. 3. to 10. Drawings taken from the course handout: Lapeyre Ch., *Cours de construction métallique pour le bâtiment. Tome 2*, ESITC Cachan.

From Intuition to Theory
fig. 1. Photo E. Beaudouin.
fig. 2. Photo N. Régnier-Kagan.
fig. 3. Source: The Peak, Hong Kong, consultation file.
fig. 5. Source: Carton d'invitation, « Casa Bloc Barcelona 1932–1939 », ETSA Barcelona, 2009.
fig. 6. Photo © Pau Bou.
fig. 7. and 8. GATCPAC, drawings: M. Kagan Architecture & Ass.
fig. 9. Source: *AC Documentos de actividad contemporanea* review.
fig. 10. and 11. Students photos, EAPB.
fig. 12. © FLC / Adagp.

A Vertical Garden City
fig. 1. Students drawings and photos, ENSA PVS.
fig. 2. Photo N. Régnier-Kagan.
fig. 3. Photo © Frédéric Druot architect.
fig. 4. & 5. Source: W. Boesiger ed., *Le Corbusier, Œuvres complètes* (Zurich: Girsberger), vol. 1, 1910-1929: 41; vol. 4, 1938-1946: 139.
fig. 6. to 12. Students photos: ENSA Paris-Val de Seine.
fig. 13. Drawing © Paul Rudolph Library of Congress. https://www.loc.gov/

Project Notebook II
fig. 1. to 11., 21. to 24., 27. Photos and students drawings, Ensa PVS.
fig. 12. Photo Pierre Léger.
fig. 13. to 20. and 25. Photo N. Régnier-Kagan.

Mental Structure, Constructive Structure
fig. 1. Drawing © Côme, Museo Civico.
Source: *Le Futurisme 1909–1916*, RMN, 1973.
fig. 2. Projet de M. O. Paux, EAG.
fig. 3. et 4. Drawings, model photos d'étudiants, EAG.
fig. 5. Drawing © John Hedjuk. Source: J. Hedjuk, *Mask of Medusa*, Rizzoli, 1989.
fig. 6a. to 6c., 8., 9. and 11. : Photos © H. Orlati, EAV.
fig. 10-11. Projet d'étudiants, F. Foucault and F. Mathieu, EAV.
fig. 12-13. @ Atelier 2/3/4.

A Tall Building in an Urban Zone: the Cimbéton Competition
fig. 1. Drawing M. Kagan.
fig. 2. Photos A.-L. Verlyk, EAV.
fig. 3. Drawings Russel Jager, ENSA Normandie, Trophée Béton.

Designing an Innovative Structure for a Parisian Tower
fig. 1., 2., 8, 9. Students drawings and photos, Politecnico di Torino.
fig. 2. Photo W. Lescaze. Source: C. Hubert, L. S. Shapiro, W. Lescaze, *Catalogue 16 IAUS*, Rizzoli-IAUS, 1982.
fig. 3. Drawing © Semapa / Ateliers Lion Ass.
fig. 4. Drawing @ Ateliers Lion Ass.
fig. 6. to 11. Students drawings and photos, Politecnico di Milano.

Metropolitan Towers as Architectural and Urban Infrastructures
fig. 1. Photo: Daniel Case, wikimedia.org CC BY 3.0
fig. 2. Students photos, Ensa PB.
fig. 3. Students drawings, Politecnico di Milano.

Urban Architectures between Paris, Milan, and Bergamo
fig. 1. to 4. and 6. Photos N. Régnier-Kagan.
fig. 5. et 7. Photos © city of Bergamo.
fig. 8., 9. and 11. Photos and students drawings, EAPB/EAV.
fig. 10. Photo © H. Orlati, EAV.

fig. 12. Source: Bovati M., Di Franco A. (dir.), « Edifici Alti e Paesaggio... », Politecnico di Milano-Maggioli Ed., 2009
fig. 13. Photo © E. Leggeri, Politecnico di Milano/EAPB.

Laboratories of Architecture: from Vibo Valentia to Athens
fig. 1., 4. and 5. Drawings: Vibo Valentia workshop. Source: L. Thermes, M. Mannino, L. Marino (dir.), « Il progetto de l'esistente... », Facolta di Architettura di Vibo Valentia, Iiriti Editore, 2003.
fig. 2., 3., 6., 12. and 13. Sketches: M. Kagan.
fig. 7. and 8. Photo and Athens plan, « Athens beyond history » workshop, city of Athens.
fig. 9. and 10. Photos N. Régnier-Kagan.
fig. 11. Photo N. Ktenas.

Open Dialogue
fig. 1. Photo N. Ktenas.
fig. 2. : Students photos, EAPB.
fig. 3. and 4. Photos M. Kagan.

The Standing City
fig. 1. to 8. Source: Eun-Seok Lee, Kwan-Seok Lee, Jae-Heon Jeong, Dae-Hee Cho (dir.), *Vertical City of Paris, 2005, 2006, 2007,* Séoul, Éd. PixelHouse, 2008 and Eun-Seok Lee, Kwan-Seok Lee, Jae-Heon Jeong and Salomon L. (dir.), *Vertical City of Paris, 2008, 2009, 2010,* Séoul, Éd. PixelHouse, 2010.
fig. 9-10. Drawings © Atelier Rotbart & Salomon

The Air of Modernity
fig. 1. Source: *Khan-Magomedov, S. O., A. Vesnine and le constructivisme*, Philippe Sers, 1986.
fig. 3. Source: *PRECIS* 4, 1983
fig. 4. Source: *PRECIS* 5, 1984
fig. 2a., 2b., 5. to 8. and 11. to 14. Students projects, Université du Québec to Montréal.
fig. 15. Photo Georges Adamczyk.
fig. 16. Photo © Pei Cobb Freed & Parnters.

The New York Years 1981–1986
fig. 1. Drawing M. Kagan.
fig. 2. Photo M. Kagan.
fig. 3. Photo Studio 7 / M. Kagan Architecture & Ass.
fig. 4. to 12. Drawings Studio 7 / M. Kagan Architecture & Ass.

On Verticality in the Korean Project
fig. 1. to 6. and 8. Photos and drawings M. Kagan Architecture & Ass.
fig. 7., 9. and 10. Sketch: M. Kagan.

Theoretical Practice
fig. 1., 2., 6., 15. and 18. Sketch: M. Kagan.
fig. 3. Drawing Studio 7 : M. Kagan Architecture & Ass.
fig. 5., 11. to 14., 16. and 17. Drawings M. Kagan Architecture & Ass.
fig. 4., 7., 8. Photos © Jean-Marie Monthiers for M. Kagan Architecture & Ass.
fig. 9. and 10. Photos © Hervé Abbadie for M. Kagan Architecture & Ass.
fig. 19. Drawing © Ateliers Lion & Ass.
fig. 20. Drawing: N. Régnier Kagan.
fig. 22. Drawing: © Nouvel R , annotations by M. Kagan Architecture & Ass.
fig. 23 Photos: N. Régnier Kagan.

Acknowledgements

I would like to thank Philippe Bach, Director of Ensa de Paris-Val de Seine, who encouraged and supported this updated edition, making it possible, through its translation, to disseminate our research and make it known abroad. I am particularly grateful to him. I would also like to thank the EVCAU laboratory, in particular Dimitri Toubanos and David Serrero, Directors, for their support.

I would like to thank again the Ensa Paris-Belleville, Jean-Pierre Bobenriether, former Director, and of course, Ann-José Arlot, architect, former Head of the General Inspectorate of Cultural Affairs, Ministry of Culture and Communication, as well as Laurence Cassegrain, former Deputy Director of Architectural Education, for the trust they placed in us for the first edition.

I thank Kenneth Frampton, who enlightened us with his thought, his knowledge, his intelligence and his profound humanity throughout our years of study, teaching and professional practice.

I would like to pay tribute to Jean-Louis Cohen, who encouraged me in the new edition of this book, and who, through his knowledge and his publications, inspired me greatly in its writing.

I thank Christian Hubert, the translator of the English edition, who met Michel Kagan in New York in the 80s at the IAUS, who managed to bring this translation to fruition despite the tedious back and forth.

I would of course like to thank Florence Petry and Pauline Nuñez, editors, who supported us in this adventure with a great deal of patience, understanding and rigour.

In particular, I would like to thank Pierre-Alain Croset for his preface to the new edition, which places the work, twelve years after the first edition, in its current context, and for the addition he made to his article, and the authors: Georges Adamczyck, Miguel Macian, Jean Mas, Pascal Hofstein and Laurent Salomon, who updated their texts and supported me in this new edition.

I would also like to thank Elena Fontanella, a former student of Michel Kagan at Ensa Paris-Belleville, now teaching at the Politecnico di Milano, for her article shedding new light on the subject, her proofreading and her help with the layout of the new illustrations.

I would particularly like to thank my colleagues at Ensa Paris-Val de Seine: Laurent Beaudouin, Jean Mas, Jean-Michel Veillerot, as well as Pierre-André Comte, Thomas Heuze, Dominique Pinon, Bruno Person, Bruno Thomas, Pierre Léger, and all the teachers in the A-Ito group, with whom I had the pleasure to teach.

My warmest thanks to all the authors who contributed to this book: Georges Adamczyk, Henri Bresler, Catherine Carpentier, Gwenaël Clément, Pierre-Alain Croset, Hervé Dubois, Kenneth Frampton, François Giraldeau, Jae-Heon Jeong, Nikos Ktenàs, Norbert Laurent, John Loomis, Miguel Macian, Jean Mas, Nancy Ottaviano, Pascal Hofstein, Laurent Salomon, Ilaria Valente, Jean-Marc Weill, each of whom has shed a nuanced light on this pedagogical theme through their texts.

I would also like to thank Édith Girard who is no longer with us, Sergio Crotti for his afterword, and Henri Ciriani for the drawing he donated especially for this book.

I would like to thank the students at Paris-Val de Seine, who took part in this teaching with enthusiasm, and who, through their research, enabled us to take a fresh look at these architectural and urban issues.

I thank again Michel Kagan's former students for taking part in the interviews for the original edition: Adrien Cosnefroy, Simon El Hage, Alexis Guilhaumaud, Grégory Gouard, Nicolas Lancereau, Sophie Maurin, Marion Nielsen, Grégoire Oberdoerffer, Aleth Pauphilet, Guillaume Renaud, Guillaume Sprenger, Cédric Thomas, Mathilde Tielman, as well as all his former students from Geneva, Lille and Belleville, and my former students from Versailles, whose projects are published here.

I would also like to thank my children Sonia and Sacha for their support, and I am infinitely grateful to Michel Kagan, for his understanding of the world, for his ethical attitude, his passion, his strength of conviction that does not allow itself to be impressed by public opinion, and for the enthusiasm that he has given me to convey in this book.

May all these people receive the assurance of my most sincere gratitude.

Thanks to the students from

École nationale supérieure d'architecture Paris Val de Seine, École nationale supérieure d'architecture Paris-La Villette, École nationale supérieure d'architecture de Rouen, Politecnico di Milano, 2011–2024:

Cecile Achard, Camille Benoit, Victoire Bergey, Raphaël Boussange, Eudes Cazaunau, Andi Cinna, Lauriane Chiri, Emma Collet, Tom Debaye, Leo Demeillers, Thomas Dietert, Emma Dufour, Solene Duplessis, Melissa Dyminat, Nora El Assaad, Maria El Tabib, Samia Filali, Raphaël Guerrier, Hayder Hamid, Russel Jagger, Sacha Kagan, Alina Kim, Antoine Kubik, Margaux Kleindiest, Camille de Labbey, Alexandre Laurent, Kevin Laurent, Sacha Luisada, Manuel Mandrille, Ekaterin Meskhi, Théo Métalli, Simon Mullot, François Nahory, David Pallaro, Paul Pelletier, Pedro Pereira, Ani Periashvilli, Kevin Pinto, Marie Prel, Théo de la Presle, Nicolas Regnard, Paloma Rodrguez, manuel Sanchez, Mathilde Schaal, Marin Segal, Joanna Souraya, Vincent Tissandier, Felicia de la Tullaye, Simon Valero, Elisa Valpreda, Irina Vilmus, Ladin Yacizi.

École d'architecture de Paris-Belleville, École d'architecture de Versailles, École d'architecture de Lille, École d'architecture de Genève, Université du Québec à Montréal, Columbia University New York, École d'architecture de Sakhu Séoul, Politecnico di Milano, Politecnico de Turin, Facolta di Architettura di Vibo Valentia. 1982–2009.

Corrado Alberi, Salvatore Amaddeo, R. Arpin, Steve Balme, Laurent Bariat, Francesca Benedetti, Roxanne Barruet, Bastien Bergramian, G. Bérubé, Josée Bérubé, Clément Blanchet, Alexis Bueno, Daiga Busmane, Colin Cathcart, Alice Sin Ha Chau, Emira Chimenti, Jin Man Choi, Diego Ciccone, Isabelle Claden, Xabi Claverie, Gwenaël Clément, Liliana Collazos, Simon Coquoz, Julien Corbin, Adrien Cosnefroy, Benjamin Cros, R. Daoust, Fanny Dohen, François Dulon, Fred Einaudi, Maurizio Grilla, Simon El Hage, Manuela Festa, Frédéric Floquet, Elena Fontanella, Florian Foucault, Tat Wai Fung, G. Gagnon, M. Gamache, Kayan Gerami, Mathias Gervais de Lafond, Maxime Gil, A. Giroux, Alain Gonin, C. Gosselin, Grégory Gouard, François Guex, Alexis Guilhaumaud, Astrid Hajrullahu, Keith Hone, Jong Hwa Hong, Éric Hugel, Young Mi Im, Ali Imanof, Matthieu Janmot, Jo Young Jeon, Jiong Jia, Ho Suk Kang, Joo Mi Kim, Young Tae Kim, Hee Jeong Koo, Theodore Kruger, Nicolas Lancereau, Annamaria Larghi, Yun Ho Lee, Seo Joo Lee, Dong Hoon Lee, You Yin Lee, Jae Min Lee, Elena Leggeri, M. A. Letarte, Manuele Mandrile, Emanuela Marinska, Florian Mathieu, Sophie Maurin, Thorsten Mischo, Marion Nielsen, Romain Nowak, Grégoire Oberdoerffer, Andrea Oldani, Barbara Oteri, Gezim Pacarizi, Davide Pallaro, Fiorina Pantusa, Sandra Parvu, Francesco Pasquino, Aleth Pauphilet, Marc Olivier Paux, Virginie Pernaut, Peter Pfau, Jean-Christophe Quinton, Cinzia Rapetto, Pauline Raurte, Guillaume Renaud, Giuseppe Rotirati, Yves Rouleau, P. Saint-Laurent, Bruno Sansotta, Raphaelle Sestranetz, Xuemei Shao, Woo Lin Shoe, Heon Yeong Shoe, Chang Woo Son, Kyu Nam Song, Guillaume Sprenger, Marc-André Tellier, Cédric Thomas, Mathilde Tielman, Sinda Tobni, César Vabre, Daniele Vacca, Elisa Valpreda, Marie Vosguimoroukian, Anne-Lise Verlyck, Chloé Wawrzyniak, Ju Sik Yang, Yoo Na Yi, Fung Tat Wai.

We regret that despite our research we were unable to identify certain student projects.

Imprint

Translation: Christian Hubert
Design: Pauline Nuñez
Fonts: Whitney
Image processing, printing, and binding: Gugler GmbH, Melk/Donau, Austria

First published in French in 2012 by Éditions Recherches, Paris:

Park Books AG
Niederdorfstrasse 54
8001 Zurich
Switzerland
www.park-books.com
T +41 44 262 16 62
E info@park-books.com

Product safety
Responsible person pursuant to EU Regulation 2023/988 (GPSR):
GVA Gemeinsame Verlagsauslieferung Göttingen GmbH & Co. KG
Post Box 2021
37010 Göttingen
Germany
T +49 551 384 200 0
E info@gva-verlage.de

Park Books is being supported by the Federal Office of Culture with a general subsidy for the years 2021–2025.

ISBN 978-3-03860-426-6

PARIS VAL DE SEINE
ÉCOLE NATIONALE SUPÉRIEURE D'ARCHITECTURE

evcAu